AUTHENTIC
Trentino-Alto Adige

TOURING CLUB
OF ITALY

Touring Club Italiano
President and Chairman: *Roberto Ruozi*
General Manager: *Guido Venturini*

Touring Editore
Managing Director: *Alfieri Lorenzon*
Editorial Director: *Michele D'Innella*
Editorial coordination: *Cristiana Baietta*

International Department
Fabio Pittella
fabio.pittella@touringclub.it

Senior Editor: *Paola Pandiani*
Editor: *Monica Maraschi*
Writer and Researcher: *Pietro Ferrario*
with Banca Dati Turistica for Pratical info
Translation and page layout: *Studio Queens, Milan*
Maps: *Touring Club Italiano*
Design: *Studio Gatelli, Milan*
Cover photo: *Odle in the Funes valley*
(O. Seehauser)

Advertising Manager: *Claudio Bettinelli*
Local Advertising: *Progetto*
www.progettosrl.it - info@progettosrl.it

Printing and Binding: *CPM, Casarile*

Distribution
USA/CAN – *Publishers Group West*
UK/Ireland – *Portfolio Books*

Touring Club Italiano, Corso Italia 10, 20122 Milano
www.touringclub.it
© 2006 Touring Editore, Milan

Code K8WOO
ISBN-13: 978 – 88365 – 3900 – 0
ISBN-10: 88 – 365 – 3900 – 9

Printed in July 2006

SUMMARY

WHAT IS THE TOURING CLUB OF ITALY?

Long Tradition, Great Prestige

For over 110 years, the Touring Club of Italy (TCI) has offered travelers the most detailed and comprehensive source of travel information available on Italy. The Touring Club of Italy was founded in 1894 with the aim of developing the social and cultural values of tourism and promoting the conservation and enjoyment of the country's national heritage, landscape and environment.

Advantages of Membership

Today, TCI offers a wide rage of travel services to assist and support members with the highest level of convenience and quality. Now you can discover the unique charms of Italy with a distinct insider's advantage.

Enjoy exclusive money saving offers with a TCI membership. Use your membership card for discounts in thousands of restaurants, hotels, spas, campgrounds, museums, shops and markets.

These Hotel Chains offer preferred rates and discounts to TCI members!

JOIN THE TOURING CLUB OF ITALY

How to Join

It's quick and easy to join.
Apply for your membership online at
www.touringclub.it
Your membership card will arrive within
three weeks and is valid for discounts
across Italy for the entire year.
Get your card before you go and start
saving as soon as you arrive.
Euro 25 annual membership fee
includes priority mail postage for
membership card and materials.
Just one use of the card will more than
cover the cost of membership.

Benefits

- Exclusive car rental rates with Hertz
- Discounts at select Esso gas stations
- 20% discount on TCI guidebooks
and maps purchased in TCI bookstores
or directly online at
www.touringclub.com
- Preferred rates and discounts available
at thousands of locations in Italy: Hotels -
B&B's - Villa Rentals - Campgrounds -TCI
Resorts - Spas - Restaurants - Wineries -
Museums - Cinemas - Theaters - Music
Festivals - Shops - Craft Markets - Ferries -
Cruises - Theme Parks - Botanical Gardens

ITALY: INSTRUCTIONS FOR USE

Italy is known throughout the world for the quantity and quality of its art treasures and for its natural beauty, but it is also famous for its inimitable lifestyle and fabulous cuisine and wines. Although it is a relatively small country, Italy boasts an extremely varied culture and multifarious traditions and customs. The information and suggestions in this brief section will help foreign tourists not only to understand certain aspects of Italian life, but also to solve the everyday difficulties and the problems of a practical nature that inevitably crop up during any trip. This practical information is included in brief descriptions of various topics: public transport and how to purchase tickets; suggestions on how to drive in this country; the different types of rooms and accommodation in hotels; hints on how to use mobile phones and communication in general. This is followed by useful advice on how to meet your everyday needs and on shopping, as well as information concerning the cultural differences in the various regions. Lastly, there is a section describing the vast range of restaurants, bars, wine bars and pizza parlors.

TRANSPORTATION

From the airport to the city
Public transportation in major cities is easily accessible and simple to use.
Both Malpensa Airport in Milan and Fiumicino Airport in Rome have trains and buses linking them to the city centers. At Malpensa, you can take a bus to the main train station or a train to Cadorna train station and subway stop.

Subways, buses, and trams
Access to the subways, buses, and trams requires a ticket (tickets are not sold on board but can be purchased at most newsstands and tobacco shops). The ticket is good for one ride and sometimes has a time limit (in the case of buses and trams). When you board a bus or tram, you are required to stamp your previously-acquired ticket in the time-stamping machine. Occasionally, a conductor will board the bus or tram and check everyone's ticket. If you haven't got one, or if it has not been time-stamped, you will have to pay a steep fine.

Trains
The Ferrovie dello Stato (Italian Railways) is among the best and most modern railway systems in Europe. Timetables and routes can be consulted and reservations can be made online at www.trenitalia.com. Many travel agents can also dispense tickets and help you plan your journey. Hard-copy schedules can be purchased at all newsstands and most bookstores.

The Dolomites are alive with amazing scenery

Automated ticket machines, which include easy-to-use instructions in English, are available in nearly all stations. They can be used to check schedules, makes reservations, and purchase tickets.
There are different types of train, according to the requirements:
Eurostar Italia Trains *ES★* : Fast connections between Italy's most important cities. The ticket includes seat booking charge;
Intercity *IC* and **Espresso** *E* Trains: Local connections among Italy's towns and cities. Sometimes   and   trains require seat booking. You can book your seat up to 3 hours before the train departure. The seat booking charge is of 3 euro.
Interregionale Trains *iR* move beyond regional boundaries. Among the combined local-transport services, the *iR* Trains are the fastest ones with the fewest number of stops. No seat booking available.
Diretto *D* and **Regionale** *R* Trains can circulate both within the regions and their bordering regions. No seat booking available.

7

DO NOT FORGET: In Italy, you can only board a train if you have a valid ticket that has been time-stamped prior to boarding (each station has numerous time-stamping machines). You cannot buy or stamp tickets on the train.

If you don't have a ticket – or did not stamp before boarding – you will be liable to pay the full ticket price plus a 25 euro fine. If you produce a ticket that is not valid for the train or service you're using (i.e. one issued for a different train category at a different price, etc.) you will be asked to pay the difference with respect to the full ticket price, plus an 8 euro surcharge.

Taxis

Taxis are a convenient but expensive way to travel in Italian cities. There are taxi stands scattered throughout major cities. You cannot hail taxis on the street in Italy, but you can reserve taxis, in advance or immediately, by phone: consult the yellow pages for the number or ask your hotel reception desk or maitre d'hotel to call for you.

Taxi drivers have the right to charge you a supplementary fee for every piece of luggage they transport, as well as evening surcharges.

Driving

Especially when staying in the countryside, driving is a safe and convenient way to travel through Italy and its major cities. It is important to be aware of street signs and speed limits, and many cities have zones where only limited traffic is allowed in order to accommodate pedestrians.

Street parking is organized using road signs and different colored street markings. No line or a white line is for free parking, blue is for paid parking and yellow is for reserved parking (disabled, residents etc). There may be time limits for both free and paid parking. In this case, use your parking disc to indicate your time of arrival. Although an international driver's license is not required in Italy, it is advisable. ACI and similar associations provide this service to members. The fuel distribution network is reasonably distributed all over the territory. All service stations have unleaded gasoline ("benzina verde") and diesel fuel ("gasolio"). Opening time is 7am to 12:30 and 15 to 19:30; on motorways the service is 24 hours a day.

Type of roads in Italy: The *Autostrada* (for example A14) is the main highway system in Italy and is similar to the Interstate highway system in the US and the motorway system in the UK. Shown on our Touring Club Italiano 1:200,000 road maps as black. The Autostrada are toll highways; you pay to use them. The *Strada Statale* (for example SS54) is a fast moving road that may have one or more lanes in each direction. Shown on our Touring Club Italiano 1:200,000 road maps as red. *Strada Provinciale* (for example SP358) can be narrow, slow and winding roads. They are usually one lane in each direction. Shown on our Touring Club Italiano 1:200,000 road maps as yellow. *Strada Comunale* (for example SC652) is a local road connecting the main town with its sorrounding. Note: In our guide you will sometime find an address of a place in the countryside listed, for example, as

"SS54 Km 25". This means that the you have to drive along the Strada Statale 54 until you reach the 25-km road sign.
Speed limits: 130 kmph on the Autostrada, 110 kmph on main highways, 90 kmph outside of towns, 50 kmph in towns.
The town streets are patrolled by the Polizia Municipale while the roads outside cities and the Autostrada are patrolled by the Carabinieri or the Polizia Stradale.
Do not forget:
• Wear your seat belt at all times;
• Do not use the cellular phone while driving;
• Have your headlights on at all times when driving outside of cities;
• The drunk driving laws are strict – do not drink and drive;
• In case of an accident you are not allowed to get out of your car unless you are wearing a special, high-visibility, reflective jacket.

ACCOMMODATION

Hotels

In Italy it is common practice for the reception desk to register your passport, and only registered guests are allowed to use the rooms. This is mere routine, done for security reasons, and there is no need for concern.
All hotels use the official star classification system, from 5-star luxury hotel to 1 star accommodation.
Room rates are based on whether they are for single ("camera singola") or double ("camera doppia") occupancy. In every room you will find a list of the hotel rates (generally on the back of the door). While 4- and 5-star hotels have double beds, most hotels have only single beds. Should you want a double bed, you have to ask for a "letto matrimoniale". All hotels have rooms with bathrooms; only 1-star establishments usually have only shared bathrooms.
Most hotel rates include breakfast ("prima colazione"), but you can request to do without it, thus reducing the rate.
Breakfast is generally served in a communal room and comprises a buffet with pastries, bread with butter and jam, cold cereals, fruit, yoghurt, coffee, and fruit juice. Some hotels regularly frequented by foreign tourists will also serve other items such as eggs for their American and British guests.
The hotels for families and in tourist

localities also offer "mezza pensione", or half board, in which breakfast and dinner are included in the price.
It's always a good idea to check when a hotel's annual closing period is, especially if you are planning a holiday by the sea.

Farm stays

Located only in the countryside, and generally on a farm, "agriturismo" – a network of farm holiday establishments – is part of a growing trend in Italy to honor local gastronomic and wine traditions, as well as countryside traditions. These farms offer meals prepared with ingredients cultivated exclusively on site: garden-grown vegetables, homemade cheese and local recipes. Many of these places also provide lodging, one of the best ways to experience the "genuine" Italian lifestyle.

Bed & Breakfast

This form of accommodation provides bed and breakfast in a private house, and in the last few years has become much more widespread in Italy. There are over 5,000 b&bs, classified in 3 categories, and situated both in historic town centers, as well as in the outskirts and the countryside. Rooms for guests are always well-furnished, but not all of them have en suite bathrooms.
It is well-recommended to check the closing of the open-all-year accommodation services and restaurants, because they could have a short break during the year (usually no longer than a fortnight).

COMMUNICATIONS

Nearly everyone in Italy owns a cellular phone. Although public phones are still available, they seem to be ever fewer and farther between. If you wish to use public phones, you will find them in subway stops, bars, along the street, and phone centers generally located in the city center. Phone cards and pre-paid phone cards can be purchased at most newsstands and tobacco shops, and can also be acquired at automated tellers.
For European travelers, activating personal cellular coverage is relatively simple, as it is in most cases for American and Australian travelers as well. Contact your mobile service provider for details.

Cellular phones can also be rented in Italy from TIM, the Italian national phone company. For information, visit its website at www.tim.it. When traveling by car through the countryside, a cellular phone can really come in handy.

Note that when dialing in Italy, you must always dial the prefix (e.g., 02 for Milan, 06 for Rome) even when making a local call. For cellular phones, however, the initial zero is always dropped.

Freephone numbers always start with "800". For calls abroad from Italy, it's a good idea to buy a special pre-paid international phone card, which is used with a PIN code.

Internet access

Cyber cafés have sprung up all over Italy and you can find one on nearly every city block.

EATING AND DRINKING

The bar

The Italian "bar" is a multi-faceted, all-purpose establishment for drinking, eating and socializing, where you can order an espresso, have breakfast, and enjoy a quick sandwich for lunch or even a hot meal. You can often buy various items here (sometimes even stamps, cigarettes, phone cards, etc.). Bear in mind that table service ("servizio a tavola") includes a surcharge. At most bars, if you choose to sit, a waiter will take your order. Every bar should have a list of prices posted behind or near the counter; if the bar offers table service, the price list should also include the extra fee for this.

Lunch at bars will include, but is not limited to, "panini," sandwiches with crusty bread, usually with cured meats such as "prosciutto" (salt-cured ham), "prosciutto cotto" (cooked ham), and cheeses such as mozzarella topped with tomato and basil. Then there are "tramezzini" (finger sandwiches) with tuna, cheese, or vegetables, etc. Often the "panini" and other savory sandwiches (like stuffed flatbread or "focaccia") are heated before being served. Naturally, the menu at bars varies according to the region: in Bologna you will find "piadine" (flatbread similar to pita) with Swiss chard; in Palermo there are "arancini" (fried rice balls stuffed with

ground meat); in Genoa you will find that even the most unassuming bar serves some of the best "focaccia" in all Italy. Some bars also include a "tavola calda". If you see this sign in a bar window, it means that hot dishes like pasta and even entrées are served.

A brief comment on coffee and cappuccino: Italians never serve coffee with savory dishes or sandwiches, and they seldom drink cappuccino outside of breakfast (although they are happy to serve it at any time).

While English- and Irish-type pubs are frequented by beer lovers and young people in Italy, there are also American bars where long drinks and American cocktails are served.

Breakfast at the bar

Breakfast in Italy generally consists of some type of pastry, most commonly a "brioche" – a croissant either filled with cream or jam, or plain – and a cappuccino or espresso. Although most bars do not offer American coffee, you can ask for a "caffè lungo" or "caffè americano", both of which resemble the American coffee preferred by the British and Americans. Most bars have a juicer to make a "spremuta", freshly squeezed orange or grapefruit juice.

Lunch and Dinner

As with all daily rituals in Italy, food is prepared and meals are served according to local customs (e.g., in the North they prefer rice and butter, in South and Central Italy they favor pasta and olive oil).

Wine is generally served at mealtime, and while finer restaurants have excellent wine lists (some including vintage wines), ordering the house table wine generally brings good results (a house Chianti to accompany your Florentine steak in Tuscany, a sparkling Prosecco paired with your creamed stockfish and polenta in Venice, a dry white wine with pasta dressed with sardines and wild fennel fronds in Sicily).

Mineral water is also commonly served at meals and can be "gassata" (sparkling) or "naturale" (still).

The most sublime culinary experience in Italy is achieved by matching the local foods with the appropriate local wines: wisdom dictates that a friendly waiter will be flattered by your request for his recommendation on what to eat and drink. Whether at an "osteria" (a tavern), a "trattoria" (a home-style restaurant), or a "ristorante" (a proper restaurant), the service of lunch and dinner generally consists of – but is not limited to – the following: "antipasti" or appetizers; "primo piatto" or first course, i.e., pasta, rice, or soup; "secondo piatto" or main course, i.e., meat or seafood; "contorno" or side-dish, served with the main course, i.e., vegetables or salad; "formaggi", "frutta", and "dolci", i.e., cheeses, fruit, and dessert; caffè or espresso coffee, perhaps spiked with a shot of grappa.

The pizzeria

The pizzeria is in general one of the most economical, democratic, and satisfying culinary experiences in Italy. Everyone eats at the pizzeria: young people, families, couples, locals and tourists alike. Generally, each person orders her/his own pizza, and while the styles of crust and toppings will vary from region to region (some of the best pizzas are served in Naples and Rome), the acid test of any pizzeria is the Margherita, topped simply with cheese and tomato sauce.

Beer, sparkling or still water, and Coca Cola are the beverages commonly served with pizza. Some restaurants include a pizza menu, but most establishments do not serve pizza at lunchtime.

The wine bar (enoteca)

More than one English-speaking tourist in Italy has wondered why the wine bar is called an enoteca in other countries and the English term is used in Italy: the answer lies somewhere in the mutual fondness that Italians and English speakers have for one another. Wine bars have become popular in recent years in the major cities (especially in Rome, where you can find some of the best). The wine bar is a great place to sample different local wines and eat a light, tapas-style dinner.

CULTURAL DIVERSITY

Whenever you travel, not only are you a guest of your host country, but you are also a representative of your home country. As a general rule, courtesy, consideration, and respect are always appreciated by guests and their hosts alike. Italians are famous for their hospitality and experience will verify this felicitous stereotype: perhaps nowhere else in Europe are tourists and visitors received more warmly. Italy is a relatively "new" country. Its borders, as we know them today, were established only in 1861 when it became a monarchy under the House of Savoy. After WWII, Italy became a Republic and now it is one of the member states of the European Union. One of the most fascinating aspects of Italian culture is that, even as a unified country, local tradition still prevails over a universally Italian national identity. Some jokingly say that the only time that Venetians, Milanese, Florentines, Neapolitans, and Sicilians feel like Italians is when the national football team plays in international competitions. From their highly localized dialects to the foods they eat, from their religious celebration to their politics, Italians proudly maintain their local heritage. This is one of the reasons why the Piedmontese continue to prefer their beloved Barolo wine and their white truffles, the Umbrians their rich Sagrantino wine and black truffles, the Milanese their risotto and panettone, the Venetians their stockfish and polenta, the Bolognese their lasagne and pumpkin ravioli, the Florentines their bread soups and steaks cooked rare, the Abruzzese their excellent fish broth and seafood, the Neapolitans their mozzarella, basil, pizza, and pasta. As a result of its rich cultural diversity, the country's population also varies greatly in its customs from region to region, city to city, town to town. As you visit different cities and regions throughout Italy, you will see how the local personality and character of the Italians change as rapidly as the landscape does. Having lived for millennia with their great diversity and rich, highly heterogeneous culture, the Italians have taught us many things, foremost among them the age-old expression, "When in Rome, do as the Romans do."

NATIONAL HOLIDAYS

New Year's Day (1st January), Epiphany (6th January), Easter Monday (day after Easter Sunday), Liberation Day (25th April), Labour Day (1st May), Italian Republic Day (2nd June), Assumption (15th August), All Saints' Day (1st November), Immaculate Conception (8th December), Christmas Day and Boxing Day (25th-26th December).

In addition to these holidays, each city also has a holiday to celebrate its patron saint's feast day, usually with lively, local celebrations. Shops and services in large cities close on national holidays and for the week of the 15th of August.

EVERYDAY NEEDS

State tobacco shops and pharmacies

Tobacco is available in Italy only at state licensed tobacco shops. These vendors ("tabaccheria"), often incorporated in a bar, also sell stamps.

Since January 2005 smoking is forbidden in all so-called public places – unless a separately ventilated space is constructed – meaning over 90% of the country's restaurants and bars.

Medicines can be purchased only in pharmacies ("farmacia") in Italy. Pharmacists are very knowledgeable about common ailments and can generally prescribe a treatment for you on the spot. Opening time is 8:30-12:30 and 15:30-19:30 but in any case there is always a pharmacy open 24 hours and during holidays.

Shopping

Every locality in Italy offers tourists characteristic shops, markets with good bargains, and even boutiques featuring leading Italian fashion designers. Opening hours vary from region to region and from season to season. In general, shops are open from 9 to 13 and from 15/16 to 19/20, but in large cities they usually have no lunchtime break.

Tax Free

Non-EU citizens can obtain a reimbursement for IVA (goods and services tax) paid on purchases over €155, for goods which are exported within 90 days, in shops which display the relevant sign. IVA is always automatically included in the price of any purchase, and ranges from 20% to 4% depending on the item. The shop issues a reimbursement voucher to present when you leave the country (at a frontier or airport). For purchases in shops affiliated to 'Tax Free Shopping', IVA may be reimbursed directly at international airports.

Banks and post offices

Italian banks are open Monday to Friday, from 8:30 to 13:30 and then from 15 to 16. However, the afternoon business hours may vary.

Post offices are open from Monday to Saturday, from 8:30 to 13:30 (12:30 on Saturday). In the larger towns there are also some offices open in the afternoon.

Currency

As in many other European Union countries, the Euro is the Italian currency. Coins are in denominations of 1, 2, 5, 10, 20 and 50 cents and 1 and 2 euros; banknotes are in denominations of 5, 10, 20, 50, 100, 200 and 500 euros, each with a different color.

Credit cards

All the main credit cards are generally accepted, but some smaller enterprises (arts and crafts shops, small hotels, bed & breakfasts, or farm stays) do not provide this service. Foreign tourists can obtain cash using credit cards at automatic teller machines.

Time

All Italy is in the same time zone, which is six hours ahead of Eastern Standard Time in the USA. Daylight saving time is used from March to October, when watches and clocks are set an hour ahead of standard time.

Passports and vaccinations

Citizens of EU countries can enter Italy without frontier checks. Citizens of Australia, Canada, New Zealand, and the United States can enter Italy with a valid passport and need not have a visa for a stay of less than 90 days.

No vaccinations are necessary.

Payment and tipping

When you sit down at a restaurant you are generally charged a "coperto" or cover charge ranging from 1.5 to 3 euros, for service and the bread. Tipping is not customary in Italy. Beware of unscrupulous restaurateurs who add a space on their clients' credit card receipt for a tip, while it has already been included in the cover charge.

USEFUL ADDRESSES

Foreign Embassies in Italy

Australia
Via A. Bosio, 5 - 00161 Rome
Tel. +39 06 852721
Fax +39 06 85272300
www.italy.embassy.gov.au.
info-rome@dfat.gov.au

Canada
Via Salaria, 243 - 00199 Rome
Tel. +39 06 854441
Fax +39 06 85444 3915
www.canada.it
rome@dfait-maeci.gc.ca

Great Britain
Via XX Settembre, 80 -
00187 Rome
Tel. +39 06 42200001
Fax +39 06 42202334
www.britian.it
consularenquiries@rome.
mail.fco.gov.uk

Ireland
Piazza di Campitelli, 3 - 00186
Rome
Tel. +39 06 6979121
Fax +39 06 6792354
irish.embassy@esteri.it

New Zealand
Via Zara, 28 - 00198 Rome
Tel. +39 06 4417171
Fax +39 06 4402984

South Africa
Via Tanaro, 14 - 00198 Rome
Tel. +39 06 852541
Fax +39 06 85254300
www.sudafrica.it

United States of America
Via Vittorio Veneto, 121 - 00187
Rome
Tel. +39 06 46741
Fax +39 06 4882672
www.usis.it

Foreign Consulates in Italy

Australia
2 Via Borgogna
20122 Milan
Tel. +39 02 77704217
Fax +39 02 77704242

Canada
Via Vittor Pisani, 19
20124 Milan
Tel. +39 02 67581
Fax +39 02 67583900
milan@international.gc.ca

Great Britain
via S. Paolo 7
20121 Milan
Tel. +39 02 723001
Fax +39 02 86465081
ConsularMilan@fco.gov.uk

Lungarno Corsini 2
50123 Florence
Tel. +39 055 284133
Consular.Florence@fco.gov.uk

Via dei Mille 40
80121 Naples
Tel. +39 081 4238911
Fax +39 081 422434
Info.Naples@fco.gov.uk

Ireland
Piazza San Pietro in Gessate 2 -
20122 Milan
Tel. +39 02 55187569/02 55187641
Fax +39 02 55187570

New Zealand
Via Guido d'Arezzo 6,
20145 Milan
Tel. +39 02 48012544
Fax +39 02 48012577

South Africa
Vicolo San Giovanni
sul Muro 4
20121 Milan
Tel. +39 02 8858581
Fax +39 02 72011063
saconsulate@iol.it

United States of America
Via Principe Amedeo, 2/10
20121 Milan
Tel. +39 02 290351
Fax +39 02 29001165

Lungarno Vespucci, 38
50123 Florence
Tel. +39 055 266951
Fax +39 055 284088

Piazza della Repubblica
80122 Naples
Tel. +39 081 5838111
Fax +39 081 7611869

Italian Embassies and Consulates Around the World

Australia
12, Grey Street - Deakin, A.C.T.
2600 - Canberra
Tel. 02 62733333, 62733398,
62733198
Fax 02 62734223
www.ambcanberra.esteri.it
Consulates at: Brisbane, Glynde,
Melbourne, Perth , Sydney

Canada
275, Slater Street, 21st floor -
Ottawa (Ontario) K1P 5H9
Tel. (613) 232 2401/2/3
Fax (613) 233 1484 234 8424
www.ambottawa.esteri.it
ambital@italyincanada.com
Consulates at: Edmonton,
Montreal, Toronto, Vancouver,

Great Britain
14, Three Kings Yard, London
W1K 4EH
Tel. 020 73122200
Fax 020 73122230
www.amblondra.esteri.it
ambasciata.londra@esteri.it
Consulates at: London, Bedford,
Edinburgh, Manchester

Ireland
63/65, Northumberland Road -
Dublin 4
Tel. 01 6601744
Fax 01 6682759
www.ambdublino.esteri.it
info@italianembassy.ie

New Zealand
34-38 Grant Road, Thorndon,
(PO Box 463, Wellington)
Tel. 04 473 5339

Fax 04 472 7255
www.ambwellington.esteri.it

South Africa
796 George Avenue, 0083 Arcadia
Tel. 012 4305541/2/3
Fax 012 4305547
www.ambpretoria.esteri.it
Consulates at: Johannesburg,
Capetown, Durban

United States of America
3000 Whitehaven Street, NW
Washington DC 20008
Tel. (202) 612-4400
Fax (202) 518-2154
www.ambwashingtondc.esteri.it
Consulates at: Boston, MA -
Chicago, IL - Detroit, MI - Houston,
TX - Los Angeles, CA - Miami, FL -
Newark, NJ - New York, NY -
Philadelphia, PA - San Francisco, CA

ENIT (Italian State Tourism Board)

Australia
Level 4, 46 Market Street
NSW 2000 Sidney
PO Box Q802 - QVB NSW 1230
Tel. 00612 92 621666
Fax 00612 92 621677
italia@italiantourism.com.au

Canada
175 Bloor Street E. Suite 907 –
South Tower
M4W3R8 Toronto (Ontario)
Tel. (416) 925 4882
Fax (416) 925 4799
www.italiantourism.com
enit.canada@on.aibn.com

Great Britain
1, Princes Street
W1B 2AY London
Tel. 020 7408 1254
Tel. 800 00482542 FREE from
United Kingdom and Ireland
italy@italiantouristboard.co.uk

United States of America
500, North Michigan Avenue
Suite 2240
60611 Chicago 1, Illinois
Tel. (312) 644 0996 / 644 0990
Fax (312) 644 3019
www.italiantourism.com
enitch@italiantourism.com

12400, Wilshire Blvd. – Suite 550
CA 90025 Los Angeles
Tel. (310) 820 1898 - 820 9807
Fax (310) 820 6357
www.italiantourism.com
enitla@italiantourism.com

630, Fifth Avenue – Suite 1565
NY – 10111 New York
Tel. (212) 245 4822 – 245 5618
Fax (212) 586 9249
www.italiantourism.com
enitny@italiantourism.com

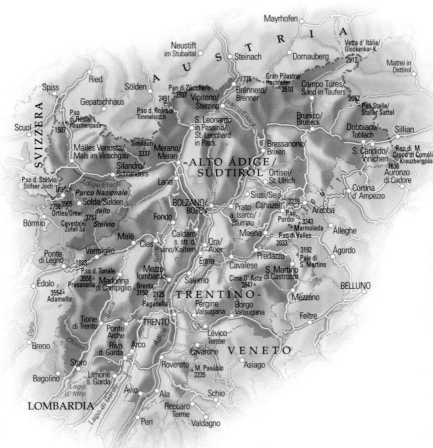

In Trentino-Alto Adige, cultural events and art flourish alongside the traditions of a mountain society where life has always been dominated by the beauty of the natural landscape. At the cross-roads between Northern and Southern Europe, the region has accumulated influences over the centuries, resulting in a legacy of cultures which may be diverse, yet have much in common in terms of the refined taste and elegance of the art-works and monuments. In this enviable natural setting, where the glistening peaks of the Dolomites

Abbey	→ Abbazia	Museum	→ Museo
Cathedral	→ Duomo	Oratory	→ Oratorio
Chapel	→ Cappella	Park	→ Parco
Castle	→ Castello	Hall	→ Sala
Church	→ Chiesa	Theater	→ Teatro
Fountain	→ Fontana	Sanctuary	→ Santuario
Hill	→ Col/colle	Valley	→ Val/valle

provide a stark contrast with the flowering meadows of the valleys, unique forms of artistic expression are to be found across the region, whether in town streets or on the shores of the crystal-clear Alpine lakes. The region is a melting pot of art embodying the cultural and artistic expressions of the peoples for whom this land is home.

Highlights

- The sumptuous stucco and fresco decoration of the Castello del Buonconsiglio in Trent
- The beautiful frescoed facades of houses in Trent
- Castel Roncolo near Bolzano
- Piazza Walther, Bolzano's elegant square and the Gothic cathedral

Inside

Bold, stars and italics are used in the text to emphasize the importance of places and art-works:

bold type **   → not to be missed
bold type *   → very important
bold type   → important
italic type   → interesting

BOZEN/BOLZANO

"For me, Bolzano is a mountain disguised as a city; whenever you move about, its appearance changes, from far away, it looks different again, and when you come back you discover it's changed yet again. It speaks different languages. It's an actress, just like the mountains, fascinating and contradictory, proud and communicative, available and cold at the same time." These words of Reinhold Messner are even more true if we consider that Bolzano is simultaneously a commercial city, a benchmark of one of Italy's finest tourist areas and a meeting-place for people from the Mediterranean and Central Europe, Italians and Germans, where speaking two languages and integration have resulted in dynamism and opening up to the outside. The bowl in which it is situated gets plenty of sunshine and is sheltered from the wind. In the Middle Ages, the town was enhanced with Gothic buildings and, in the following

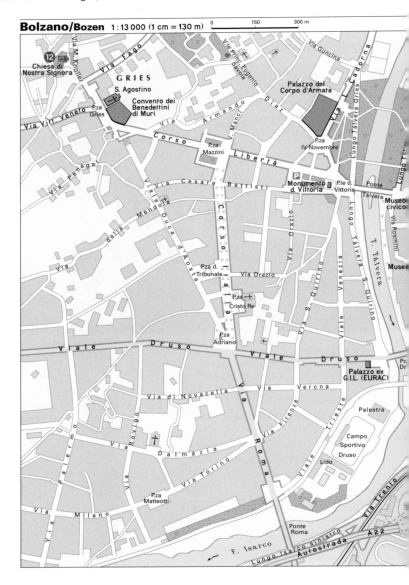

centuries, the Gothic structure wasn't altered significantly. In fact, you can still recognize it in the typical market-street of that time, with narrow, deep porticoed houses that combined commercial and residential functions. The wealth, which circulated in the streets and the workshops, 2 patronage, so that artisans were entrusted with the task of embellishing the city. Here again, Bolzano confirmed its vocation as a bridge between cultures. Beside works of the Giottoesque Schools, especially in the Dominican monastery, we find excellent creations of Gothic art: the filigreed spire of the bell tower and the sandstone pulpit created by the Swabian sculptor, Hans Lutz, for the cathedral. In the 19th century, the city's increasing fame as a health resort boomed. The small medieval town was quickly transformed by the addition of new buildings in the Oltradige style. In the early 20th century, the tourist infrastructures were regarded as being some of the most advanced in Europe: Bolzano had cutting edge skiing facilities (the electric rack at Renon, 1906; the cable-car at Colle, 1908).

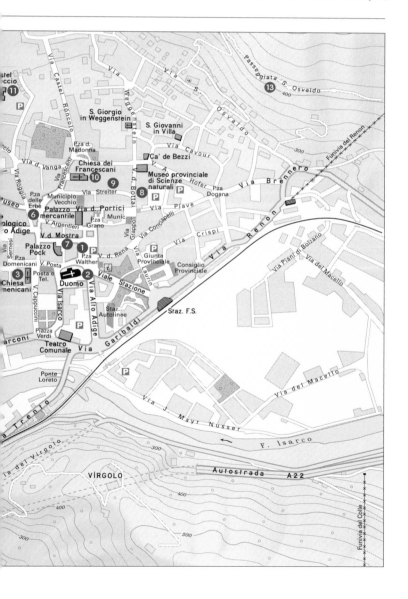

Piazza Walther ❶

The central square, located between the apse of the cathedral of Santa Maria Assunta and little Piazza del Grano, is named after Walther von der Vogelweide (1170-1230), one of the greatest medieval German poets. A statue of the poet, a neo-Romanesque work in white Lasa marble by Heinrich Natter (1889), a sculptor from the Venosta valley, stands in the center of the square. Many of the buildings around the square were reconstructed after bomb damage in 1943-45.

Duomo ❷

On one side of Piazza Walther stands the cathedral of Santa Maria Assunta. It was begun in 1280 in the Romanesque style by Lombard masons. In 1340, the building work was taken over by Swabian craftsmen, who gave the building its present Gothic forms. It has beautiful **exterior** decoration. On the left side is a Romanesque doorway, with a *Crucifixion* by a 14th-century German painter in the lunette. On the right side, a Gothic doorway with a fresco of the *Annunciation* stands between the bell tower and the **Wine door***, the name of which refers to a privilege awarded to the Parish in 1387 to sell wine at the church. The little door with a pointed arch has a spired tympanum with perforated decoration, at the sides of which are various statues in niches. The fine 16th-century **bell tower*** rises up from the roof of the church with two storeys of Gothic windows, above which a balustrade and slender rampant arches lead up to the hexagonal upper part of the tower. Its perforated spire exploits the whole range of Gothic decoration to great effect, since most of the stone appears to have been chiseled out. Near the base of the spire is an inscription with the name of the master-builder, Hans Lutz, who supervised the building work between 1501 and 1519, according to the design of Burkhard Engelberg.

The *apse*, begun in 1380, is surrounded by buttresses ending in small spires connected by a balustrade, with tall windows in-between. The *facade*, with its sloping roof and porch, belies the Romanesque origins of the building (however, the bronze doorway dates from 1989); the *polychrome roof*, covered with glazed tiles, dates from the late Gothic period. The nave and two side-aisles of the **interior** are divided into six bays by pillars supporting cross vaults. The first bay contains a large gallery with a parapet adorned with sculptures (1953); beside the doorway are fragments of frescoes by Konrad Erlin (1424) and Friedrich Pacher (*Stories of St Christopher*; 1498). On the wall of the south aisle, below the 15th-century wooden *crucifix* are Renaissance frescoes of the Bolzano School (c.1520). In the fourth bay, the *Stories of St Dorothy and St Mary* date from the mid-14th century. The frescoes depicting *Pope St Urban V* date from c.1370. In the nave, the Gothic sandstone **pulpit*** is by Hans Lutz (1514). The *chapel of the Grazie*, located behind the presbytery and the monumental Baroque high altar in polychrome marble (1710-20), was added in 1743-45 and decorated with frescoes by Carl Henrici (1771). The small marble statue on the altar, depicting *Mary Nursing the Holy Child*, dates from the 12th century.

Chiesa dei Domenicani ❸

About 100m from the cathedral stands the church of the Dominicani, dating from around 1270. It was partially rebuilt after damage incurred during the last war. It was one of the city's first Gothic buildings. In the *chapel of the Mercanti*, above the

Piazza Walther, with the Gothic apse and bell tower of the cathedral

An Annunciation in the fresco cycle of the chapel of St John in the Church of the Dominicans

altar of 1642, is the altarpiece of the *Vision of Soriano* by Guercino. On the right wall are important fragments of frescoes (*Castelbarco fresco*), from the late 14th century, marking a period in the painting of the Bolzano School, which was strongly influenced by painters of the Verona School. Next to the choir, the **chapel of San Giovanni**** is decorated with works by 14th-century painters. In the first bay, the frescoes depict the *Stories of St John the Baptist*; those in the second and third bays depict scenes from the *Life of the Virgin Mary*; in the vaults, the *Symbols of the Evangelists*, the *Fathers of the Church* and the *Prophets*. On the opposite wall, the second and third bays contain frescoes by the Maestro del Trionfo della Morte, who was obviously influenced by Giotto in his depiction of the background, and the sculptural quality of the main figures, who are extremely expressive (*Calling of St John, Wedding at Cana*, the **Vision of the Apocalypse***). The square **cloister** has paintings by Friedrich Pacher (1496). Next to the chapter house is the **chapel of Santa Caterina**, which contains works (*Stories of Jesus, the Annunciation*) by the same 14th-century masters who decorated the chapel of San Giovanni.

Museo Archeologico ④

The archeological museum covers the history of the South Tyrol from the end of the last glacial period (15,000BC) up to the time of Charlemagne (800AD). Models, reconstructions, film and multimedia facilities add to the interest. It contains some very important exhibits, such as the only complete Bronze-Age smelting kiln ever to be found in Europe, and Ötzi, the museum's most famous exhibit. Ötzi lived between 3000 and 3300BC and was discovered in 1991 at an altitude of 3,210m, emerging from the ice. His mummified body is virtually intact and, with the aid of modern analysis techniques, it has proved possible to examine his anatomy and pathological alterations in detail. Experts have also studied his clothing and equipment, resulting in an enormous amount of new information, which has enhanced our knowledge about the Bronze Age. Ötzi is kept in a special refrigerated cell at a constant temperature of -6C°/21F° and 98% humidity. Visitors to the museum can observe him through a small window.

Museo Civico ⑤

The civic museum, opened in 1905 in a building inspired by the Oltradige style, houses an important historical and art collection. It includes archeological finds,

BOZEN/BOLZANO
IN OTHER COLORS...

■ **Ski:** pages 70-101
■ **Itineraries:** pages 125, 129-134
■ **Food:** pages 165, 170, 176, 181
■ **Shopping:** pages 193, 195
■ **Events:** pages 198, 201
■ **Wellness:** pages 210-213
■ **Practical Info:** page 217

ÖTZI, THE ICE MAN

One day a man was making his way up the Senales Glacier, below the Similaun massif, on today's Italo-Austrian border, when he met his death. More than 5,000 years later, in 1991, two climbers came across his remains and, when they saw his clothes and equipment, immediately realized that they had found something very special. The studies conducted in recent years have confirmed the enormous value of the discovery because, for the first time ever in the history of archeology and medicine, it proved possible to examine a corpse that had been conserved in a humid environment, providing new information about the life of people who lived in the Copper Age (3500-2300BC). Ötzi (named after the Ötztal Mountains where he was found) was about 40 years old and 160cm tall (the photo shows the reconstruction made by the Museo Archeologico). When he made his last journey, he was carrying with him a great deal of equipment, which would have enabled him to survive for a long time far away from his habitual place of residence, procure what he needed, and repair damaged objects or make new ones himself. He wore a bearskin cap, a fur jacket, a cloak made of woven grass, leather gaiters and a leather belt, a loincloth and shoes (sewn together with thread made from animal tendons or made of plant matter). He was armed with a bow and quiver with 14 arrows with viburnum shafts, a copper axe with a yew handle, and a flint knife with an ash handle and sheath. At first it was thought that he died due to natural causes. Later, tests revealed that he had fractured ribs, some cuts on his right forearm and hand and, more particularly, a deep wound caused by a flint arrow-head which was still embedded in his left shoulder. According to the most recent reconstructions, Ötzi died after a bloody fight: one of his arrows bears traces of the blood of two people and the knife of a third person. The fact that he had weapons with him, especially the precious copper axe, suggests that he defended himself and managed to escape. While he was running away, he was hit from behind by an arrow. Now wounded, he sought refuge high in the mountains, in places he presumably knew well. Then, weakened by the loss of blood, he dropped to the ground and died.

art-works from the medieval period (stucco decoration, wooden statues and altars, detached frescoes) up to the 19th century (paintings and engravings, but also fine furnishings and household goods), objects associated with folk art and folklore (decorated stoves, wooden *Stuben* interiors, portraits, glassware, traditional costumes and masks), as well as exhibits associated with the history of Bolzano and the South Tyrol. The building is being restored. When it re-opens, its collection will include that of the *Museo della Scuola*, which documents aspects of everyday life in Tyrolean schools between 1800 and 1900.

Piazza delle Erbe ⑥

This square at the top of Via Museo is where the colorful fruit and vegetable market is held. The space for the square was created in the 13th century by filling in the moat which once surrounded the town walls. The neo-Gothic building on the corner of Via Museo occupies the site of the "Zur Sonne" hotel, mentioned by Goethe in his "Italian Journey". The bronze *Neptune fountain* (1746), has been jokingly nicknamed "Gabelwirt" (or "innkeeper with a fork"). **Via dei Portici*** leads off the square: this porticoed commercial street is the heart of the old town and one of the town's most popular shopping areas. In the 12th century, so as to use the limited space as economically as possible, long, narrow streets were built with shops and porticoes on the ground floor, two layers of cellars below ground level, dwellings on the upper floors, store-rooms behind the shops and cowsheds at the back, with tiny courtyards and skylights which provided light. The houses were rebuilt several times: the ones we see today, with their simple facades adorned with *erker* (splendid projecting windows typical of late-Gothic buildings) and stucco decoration, date from the 16th and 17th centuries. No. 46 is the *Farmacia dell'Aquila Nera*, a pharmacy that opened in 1317, and now has an Art Deco interior. At No. 30, only three Gothic arches remain of the original *Municipio Vecchio* (old town hall), which has been rebuilt several times. Across the street is the elegant five-arched facade of **Palazzo Mercantile**. The facade (1708-28), with a large balcony, has two doorways accessed by flights of stone steps, giving it a particularly majestic appearance. The internal courtyard is overlooked by two tiers of loggias, with rooms leading off them. In the Salone d'Onore, with its inlaid wooden doors, fine furniture and chandeliers, are portraits of Austrian princes, with elaborate frames, and works by 18th-century painters such as Martin Knoller, Antonio Balestra and Alessandro Marchesini (*Justice and Peace Unite Italy and Germany through Commerce*). The paintings on the ceiling of the Chancery are by Ulrich Glantschnigg. Some of the rooms now house the *Museo Mercantile*, which is devoted to Bolzano's economic history. The exhibits illustrate the trade fairs held in the town and the activities of the mercantile magistracy. On the corner of Piazza del Grano, the *Farmacia della Madonna* has been operating since 1443 and has occupied its current premises since 1602. The *Madonna* for which the pharmacy is named is a 17th-

century wooden sculpture. Narrow lanes connect Via dei Portici to the parallel street, **Via Argentieri** (Silbergasse), which follows the line of the moat around the old town. One of these lanes provides access to **Casa Troilo**, which was once entirely covered with frescoes. The large fragments of 16th-century red and white geometrical decoration are typical of the frescoes which once adorned many houses in the town. In the late 18th century, the house was completed by adding an *erker* in the shape of a turret.

Via and Piazza della Mostra ❼

Via della Mostra was where the town's wealthier citizens chose to build their houses. *Palazzo Menz* dates from 1760. The Great Hall was frescoed in 1776 by Carl Henrici with a *Masked Ball*, employing the *trompe l'oeil* technique. Across the street, *Palazzo Campofranco* (c.1760) has a large skylight. In little Piazza della Mostra, *Palazzo Pock* (1759) is an elegant L-shaped building, with windows surrounded by stuccoes and stone decorative features emphasized by the building's otherwise plain facade. In *Piazza del Grano* is *Casa della Pesa*. On its facade with two-light windows are the remains of 17th-century frescoes. We can return to Via dei Portici along a narrow lane spanned by strong arches and continue towards *Piazza del Municipio*.

Bolzano: view of the old houses on Piazza del Municipio, where the Friday market attracts many tourists

Via Portici

The layout of Via Portici, right in the heart of the town center dates from the 12th century, when the bishop-prince of Bressanone gave some of the land to the north of the cathedral to the town's merchants. Lining the sides of the street are the merchants' houses which, in order to exploit the little space available, were built with a few long, narrow rooms, illuminated by inner courtyards and skylights. The ground floor, accessed from the portico, was the shop, while the daily life of the merchant's family unfolded upstairs. The facades are the result of a number of superimposed architectural styles: stern, simple medieval facades decorated only by the occasional and very characteristic *erker* are found next to richly decorated facades with stuccoes, elegant wrought-iron decoration and harmonious sandstone balustrades. Palazzo Mercantile, built in 1727 according to a design by the architect Francesco Perotti, was used for the sessions of the Mercantile Magistrature, whose task it was to apply the laws regulating the trade fairs held in Trento. The heart of this elegant Baroque building, now the seat of a museum, is the Hall of Honor, splendidly decorated with paintings with mythological themes and portraits of members of the Austrian Imperial family.

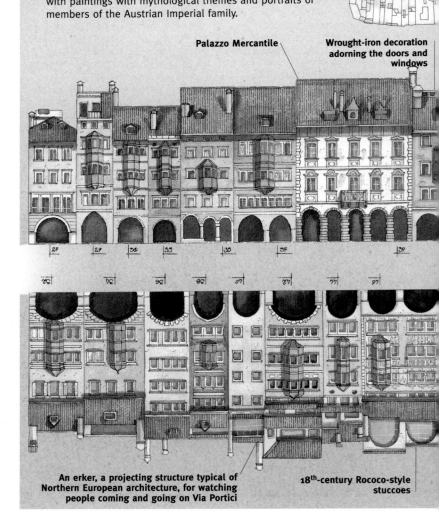

Palazzo Mercantile

Wrought-iron decoration adorning the doors and windows

An erker, a projecting structure typical of Northern European architecture, for watching people coming and going on Via Portici

18th-century Rococo-style stuccoes

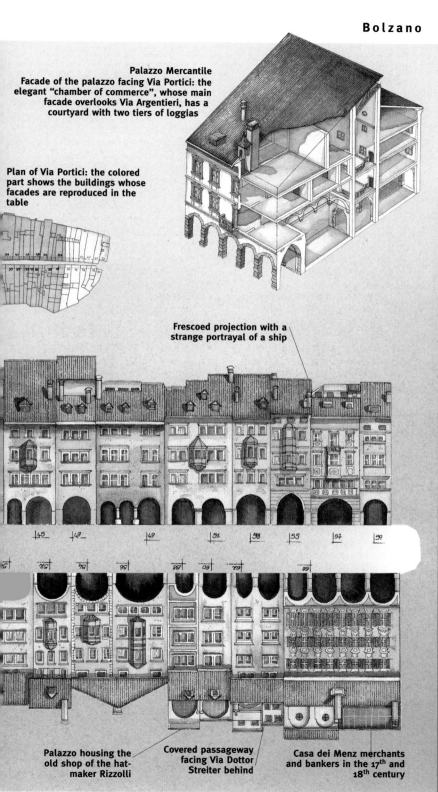

Palazzo Mercantile
Facade of the palazzo facing Via Portici: the elegant "chamber of commerce", whose main facade overlooks Via Argentieri, has a courtyard with two tiers of loggias

Plan of Via Portici: the colored part shows the buildings whose facades are reproduced in the table

Frescoed projection with a strange portrayal of a ship

Palazzo housing the old shop of the hat-maker Rizzolli

Covered passageway facing Via Dottor Streiter behind

Casa dei Menz merchants and bankers in the 17th and 18th century

Here stands *Palazzo Municipale* (Town Hall) (1907), built in the neo-Baroque style with features of the *Jugendstil*, the art style which emerged in Germany in the late 19th century and had much in common with the various European expressions of Art Nouveau.

Via Bottai ⑧

This street, which used to lead into the town from the direction of Isarco valley once thronged with taverns and inns, as the elaborate wrought-iron signs still hanging on the facades show. Near the beginning of the street, *Casa Amonn*, with an *erker*, was frescoed in 1930 by Rudolf Stolz. On the corner with Via Ca' de Bezzi, *Palazzo di Massimiliano I* (1500-12), with an *erker* in the shape of a turret, houses the **Museo Provinciale di Scienze Naturali**. The museum illustrates the geological history of the South Tyrol and the formation of the natural environment through scale models, information panels, dioramas and multimedia facilities. The collections include a wide range of minerals, fossils, beetles, butterflies and moths, shells and some herbariums.

Via Streiter ⑨

The houses here are joined by arched passageways spanning the street. The building with merlons and a broken arch is a 16th-century reconstruction of one of the towers of the old town walls. Opposite is the facade of the *Municipio Vecchio* (old Town Hall), with wooden ceilings, frescoes and paintings by local artists. Near Piazza delle Erbe are the stone tables of the old fish market.

Chiesa dei Francescani ⑩

The original church dates from the 13th century but has been altered several times since. Inside there is a Gothic choir (rebuilt, with modern windows) and an interesting fresco of *Celebrated Franciscans* (c.1500). The organ doors depict *Stories of the Infant Christ*, an important work by Georg Vischer (early 17C). Next to the choir, the *chapel of the Vergine* contains the **altar of the Nativity****, with a fine carved wooden altarpiece with doors, by Hans Klocker, dated 1500. The main part of the altar contains a scene of the *Nativity*, with a *Journey of the Magi* in the

background; the four low reliefs on the doors depict the *Annunciation*, the *Presentation at the Temple*, the *Circumcision* and the *Death of the Virgin*. In the monastery, the *chapel of S. Erardo* is decorated with 14th-century frescoes. In the **cloister***, which has 14th-century trilobate arches, there are other important paintings: a *Deposition* by the same painter who executed the works in the chapel of S. Erardo, a *Crucifixion* by a painter of the Giottoesque School, another late-Gothic *Crucifixion* and various scenes in the Mannerist style by Ludwig Pfendter, including an **Adoration of the Magi** (1609).

Castel Mareccio ⑪

The name of this unusual example of fortified architecture in the plain, surrounded by vineyards, Maretsch, comes from the word *muretes* (stone walls) which used to protect the vineyards from flooding when the Tàlvera river was in spate. Built in 1200, the castle was converted into a prestigious residence in 1549, when towers were added to the corners and a loggia was created in the courtyard. The interior was elaborately decorated with **cycles of frescoes*** which constitute some of the most important examples of 16th-century painting in the Tyrol. Some paintings contain numerous references to Greek and Roman Antiquity, and many others depict religious scenes. Furthermore, the many crests of Tyrolean families (in the Sala Kaspar) provide valuable information about heraldic traditions.

Near the castle, the *manor of Gerstburg* was decorated in 1700 by Martin Knoller, who also painted the neo-classical scenes in the hall depicting the *Triumph of Aurora*, as well as the medallions, the decoration above the doors and the painted statues. Between Castel Mareccio and the Tàlvera river, there is a panoramic hike with lovely views of the mountains around the town and the Dolomites.

Chiesa di Nostra Signora ⑫

The origins of the church are very old. Archeological excavations have unearthed a choir (below the current one) from the 10th-11th centuries, and foundations of a Roman building dating from the 2nd-3rd centuries. The church assumed its Gothic appearance in the 15th and 16th centuries.

The altar-piece by Michael Pacher in the Church of Our Lady

The polygonal **choir** with large windows and perforated decoration dates from 1410, the *chapel of S. Erasmo* from 1519, and the two remarkable **doorways with porches** (on the south side of the nave and the west side of the chapel) date from the same period. Inside are two 16th-century frescoes (*St Christopher* and the *Last Judgement*) and a wooden **crucifix** from the 13th century. The chapel of S. Erasmo contains an **altarpiece**** (1471-75) by Michael Pacher, a masterpiece of Gothic art. The main part of the altarpiece contains a relief of the *Coronation of the Virgin*. Only two of the original four low reliefs on the doors remain: an *Annunciation* and an *Adoration of the Magi*.

Passeggiata S. Osvaldo ⑬

On the slopes on the hills around Bolzano and in the valley itself there is an extensive network of footpaths running through the luxuriant vegetation, all of which can easily be accessed from the old town center. The walks are delightful and include St Oswald's Hike. The route leads through vineyards and sub-Mediterranean vegetation, and rises to 4,000m, with spectacular views. If you wish, you can continue to contour across the hillside on the path known as Petrarch's Hike to the Romanesque *church of S. Maria Maddalena* (c.3km), which has fine 14th-century frescoes in the apse and the nave.

Passeggiata del Guncina (off map)

This route (3.4km; vertical change 250m; about 45 minutes' walk) climbs steeply up the green hillside, with fine views over the town. It's a great hike for botany enthusiasts, amid luxuriant sub-Mediterranean vegetation, which benefits from this area's exposure to the sun. At the end of the trail is the *Reichrieglerhof*, or Albergo Guncina (1912). On the hillside, notice the *Maso Mauracher*, a building with late-Gothic features.

San Genesio Atesino (off map)

This holiday resort (1,087m), with its hotels and skiing facilities, which can easily be reached from the center of Bolzano, is situated on the Salto plateau. This is part of the southern part of the Tschögglberg plateau, between the Sarentina and Adige valleys. If you want to enjoy its splendid views to the full, take a cable-car trip up to the top, where the views over the town, the valley and across to the Dolomites are even more spectacular. The plateau is a perfect place for hikers and there are plenty of footpaths passing through meadows of lush grass and shady woods. You can also stop to admire the *Parish church*, with its 15th-century bell tower, 19th-century paintings and a Gothic tabernacle made in Bavaria in the 16th century. Not far from the bottom of the San Genesio cable car, a small road leads up to the ruins of *Castel Sarentino/Schloss Rafenstein*, built on a spur and dating from the 13th century. The path leads across the Tàlvera via the S. Antonio bridge and, where the path crosses the Lungo Tàlvera Bolzano, stands the manor of *Castel S. Antonio/ Klebenstein*, the starting-place of yet another hike.

Castel Roncolo (off map)

Situated perpendicularly above the Tàlvera, Castel Roncolo/Schloss Runkelstein was built in 1237, then rebuilt and decorated with frescoes in the late 14th century. The frescoes here are the finest examples of medieval secular painting in the Tyrol. In *Palazzo Occidentale* the frescoes celebrate courtly and chivalrous ideals, depicting festivals and everyday activities in a very ritual, symbolic way: dances and games are depicted against a background of landscape, one of which features Castel Roncolo (*Stanza dei Giochi*), men and women dressed according to the fashion of the time looking out of loggias, real and imaginary animals, noble crests, hunting and fishing scenes and a marvelous jousting tournament (*Sala del Torneo*). The paintings date from 1390-1395, although additions were made in the early 16th century. The *Casa d'Estate* (a building with a loggia on the ground floor, and three rooms and a balcony on the first floor) has paintings executed between 1400 and 1405 (with 16th-century additions). Here the frescoes depict crests and busts of emperors, a series of historical and legendary heroes, and episodes from the stories of *Tristan and Isolde*, *Garello*, and the *Knights of the Round Table*. Finally, in the Romanesque *chapel*, are some religious frescoes.

Niederhaus and Castel Flavòn
(off map)

The paintings at Niederhaus are contemporary with the paintings of Castel Roncolo and similar in style, but less numerous. Some of the details in the paintings (e.g., a tin bath and a picnic in a wood) give them a more "domestic" dimension. The manor of Niederhaus is at Oltrisarco, in the area beyond Roma bridge, below Castel Flavòn/Haselburg. The latter has 16th-century frescoes depicting mythological scenes and others from Roman history.

Colle (off map)

Colle/Kohlern (1,136m) is situated on a peak with splendid **views** of the Bolzano valley and the mountains which surround it, and across to the glaciers of Cevedale and the Dolomites. It can be reached by the cable car located in Via Campiglio. This was the first cable car in the world to be built, in 1908. In those days it had wooden pylons and open-air, six-seater cabins. A reproduction of the original cabin can be seen near the upper cable-car station.

DAY TRIPS

BRIXEN/BRESSANONE [40 km]

In the broad, sunny plain at the confluence of the Isarco and Rienza rivers, surrounded by hillsides cultivated with vineyards and orchards, Bressanone is the oldest town in the South Tyrol. Its defensive walls, built in 1015-39 on the right bank of the Isarco river once surrounded the cathedral, the bishop's castle, and the dwellings of the town's clergy and the merchants. Today, this early nucleus can still be recognized, although only three gates of the original fortifications survive. Between 1500 and 1600 the bishop-princes transformed the medieval fortified town into a beautiful, albeit tiny, Renaissance capital, which was gradually altered to the Baroque style. The work done on the residence of the bishop princes and, later, the rebuilding of the cathedral provided an example for the nobles and rich citizens of Bressanone. In private and public buildings, they superimposed or replaced Gothic features with the gentler, more spacious style brought by architects and artists from Italy. In the second half of the 19th century, Bressanone

Bressanone: Cathedral

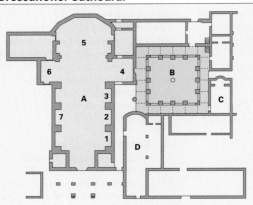

A Cathedral
B Cloister
C Church of St John the Baptist
D Church of the Virgin in Ambitu
1 *Crucifixion* by Josef Schöpf
2 *St John Nepomucene being thrown off the bridge over the Moldava in Prague* by G. B. Cignaroli

3 *Transfiguration* by Cristoforo Unterperger
4 *Madonna of the Rosary* by Francesco Unterperger
5 *Death of the Virgin* by Michelangelo Unterperger
6 *Martyrdom of St Cassian* by Paul Troger
7 *Martyrdom of St Agnes* by Cristoforo Unterperger

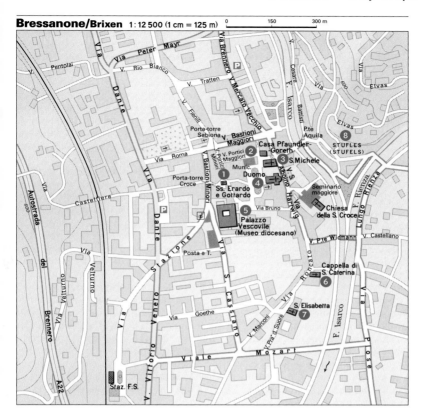

Bressanone/Brixen 1:12 500 (1 cm = 125 m)

became a health resort. Later, tourism became a decisive part of the economy and a further boost was given by the construction of the Plose cable car, leading up to ski runs with excellent facilities. Entering the old town center through Porta Croce (or Porta Sole), you immediately encounter the *church of Ss. Erardo e Gottardo*, the earliest evidence of which dates from the 9th century. Turn left into **Via dei Portici Minori** ❶: the houses, with elaborate *erker* and merloned facades, date from the late medieval period, and were built quite high for reasons of space. Shops and workshops were located under the porticoes, the dwellings were on the upper floors, the storerooms and service rooms were at the back and were illuminated by small, inner courtyards. At an intersection there is a strange 16th-century statue, the so-called *Uomo selvaggio* (wild man), a three-headed giant, which was probably once an inn sign. On **Via Portici Maggiori** ❷, *Casa Kaltenegger* is a Gothic building, which

has been altered several times. The other side of the house, with a merloned facade and a tower, overlooks Piazza del Duomo. It contains interesting frescoes depicting scenes from the history of Bressanone (1901). At the end of the street stands one of Bressanone's most beautiful buildings, the **Casa Pfaundler Goreth**, an excellent example of the transition between the late Gothic and Renaissance styles. The facade, decorated by polygonal *erker*, has arched windows framed by fine wrought-iron work; on the top floor you can see the remains of frescoes. Not far away, the facade of the **church of S. Michele** ❸ is decorated with a rose window and three blind niches, lending even greater importance to the elaborate marble doorway below. The *bell tower*, called the Torre Bianca (White Tower), was built in 1459. 72m high, its profile is marked by projecting windows with sloping roofs. The bell tower is one of the symbols of the city, together with the towers of the cathedral. The interior of

27

A detail of the frescoes in the cloister of Bolzano cathedral

the church is a riot of 18th-century Baroque decoration, with frescoes, stuccoes, polychrome marble and altarpieces. Nearby, the **cathedral*** ❹ is a combination of several buildings which has been altered over the years. The first church was built in the 10th century. The building is instantly recognizable because of the bell towers on either side of the facade. In the center is a round window and, above it, a niche with a polychrome wooden statue of the *Madonna*. Five arches and a cornice with stucco decoration and statues form the narthex, dating from 1783-85. The sumptuous interior consists of a single broad nave with side-chapels. The marble (33 different types), stucco decoration and *paintings* are quite overwhelming. The *frescoes* in the vaults above the nave, in the gallery, the transept, the choir and the sacristy, executed between 1748 and 1750 by Paul Troger, are some of the most important Baroque paintings in the Tyrol. Particular attention should be devoted to the frescoes above the nave, covering an area of 250m². From the square, you enter the **cathedral cloister**** by way of a corridor with tombstones and the remains of frescoes. This runs along the side of the *church of the Vergine in Ambitu*, which dates from the 13th century and was altered in the following century (note the fine Romanesque

frescoes above the Gothic vault). Between the 20 arches of the cloister (pointed arches supported by small paired columns) are 15 wonderful Gothic **frescoes** painted in the late 14th and 15th centuries. The paintings are not organized according to any iconographic scheme. The frescoes in each bay have a different theme, dictated by the various donors. The south corner of the cloister leads into the little **church of S. Giovanni Battista**, formerly the chapel of the old bishop's palace. The frescoes on the upper part of the walls of the nave date from the 13th century. Beyond the *Colonna del Millennio*, a column erected to mark the town's thousandth anniversary, you come to *Hofburg*, the **Bishop's Palace*** ❺. Hardly anything remains of the original 13th-century building. The current sumptuous palace (1595) is built around a **courtyard*** with two tiers of Renaissance loggias on the north and south sides. The rooms of the apartments are decorated with stuccoes and frescoes: in particular, the reception hall in the apartment reserved for the Habsburgs contains a series of precious tapestries and a ceiling with optical illusions painted by Antonio Gresta (1710). The rooms of the building house the **Museo Diocesano****, which has works of sacred art. The collections include masterpieces produced between the Middle Ages and the mid-19th century: beautiful *crucifixes* (particularly the fragment of the **crucifix** from Lamprechtsburg, near Brunico, dated between 1140 and 1150), late Romanesque and Gothic wooden sculptures, paintings on panels and canvas, sacred furnishings, gold- and silver-ware. The museum contains a wide range of historical exhibits and art-works from the town and the surrounding area. One section is devoted to Christmas cribs (Nativity scenes, 18C), with thousands of painted wooden figures. By walking along Via Bruno and Via Hartwig, you reach the *Seminario Maggiore* (Great Seminary), situated between the center of the old town and the Isarco river. This 18th-century building has a fine library frescoed by Franz Anton Zeiller, who also executed the decoration in the *church of the Santa Croce* next-door. By continuing along Via Roncato, you come to the *chapel of S.*

Caterina ❻ and the *church of S. Elisabetta* ❼: the first contains an altarpiece, the second a fine *Stations of the Cross* by Francesco Unterperger. This painter was also responsible for the cycle of the *Life of St Clare* in the *convent of the Clarisse*, next to the church of S. Elisabetta. The *convent of Francescani* contains a remarkable *carved wooden altarpiece by* Hans Klocker (15C). Turning back towards the town center, behind the church of S. Michele, is the *Museo della Farmacia*, which has exhibits dating back more than 400 years illustrating the history of the art of the pharmacist. The little town of *Stufles* ❽, beyond the river, has old houses and fine manors. There are also some interesting 19th- and 20th-century buildings, including some examples of *Jugendstil*, in the area of Via Stazione.

BRUNECK/BRUNICO [74 km]

Brunico was built in about 1252 as a fortified town surrounded by walls and a moat below a castle, on the right bank of the Rienza river. It has the usual plan of a medieval town, can be accessed through four town gates and has a single main street, Via Centrale (Stadtgasse), which is still one of the most beautiful, lively streets in the South Tyrol. Brunico was the center of thriving trade and craft activities, which have continued to flourish over the centuries. Today, the little town is one

of the region's most important centers for supplying ski resort equipment, which is distributed to the Piana di Riscone (cross-country skiing) and the slopes of the rounded and panoramic **Plan de Corones/Kronplatz**, one of the finest downhill skiing areas, with almost 100km of ski runs. The **church of Salvatore alle Orsoline** ❶, built in the 15th century, used to stand right next to the walls. In fact, the bell tower formed part of the defensive structure, as we can see from the part of chemin-de-ronde with loopholes at the bottom of the spire. On the facade, the Gothic doorway with a decorative gable is preceded by a flight of steps. On the neo-Gothic high altar, are some *reliefs* which belonged to a wooden altarpiece dating from about 1435. Next to it, on the *Porta delle Orsoline (Gate of the Ursulines)*, once part of the old defensive walls, are painted family crests and a *Crucifixion* from about 1420 by Giovanni da Brunico. **Via Centrale** ❷ runs between Porta delle Orsoline and Porta Ragen, forming an arc around the castle hill. The harmonious buildings, which are two- or three-storeys high, have only a few decorations, usually simple *erker* or frescoed cornices. No. 43 was once a **Trinkstube***, an exclusive meeting-place for a group of citizens. These 'clubs' were common all over the German-speaking part of Europe, but few of

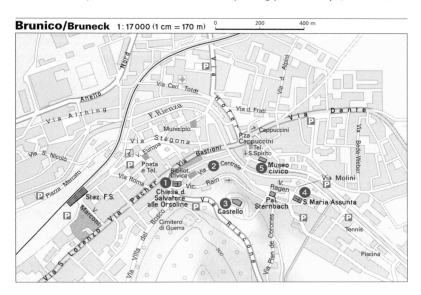

Brunico/Bruneck 1:17 000 (1 cm = 170 m)

Brunico, with its castle and the churches dedicated to the Assumption and St Catherine

them are still so well preserved. The painted decoration, by Ulrich Springenklee, dates from 1526 and depicts family crests and scrolls with names and mottoes, surrounded by ingenious compositions, which allude to wine. Naturally the family crests correspond to the places at the table occupied by the members of this merry society. The **castle** ❸ was built in 1252, extended in the 14th century, and surrounded by defensive walls in 1518. In the courtyard stands a round tower with an internal staircase leading to the upper floors. The **church of S. Maria Assunta** ❹, in the neo-Romanesque style (1866), is decorated with *frescoes*. Some of the older art-works include a sculpture of the *Pietà* (1410-15), *Christ with the Cyrenian* (15C), and a *crucifix* of the school of Michael Pacher. In the refurbished stables of the old post inn, the **Museo Civico** ❺ exhibits works by Michael and Friedrich Pacher, the Maestro di Uttenheim, Simone da Tésido and other painters of the Pusteria valley and elsewhere in the Tyrol. Great emphasis is given to the collection of drawings by contemporary artists of the region.

DEUTSCHNOFEN/ NOVA PONENTE [25 km]

Situated on the plateau between the Ega and the Adige valleys, Nova Ponente has several treasures worth visiting. First, the *Parish church of S. Benedetto* contains four **panels** belonging to a wooden altarpiece by Hans von Judenburg

(1421-25; the main part of the altar and predella have been lost), depicting the *Nativity*, the *Adoration of the Magi*, the *Presentation at the Temple* and the *Dormition*. In the *manor of Thurn*, the *Museo Territoriale* contains works of sacred art, archeological remains, and documents about local history. About 2.5km from the town, a small road leads to the **church of S. Elena****, which was built in the 12th century, and is situated in a panoramic position with views of Latemar. The small church contains *frescoes* by a 15th-century painter associated with Hans Stotzinger, which are regarded as some of the most important Gothic works of the Bolzano School. In *the church of S. Agata*, about an hour's hike from the town, there are fragments of 14th-century frescoes.

ENNEBERG/MAREBBE [84 km]

East of the Badia valley, the Marebbe valley carves its way steeply between the Fanes and Senes Dolomites. The upper valley has retained its old appearance, with its *viles* (a Ladin word used to describe small clusters or villages of buildings built in a particular way: usually they are situated on the tops of hills and are adapted according to the lie of the land and exposure to the sun). The most famous village is *San Vigilio di Marebbe/Al Plan*, an important summer-holiday and ski resort. Here, the **church of S. Vigilio** (1781) is decorated in a luminous Rococo style, which has much in common with the Bavarian Baroque. Inside, lofty *frescoes* are emphasized by white and gold stucco decoration to great effect, especially in the two domes. At *Corte/Curt*, the *maso* of the same name is a very old building, cited in a document of 1296. At *Pieve di Marebbe/La Pli de Mareo*, the *manor of Moreck*, called *Gran Ciasa*, is a massive 16th-century building with fresco decoration inside. The Gran Ciasa is the starting-point for a hike that crosses meadows and woods to the *viles* of **Ciaseles**, **Frontü**, **Fordora** and **Frena**.

EPPAN AN DER WEINSTRASSE/ APPIANO SULLA STRADA DEL VINO [10 km]

Appiano, whose administrative territory includes several villages, is distinctive for its concentration of castles and manors: the former because of its position, at the entrance to the Bolzano valley; the latter to the wealth generated by the agricultural estates, which had been farmed for centuries, especially with vineyards. As you enter *Cornaiano/Girlan* note the *manor of Breitenberg* (1650), which features a late use of the Oltradige style. At *San Michele/St. Michael* are the manors of **Wohlgemuth** (1620), **Thalegg** (1546) and **Altenburg** (1592). At *Monte/Berg* the **manor of Reinsberg** (17C), with *chapel of S. Croce* attached, is one of the finest examples of the Oltradige style, on account of the balanced use of Gothic

San Paolo's most striking building is undoubtedly the lovely parish church (pieve) in the center of town

and Renaissance features and the simultaneous use of Baroque features. At *Ganda di Sotto/Untere Gand* stands the remarkable **manor of Kreit** (1597), surrounded by green vineyards. At *San Paolo/St Paul* the bell tower of the monumental **Parish church** (1460-1550) is incorporated into the facade, which exploits the symmetry of the buttresses and stringcourses. Wooden sculptures inside the church include a **Madonna and Child** (c.1460), holding a bunch of grapes, symbolizing the town's prosperous farming tradition. To the west, below the mountains, are the **castles**, starting at *Predonico/Perdonig*, with *Castelforte/Festenstein* (13C), and, at *Missiano/Missian*, **Castel d'Appiano/ Hocheppan****, built in the 12th century and overlooking a sheer drop. This remarkable example of defensive architecture, with its 30m-high pentagonal keep, contains a chapel entirely decorated with fine Romanesque *frescoes*, in which the influence of painters from Verona and Aquileia can be detected. Continuing south from here are *Castel Corba/Korb*, a 13th-century fortified tower-house, and *Castel Boymont*, a fortified Romanesque manor which, despite the fact that it is ruined, was obviously once a fine building. At *Pigenò*, *Castel Ganda/Gandegg* is memorable on account of its richly decorated interior and for the **chapel of the Madonna della Neve** (1698), a masterpiece in the Baroque style. At *San Paolo*, *Castel Wart* dates from the 12th century and probably formed a single system of fortifications along with the *Altenburg* nearby. From San Michele a country road leads through vineyards and then woodland (5km) to the small *lakes of Monticolo*. In a wooded area not far from Castel Ganda are the *buche di ghiaccio* (literally "ice holes"). This curious phenomenon is the result of the presence of deposits from landslides with very large stones between which currents of cold air form underground. When these rise to the surface they alter the microclimate. When you approach, you will notice a change in the temperature and the level of humidity, while the vegetation changes from sub-Mediterranean to Alpine.

LADIN

Ladin, also known as Rhaeto-romance, is not a dialect, as many people think, but a collection of similar neo-Latin languages, spoken in the central and eastern parts of the Alpine Chain, from Switzerland to Friuli, by about 700,000-900,000 people. In the year 15BC, the Romans conquered this Alpine region. The development of the Ladin language began as a result of the superimposition of the Roman culture and language over the language and culture of the Celts (the Raeti) and may have taken hold very early, even during the early centuries of the Christian era. During the Middle Ages and in modern times, the geographical position of Ladinia between the Italian and German linguistic spheres heavily influenced its later development. The fact that most people in the area were German-speaking meant that German became predominant, and that Ladin became confined to the more isolated side-valleys. The Ladin spoken in the Dolomites can be divided into five main streams: the fascian of the Fassa valley in the Trentino, which is considerably influenced by Italian; the gherdëina of the Val Gardena and the badiot of the Badia valley and the Marebbe valley, which have been more influenced by German; the fodom of Livinallongo and the ampezan of Cortina, which are strongly influenced by the dialect of the Veneto. The Province of Bolzano (Bulsan) officially recognizes the Ladin language and the minority is protected under various laws, which also concern education in state schools. In fact, in the schools of the valleys in the South Tyrol where Ladin is spoken, Ladin is the language used for teaching, along with German and Italian. There are also various publications in Ladin, (books and newspapers), radio news broadcasts and television programs. A Provincial law passed in 1976 led to the foundation of the Istitut Ladin "Micurà de Rü", based in San Martino in Badia, "with the aim of conserving, protecting and studying the language, culture and ethnic characteristics of Ladin". The institute conducts scientific research into the language, history and culture of the Ladin people of the Dolomites, and encourages the use of the written and spoken language, partly through the mass media, partly through publications and the organization of cultural events. There is also an Istitut Pedagogich Ladin, based in Bolzano and Ortisei, which is concerned primarily with organizing Ladin activities in schools.

GADERTAL/VAL BADIA [75 km]

San Leonardo/San Linard in the Badia valley was where Franz Singer and Matthäus Günther worked. These men were responsible for designing and decorating the *Parish church of Ss. Giacomo e Leonardo*. At *La Villa/La Vil*, in the bowl below Gardenaccia and Piz la Villa, stands *Castel Colz*, a square, 16th-century manor surrounded by walls with small round turrets. In the hollow sheltered by the rocky pyramid of Sassongher (2,665m), with a view of the great buttress of the Sella range, Corvara in Badia/Corvara is a famous ski resort, with cutting edge facilities and a wide range of excellent accommodation. In the late Gothic *church of S. Caterina*, with a neo-Gothic loggia, 15th-century frescoes have been discovered below later layers of decoration in the nave, the choir and on the triumphal arch. The carved wooden **altarpiece***, dated 1519, is by the workshop of Michael Parth. In the village of *Colfosco/Colfusc*, the church of

S. Vigilio has a high altar, which is a combination of 15th- and 18th-century features. From here you can continue towards the Gardena Pass (2,121m) and the Plan de Gralba with spectacular **views** of the Dolomites.

GLURNS/GLORENZA [83 km]

Surrounded by a massive set of fortifications (7m high and 1.5m thick) with round towers and square tower-gates, Glorenza is one of the finest examples of a fortified town. The porticoes, houses, manors and churches all date from the time when the town was a compulsory stopping-place for the trade between southern Germany, Switzerland, the Tyrol and Italy. The Empire renewed the fortifications in the 16th century, adapting them to withstand cannon fire. Look out for the manors of *Fröhlich* (c.1570), *Hössische Behausung*, (originally late Gothic but with Baroque additions) and the 16th-century *Hendlspurg*. The *Parish church of S.*

Pancrazio, built in 1481, lies outside the walls. Its 14th-century bell tower (to which a Baroque spire was added) is frescoed with a *Last Judgement*, dated 1496.

INNICHEN/SAN CANDIDO [106 km]

In 1143 work started on the great church of San Candido, and continued until 1284, resulting in the most important Romanesque building in the region. The **collegiate church of Ss. Candido e Corbiniano**** has a facade flanked by a massive bell tower (1325) decorated with a rose window. Behind the facade, a 15th-century narthex leads through a Romanesque doorway with sculpted capitals into the church. The interior, with a nave, two side-aisles and a triple apse, has a raised presbytery above the crypt. The frescoes in the vault of the dome date from the 13th century (*Story of the Creation*). Above the altar is a carved wooden altarpiece of the **Crucifixion**. This work is of great historic and artistic importance because, although it was carved in about 1250, its original colors have been preserved. The *frescoes* in the

gallery are by Leonardo da Bressanone (c.1470). The south door, known as the Porta dei Veneziani (Venetians' door) because it faced the road leading to the Veneto, has a lunette with a Romanesque relief depicting *Christ and the Symbols of the Evangelists*; the fresco above the arch, which dates from 1475, is by Friedrich Pacher. On one side of the transept, by the cemetery fence, which surrounds the church, the former chapter granary now houses the *Museo della Collegiata*, with a collection of historical documents, art-works, objects from the Treasury, and a library of books dating from the 14th to 17th centuries. In the cemetery, a shrine near the western entrance contains frescoes of a *Last Judgement* by Leonardo da Bressanone. Another *shrine* with a pyramid-shaped roof contains 15th-century paintings. Opposite the collegiate church, the *Parish church of S. Michele*, rebuilt after a fire in 1740, has a round bell tower. Behind its fine Baroque facade, the nave is richly decorated with *frescoes*. At the entrance to the town, the *Ausserkirchl* (17C) is an unusual example of Baroque religious architecture: it consists of two chapels joined by a central chamber. At the confluence of the Sesto stream and the Drava river, the *church of S. Leopoldo* adjacent to the Franciscan monastery contains a valuable *Madonna and Child with Sts Francis and Leopold* (1764). Villa Wachtler houses *Dolomythos*, a museum about the local area with information about the geological history and wildlife of the Dolomites.

KALTERN AN DER WEINSTRASSE/CALDARO SULLA STRADA DEL VINO [15 km]

In the territory of Caldaro, numerous fine manors were built in the 16th and 17th centuries. In the town center, note the former inn of **Zum Weissen Rössl** (1586, with a lovely 18th-century wrought-iron sign) and the manor of *Reich an Platz*; at *Monte di Mezzo/Mitterdorf*, *Castel Campan/Kampan*, with its courtyard and loggias; at *Pianizza di Sopra/Oberplanitzing* and *San Giuseppe al Lago/St Josef am See* the manors of *Andergassen* and *Ringberg*, both dating from the 17th century. The *Parish church of the Assunta*, dating from the late 18th century, has a Gothic bell tower. The

San Candido: Collegiate church of Sts Candidus and Corbinian

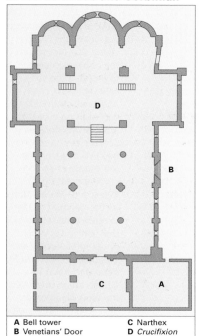

A Bell tower   **C** Narthex
B Venetians' Door   **D** *Crucifixion*

ceilings of the nave and the choir are frescoed by Josef Schöpf (1792), and there are altarpieces by Michelangelo Unterperger (*Madonna of the Rosary*, 1740) and Johann Georg Grassmair (*The Magi*, 1728). Nearby, the **Museo Provinciale del Vino** occupies the wine cellar of a medieval building. It contains tools, equipment and paintings associated with winemaking. The *church of the Santa Croce al Calvario* (1720) has an altarpiece by Paul Troger (now replaced by a photograph) with a beautiful gilt carved wooden frame (with cherubs and bunches of grapes). There are good frescoes in the *church of S. Caterina* (Hans Stotzinger, 1414) at Villa di Mezzo; the *church of S. Nicolò* (1529-36) and the *church of S. Antonio Abate* (of the 14th and 15th centuries) in the villages of the same name; and the *church of S. Leonardo* (c.1380) at *Pianizza di Sotto/Unterplanitzing*. From Caldaro a funicular leads up to **Méndola**, a health resort with a very long tradition. Southeast of the town is **Lake Caldaro**, a nature reserve, where birds stopover when migrating and breed.

MALS IM VINSCHGAU/ MALLES VENOSTA [85 km]

In the Venosta valley, Malles Venosta can be distinguished by its many bell towers. Among them rises the round tower of *Castel Fröhlich/Fröhlichburg*, documented as early as the 14th century. Although there are many fine buildings in the town, it is particularly memorable for its lovely Romanesque churches. **S. Benedetto**** dates from the 8th century and has a 12th-century bell tower. The *frescoes* and the remains of stucco and marble decoration are some of the oldest in the whole of the German-speaking cultural area, and date from just after the year 800. The *church of S. Martino*, altered in the 15th and 16th centuries, has a Romanesque **bell tower** dating from the 12th century. From the same period, the **bell tower** of the *church of S. Giovanni* has stood alone since the church was demolished in 1799. The Gothic bell tower of the *Parish church of the Assunta* dates from 1523-1531. The ceiling of the choir is decorated with frescoes, which have strong affinities with the *Jugendstil*.

MARIENBERG/ MONTE MARIA [5 km]

The finest treasure of the Venosta valley and one of the most important in the Tyrol is the Benedictine Abbey of Monte Maria, whose white form and onion-shaped domes stand on the right bank of the Adige at the bottom of the Slingia valley. The oldest part of the abbey complex, founded in the 12th century, is the crypt, above which the church was built on a basilica plan. It was finished in 1201. In the *crypt*, which has five bays, is one of the treasures of 12th-century painting. The Maestro di Monte Maria, as the painter is called, executed the fresco on the ceiling depicting *Christ in Mandorla with Cherubs, Angels and Sts Peter and Paul*. The figures stand out against the lapis lazuli blue background dotted with stars, emphasizing the stark contrasts in color

SPRING IN VENOSTA VALLEY: MAGIC OF FLOWERS AND ICE

The Venosta valley is the kingdom of apple farming par excellence. The farmers here use organic farming methods, insects, to combat parasites. In fact, the ladybird has become the symbol of this high-quality production area. In spring, when the apple orchards begin to flower, this valley offers a fascinating spectacle of rare beauty. High up, the peaks are still covered in snow, while down in the valley, the delicate pinkish-white flowers of the apple-trees emanate their sweet, intense perfume, particularly in the evening. The irrigation system used to defend the crops from the frost is quite amazing. During the clear, cold nights, the delicate flowers would otherwise be damaged by the frost. The method is based on the phenomenon known as "freezing heat": water which freezes produces heat which, below a thin layer of ice, prevents the temperature of the buds from falling below one degree below zero. Seen with the naked eye, the effect is unforgettable: an enchanted forest of frozen flowers sparkling in the early-morning sun.

REINHOLD MESSNER'S CASTLE

Castel Juval is perched on a steep rocky spur and has stood in this for more than 700 years. Built in about 1278 by Hugo von Montalban, it occupies a towering position dominating the Venosta, Passiria and Senales valleys. The views from its windows are spectacular. Since 1983, it has been home to the famous mountaineer, Reinhold Messner, who has restored the castle to house his considerable collections, the result of his many travels and his passion for nature: collections of art-works from Tibet, masks from all over the world, a photographic exhibition of his mountaineering exploits and a botanical trail.

Today the castle even looks rather like a Tibetan monastery but, surrounded by its network of Waalwege (paths following irrigation channels), a maso (alpine farmhouse) with its vineyards and nearby tavern, it still preserves some of the oldest traditions of this area.

gateways is all that remains of the medieval wall demolished in the 19th century. The **cathedral of S. Nicolò*** ❶ (1302-1465), which is Gothic with a crenellated facade, has a majesty which is enhanced by the massive *bell tower* (83m high), with seven clocks, arranged in pairs on the sides and at the bottom of a pointed arch (with frescoes). On the south side of the church are two 15th-century *doorways*. The inside is worth visiting to see the 14th-century choir, with *stained-glass windows*, two of which date from the late 15th century (the others are neo-Gothic, from the 19C). Between the cathedral and Piazza del Grano, **Via dei Portici** ❷ is a market-street, with rows of porticoed 16th- and 17th-century buildings with *erker*. Note *Casa Mahlknecht* with its *Jugendstil* decoration and the *Palazzo Municipale* (*Town Hall*) (1927-31). The *Museo della Donna "Evelyn Ortner"* contains a vast

and the refined drawing technique; on the west wall is a fresco of *Celestial Jerusalem*. The *church of Nostra Signora*, altered in the 17th century, is decorated with white, yellow and gold stuccoes. The *pulpit*, with gold statues of saints and a canopy with angels on the top dates from the 18th century. In the monastery buildings, the *refectory* is lined with wooden paneling with architectural scenes in low relief (c.1630); the *Sala Principesca*, which corresponds to the *erker* on the southwest corner, has elegant Rococo frescoes.

MERAN/MERANO [28 km]

Merano, in the Passiria valley, is famous as a beauty spot and for its mild climate. The little town is popular because of its geographical position, in a deep hollow sheltered by the mountains, facing south, with low rainfall, not much wind, and thermal springs. Merano, a true garden city, has an eclectic architectural style and, despite the increasing number of tourist initiatives, one of the most recent being the building of the Merano 2000 ski resort, it has managed to preserve its true character. You enter the town through the *Bolzano gateway*, which with the *Venosta* and *Passiria*

Porta di Val Venosta, together with Porta Bolzano and Porta Passirio, is all that survives of the medieval walls demolished in the 19 century

35

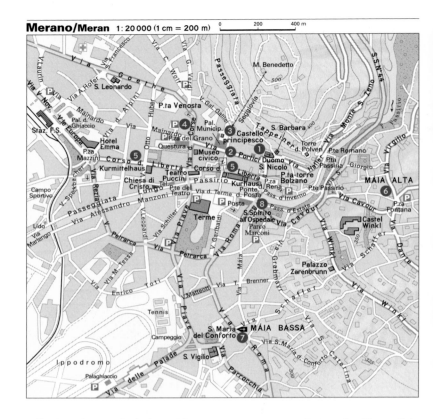

Merano/Meran 1:20 000 (1 cm = 200 m)

collection of women's clothes and costumes dating from 1820 to the present day. Behind the Town Hall, the **Castello Principesco (Prince's Castle)** ❸ is a small palace built in about 1470, above earlier foundations. It contains an exhibition of furniture, and collections of weapons and musical instruments. Other rooms of note include the *Emperor's room*, lined with wood paneling, with a huge majolica stove dating from the 15th century. In the chapel there is a *St George and the Dragon* by the Bressanone School, (1455). In Via Galilei, opposite the castle, is the station of the cable car, which goes up to Mt Benedetto (it can also be reached in 20 minutes on foot by climbing the steps behind the cathedral), a beautiful spot with **wonderful views**. In **Via delle Corse** ❹, between Venosta gateway and Piazza del Teatro, there are some beautiful buildings with *Jugendstil* decoration on the facade, including the *Schwarze Katz* and a small palace. The former Roter Adler inn, painted with red and white

squares, now houses the **Museo Civico**, with its collections of prehistoric remains, Gothic wooden sculptures, painted panels from the 14th and 16th centuries, and paintings by the region's most famous painters. From Piazza del Teatro Puccini (1899), built in the *Jugendstil*, you enter **Corso Libertà** ❺, the scene of merrymaking in the late 19th century. The **Kurhaus*** overlooking the river is a magnificent building (1874) which had an area for bathing and another for entertaining its guests (ballrooms for concerts and shows). The colonnaded facade has a tympanum and a sculpture of the *Dancing Graces*, above which is a dome. Together with the wing built in 1914 with a nave and two side-aisles, it resembles a basilica built to celebrate the worldliness of the Belle Époque. Via S. Giorgio and Via Cavour both lead to the area of **Maia Alta/Obermais*** ❻, where prestigious villas and manors were built. Note *Castel Rundegg* (15C), the residence of *Reichenbach*, documented in 1380, *Castel Rottenstein*

NATURE AND BEAUTY

Sissi is the name affectionately coined by the Austrian people to refer to
Elizabeth of Austria, one of the best-loved sovereigns ever to sit on a throne.
Her personality still seems to haunt the gardens of Castello Trauttmansdorff
(in the photo), where she came in 1870 to nurse her ailing health. Here,
nature is an expression of art, an elect place for the soul, a man-made paradise
for meditating and drawing inspiration, where architects and botanists have
created a setting for the plants of every conceivable continent and latitude.
Finding your way around the 12 hectares of garden, which opened to the public
in 2001, is easy because it's divided into four distinct sectors: there are
the plants of sun-kissed lands, with olive- and lemon-trees, vines, fig-trees,
holm oaks, lavender and the succulents of desert habitats; there are the landscapes
of the Tyrol; then water gardens and the forests of the world, with trees from all over
the globe. More than 6km of carefully designed footpaths thread their way through
this botanical garden interspersed with steps, pavilions and ravines. Thousands of
species are represented. The garden is dominated by the castle,
which houses the Touriseum, a museum that provides interesting information
about 200 years of alpine tourism. The castle lies 2km east of Merano,
30km from the A22 highway (crossing the Brenner Pass).

(14C) and the manor of *Rosenstein*
(1602). The area of Piazza Fontana
leads to *Castel Winkl*, dating from the
14th century. Between Via Schaffer and
Via Dante, the manor of *Knillenberg*
(1616) was frescoed in the 18th century.
In Via Schaffer, **Palazzo Zarenbrunn**
with its onion-shaped dome houses the
Greek Orthodox *church of S. Nicola
Taumaturgo*, with a wooden iconostasis
and a precious *collection of icons*,
sacred vestments and documents.
Where Via Schaffer and Via Roma
cross, in Maia Bassa/Untermais, is the
church of S. Maria del Conforto ** ❼ ,
which dates from the 12th century. On

the south side of the exterior is a *cycle
of frescoes* dating from the late 14th
century. Inside, on the triumphal arch
and the adjacent walls, are paintings
which are unique in the region: the
Stories of the Virgin Mary and the
Council of Apostles are works executed
by painters in the late 12th and early
13th centuries and incorporate
Byzantine motifs which have
similarities with eastern art. The **church
of the S. Spirito all'Ospedale** ❽ , one of
the most interesting late Gothic
buildings in the region (1483), has a
hanging bell tower on the facade and a
doorway with elaborate sculptural

decoration. On the south side of the church, a *Crucifixion* painted by Ambrosius Gander (c.1450) was found. Inside is a 14th-century wooden *crucifix* and four *reliefs* by Jörg Lederer (1524), as well as various wooden sculptures dating from the 15th and 16th centuries. There are six **Passeggiate** (hikes) from Merano: the *River Passirio Hike* stretches between the Teatro and Ferrovia bridges, and follows the right bank of the river. The *Winter Hike* starts at the Posta bridge (1909, in the *Jugendstil*) and ends at the Romano bridge (19C): note the elegant design of the **Wandelhalle***, a portico built of iron and wood (1892). The Romano bridge is the starting-point of the *Gilf Hike* towards the Gola del Passirio below the crag of Mt San Zeno. These two hikes link up with the **Tappeiner Hike**, which runs along above the old town center (with views across the valley and the Adige) below eucalyptus, strawberry trees, bamboo and Japanese palms. On the left bank of the Passirio, opposite the Winter Hike, is the *Summer Hike*, which wanders through the shade of cedars of Lebanon, poplars, pines and sequoias. The last hike is the *Sissi Route*, which runs between the town and the gardens of Castello Trauttmansdorff.

NEUSTIFT/NOVACELLA [45 km]

Founded in 1142, the Abbey of Novacella, just north of Bressanone, has been a key center of Tyrolean culture and spirituality for centuries. More than 800 years of history have left their mark in this vast complex of buildings, where many different styles exist side by side, from the Romanesque to the Rococo. The visitors' route starts in the *central courtyard*, which dates from the 18th century and is dominated by the Romanesque bell tower of the abbey church. In the center is the *well of wonders*, a well covered with an octagonal shrine (1669) with a frieze depicting the Seven Wonders of the Ancient World, to which an eighth, the abbey, has been added. A door on the east side leads into the *art gallery*. There are eight important panels depicting the *Stories of St Augustine* and the **wooden altarpieces of St Catherine** (1480) and *St Barbara*. The *museum* next to the gallery contains astronomical instruments; plan spheres and geographical maps dating from the 17th and 18th centuries. The **library**, built in 1773 and decorated with stuccoes in the Rococo style, contains approximately 76,000 volumes, including choir-books and codices illuminated by the monks of

Abbazia di Novacella: in the past, because of its isolated position, the abbey's 12th-century chapel of St Michael was used as a hospice for pilgrims

the abbey. The **church of the Assunta** was originally Romanesque but only the walls of the nave and the bell tower remain from this period. The Baroque church was built between 1735 and 1773. The interior is decorated with **frescoes** and stuccoes. On the south side of the church, the *cloister* has paintings on the ceilings and walls dating from the late 13th and 15th centuries. Off the cloister is the *chapel of S. Vittore*, with fragments of Gothic wall paintings executed in the 14th century. The unusual round building (which is in fact a polygon with 16 sides), just outside the wall at the entrance to the abbey, used to be a hospice for pilgrims. Built in the late 12th century, it is now called the *fortified chapel of S. Michele*. The merlons and the turret were added later, in the 15th century, when walls were built around the abbey, in the hope of defending it from the threatened invasion by the Turks. This also explains why the building inside the walls, behind the old furnace, is called the *Torre dei Turchi* (Turks' Tower).

The earth pyramids at Renon

RITTEN/RENON [15 km]

Renon is a gently undulating plateau, covered with meadows and woods, with a mild climate. Justly famous for its splendid views, it hangs like a balcony above Bolzano and the end of the Isarco valley, looking across to the Dolomites from a very favorable position. From here you can see the most spectacular views of Sciliar, the majestic crag between the Catinaccio massif and Alpe di Siusi. In the 16th and 17th centuries, the towns under the administrative power of Renon were chosen by the merchants of Bolzano so that they could escape from the heat and spend the summer in villas which they built here as a sign of their economic and social prestige. A few of them remain, especially in the area of Soprabolzano. These small villages are still popular today as holiday destinations with the people of Bolzano. Many Italian and foreign tourists come here, even in winter, to take advantage of the ski facilities of Corno di Renon. At **Auna di Sotto/Unterinn** and **Costalovara/**

Wolfsgruben many buildings date from the 15th and 16th centuries. A Bronze Age settlement was discovered at San Sebastiano: prehistoric settlements were also discovered on the shores of *Lake Costalovara* and at Wallnereck hill. At Costalovara, the **Plattnerhof*** is a late Gothic *maso* with a Baroque *Stube*, which houses the *Museo dell'Apicoltura* (Bee-keeping Museum). The rooms of the museum provide a glimpse of everyday life in these old farmhouses, and contain a collection of tools, beehives and bee-keeping equipment. There is a special open-air exhibition for children outside. The cable car leads up from Bolzano to **Soprabolzano/Oberbozen**, where there are many fine manors and villas with beautiful gardens. Many of them have rooms with fresco decoration and painted wooden ceilings, often of very high quality. One with very original decoration is the 18th-century **Villa Toggenburg**, with a *room of the hunt*. In the garden of Villa Huyn, the *Casino del Bersaglio* has a remarkable collection of targets for sharp shooting. These painted wooden disks depict allegorical and mythological scenes, and some depict landscapes or scenes of social life. Also worth visiting are the *churches of S. Maria Assunta, S. Maria Maddalena* and the Romanesque *church of Ss. Giorgio e Giacomo*, which has beautiful 13th-century frescoes in the apse. From the *church of the Assunta* (Maria Himmelfahrt) a marked footpath leads to the **earth pyramids***, strange geological formations resulting from erosion by rainwater. When the ice withdrew at the end of the last glacial period, it left enormous deposits of debris. This loose material was usually washed away by the rain unless it was protected by more solid objects. Large boulders were enough to allow these strange pinnacles to form.

Collalbo/Klobenstein is situated on an undulating plateau, with views of Sciliar and Catinaccio. Two of the side-chapels in the *church of S. Antonio* (1672) are decorated with altarpieces by Francesco Unterperger (1747-48), who also created the altarpiece in the little *church of S. Pietro* at

Siffiano/Siffian. Stein am Ritten (Castelpietra), perched on a rocky spur dominating the Isarco valley, is the ruin of a fortified house with a tower dating from the 13th century. At *Longomoso/Lengmoos*, the Commenda dell'Ordine Teutonico is a 17th-century building with stucco decoration on the ceilings and painted tapestries (1730). The *church of S. Nicolò* at *Monte di Mezzo/Mittelberg* has frescoes dating from 1450 attributed to Leonardo da Bressanone. At **Longostagno/Lengstein**, the *church of S. Ottilia*, documented since 1117, has a Gothic choir and a 15th-century bell tower. The facade, furnishings and stained-galss windows are neo-Gothic. A footpath leads from here to the Corno di Renon (4 hours). In the hamlet of **Pietra Rossa/Rotwand** the *church of S. Verena*, which dates from 1460 but was rebuilt in the 18th century, is situated in one of the best viewpoints on the plateau, looking down into the Isarco valley and across to Sciliar. There are also good views from the *church of S. Andrea*, south of Longostagno, with 15th-century frescoes.

THE WITCHES OF SCILIAR AND ALPE DI SIUSI

Throughout the Alpine Chain, there is a tradition of stories about witches, but on the Sciliar plateau and at Alpe di Siusi, such stories, sadly, have a basis of truth.
In Presule, between 1506 and 1510, seven women were tried for witchcraft.
They practiced the ancient art of healing using medicinal plants and used ancient propitiatory rites, which were a legacy from the pre-Christian era.
These unfortunate women, considered capable of practicing witchcraft and accused of meeting with the devil in person, were condemned to death at the stake. The places, which, according to tradition, were used for the witches' rites, have place-names which reflect this belief. In the area of Castelrotto and Bullaccia, we find the Hexenstühle ("witches' chairs"; in the photo) and the Hexenbänke ("witches' benches"). These are actually rock formations strangely eroded in the shape of seats, which have kindled people's imagination for centuries. Today, there are guided tours in the witches' footsteps for adults and children alike. Anyone wishing to learn more about the legends and the historical facts should visit the Museum de Gherdëina in Ortisei.

The Benedictine Monastery at Sabiona, in the center; in the foreground, the octagonal church dedicated to the Madonna

At **Auna di Sopra/Oberinn**, the highest hamlet of Renon, the church of S. Leonardo, has a 13th-century bell tower and a Gothic 15th-century choir. However, the decoration and furnishings were altered in the neo-Gothic style in the late 19th century.

SÄBEN/SABIONA [30 km]

A road leads up from Piazza S. Andrea di Chiusa to the *Torre del Capitano* (13C), where it begins to climb towards the Monastery of Sabiona, one of the South Tyrol's oldest monuments (6C). The view of the complex is exceptional. The first building you encounter on the way up is the octagonal *church of the Madonna* (1652-58), enclosed within a fortified wall, which surrounds the whole complex (now mainly used as orchards and vegetable patches). Inside the church, in the vault of the dome, are remarkable *frescoes,* stuccoes and other decoration. Next to it is the Romanesque *chapel of Maria*, a single chamber with a round apse. In the higher part of the plateau, the *monastery* and the *church* were created by incorporating some existing buildings. One of the corner towers was adapted to serve as a refectory and a chapter house. In the church, the oldest features are the Romanesque two-light windows in the south wall. The *church of the Santa Croce*, which occupies the highest point on the site, was built above the foundations of a Romanesque building. The Baroque *frescoes* inside dilate the space by using *trompe l'oeil* architectural features and tricks of perspective. Next to the church is the *Torre di S. Cassiano*, the only building in the complex which has not been altered since the 13th century. Another hike from Chiusa leads to the little town of **Villandro/Villanders**, which has many fine medieval buildings.

SANKT ULRICH IN GRÖDEN/ ORTISEI [35 km]

Ortisei, one of the area's best-known holiday and ski resorts, is situated in a splendid position in a hollow surrounded by meadows and forests and views of Sasso Lungo and Sella. Via Rezia, lined with hotels, shops and brightly painted houses, traverses the town center. In Piazza S. Antonio, the little *church of S. Antonio* dates from the 17th century. Further on, in Piazza Durich, the *Parish church of S. Ulrico* (1796, enlarged in 1907) has a nave and two large chapels at the sides of the presbytery. The church is richly decorated, with many wooden sculptures carved by craftsmen of Val Gardena in the 19th and 20th centuries. The **Museo di Ortisei/Museum de Gherdëina***, is a key benchmark for modern Ladin culture. Organized with the aim of collecting the most significant expressions of the art and craftsmanship of Val Gardena, it has an important library, a collection of archeological finds, and collections of

41

minerals and paleontological specimens. In the Palazzo dei Congressi there is a *permanent exhibition of local crafts*, with works by wood-carvers and sculptors.

SARNTAL/VAL SARENTINA

Bolzano was immersed in the Sarentina valley, hugged between steep rock walls above which you can catch glimpses of wooded terraces. At the top of a porphyry spur high above the Tàlvera is the shape of *Castel Vanga/Schloss Wangen-Bellermont*, which was built at the beginning of the 13th century. On another rocky promontory stands the 16th-century *church of s. Giovanni Battista am Kofel*. Further on, a road climbs up to the Renon plateau, passing the village of *Vanga/Wangen*. Dominating the town is the *church of S. Pietro*, the origins of which are 13th-century. The church was altered in the 16th century and then decorated in the second half of the 18th century with frescoes by Carl Henrici (triumphal arch). Now, the valley begins to open out, and the slopes become gradually less steep.

Sarentino/Sarnthein, the largest town in the valley, looks forward every year to the annual festival held in September. The Sarntaler Kirchtag is attended by all the town's inhabitants dressed in traditional costumes, which are considered to be the most beautiful and elaborate in the Tyrol. In the town center, the *Albergo Zum Hirschen* (Stag Inn) has a Gothic *Stube* dating from the late 15th century, which is regarded as being representative of the many *Stuben*

that survive in the *masi* and residences of the valley. The little *church of S. Cipriano*, dating from the 13th century, is decorated in the Gothic style. The nave is decorated with *paintings* from 1395 by a Giottoesque artist. From the town, you can climb up to the 13th-century **Castel Regino/Schloss Reineck**, with its high walls, a mighty keep and a manor. In the chapel with two floors, the *frescoes* covering the triumphal arch are thought to date from the 13th century, while those in the apse date from the late 14th century. Another building of note is *Maso Moser*, south of the town in the village of *Stetto/Steet*. The 14th-century building incorporates a tower. Other medieval towers can be seen in the older *masi* of the area.

SEXTEN/SESTO [110 km]

From here there are splendid views of the old farmhouses and the broad expanses of larch forest, which cover the hillside, and the peaks of the Dolomites. At **Sesto/Sexten**, situated in the valley of the same name, you enter some truly breathtaking mountain scenery and one of the most famous areas of the Dolomites. In the higher part of the town, above the typical alpine houses with their balconies laden with flowers, its worth visiting the round building at the entrance to the cemetery, which is frescoed with a vivid *Dance of Death*. In the town square, the *Museo "Rudolf Stolz"* contains 160 works by the painter from Bolzano, who was also responsible for the frescoes in the *church of*

LakeValdurna, in a side-valley of the Val Sarentina, which leads down from the Forcella di Vallaga

S. Giuseppe at Moso/Moos, a small village that has become a large ski resort.

STERZING/VIPITENO [70 km]

In a broad hollow at the meeting-point of the Isarco, Ridanna and Vizze valleys, Vipiteno has the typical openness and beauty of Tyrolean valleys, and has retained the aura of a thriving mining and market town. The town is an important winter sports center. **Via Città Nuova** and **Via Città Vecchia** traverse the town on either side of the *Torre Civica (Civic Tower)*, lined by fine houses with *erker*, following the usual market-street plan. Above the doors are family crests or crests of mining companies, some of which incorporate silver nuggets. There are many splendid gilt and painted wrought-iron signs with imaginative designs. The *Palazzo Comunale* (Town Hall), with an *erker* on the corner, has a council chamber lined with wooden paneling and a Renaissance coffered ceiling. In the open courtyard is a marble *relief of Mythras* dating from the Roman period. Next to the Town Hall is a statue of St John Nepomucene (1739). In Piazza Città the nave of the *church of S. Spirito* is decorated with **frescoes** (1410-15) that constitute the largest surviving fresco cycle by Giovanni da Brunico. In the area near the Civic Tower, in Via Cappuccini, the *Jöchlsturm* is regarded as one of the most beautiful late-Gothic patrician residences. The carved gilt ceilings on the second floor are particularly beautiful. Next to the residence is the *church of Ss. Pietro e Paolo*. Continuing from Via Città Nuova into Via Gänsbacher, you come to the *Commenda dell'Ordine Teutonico*. This 13th-century building now houses the Museo Civico and the **Museo Multscher**, which contains the surviving parts of the wooden altarpiece from the high altar of the Parish church, by Hans Multscher (1458). There are **eight panels**** which once adorned the doors and some sculptures: the large paintings are very realistic, yet executed with balanced restraint. In the adjoining rooms of the **Museo Civico** the exhibits and documents illustrate the town's history. Next-door to the Commenda is the *church of S. Elisabetta*. The **church of S. Maria della Palude**, just beyond the Commenda, is a building of Romanesque origin which was enlarged and transformed in the 15th and 16th centuries. The interior was altered again in the 18th century and Hans Multscher's altar was removed; however five of the statues from it still adorn the neo-Gothic high altar.

TAUFERS IM MÜNSTERTAL/TUBRE [92 km]

In the *Monastero valley/Münstertal*, the ruins of the Rotund and Reichenberg castles dominate Tubre. The town came into being in the 11th century around the **hospice of S. Giovanni***, one of the few medieval hospices which has survived. The church of the complex has Romanesque *paintings*, dated 1220-30, which is clearly influenced by Venetian mosaics and Byzantine culture. In a room on the first floor, which leads into the presbytery through an arch, there are Gothic frescoes dating from about 1385, executed by a painter who was influenced by the Lombard tradition. The frescoes in the little *church of S. Nicolò* are also Gothic, but later. The *Parish church of S. Biagio* with fine paintings, stuccoes and carvings dates from the 17th century.

TOBLACH/DOBBIACO [101 km]

Situated below the *Landro valley/Höhlensteintal*, between 1800 and 1900, Dobbiaco became a favorite holiday place for the Habsburg nobility and bourgeoisie. The old town lies to the north, in the short San Silvestro valley, clustered around the **Parish church of S. Giovanni Battista***. The church was built between 1764 and 1774 in a particularly harmonious Baroque style, with clear architectural lines and refined stucco and fresco decoration. The *Herbstenburg* castle, built around a medieval tower, was enlarged in the 16th century conserving the massive appearance of a fortress. Just outside the town, the *Stations of the Cross*, comprising five shrines and a chapel with polychrome stone reliefs, date from 1519. The *Landro valley* is popular with hikers bound for the Lakes *Dobbiaco* and *Landro*. Many places in the valley have spectacular **views** of the ridges and peaks of the Dolomites.

LAURINO'S ROSES

A poetic legend explains the phenomenon called enrosadira by the locals.
In the valleys where Ladin is spoken, the word refers to that special time of evening, just before dusk, when the last rays of sunshine illuminate the rocky walls of the Dolomites. The really special aspect of this time of day is that the mountains become a marvelous crimson-orange tinge. This amazing sight occurs because the rocks contain iron minerals, or silver-bearing veins. The phenomenon is quite unique and can only be seen in the Dolomites. On Catinaccio (in the photo), where, even now, a large patch of snow can be seen cradled, as if in the vault of an apse, until quite late in spring, there was once a rose-garden.
It belonged to Laurino, the king of a community of dwarfs, who used to tunnel into the depths of the mountain in search of crystals, silver and gold.

King Laurino wasn't very tall, and rode a horse no bigger than a goat, but he wore armor, which made him invisible, and a belt, which gave him the strength of twelve men. One day, the king of the Adige, who wanted to choose a husband for his beautiful daughter Similde, invited all the nobles of the area to a huge feast. King Laurino, who was not invited, decided to participate anyway as an invisible guest. When he spotted Similde on the jousting ground, he fell in love with her instantly and ran away with her. The knights followed him to the garden and realized that they could tell where he was by watching the rosebushes move as he passed. They succeeded in capturing him and removing his magic belt. Laurino, furious, cast a curse over the roses, which had betrayed him: no one would ever be able to admire them again, neither by day nor by night. But he forgot to include sunset and dawn in his curse. So the beautiful rose-garden can still be seen today, albeit for a few precious moments.

WELSCHNOFEN/ NOVA LEVANTE [20 km]

The history of Nova Levante, a holiday and ski resort, is illustrated in the *Museo Locale*, with an exhibition of paintings and objects associated with local folk culture and traditions.
The town is famous for its splendid **views** of the Dolomites of Latemar and Catinaccio. In particular, the woods and mountains are reflected in the waters of the little **Lake Carezza***, which was already famous in the late 19th century. It's almost as if this tiny lake was created specially (by a glacial cirque) to enhance the fantastic shapes of Latemar, its colors ranging from the bluish-gray of the rocks to the green of the conifers which adorn its slopes. This is the starting-point for many hikes, including a circuit of the lake, and another

to the Labirinto, an area where huge boulders have rolled down from Latemar, creating a kind of natural maze. A couple of kilometers away, the *Costalunga Pass* leads across into the Fassa valley. From the top, the view stretches across to the mountains of Marmolada and the Pale di San Martino.

WOLKENSTEIN IN GRÖDEN/ SELVA DI VAL GARDENA [42 km]

Selva di Val Gardena is situated in a hollow surrounded by coniferous forests, which provide a contrast with the dolomitic rocks of Sella and Sasso Lungo. There are plenty of chairlifts and cable cars to take hikers up to the start of their hikes.
At the edge of the town, at the beginning of the *Vallunga*, are the ruins of the 13th-century *Castello Wolkenstein*, an unusual building which was once a fortified cave.
On the side of Piz Culac (2,086m) is the lovely Plan de Gralba (1,810m), a large ski resort with excellent hotels and skiing facilities. The **Gardena Pass** (2,121m) is worth the expedition. This broad, grassy depression is dominated on one side by the rocky ridge of Pizzes da Cir and on the other by the rock walls of Sella. The pass leads across into Badia valley and forms part of the circuit surrounding the whole Sella massif called the **Sella**

Ronda, along with the passes of Sella, Pordoi and Campolongo. This is one of the most beautiful drives in the Dolomites, because of the exceptional **views**. The name is also applied to the skiing area nearby which, with about 600km of ski runs, is one of the most extensive in the Alps. The **Sella Pass** (2,213m) has **views** of Sasso Lungo and Sella, Gran Vernel and the glacier of Marmolada, the mountains of the Fassa valley in the Trentino and the Odle Mountains. On the northern slopes of Sciliar, the 16th- and 17th-century houses of **Castelrotto/Kastelruth** are clustered around the square of the *church of Ss. Pietro e Paolo*. The church has a 18th-century bell tower incorporating a chapel at the bottom. **Siusi/Seis** has been a popular summer resort for more than a century. It's a 40-minute hike through the woods to the ruins of *Castelvecchio/Hauenstein*. A few hundred meters out of the town, another path climbs up to the *church of S. Valentino*, which has frescoes dating from the 15th and 16th centuries by artists of the Bolzano School. Another footpath (4 hours) leads up to the **Bolzano mountain refuge** (2,450m). The hut is the starting-point for the climb to **Pez** (2,563m; 30 minutes), the highest peak in the Sciliar range. From the top, the **views*** stretch for miles across the Alps.

Rock pillars and forest reflected in the waters of the little Lago di Carezza (of glacial origin), already a tourist destination in the late 19th century

TRENT/TRENTO

The peaks around Trent already have much in common with the Alps, in fact it is very like other typical "mountain" cities in northern Italy. But Trent is different. It was here that an important part of the history of the Church of Rome was played out. At the Council of Trent, (1545 and 1563), the Church opposed the revolutionary entreaties from North of the Alps, sustained by Martin Luther and his followers, and established dogmas and papal rights, as well as religious rules, which Roman Catholics still conform to today. Almost paradoxically, that proved to be the "golden age" of the town founded by the Romans with the name of Tridentum (in 23BC), on the crossroads between the Via Claudia Augusta and the road following the valley of the Adige river. Effectively, it inherited the control over an area, which, in Neolithic times, had been held by the castle on Doss Trento (a small hill 310m high, whose real name is Mt Verruca, situated on the left bank of the Adige river, near Trent). As soon as the power of the Roman Empire began to decline, the first incursions by tribes living north of the Alps began. However, we can only talk of true Germanic dominion after the year 952, when the Bavarian King Otto I took Trent from Berengarius II. Under him, the medieval renaissance of the town began, following the axes of the Roman colony and "re-using" the early-Christian places of worship dedicated to St Vigilius (now the cathedral) and St Mary (now the church of S. Maria Maggiore). The relaunch of the town was also crowned by success in the commercial sphere, and reconfirmed in 1027 by Conrad II the Salic with the creation of the prince-bishopric of Trent. In the early 13th century, the cathedral and the surrounding buildings were rebuilt, and, at the same time, a set of fortifications was erected around the town. Next to this, the nucleus, which later became the Castello del Buonconsiglio, was built. When, in 1516, Bishop Bernardo Cles began his rule, the town had looked like a medieval town for several centuries. However, the bishop wrought far-reaching changes according to the tenets of Italian Renaissance culture. And while he was busy transforming blocks of Gothic houses into noble palaces, and enlarging the Castello del Buonconsiglio, he found the time to support the candidature of Trent as seat of the Council, although it did not actually exist any more when the first session was held (1545). The arrival of the French in Trent (in 1796) put an end to religious rule. It was subsequently annexed by the kingdom of Bavaria (1806-1809), and by the Napoleonic kingdom of Italy (1810-1813) and then by the Austrian government (1815), sparking a period marked by a renewal of the urban fabric.

Piazza del Duomo ❶

Piazza del Duomo immediately conveys the impression of being the heart of the town. In fact, in the past, it was here that religious and civilian powers used to challenge each other, having come here to contest control of the square. The marble strip in the paving shows where the stream known as the Roggia Grande, now filled in, used to be. In the old days, it marked the border between the two spheres of influence. The *Fontana del Nettuno (fountain of Neptune)* was not put there until 1769. Not far away, the Case Cazuffi are the most important example of the secular part of Piazza del Duomo, although they no longer bear any of their original Gothic features. They were rebuilt in the 15th century and redecorated with frescoes in 1531-33 (the monochrome frescoes of *Justice* and *Fortune* on the left-hand facade are attributed to Battista Dossi, whereas Marcello Fogolino executed the frescoes

of *Virtue*, *Time* and, again, *Fortune*. Casa Balduini has an example of a facade frescoed in the Venetian Lombard style, dating from the mid-15th century.

Duomo ❷

The side of the cathedral (1212) facing the square looks more like the main facade because of its decoration: the gallery with small arches is typical of the Romanesque period, as is the relief by sculptors from Campione below the 16th-century porch known as the *Bishop's door*, and the rose window of the transept known as the *Wheel of Fortune*. The main facade with its austere lines is asymmetrical, with a tower on only one side (the onion-shaped dome on the top gives it an Austrian flavor); on the right-hand side, three human figures and a lion support the porch beside the right apse. The top of the apse is decorated by a gallery of little arches, a continuation of the arches running along on the left side

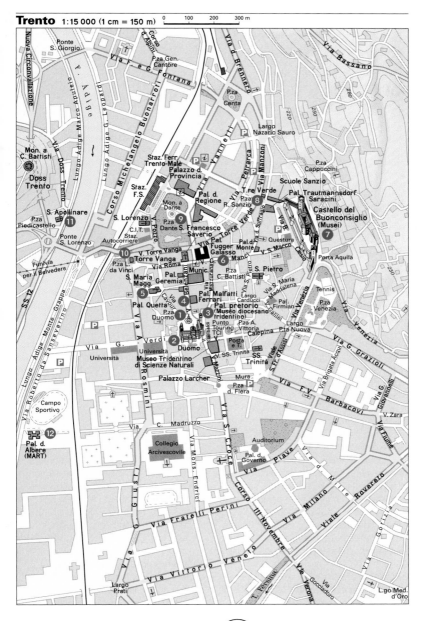

Trento 1:15 000 (1 cm = 150 m)

of the cathedral, the center by splayed one-light windows and, the bottom by small blind arches and more splayed one-light windows. From this angle you can see that the left apse of the church has been incorporated in the *Castelletto*, the crenellated building with the slender Torre di S. Romedio (tower). Gothic forms dominate the interior, both in the division of the church into a nave and two side-

Piazza Duomo is the throbbing heart of the city. Formerly it was the scene of clashes between ecclesiastical and secular powers

aisles and in the cross vaulting above; on the beautiful stairs with loggias leading up from the aisles are 16th-century tombstones. The canopy above the high altar is Baroque, while the Romanesque reliefs at the sides of the apse date from the reconstruction of the church in the 13th century. The frescoes (*Stories of St Julian*) by Monte da Bologna are the most interesting of the 14th-century frescoes which still decorate the transept. Below the high altar of the cathedral, you can see the foundations of the early-Christian basilica on which it was built, but also part of the floor, which consists of some stone burial slabs and, near the presbytery, fragments of original mosaics.

Palazzo Pretorio ❸

Palazzo Pretorio bears the thumb-print of Bishop Federico Vanga, who commissioned the rebuilding of a previous (9-10C) bishop's palace. However, it was not he who named the palace "Pretorio". It acquired the name in the following century, when the Castello del Buonconsiglio became the residence of the bishops, and this palace was used for judicial proceedings. Then, Mannerist and Baroque decorations were added, but they were removed in 1963 to restore the "medieval" appearance of the complex.

Now the building stands between the *Torre Civica (Civic Tower)*, erected in the 11th century, and the Castelletto. It is now the **Museo Diocesano Tridentino**. One part of the museum focuses on the Council of Trent held here in 1534 with the aim of reforming the ecclesiastic institutions, which had been shaken by the spread of Protestantism. The other exhibits are paintings and sculptures by local artists. The exhibits date from the medieval to the neoclassical periods and document Lombard, Venetian, and Austrian influences. The pride of the collection is a series of tapestries depicting *The Passion*.

Via Belenzani ❹

This street is lined with noble palaces. One of the most interesting buildings stands beyond the *church of the SS. Annunziata* (1715) and *Palazzo Malfatti Ferrari* (early 18C), and is known as **Palazzo Quetta**, or Casa Colico Alberti. You can recognize it from its decoration (fake architectural features, festoons and bundles with cherubs, and busts) and it has a door with a three-light window above it. Another historic residence is *Palazzo Thun*, the stern facade of which confirms its 16th-century origins. There are more *frescoes* on the

Trento: Cathedral

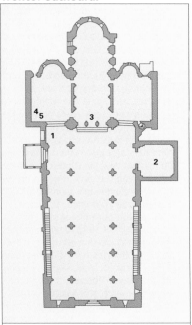

1 Tombstone of Bernardo Cles
2 Chapel of the Crucifix
3 High altar
4 Stories of St Julian
  by Monte da Bologna
5 Statue of the Madonna of the Drowned

facade of the 15th-century **Palazzo Geremia***. The *church of S. Francesco Saverio* is the highest expression of the Baroque style in the city, a building with the typical lines of the Counter-Reformation.

Chiesa di S. Maria Maggiore ⑤

Antonio Medaglia rebuilt the church in 1520 over a previous 6th-century church. Built in the Lombard Renaissance style (however the bell tower is a re-used medieval tower), both the exterior (the doorway dates from 1539; the fresco in the lunette is by Martino Teofilo Polacco) and the basilical interior have classical lines. The *organ doors* on the back of the facade were painted by Giovanni Maria Falconetto, the *Nativity* (1st altar on the right) and the *Ecstasy of St Theresa* (3rd altar on the right) by Giambettino Cignaroli, with a *Dispute with the Doctors* by G.B. Moroni (2nd altar on the right, 1551) which already expresses the matters associated with the famous Council. The *Assumption* by Pietro Ricchi (above the high altar) and the frescoes by Il Polacco (in the apse) fade slightly into the background in the presence of the **choir gallery** on the left with its beautiful reliefs executed by Vincenzo Grandi in 1534. Francesco Sebaldo Unterpergher painted the *St Joseph* above the 3rd altar on the left; the *Adoration of the Magi* above the 1st altar on the left is attributed to Domenico Brusasorci.

Via Manci ⑥

Via Manci is the other section of the street linking the cathedral to the castle. Like Via Belenzani, this is a medieval street, which was included in the town-planning reforms under Bishop Bernardo Cles (1485-1539). It was widened, the medieval porticoes were removed and

Trent cathedral, with its delicate arch motif

the blocks of Gothic houses were combined to create noble palaces. One example is **Palazzo Fugger Galasso,** "created" before 1608, with its late Mannerist forms: the lower part of the facade has smooth rustications (the doorway stands between the columns supporting the balcony) and is divided by pilaster strips which frame the windows on the upper floor with broken curved pediments. The 16th-century *Palazzo Saracini Pedrotti* was also involved in the Bishop Cles' rebuilding program, the external decoration of which imitates rustication. It is now the *Museo della SAT* where old photographs and climbing equipment tell the story of the founding of the Società degli Alpinisti Tridentini (Trent Climbing Club); so was *Palazzo Salvadori*, which was rebuilt in 1515 (the two medallions above the doors date from the 18th century). The *Labors of Hercules* on the facades of *Palazzo Del Monte* were painted in about 1540. This palazzo and the 15th-century *Casa Bazzani* (the *Deposition* on the facade below the sun-dial is by Martino Teofilo Polacco) form the *Cantone* (Street-corner), a popular meeting-point within the walls.

Castello del Buonconsiglio 7

The Castello del Buonconsiglio is the monument which symbolizes the city and has been perched on its rocky hill since at least 1240, the year from which the earliest part of the fortress dates. Not until the 15th century did the building acquire a more residential character, through the creation of an internal garden and the building of the Torre dell'Aquila (Eagle's Tower). The internal courtyard was built In the second half of the same century. The Magno Palazzo was built in 1528-36 and was lavishly decorated inside. In 1688 it was decided to join Castelvecchio to the Magno Palazzo. The *Museo Storico in Trento* is located in the Marangonerie (formerly carpenters' workshops). The exhibits document the Italian culture of this city and the surrounding area and

also illustrates how it became autonomous after the II World War. The Castello del Buonconsiglio houses the **Monumenti e Collezioni Provinciali,** with archeological collections and majolica stoves of the 16th-18th centuries, wooden sculpture from Trentino and the South Tyrol dating from the 14th and 15th centuries, and some fine paintings, for which frescoes and reliefs provide the "background". The heart of **Castelvecchio** is the **courtyard,** with three tiers of loggias (the highest one is the famous Venetian Gothic panoramic *loggia* facing the city). High up on the wall of the loggia is a painting of *Charlemagne Enthroned*; the band below it with portraits of bishops extends into the third loggia and the Bishops' Hall, so numerous were the "lords" of the city. From the first loggia of the courtyard, a passageway leads into the **Magno Palazzo,** through the *Chapel entrance* with frescoes of the *Gods of Olympus*; on the right, is the *Courtroom*. This leads into the **Giunta Albertiana,** with its lavish Baroque decoration of stuccoes and frescoes; on the left in the frescoed *Room of the Black Fireplace*, the *Audience Chamber*, in the *Room of the Figures*, named after the half-

A fresco in the Eagle's Tower depicting the month of December at the Castello del Buonconsiglio

TRENTO CARD

The Trento Card is a prepaid card which gives visitors the right to use various services and benefit from special discounts. The card includes a ticket for public transport and an information kit containing all the information about the services on offer. The card is valid for 24 or 48 hours and can be used for museums, transport, restaurants, sports facilities, guided tours, wineries and shopping. The Trento Card is available at the Tourist Information Office in Trent (Via Manci 2, tel. 0461983880, www.apt.trento.it) and at Monte Bondone (località Vaneze, tel. 0461947128), at the city's main cultural institutions and at the hotels and restaurants, which belong to the scheme.

relief figures on the ceiling, and in the *Room at the Bottom of the Great Tower* (1532-33). From the Chapel entrance you emerge into the **Lions' courtyard**; the *loggia* at the end was frescoed in 1531-32, and from here you can drop down into the *ditch of the Martyrs*. The decoration continues in the first section of the stairs leading towards the **Great Hall**, with a frieze by the Dossi family and a *fireplace* by Vincenzo Grandi (1532). Both the appearance of the *Hall of Mirrors* and the frescoes of the *Stua Granda* are 18th-century, whereas those in the *Room of the Scarlatti* are again by the Dossi family. From the entrance to the Great Hall you can access the private apartment of the prince-bishop, where the *library* still has its original ceiling. In the *Torre del Falco* (Falcon's Tower) (c.1400) they have discovered frescoes reflecting German culture (post-1530); in the *Eagle's Tower*, erected in the 15th century, is the **fresco cycle depicting the Twelve Months****. It was probably executed by a painter of Bohemian origin in the early 15th century and is one of the finest examples of International Gothic painting.

Piazza Sanzio ⑧

The *Torre Verde* (Green Tower), once part of the city's fortifications, was thus named because of the color of the majolica tiles on its pointed roof. When Adalberto Libera built the *Scuole Raffaello Sanzio* in 1932, he based his design on the Castello del Buonconsiglio. The 16th-century *Palazzo Trautmannsdorf Saracini* can be recognized by the doorway, framed by twisted columns which support a balcony.

Piazza Dante ⑨

There's a reason why all the buildings on Piazza Dante date from the second half of the 19th century. In fact, the Adige river used to flow through this spot before it was moved west and the area of reclaimed land was landscaped to include the station and some of the city's administrative buildings. Having completed the difficult task of erecting a Rationalist building next to the city's main monument, Adalberto Libera was entrusted with designing *Palazzo della Regione* (1954). The neoclassical **Palazzo della Provincia** nearby was built in 1874. It is used for exhibitions and contains several paintings by Depero. The *monument to Dante* in the gardens dates from 1896. The *station*, built in 1934, has a *Mostra Permanente del Modellismo Ferroviario* with a series of model trains built by Arnaldo Pocher. It was the Benedictines who founded the monastery in the *church of S. Lorenzo* in 1146. In a short time they became so influential that they clashed with the bishops. All that remains of their glorious past is the Romanesque church, with its bare interior.

Torre Vanga ⑩

The tower was once part of the city walls, but it was also used for controlling the bridge over the river that enabled the inhabitants to escape in times of danger to Doss Trento. Its medieval appearance is enhanced by the low 13th-century building nearby with two- and three-light windows.

S. Apollinare ⑪

The church was begun in 1320, in the Romanesque Gothic style, on the site of a previous 12th-century church. It has a plain facade with a sloping roof and, at the bottom of the bell tower, is a

Castello del Buonconsiglio

The earliest part of the building is Castelvecchio, a fort begun in the 13th century and built around the massive Augustus Tower, formerly the keep of the town's ring of fortifications. With the passing of time, the castle, now the seat of a bishop, gradually began to look like more like a noble residence. The first changes were made in the 15th century when the Eagle's Tower was added, and the interior was richly decorated with splendid fresco cycle depicting the Twelve Months of the year, one of the most important examples of late-Gothic painting in Europe.

Next to Castelvecchio stands the Magno Palazzo built by Bernardo Cles in the 16th century as the representative seat of his political and cultural power. Magnificent, delicate fresco cycles were painted by artists in great demand in the Renaissance courts of that time the walls of the most important rooms in the palace. Some of the finest achievements here are the Loggia designed by Alessio Longhi and enhanced by the splendid frescoes Romanino, and the decoration by Dosso Dossi in some of the rooms inside the building Finally, in the 17th century, the bishop-prince Francesco Alberto Poia decided to build the so-called Giunta Albertiana, linking Castelvecchio and the Magno Palazzo. It is decorated with Baroque stuccoes and elaborate frescoes celebrating the victories against the Turks, painted by Giuseppe Alberti.

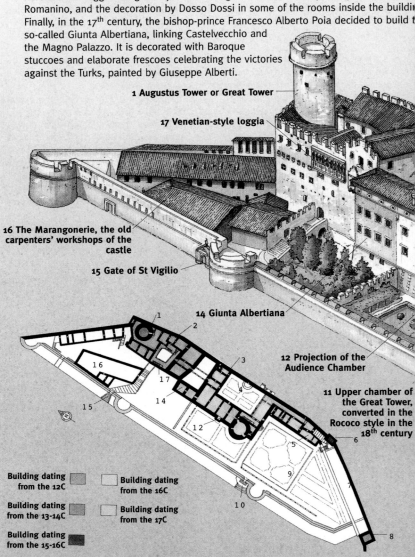

1 Augustus Tower or Great Tower

17 Venetian-style loggia

16 The Marangonerie, the old carpenters' workshops of the castle

15 Gate of St Vigilio

14 Giunta Albertiana

12 Projection of the Audience Chamber

11 Upper chamber of the Great Tower, converted in the Rococo style in the 18th century

Building dating from the 12C

Building dating from the 13-14C

Building dating from the 15-16C

Building dating from the 16C

Building dating from the 17C

Loggia del Romanino

The ceiling of the Loggia created by Alessio Longhi was frescoed by Romanino between 1531 and 1532. The walls above the columns supporting the five arches facing the Lions' courtyard were decorated with four medallions depicting the profiles of members of the ruling Habsburg family: Maximilian I, Philip the Handsome, Charles V and Ferdinand I.

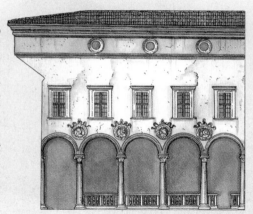

2 Castelvecchio

3 Magno Palazzo

13 The Great Hall of the Magno Palazzo with the fireplace by Vincenzo Grandi

4 Lions' courtyard

5 Garden loggia

6 Falcon's Tower or Owl's Tower

7 Chemin-de-ronde

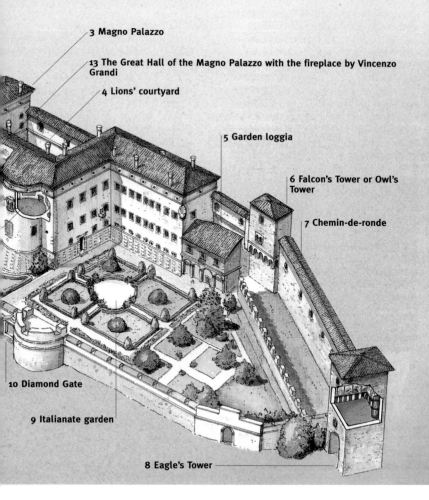

10 Diamond Gate

9 Italianate garden

8 Eagle's Tower

Palazzo delle Albere, now the Museo d'Arte Moderna e Contemporanea di Trento e Rovereto (MART)

sarcophagus dated 1320. Above the left-hand altar is a fresco of the *Madonna and Child* by Nicolò da Padova; above the high altar, a *St Apollinaris* by Albrecht Altdorfer (1517); opposite, on the back of the main facade, a *Pietà* by the same artist. Just above the church, *Doss Trento*, set on a rocky knoll, has always provided shelter for the citizens of Trent in times of danger. It can be seen from all over the city, thanks partly to the *mausoleum of Cesare Battisti*, built in 1935. On the top of the hill you can still make out the foundations of the early-Christian *basilica* (6C), and the former Austrian *munitions dump*, which, since 1958 has housed the *Museo Storico delle Truppe Alpine (Historical Museum of the Alpine Regiments)*.

Palazzo delle Albere ⑫

Palazzo delle Albere, a suburban residence built in about 1535, is named after the avenue of poplars (*àlbere* in dialect) which formerly led up to the entrance. The building, which looks more like a fortress than a villa, is surrounded by a moat. The four facades, the lower part of which is rusticated, have square towers at the corners. You can still see some of the splendid *fresco cycles*, which once adorned the exterior, inspired by the typical themes of the Humanist culture of that time. It is now the **Museo d'Arte Moderna e Contemporanea di Trento e Rovereto** (MART), and contains about 1,700 works and numerous temporary exhibitions illustrating the main artistic genres of Italian 20th-century painting.

DAY TRIPS

ARCO [35 km]

The town, situated below its medieval castle in the Sarca river valley, has retained its characteristic arched shape. Next to the remains of the *Archduke's Villa* is the Parco Arboreto, a garden worth visiting for its rare species of plants. A road climbs up past olive groves and cypress trees to the **Castle*** ❶, proof of the "Mediterranean" climate prevailing in this corner of Trentino. The castle dates from the 12th century and has International-Gothic style frescoes in the *Games Room*. Other monuments worth seeing in the town include the *monument to the painter Giovanni Segantini*, the former *Casino* (late 19C) and the neo-Gothic *Evangelical church* (1897). The architecture of the **Collegiata dell'Assunta** ❷ has obvious references to the Palladian style, despite being built in 1613-71. Inside, the pillars, the entablature and the fake-coffered ceilings above the altars are in the Baroque style. In front of the church, in Piazza III Novembre, the *Fontana del Mosè (fountain of Moses)* is also Baroque. Hidden to the left of the church is the 16th-century **Palazzo Marchetti** ❸, with traces of a frescoed frieze on the facades and in the courtyard. Church enthusiasts should walk along the right bank of the Sarca river to the *church of S. Apollinare* (14C), to see the fresco cycle by painters of the Verona School executed in the late 16th century. They should then proceed to *St Paul's Hermitage*, set amid olive-trees and holm oaks on the hillside since the 12th century. Geology enthusiasts, on the other hand, should continue further, to see the **marocche**, clusters of boulders surrounded by moraines.

CASTEL BESENO [15 km]

About thirty fortresses were built in the Lagarina valley to control the Adige river. One of them, Castel Beseno (12C), is perched on the top of a hill overlooking the beginning of the Folgaria plateau. Within its walls, you eventually reach the Court of Honor, where the *Palazzo dei Mesi* is named after the 15th-century fresco which adorns its facade. There are magnificent views from the chemin-de-ronde. Not far from Castel Beseno is *Castel Pietra* (may be visited on request), probably founded in the 13th century. The frescoes in the Hall of

Judgment (a cycle depicting secular themes) were painted two centuries later. Close by is **Lake Lavarone**, a karst phenomenon, with a shady path running around its perimeter and two beaches with picnic tables.

CASTELLO DI AVIO [50 km]

Vineyards cover the slopes leading up to the Castello di Àvio, which, from 1053 (when it was first documented) until 1977 (when it was donated to the State) belonged to the most important noble family in the area. In the 13th century, a circle of walls was built around the earliest part of the castle and the keep, forming a formidable fortified complex, which could be seen on its hilltop perch from miles around. Only a few fragments remain of the frescoes which once adorned its walls in the *Guard Room* (**Battle Scenes around the Castle**), on the left before entering the main part of the castle, and in the *keep* (**Story of Knightly Love** interspersed by **drapes**). The frescoes were painted by a master

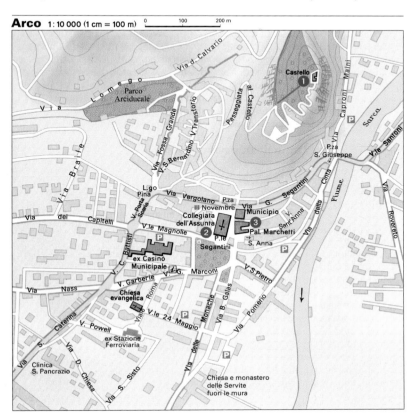

Arco 1: 10 000 (1 cm = 100 m)

from the Verona area in the second half of the 14th century, according to the tenets of the International-Gothic style. The frescoes in the *chapel* were painted a century later.

Other frescoes, dating from the 14th and 15th centuries, and partly influenced by the Giotto School, adorn the *Parish church of the Immacolata* at **Àvio**, first documented in 1145.

FOLGARIDA [6 km]

The resort of Folgàrida (1,270m) has special facilities for snowboard enthusiasts. In fact, it has designated runs so that snowboarders can exert themselves in complete freedom. Of course, people still come here to ski. Sometimes they come straight from Madonna di Campiglio with a ski pass valid for both sides of Mt Vigo (2,179m).

MADONNA DI CAMPIGLIO [14 km]

Madonna di Campiglio is an extremely fashionable resort, particularly popular with tourists from north of the Alps, especially Austrians. It is situated in a basin where the emerald green of the meadows provides a contrast to the darker green of the spruce forest. Not only foreign tourists come here: there are also many Italian ski enthusiasts, all of whom can use cable cars and chairlifts which leave from the town

center to ski on the more than 90km of runs. In the nearby *Campo Carlo Magno* (1,681m), there are more than 30km of tracks for cross-country skiing. There is no season when Madonna di Campiglio isn't crowded, partly because the views of the Brenta Dolomites are indescribably beautiful. Above the town, the **route of the five lakes** follows the mountain chain, which separates the Nambrone valley from the glaciers of Presanella, with spectacular views of the crystal-clear waters of *Lake Ritorto*, *Lake Nero*, *Lake Seròdoli*, *Lake Gelato* and *Lake Nambino*.

PASSO DEL TONALE [90 km]

You can ski all the year round on the Presena Glacier, which is almost as high as the pass (1,883m) linking Trentino to Lombardy. According to the legend, in the 15th century, witches used to congregate here. The Romans and the Franks both crossed this pass and, in 1166, Frederick Barbarossa. The pass was the scene of fierce fighting during the Great War, as testified by the *Sacrario Militare* (Military Cemetery, 1924) and the Austrian fortifications, the remains of which can still be seen among the peaks.

PIANA ROTALIANA [20 km]

Piana Rotaliana or Campo Rotaliano is the only

THE MULTIFUNCTIONAL BROZ

This rather strange name refers to one of the most common means of transport in the mountains of the Trentino. Basically, it is a two-wheeled cart with some special devices, which enable it to negotiate any kind of ground and transport any kind of load.

For going downhill, two hard wooden poles are lowered to the ground, acting as a sort of brake. On flat land, the poles are attached to the shafts linking the Broz to the draught animal. To transport dung or other products which can be stored in deep containers, the two central planks of the back of the cart can be removed to allow space for a large basket made of ash branches. For carrying hay or wood, they add two beams 3-4m long held together by a curved piece of wood, thus creating the space for a very broad load.

Riding across the snow towards Passo del Tonale

plain in Trentino, a seemingly endless expanse of vineyards. The towns of **Mezzocorona** and **Mezzolombardo** are situated on the lower slopes of the mountains. Part of the sheer rock wall above Mezzocorona, where you can visit the remains of a late 1st-century farm, was excavated in the 12th century to build **Castel S. Gottardo**. Hidden among the houses of Mezzolombardo is the *Castello della Torre* (16C). At *Spormaggiore*, the area of Maso Fratton-Valaia, on the border with the Parco del Brenta, is home to the few remaining brown bears in Trentino. **Lake Molveno** is the largest Alpine lake in Italy above 800m. Surrounded by breathtaking landscape, it offers plenty of scope to hikers and mountain-bike enthusiasts. Footpaths criss-cross the woods and lead up to the peaks of the Brenta Dolomites and *Mt Gazza* (2,034m), where the ski facilities are excellent. The rocky peaks of the Brenta Mountains are reflected in the still, clear waters of the lake, where visitors can practice water sports, fish or relax on its lovely grassy beaches. A series of hairpin bends leads up to *Dosso Alto* (1,550m) and another wiggly road winds its way between this mountain and *Paganella* (2,098m), dominating **Fai della Paganella**. Here, the ruins of a *village* show that humans settled here as early as the 5th-4th centuries BC. When you reach **Àndalo**, the sight of the little karst lake (only possible at certain times of year) makes you feel that all the effort to get

there was worthwhile. At **Lake Molveno**, the Brenta Dolomites, the delight of the mountaineers who have been coming here to climb since the mid-19th century, and which form part of the Parco Naturale Adamello-Brenta, dominate the landscape. There are even late-Gothic frescoes on the 13th-century *church of S. Vigilio*, situated close to the edge of the lake, which is famous for its clear, warm water. The waters of the lake contain a 3,000 year-old petrified forest.

RIVA DEL GARDA [41 km]

At Riva del Garda a gentle breeze blows off the lake, keeping the temperature mild and giving the town a natural vocation as a health resort. The fact that **Piazza III Novembre*** ❶ faces the harbor shows more than anything else how close the ties between the town and the lake are. The lines of Lombard Venetian houses facing Lake Garda have porticoes on the ground floor, like the *Town Hall* (1482), which forms a single block with *Palazzo Pretorio* (1375), as does the *Torre Apponale*, built in the 13th century. From the square you can also see a round *bastion* dating from the 16th century and, on the shore of the lake, the *Ponale Hydroelectric power plant* (20C). Walking along **Via Fiume** ❷ is one way to discover the old part of Riva del Garda, a dense maze of narrow streets with Baroque facades. The *Parish church of the Assunta* dates from 1728, although the original church was much older. Giuseppe Alberti painted the frescoes on the right-hand wall of the chapel of the Madonna (the *statue* of the Madonna dates from the 16C); Giuseppe Craffonara painted the *Assumption* (above the high altar) and *Our Lady of Sorrows* (4th altar on the left); Giambettino Cignaroli painted the *Madonna of the Rosary and Saints* (2nd altar on the left). *St Michael's door* dates from the 12th century. But the real treasure of the Baroque here is the **church of the Inviolata** ❸, built in 1603-1636. Everything inside the church, built on an octagonal plan, points to the language of the Counter-Reformation: the frescoes on the ceiling (Martino Teofilo Polacco), interspersed with stuccoes, and those in the niches (Pietro Ricchi), which frame altars with works by Palma the Younger (who painted the *St Onofrius* above the 1st altar on the right, the *St Jerome* above the 2nd on the right and the *St Carlo Borromeo* above the 2nd

today, more than 800 years since it was built (it was begun in 1124), with its 13th-century keep and its four corner towers. Inside, some of the rooms, which still bear traces of 16th-century frescoes, now house the *Museo Civico*. The art gallery contains paintings, frescoes and sculptures dating from the 15th to 20th centuries. There are a number of paintings by Pietro Ricchi and Giuseppe Craffonara, the greatest exponent of neo-classicism in the Trentino. Northwest of Riva del Garda there are several small towns. On the right bank of the valley of the Magnone river, *Varone* is famous for its *waterfalls*, 87m high. In *Cologna*, the sidewalls of the 13th-century *Parish church of S. Zeno* bear the remains of 15th-century frescoes. **Tenno** has a *castle* dating back to the 12th century. If you explore the old town center, which is well-preserved, you eventually come to the **church of S. Lorenzo**. Set in a solitary position overlooking the valley,

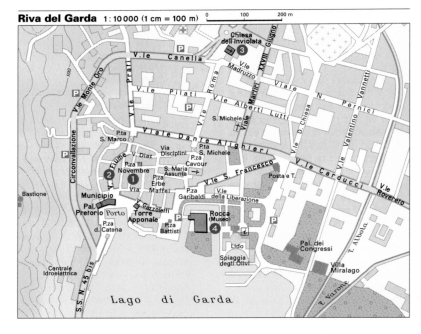

Riva del Garda 1:10 000 (1 cm = 100 m)

altar on the left). The **Rocca*** ❹, a perfect example of a castle-cum-fortress, is surrounded by a broad moat which made it impregnable (it can only be entered via a single bridge). It still looks like a fortress

the church's early medieval origins (8-9C) are betrayed by the remains embedded in the outer walls and the frescoes from the 11th, 14th and 15th centuries. *Lake Tenno* was created in the late 15th century as the result of a

The medieval center of Riva del Garda: the Rocca, a perfect example of a fortified castle surrounded by a moat, could only be accessed by a single bridge

landslide. **Lake Garda,** the largest lake in the region, was defined by Goethe as a "majestic spectacle of Nature", but is only one of the approximately 300 lakes in Trentino. Different in terms of size, climate, flora and fauna, the lakes of Trentino all have one thing in common: extremely pure water. Lake Garda, surrounded by imposing mountains, has a Mediterranean climate, which has resulted in very unusual flora, with olive-trees growing next to pinewoods. Another peculiar feature of the lake is the *ora*, a constant wind that blows every day and is very popular with sailing enthusiasts. The area around the lake is surprisingly rich in terms of cultural and natural heritage, with many picturesque medieval towns with churches, noble palaces and charming little streets. There are also many beautiful **viewpoints** overlooking a gentle landscape criss-crossed with footpaths, ideal for hiking. There are also many cycling routes crossing woods, meadows and beaches, and *vie ferrate* (equipped climbing routes) leading up to the tops of the peaks.

ROVERETO [24 km]

The fact that Trentino's second largest town has four museums says a great deal about Rovereto's vocation as a cultural center. And when we discover that its vocation was of Austrian origin and that it was here that Mozart performed his first two concerts in Italy (1769), there is no doubt that it merits its nickname of "Athens of Trentino". Another feather in its cap is the fact that the philosopher Antonio Rosmini was born here.

The **Castle*** ❶ is set in a strategic position and looks like a fortress. It was built in the 14th century by "recycling" a 12th-century fortification, but its current appearance and characteristic polygonal shape, the chemin-de-ronde for the cannons, the towers and the spur (from it you can see the whole of the old town, with its various stages of growth), date from when it was conquered by the Venetians. The Austrians continued to use it for military purposes and helped to preserve its fortified character. Almost in acknowledgement of its military role, it now houses the **Museo Storico Italiano della Guerra**, the exhibits of which describe wars and the atrocities

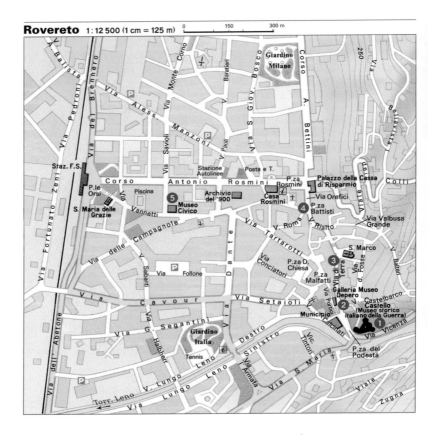

Rovereto 1:12 500 (1 cm = 125 m)

associated with them. Anyone wishing to gain an insight into the genius of the Futurist artist Fortunato Depero should visit the **Galleria Museo Depero ❷**, the only museum in Italy devoted to Futurism. Everything in the museum was created by the artist: the wall decoration, the mosaic floors, and the furniture, which blend with his tapestries, paintings and advertising posters, as if to describe the sectors in which the movement flourished. Palazzo Pretorio is used as the *Town Hall*. It was built in 1417, altered in the late 16th century (windows) and in the 18th century (door). *Via Portici* is the pleasant main shopping street of the town. There are some early buildings in **Via di Terra ❸**. For example, the *Torre Civica*, built in the 16th century and incorporating one of the entrance-gates of the town walls. The *church of S. Marco*, with its Baroque interior, was founded in the previous century. **Piazza Battisti ❹** marks the place where the medieval part of Rovereto meets the new part of the town

built in the 18th century. The *Fontana del Nettuno (Neptune's fountain)* on the square already dates from the 18th century, but so does *Corso Rosmini*, which starts at the neo-Renaissance *Palazzo della Cassa di Risparmio*. A statue of Rosmini stands opposite the house where he was born, a converted country house from the 17th century. The *Archivio del '900* rotates the exhibits from the collection of works by Futurists of the **Museo d'Arte Moderna e Contemporanea di Trento e Rovereto (MART)**. The collection, displayed in a modern building, includes works by Fortunato Depero, Luciano Baldessari, Gigiotti Zanini and Gino Severini. Nearby is the 18th-century *church of S. Maria delle Grazie*. The **Museo Civico ❶** is Rovereto's pride and joy, and the third-oldest museum in Italy. It houses exhibits from the surrounding area associated with mineralogy, paleontology, zoology and botany, as well as archeological finds, mainly from Greater Greece. In the **Vallarsa** is the

Hermitage of San Colombano, set in a wild landscape, which was dug out of the rock in the 11th-12th century and rebuilt later.

TRIENTER DOLOMITEN [20 km]

In eastern Trentino, the landscape is enhanced by the spectacular peaks of the Dolomites that tower above the green valleys of *Primiero* and *Vanoi*. An atmosphere of days gone by prevails in the small, picturesque towns in the valley. They make an ideal base for hiking in an area where the wildlife and the landscape are unique. At **Pèrgine Valsugana** there are some surprisingly luxurious buildings on *Via Maier*. They testify to the time when, from the 16th century onwards, the minerals mined in Piné and Mòcheni valleys were brought here to be processed. But the two centers of local power here also testify to the town's wealth. In Piazza del Municipio, the *Palazzo Comunale* (Town Hall, 1697) has a double staircase and complex railings and wrought-iron work; in Piazza S. Maria, the complex comprising the *Parish church of the Natività di Maria*, built in 1550 in the Late-Gothic style by Lombard masons, the *church of S. Antonio Abate*, which

was altered in the 18th century, and the 16th-18th-century *church of S. Carlo*. The history of *Pèrgine Valsugana* prior to the "mining boom" focuses on the *castle*, (supposedly based on an earlier castle), which subsequently became the center of a Roman settlement. The town first appears in documents in the 12th century and, since then, very few changes have been made to the Romanesque-Gothic street plan.

A small road winds up to *Serso*, site of a settlement of the Raeti (5th -1st century BC), and then into the **Mòcheni valley**, where the typical *masi* (farmhouses) date from the time when people of Germanic origin came to work in the mines. The area has splendid views of utterly unspoiled Alpine scenery. From **Palù del Fèrsina**, a bus service enables visitors to see the *mine* where pyrite was extracted in the 16th and 17th centuries. On warm summer evenings, people like to drive from Trent to **Lake Caldonazzo**, to escape from the heat of the city and enjoy the many night venues in the area. In the dark, not much can be seen of the mountain landscape surrounding the lake, or the many villas and holiday houses. This broad lake is perfect for water sports because it is sheltered from

The 14-C castle is now the largest museum war museum in Italy. During the First World War, the area of Rovereto was the scene of fierce fighting

THE LEGEND OF MAZARÒL

A local legend tells the story of a girl from Primiero and involves a character known as Mazaròl, a little man dressed in red that used to kidnap people and employ them as servants. One day, having trodden on one of Mazaròl's footprints, this girl suddenly found herself face to face with him.

When he breathed on her face, she immediately forgot her previous life and then spent many years working as his slave. Mazaròl taught her how to make butter, cheese and ricotta and promised her that, some time in the future, he would teach her how to make wax out of whey, but never found the time.

One day, a hunter recognized the girl and took her back to Primiero. But unfortunately, despite many attempts, no one knew how to restore her memory. Then, finally, an old lady told her to drink the milk from a white goat, and she instantly recognized her village and her family again.

She was so happy that she taught everyone in the community what she had learned from Mazaròl: so they started to produce butter, cheese and ricotta, but no one yet knows how to make wax out of whey. So be careful if you find small, pigeon-toed footprints because they belong to Mazaròl.

If anyone has any doubts about the existence of this evil little man, you can be quite sure that he does really exist. He may not kidnap young women any more but his evil power lives on. In fact, if someone's going through a bad time, it's quite common for the locals to ask: "Atu pestà te la pèca del Mazaròl?" (Have you trodden on one of Mazaròl's footprints?).

the wind. The choice of activities is bewildering: canoeing, swimming, sailing, kayaking, water-skiing, fishing. In addition, the natural landscape around the lake is ideal for hiking, horse-riding and biking.

Towns were established years ago on its southwest shore. **Calcerànica al Lago** dates from Roman times. In fact, the *church of S. Ermete* is said to have been built on the site of a pagan temple and still contains a votive altar from that period. In the 13th century, at **Caldonazzo,** the *Magnifica Corte*, a fortified house rebuilt in the 15th and 16th century, was already there. If you follow the road leading to the Monte Róvere Hotel, you will discover a pristine natural environment. The *Vézzena Pass* (1,402m) is only used for cross-country skiing, and, in winter, there are more than 50km of tracks.

Lèvico Terme is a health spa overlooking the green waters of the **Lake Lèvico.** Trees, some of them exotic species, dominate the town. In the spa park, nestling among the trees is the *Grand Hotel*, dating from the early 20th century. It was built 200 years after the spring water, containing arsenic and iron was discovered. The first spa establishments began to tap the water in 1860. **Lake Lèvico,** framed by luxuriant vegetation that tinges its waters with emerald green, is an ideal place for the family to relax. In summer, the average water temperature is 23 C°/ 73 F° and there is plenty for kids to do on the beach. In the surrounding hills, you can visit the 14th-century *church of S. Biagio*, decorated with frescoes dating from the 14th to 16th centuries, of clear Venetian influence, and the ruins of *Forte delle Benne*.

The pure, green waters of Lake Lèvico

However, the record for the highest water spa in Europe goes to *Vetriolo Terme*, which exploits the same mineral water springs as *Lèvico Terme*. From here, you can also access the ski runs of *Panarotta*.

San Martino di Castrozza*, the elegant, lively capital of skiing and hiking, has splendid views of the pinnacles known as the **Pale di San Martino**, which rise up steeply behind the town, forming the background for the clear waters of the **Fradusta** small lakes. The town, surrounded by dense forests, has the typical atmosphere of a mountain town, and a long history as a holiday resort (the circuit of the Malghe and Rolle Pass is a must for downhill-skiing enthusiasts; the traverse of the Pale plateau and the climb to Colbricòn Piccolo is a must for ski-mountaineering enthusiasts) and the views are difficult

VAL DI FASSA [70 km]

The Fassa valley, in the northwest of Trentino, is overlooked by mountains of rare beauty: **Roda di Vael** and **Cantinaccio**, the majestic peaks of **Sassolungo**, the imposing **Sella** and **Marmolada**, the "queen" of the Dolomites. To the south, the Mountains Valacia and the spurs of the Monzoni Range complete the circle. The land among these peaks is home to the Ladin people, whose ancient cultural tradition has handed down a rich heritage of charming anecdotes and mythical characters. The landscape around **Predazzo** is known as the "geological garden of the Alps". Scholars come here from all over the world to analyze the phenomena of crystallization resulting from the contact between sedimentary and volcanic rocks. Here, a visit to the **Museo Civico Geologia e Etnografia**,

Rifugio Pedrotti, one of the many huts on the Pale di San Martino massif

to beat, for example, the views from *Cima della Rosetta* (2,743m), *Alpe Tognola* (2,163m) or *Ces peak* (2,230m), slightly lower than *Mt Colbricòn* (2,603m) where a Mesolithic hunters' bivouac was discovered. Not only is the natural landscape spectacular, but also the flora and fauna. To complement the natural wealth of the region, interesting events are organized for visitors, such as concerts at mountain venues, typical village festivals (*sagre*), and historical re-enactments in period costume, craft fairs, gastronomic events and afternoon literary initiatives.

which explains the geological and natural peculiarities of the area, is a must. Rock samples, which, in past centuries, were much sought after by collectors from Italy and abroad, are accompanied by the footprints of reptiles and amphibians, a slab with the imprints of 33 fish from the Upper Permian period (270 million years ago) and fossils of invertebrates which lived 235 million years ago. In the center of the town, the houses have pretty, frescoed facades, often with Gothic doors and windows. Not far away, the mountain landscape of the **Travignolo valley** (on the right is

A VERY SPECIAL OPEN-AIR MUSEUM

After all, these are the Dolomites, a unique geological museum, but views of them from the valley floors and the exhibits in the Museo Civico in Predazzo only give you a vague idea. That's why you can't say you know this corner of the Alps until you've taken one of the guided hikes (organized in the summer, either for half a day or all day) which wind their way along some very special paths among the peaks of the Fiemme and the Fassa valleys.

One of the best hikes is around Doss Cappèl (2,264m), which you can either hike up to from Alpe di Pampeago or reach by chairlift from Predazzo: on the hike, the guide explains the volcanic history of these mountains, shows you the main types of rock and talks about the geological phenomena behind the formation of the Western Dolomites. Otherwise, try the geological route associated with the Miniere della Bedovina, where you can see the intrusive and extrusive rocks which are typical of this central area of the volcano of Predazzo and the mineral forms associated with it (copper, tungsten and veinstone minerals were extracted from the mines of Bedovina). And your knowledge still won't be complete unless you follow the Màlgola geological route, and another on the south side of the Monzoni range.

Colbricòn and, in the distance, the silhouette of the Pale di San Martino) is softened by the spruce woods managed by the Parco Naturale Paneveggio-Pale di S. Martino. The Paneveggio wood consists of more than 4,000 hectares of meadows and woods. At sunset and at dawn, when the peaks are illuminated with red, it is obvious why the town of **Moena** is also known as the "fairy of the Dolomites". Here, the Avisio stream still looks as if it has only recently left its source, the meadows are extensive and, despite the spread of building development, woods still cover half the land. This is particularly noticeable in the side-valleys, where the forests are dominated by a ring of mountains including Catinaccio, Sasso Lungo, Sella and Marmolada. In the town, the *church of S. Vigilio* was founded in the 13th century and contains painted decoration. Nearby, **S. Volfango** is entirely decorated with *frescoes* with a religious theme. Both churches are very old. The ancient tradition of making wooden receptacles is alive and well at the *Botega da Pinter*, where vats are still made. The flavors of days gone by are brought to life when you taste the typical local cheese called *Puzzone* (the Stinker). Whether you are there hiking in the summer or skiing in winter, it's worth heading for the *San Pellegrino Pass*. There are splendid views of Marmolada from **Vigo di Fassa**, (Vich in Ladin), a popular destination for skiers and hikers. The energetic can

head for the cable car which leads up to the paths to *Rifugio Campediè* (1,997m); art lovers can visit the *church of S. Giuliana*, built in the 13th century but Gothic in appearance (the frescoes in the apse and on the ceiling are by Bressanone), and the nearby *chapel of S. Maurizio*, the oldest church in the valley (1297). To explore the peaks of Catinaccio and *Lake Antermoia*, the best base is **Pozza di Fassa**. At *Pera di Fassa*, you can visit the *Molin de Pezòl*, an old mill which has been renovated and is now open to the public. Just beyond this small village, the Vajolét valley merges with the Fassa valley, penetrating the mountains and affording magnificent views.

At **Campitello di Fassa**, a museum has been created in one of the cable-car stations, paying homage to the sport, which has turned the town into one of Italy's top ski resorts. The *Museo degli Sci* may be seen by anyone catching the cable car to the *Rodella hill* (2,387m), which is connected by other facilities to the Sella Pass. Hidden among the houses which are proof that the town has become a key holiday resort is the *church of Ss. Filippo e Giacomo* (13-19C). Its frescoes show the strong Tyrolean influence – used by Bressanone – of local art. At **Canazei**, again the mountains reign supreme, both in terms of landscape, with Marmolada to the southeast, the Sella range to the northeast and Sasso Lungo to the northwest, and in terms of opportunities to practice sport, especially skiing. Here, roads set off in the direction of three Alpine passes. People don't come here to enjoy art or architecture. The Dolomites themselves are the masterpieces, and can be seen at their best from the cable car leading up to Pecol and from the next one leading up to Belvedere (2,349m).

VAL DI LEDRO [40 km]

Lake Ledro renders the Ledro valley, which lies in the shadow of the peaks of Brenta, even more beautiful. During the Bronze Age, a pile-dwelling settlement was built on its shores at Molina di Ledro. Other interesting archeological finds from the site are kept in the *Museo delle Palafitte*: necklaces, tools, ploughs and canoes. The **lake** provides opportunities for fishing and various sports, including canyoning on the Pàlvico stream and the Nero river.

VAL DI SOLE [40 km]

This deeply religious land is now a popular tourist area in winter and summer. Yet this somewhat radical change has not entirely altered the local farming economy based on fruit farming.

The branches of an apple tree appear on the crest of **Malè**, a modern-looking town, as the result of a fire which broke out in 1892. If you want to learn more about life in the valley, visit the *Museo della Civiltà Solandra* where you can see reconstructions of the interiors of local dwellings and the tools that were once used. If you follow the course of the Noce towards Cles you come to the **Castello di Caldès**, a 13th-century fortified house which as converted into a residence in the mid-15th century. If you follow the Rabbiès stream, passing meadows, woods and rock walls, you enter the **Rabbi valley***, where the *maso* with a stone base and upper floors made of wood is almost the only sign of human occupation. Tourism didn't arrive until the 19th century, a century after the healing properties of the water of *Bagni di Rabbi* had been discovered. **Lake Corvo**, the three **Sternai lakes** and **Lake Rotondo** are all worth a visit. The mountains opposite them lie within the territory of the Parco Nazionale dello Stelvio.

VALLE DI CEMBRA [20 km]

You should try to come to the Cembra valley when the vineyard terraces are covered in snow. This snow not only

In the Val di Fassa, despite recent development, meadows and woods occupy more than half the land, especially in the side-valleys

envelops them but also delicately marks out the edges of the different pieces of land. The poles, which support the vines, are the only reminder that, in spring, the plants that seem dead in winter will actually come to life again and produce the grapes for making quality wines and excellent grappas. Below the terraces, the Avisio has carved a deep gorge; above them, orchards keep the vineyards company, with the forest above.

At **Lisignago** the Gothic *church of S. Leonardo* was frescoed in the 15th century. At **Cembra**, the frescoes in *S. Pietro* are of the same date (however the Romanesque bell tower suggests that it was founded earlier; the *scenes of the Life of Jesus* on the wall of the presbytery date from the 16th century, while the *Last Judgement* opposite dates from the 18th century). The *Parish church of the Assunta* also dates from the 15th century. Outside the town is a broad flat floodplain, which is traditionally left uncultivated. There are 15th-century frescoes (but also a 16th-century wooden statue of the *Madonna of the Grapes*) in the late-Gothic *Parish church of the Immacolata* at *Piazzo*. Just beyond the town, only a few ruins remain of the *castle* built after 1216 to control the traffic passing between the Adige valley and Valsugana. In a nearby side-valley, the **earth pyramids of**

The strange earth pyramids at Segonzano

Segonzano are a phenomenon resulting from erosion. Some of the formations, each with a slab of stone on the top, are 20m high. In the Cembra valley the **Piné lakes** are immersed in the green plateau of the same name. *Lake Serraia* is popular for water sports and fishing, while nature-lovers can follow the path around the lake through woods and reed-beds. *Lake Piazze*, surrounded by meadows, offers the same opportunities for

THE LEGEND OF CAURIOL

In Fiemme valley there's a mountain, which is very dear to the hearts of the people of Trentino because many soldiers from the Alpine regiments ("Alpini") died on its summit (2,495m) during the Great War. The mountain is part of the Lagorai range and can be climbed from Ziano. Its name, "Cauriol" means roe deer in Trent dialect. A legend tells the story of a beautiful girl called Fogliadirosa ("Roseleaf"). Her mother had died and she lived with her father who adored her. One day, during a hunting expedition, there was a terrible storm and her father sought refuge at the castle of an evil, very cunning old widow, who gave him a magic potion that made him fall in love with her. The woman insisted on a very extravagant wedding during which her three daughters rode on the backs of three camels. When her father died, the girl had to escape from the castle. She knew that her stepmother and her stepsisters were jealous of her beauty and wanted to harm her in some way. She received protection from a kindly witch who lived in the forest. The girl's stepsisters followed her footprints and spied on the house. Fogliadirosa hid in the house for such a long time that she lost her lovely pink complexion. In order to let her out, the witch changed her into a roe deer, explaining that she could become a young woman again if she ate rose-leaves. Once, having encountered a hunter whom she liked, she changed back into a girl, but the hunter ran off, terrified by what he had seen. The stepsisters heard about this and realized that the girl must be Fogliadirosa. So they went to Mt Cauriol and destroyed all the roses there. Today they still say that there is a roe deer wandering about on those rose-less peaks.

leisure, and also has a path around its perimeter. At **Cavalese** you can admire the view of mountains covered in snow almost all the year round, which has made the **Fiemme valley** famous all over Europe. This broad, sunny valley, dominated by beautiful peaks such as the **Pale di S. Martino** and **Latemar**, stretches into the northeast Trentino, between the forest of the **Parco del Monte Corno** and the "Foresta dei Violini" of the **Parco di Paneveggio-Pale di S. Martino**. The first forest contains

Vigilius Enthroned, is the crest of the Community: six horizontal stripes topped by a cross. Over the years, the palace was used as a prison and a salt warehouse. Inside, the wooden ceilings and frescoed friezes have survived, while the paintings from the palace, works by the school of painters from the Fiemme valley, which flourished in the 17th and 18th centuries, now form part of the art gallery. To see other works of this school, you should visit the 17th-century *church of S. Vigilio* situated on

Summer is a riot of color in the Fiemme valley

many species of birds, while the second, famous for its woods of hazel spruce, used by Stradivarius and the finest violin-makers to create string instruments, has a healthy red deer population. Lying between the two parks are unspoiled areas such as the *Lagorai range*, where the abundant supply of water has led to the formation of delightful little lakes (there are about 80 of them in this mountain chain). **Lake Cima d'Asta** is particularly famous for its beautiful clear water. Many of the *malgas* in the area produce cheese. Some of the first to fall in love with this extraordinary mountain scenery were the bishop-lords of Trent, who built a residence at Cavalese. It is the medieval **Palazzo della Magnifica Comunità di Fiemme**. On the facade, in addition to *St*

the edge of the town. To see where the Community used to meet, starting at the palace, walk along Via della Pieve towards *'l Pra*, the park where six blocks of stone are arranged around a table in the center, known as the *banc de la Reson*. Nearby, the first stone of the *Parish church of the Assunta* was laid in the 12th century, however only a few Romanesque features in the doorway remain, and the church has been altered many times since. In this area, skiers are spoilt for choice. Either you can take the cable car from the town straight up to *Alpe Cermìs* (2,000m), which has lovely views over the valley, or you can drive to the *Lavazè Pass* (1,805m), pausing at **Varena** on the way to see the 15th-century frescoes in the *church of Ss. Pietro e Paolo*.

The Italian skiing industry really dates from the 1950s and 1960s, although it was not until the 1980s that shrugged of its modest beginnings and exploded into a fully fledged and flourishing sector of the tourist industry. In Trentino-Alto Adige, the widespread network of skiing areas, the cohesion between the different ski-lift operators and service providers, the stunning views and the extremely modern and technologically advanced facilities ensure that everything is of the highest standard. The planned development of the current network, the increasing number of high-capacity lifts and the careful grooming of the ski runs make the region one of the prime

DISABLED

SKI

Ski

destinations for Alpine sports. In short, it is not by chance that some of the ski runs have become worldwide skiing classics, such as the Gran Risa dell'Alta Badia, which hosts an annual World Cup event for giant slalom, or Saslong in Val Gardena, for downhill.

Highlights

- ■ The breathtaking views from the ski runs
- ■ The extremely well organized and comfortable ski-lifts
- ■ Certain legendary ski runs: the Trametsch at Plose near Bressanone/Brixen, or the Silvestre and the Herrnegg at Plan de Corones on the slopes of Brunico/Bruneck
- ■ The wonderful array of cross-country skiing trails in delightful surroundings

Inside

ALTO ADIGE

The smooth ski runs, very comfortable ski-lifts and numerous skiing areas make Alto Adige a "must" on any ski enthusiast's list. A key element is the Dolomiti Superski pass, invented in 1973, revolutionizing the concept of skiing. The basic idea is that a federation-consortium combines hundreds ski-lift operators, which are then grouped into smaller consortium based on valleys and centered on main hubs. Further information is available at www.dolomitisuperski.com

Sulden/Solda-Trafoi

ski-lifts open from November to May

Solda is one of the few ski resorts where the hotels, ski-lifts and related facilities do not tarnish the appeal of the mountains. By contrast, they almost blend into the surrouding monoliths of Ortles (3,905m) and Gran Zebrù, which overlook this delightful Alpine basin. The valley starts where the bends in the road up to the Stelvio Pass begin (closed in winter), in the Trafoi valley, which then becomes the Venosta valley at Prato allo Stelvio. There are numerous open spaces here, making cross-country skiing a real and interesting option for those who favor the thinner skis.

Hiking, exploring and mountaineering have been pursued in these parts for more than a century. Skiing, by contrast, is a more recent development and has led to the creation of comfortable hotels, including some

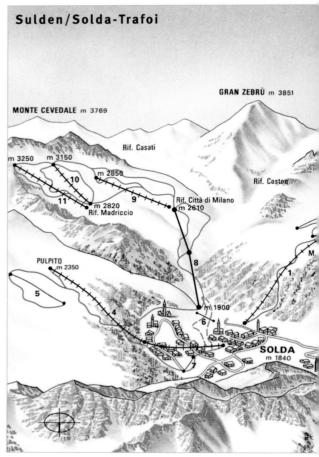

Sulden/Solda-Trafoi

SKI RUNS
Downhill skiing
55km (40 at Solda and 15 at Trafoi), including 17 covered by artificial snow spraying
blue **16** red **10** black **5**
Cross-country skiing
13km of trails of varying difficulty
Snowboarding
1 Snow park at Solda

LIFTS
Solda
Cable cars **1**
8   Solda Sezione I and II
      1900-2610
Chairlifts **5**
1   Orso 1850-2350
4   Pulpito 1920-2350
9   Madriccio 2610-2850
10   Beltovo I 2820-3150
11   Beltovo II 2820-3250
Ski-lifts **5**
2   Des Alpes 2320-2490
3   Marlet 2310-2430
5   Solda 2200-2450
6   Cevedale 1900-1920
7   Sole 1860-1910
Trafoi
Chairlifts **1**
21   Forcola 1520-2153
Ski-lifts **3**
22   Thoeni 1530-1570
23   Schölmental
2200-2352
24   Belvedere 2154-2539

notable ones, and other holiday accommodation, such as flats-to-rent, that fits in delightfully with the surroundings. The Solda skiing area is the skiing hub of the Ortler Ski Arena and, thus, of the western Alto Adige region. Some of the ski runs start from as high as 3,250m and the snow is always good and soft. Since 2000, the growth in the number of new ski-lifts has been noteworthy, with the cable car up to Madriccio being the best example. Madriccio itself is the main one of three skiing sections that comprise the 40km of ski runs in Solda. From the cable station (2,610m), you can take the black run with some technically demanding stretches (occasionally closed when avalanches are a risk) or a notable red trail with a 700m vertical drop. From the upper cable station, three modern

A break to admire the view of Gran Zebrù

chairlifts climb up a wide, snow-covered basin to the beneath the Beltovo peak. The main Madriccio lift rises to 2,850m and is both a connection to the Beltovo I and II chairlifts (moderate ski runs; between

Carving is one of the latest trends in skiing

ones). These are favored by the general public and so get quite busy. For those who so desire, there is a descent (Hochleiten no. 5, unchecked ski run) that takes you from Madriccio to the middle cable station via a narrow channel. The other sections of Solda are centered on two chairlifts that depart from near the church. A number of trails that can be skied (sometimes a little pushing is needed) run across the basin, connecting the three sections and greatly increasing the number of options for skiers who like diversity. The Orso chairlift departs from near Ortles and goes to 2,350m. From there, two further lifts take you up to 2,500m, where you can practically touch the colossal ice and rock structures while enjoying the notable view. These are not heavily used ski runs, but enjoyable because

3,150/3,250m and the Madriccio mountain refuge) and the lift to reach some wide, gentle slopes of 1.5-2km (or longer, if you start from 3,250m along the no. 1 and 1/a, the outer

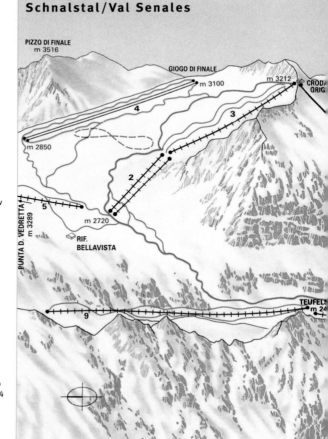

Schnalstal/Val Senales

PIZZO DI FINALE
m 3516

GIOGO DI FINALE

m 3100

m 3212

CROD/
GRIG

4

3

m 2850

2

PUNTA D. VEDRETTA
m 3289

5

m 2720

RIF.
BELLAVISTA

TEUFEL
m 24

9

SKI RUNS
Downhill skiing
35km, including 18 covered by artificial snow spraying
blue **5** red **12** black **4**
Cross-country skiing
20km of easy to intermediate trails
Snowboarding
1 Snow park with half pipe

LIFTS
Cable cars **1**
1 Gletscherbahn
   2011-3212
Chairlifts **7**
2 Gletschersee I and II
   2720-3000
3 Grawand 3013-3200
5 Hintereis 2774-3258
6 Lazaun 1999-2430
8 Roter Kofl 2027-2450
9 Teufelsegg 2444-3034
Ski-lifts **4**
4 Finail I and II
   2863-3113
7 Glocken I and II
   2010-2073

of the snow quality and gradient variations. The lovely Bosco red run leads down into the valley. From the other side, you climb to the Pulpito zone, with ski-lifts higher up. There is a lovely, medium-easy run of about 3km through the wood.

Cross-country skiing is possible at Solda, but the area is particularly loved by snowboarders. The open spaces make it possible for even relatively inexperienced boarders to enjoy the higher mountain reaches, with long, never overly difficult runs, such as from the Solda peak or on Cevedale.

Trafoi (elev. 1,543m) lies in the valley of the same name and is an alternative place to stay in the zone. It has its own, small skiing area with four lifts and about 15km of runs (varying difficulty) between 1,520 and 2,540m.

Schnalstal/Val Senales

ski-lifts open January-December
The Senales valley is one of the few Alpine skiing areas that is regularly open for more than 10 months a year. The core is the Croda Grigia-Giogo Alto Glacier. It is enclosed by imposing massifs, such as the Tessa Mountains and Silmilaun to the northeast and Palla Bianca to the west, and opens into the Venosta valley via an inaccessible 3km gorge a little upstream from Naturno. In the area where the gradient become slightly less steep, amid larch trees and open fields, small villages are dotted around while the slopes are home to ancient farmsteads. Vernago lies in an artificial basin and is where the first major hotels can be found, although the tourist structures become more evident where the valley ends. The Maso Corto

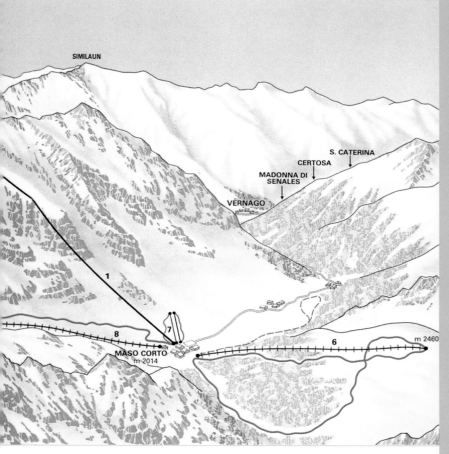

settlement rises at 2,020m and has various modern, functional hotels and other holiday accommodation. If you are looking for a vacation with a different flavor, the valley has various farm holiday options where you can lodge in refurbished farm accommodation.

The ski-lifts, serving about 35km of runs, almost all function until early May. They reopen in late June for summer skiing on the higher runs (about 9km) between 3,200 and 2,770m. The only areas for skiing in the heart of summer are the 5km of runs above 2,860m. To reach the glacier from Maso Corto, take the 100-person cable car that, in a mere 6 minutes, rises 1,200m. From the upper cable station, which is annexed to a display area with an exhibit on Ötzi and a hotel with one of the highest pools in the world, you can head straight onto the ski runs. The way back up is via the quad Grawand chairlift. Further down, there are two parallel T-bar ski-lifts, Finail 1 and 2 (open in summer) that are 1,500m long. The ski runs next to the lift seem to be flat, but this is an optical effect created by the enormous open spaces of the glacier.

Wide blue and red runs, with soft and good snow, take you down to 2,720m. Here you have two options: head back up the glacier using the Gletschersee 1 and 2 chairlifts from 2,720m in the small, facing valley; alternatively, on the other side, you can take the long, fixed Hintereis chairlift. To descend, you need to take a moderately difficult and varied route across a dazzling, snow-covered landscape. By taking a detour, you can head to the Bellavista mountain refuge, from where you can make a seemingly endless descent, known as *Contrabbandieri* (smugglers), down to Maso Corto. It is classified as a black run, although it is relatively easy except for the wall just above Maso Corto. This run can also be reached, at 2,444m, by a quad chairlift from Maso Corto. Once again from 2,444m, at the Teufelsegg mountain refuge, you can take another, new quad chairlift up to 3,034m and try the two black runs with a 590m vertical drop. This area is no longer the gentle,

The ski-lifts in the upper Senales valley, in the background, to the right, the Croda Grigia (3,202m)

overhanging glacier, and it is definitely the most technically challenging and stimulating section of the skiing area. From Maso Corto, but on the other slope, you can take the Lazaun chairlift, to access a lovely run. The chalet with the same name (2,430 m) has a stunning view. A sled run (3.3km) starts from Lazaun.

The snowboarding scene is lovely, with a well-equipped center at Maso Corto. For cross-country skiing, there are 4 different circuits (for a total of 20km) at varying altitudes.

A well-known ski-mountaineering expedition leaves from Vernago and heads to the Tisa ridge and Similaun, near where the famous mummified body of a Copper Age resident of the zone, known as Ötzi, was found. The vertical drop and the harsh environment makes this excursion particularly taxing. It is also worth visiting Archeoparc, in Madonna, with displays on the environment and daily life in the age of Ötzi.

One final aspect to note in the Senales valley are the 86 *masi chiusi* (literally, closed farmhoues, but indicating a farmstead that cannot be divided up among heirs), which are some of the highest and oldest permanent settlements in the Tyrol.

Brixen/Bressanone-Plose

ski-lifts open December-March

The Isarco valley is a meeting point for the northern and Mediterranean cultures because of the Brennero (Brenner), the most used pass in the central-eastern section of the Alps. For centuries this route, cutting through a valley rich in history, has been used by traffic and trade. This past is still visible in the ancient inns, or Gasthaus, with their typical wrought-iron signs. In the Bressanone basin, at the confluence of the Rienza (Pusteria valley) and Isarco rivers, you enter a land of vineyards, fruit orchards and chestnut trees. Bressanone lies at a mere 560m, but it is the cultural and religious center for the Tyrol area, with its own flourishing culture and trade. The Bressanone ski runs are a little higher, with the ski-lifts departing from Sant'Andrea (about 1,050m). From the valley, you can make out the famous, snake-like Trametsch black trail through the wood. This combination of city and mountain makes Bressanone a particularly intriguing destination. You can choose to stay in hotels with centuries of history that are sumptuous and bathed in tradition, or recently refurbished ones. Alternatively, small, family-owned accommodation (rooms-for-rent, bed&breakfasts, farmstay options) can be found amid the vineyards, on the Naz-Sciaves plateau, in the villages on the slopes of Plose and on the right slope of the Isarco valley, especially at Velturno and Villandro. Sant'Andrea, lying at the foot of Plose, has relatively good facilities. If you are looking for an authentic, Alpine experience, then you must try the Luson and Funes valleys. Both have lovely hotels and the latter, lying further south, is "crowned" by the jagged top of Odle. The view is one of the classic Dolomite views. The Luson and Funes valleys are near Plose, Marazan and Valles (and Val Gardena), but unlike most winter resorts in Italy, local tourism is not based on downhill skiing and, indeed, there are only small, local ski-lifts. The area, along with Maranza-Gitschberg and Valles-Jochtal, forms part of the northwestern edge of Dolomiti Superski (81km of ski runs), with a single ski pass and the

spraying of artificial snow as needed. The skiing area lies on the southwest facing slopes of Plose and on the adjacent Mt Fana. The highest point for skiing is a respectable 2,500m. Plose is a wooded massif with a barren summit that has a number of moderately difficult ski runs located between 2,050 and 2,500m. The main lift is the Valcroce chairlift. In the higher reaches, of the various interesting red trails, the highlight is the route starting from Mt Fana and heading down to the Ski Hütte, a 600m vertical drop over 4km. The run takes you on enjoyable jumps, around sharp curves in the wood and gives you a stunning view of Odle, one of the Dolomite's finest mountain groups.

The jewel, though, is the Trametsch black route that heads down into the valley. From the top of Plose (CAI mountain refuge, 2,445m) down to

Skiing in fresh snow

Sant'Andrea, the vertical drop is practically a record-breaking 1,400m. Yet, the true trail starts from the gondola lift (the variant, higher black run, no. 1, is often closed). From here, you head down through the wood on a winding trail with a constant gradient and good snow. The combination of length and difficulty make this a classy trail. The other highlight of Plose is the various chalets, with Rossalm and the lively S' Stubele (near the lift station) being the most popular.

Plose is much loved by snowboarders

who like to meet, at the end of the day at the Igloo Apres Ski that lies down in the valley.

In the Bressanone area, there are a further 5km of runs, served by a series of single lifts, at Luson, Funes and Velturno.

The Funes valley is ideal for a vacation immersed in nature: over 20km of cross-country skiing circuits, 4 sled runs and delightful snow walks in the Parco Naturale Puez-Odle, dotted with beautiful mountain refuges at the foot of the fabled Odle.

Cross-country skiers can find some interesting and rewarding circuits on Rodengo-Luson (from where you get some wonderful views of the Dolomites) and, on the opposite slope, Villandro. The unusual feature here is

Brixen/Bressanone-Plose

SKI RUNS
Downhill skiing
43km, including 35 covered by artificial snow spraying
blue **5** red **11** black **1**
Cross-country skiing
35km of trails of medium difficulty
Snowboarding
1 Fun park

LIFTS
Cable cars **1**
1 Sant'Andrea-Valcroce
   1067-2046
Chairlifts **7**
2 Valcroce-Schönboden
   2025-2320
4 Plancios-Valcroce
   1705-2060
5 Skihütte 1900-2226
6 Plose 2195-2445
7 Rossalm-Monte Fana
   2195-2506
8 Pfannspitze 2143-2477
– Trametsch 1614-2112
Ski-lifts **2**
3 Randötsch 1065-1108
9 Heini 2370-2500

the altitude: the routes run across panoramic, open plateaus that are located between 1,800 and 2,000/2,100m. Plose also has some options that are combined with those in the Funes valley, in the Erbe Pass area. From Villandro, a difficult ski touring trails goes to Renon. There are also some lovely mountain refuges used by hikers.

Welschnofen/Nova Levante-Karersee/Carezza al Lago

ski-lifts open December-March

Nova Levante, sitting within sight of some famous summits, is an ideal location for a Dolomite holiday and is the skiing hub of the Ega valley. The "upper section" is Carezza al Lago, near the Costalunga Pass (1,752m) leading into the Fassa valley. The Ega

A chalet at Carezza, with Catinaccio in the background

valley is the heart of tourism in Rosengarten-Làtemar (6,500 beds in hotels). For a number of years, the two skiing hubs of this valley, Carezza al Lago and Obereggen, have been marketed together with the Tires valley and the Regglberg plateau (Nova Ponente, Monte San Pietro and some minor towns like Aldino and Redagno). The area is characterized by a series of undulating mounds, reaching 1,000m to 1,700m, above which rise the Catinaccio and Làtemar Dolomites, separated by the Costalunga pass. These mountain groups dominate the surroundings, creating classic Dolomite scenes with majestic forests on the lower slopes and small churches amid fields and pastures. Nova Levante lies in the sunny section of the valley,

along the "Great Road of the Dolomites" that starts from a little north of Bolzano, "violating" the porphyry ravine of the Ega river. A little higher up, you come across the timeless setting of Lake Carezza, in which, during summer, you can gaze in awe at the reflection of Làtemar (in winter, of course, the lake is frozen over). The town (1,150m to 1,200m) has good accommodation ranging from farmstay options to hotels with wellness centers, both in the actual town and environs. You can enjoy another spectacular view, this time of Catinaccio in the parallel Tires valley, by using the Nigra Pass. This town, at the edge of the Parco Regionale dello Sciliar, has some delightful hotels even though there are no ski runs. If you want to enjoy the snow, there are many snow-walks, such as: in the untamed Ciamin valley, in the heart of the nature park; or the route to the Wuhnleger viewpoint, where you can savor a stupendous view of Catinaccio.

The skiing hub of the area is Carezza, lying beneath Catinaccio and alive with hotels, ski-lifts, related facilities and residential areas. For the last few years, the lifts at Nova Levante have been closed, but they are due to open soon. From the town, you cannot

The Làtemar chalet at Skicenter Làtemar

access the skiing area directly, so you need to take the ski-bus or a car up to Carezza, but you can return on your skis, via a blue route. There are 29km of runs, forming part of the Fassa-Carezza del Dolomiti Superski ski pass. The main lift is the Paolina covered quad from Carezza. The Paolina ski run extends out in front of you. It starts from the Paolina mountain refuge (2,126m) and heads down for 2km on the open slopes at the southern edge of the famed Catinaccio, at Roda di Vael. The first section (black then red) has some tight bends where speed control is vital, but then the slopes flatten out slightly and you can race down the hill, cutting perfect curves. About halfway down, the terrain becomes a natural half pipe and it can be great fun "swinging" from side to side. This is where the Italian Karen Putzer, a champion skier, learned her sport. The upper sections are

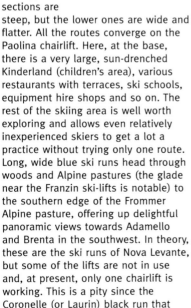

The training slope at Carezza

steep, but the lower ones are wide and flatter. All the routes converge on the Paolina chairlift. Here, at the base, there is a very large, sun-drenched Kinderland (children's area), various restaurants with terraces, ski schools, equipment hire shops and so on. The rest of the skiing area is well worth exploring and allows even relatively inexperienced skiers to get a lot a practice without trying only one route. Long, wide blue ski runs head through woods and Alpine pastures (the glade near the Franzin ski-lifts is notable) to the southern edge of the Frommer Alpine pasture, offering up delightful panoramic views towards Adamello and Brenta in the southwest. In theory, these are the ski runs of Nova Levante, but some of the lifts are not in use and, at present, only one chairlift is working. This is a pity since the Coronelle (or Laurin) black run that

starts from Frommer is one of the most romantic trails in the Dolomites. At the summit, at the Fronza Coronelle mountain refuge (2,320m), you can truly enjoy the magic of the *Enrosadira*, but for now, it can only be reached by ski-mountaineers. There are three cross-country skiing circuits, covering 17.5km, winding through some charming scenery.

Deutschnofen/Nova Ponente-Obereggen/San Floriano
ski-lifts open December-April
Obereggen is one of the most dynamic and lively resorts in the Dolomites. It has high-capacity lifts, about 10 lively chalets and a range of sporting events (and more). It is one of the three hubs of the Ski Center Làtemar with Pampeago and Predazzo, both in Trentino in the Fiemme valley. Obereggen lies on the lower slopes of Làtemar, at the end of the left side of the Ega valley, upstream from San Nicolò d'Ega (elev. 1,126m). There is, however, no real town at Obereggen, but rather a settlement around a number of extremely well equipped hotels near the lower lifts (1,550m). The main towns in the area are Nova Ponente (elev. 1,357m) and Monte San Pietro, more remote and scattered across the so-called Regglberg plateau. This is a delightful undulating area southeast of Bolzano and the Ega valley, amid Corno Bianco, Corno Nero, the Oclini Pass and the Adige valley. By continuing south, you come to the Fiemme valley on the other side of the Lavazè Pass, between Corno Bianco and Pala di Santa. The Obereggen ski runs (Fiemme Obereggen del Dolomiti Superski ski pass) cover about 40km on the western and northwestern slopes of Làtemar and towards Pampeago and the Feudo-Predazzo Pass. The modern and busy skiing area is also favored by

snowboarders (150m half pipe). To uncover the magic of the Dolomites, all you need do is take the Oberholz quad chairlift or the Ochsenweide cable car, which stops further down. Above the fir woods, you can see the snow-covered screes and "chilly" rocks of Làtemar. The Oberholz (600m vertical drop) is probably the most interesting ski run in the zone. The most spectacular stretch is the initial, wide wall to the fork for Pampeago. From here to the end, the route is easy and undulating as it moves through the wood. From the fork, via chairlifts and some easy ski runs, you come to the keystone of the area, at the Pampeago Pass (2,056m), marked by a grid of gentle pastures and some lively chalets. Another delightful run, albeit quite short, is the Reiter red trail. In general, the area has red and blue runs, aside from the black Pala di Santa (see Predazzo), which are notable for the grooming, safety and markings.

At Nova Ponente and Monte San Pietro, near the houses, are two short ski-lifts. The cross-country skiing circuits are notable, forming a vast network in the Regglberg plateau. Some of the routes, which are partially connected, are around the towns (25km at Nova Ponente, 11km at Monte San Pietro) but the best ones are from Pietralba to the Lavazè Pass and Oclini (see Cavalese), covering a total of 70km. The scenery is fabulous and the routes are dotted with chalet-restaurants.

SKI RUNS
Downhill skiing
38km, including 25 covered by artificial snow spraying
blue **11** red **10** black **1**
Cross-country skiing
70km of easy to interme-diate trails

LIFTS
Monte Croce di Comelico Pass
Ski-lifts **2**
1   Kreuzberg I 1656-1806
2   Kreuzberg I Bis 1656-1806
Sesto
Gondola lifts **1**
3   Bad Moss-Rotwand-wiesen 1356-1920
Ski-lifts **6**
4   Rotwandwiesen 1900-2000
5   Porzen 1780-1977
6   Moss 1339-1398
7   Bruggerleite 1345-1427
8   Waldheim I 1328-1415
9   Waldheim I Bis 1328-1415
Monte Elmo
Cable cars **1**
10   Sesto-Monte Elmo 1320-2055
Gondola lifts **1**
11   Versciaco-Monte Elmo 1130-2055
Chairlifts **4**
13   Raut-Kegelplätze 1680-2043
14   Ubungslift 1915-2043
15   Helm 1950-2199
17   Raut 1141-1273
Ski-lifts **1**
12   Hahnspiel 2103-2205
Rope tow **1**
16   Wiese 1140-1150
San Candido
Chairlifts **1**
18   Haunold 1175-1496
Ski-lifts **4**
19   Doris 1317-1491
20   Untertal 1467-1611
21   Lärchen 1407-1491
22   Erschbaum 1175-1200

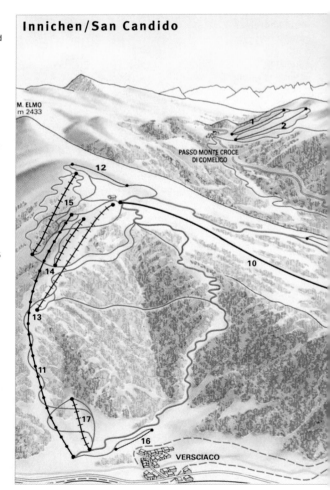

Innichen/San Candido

Innichen/San Candido

ski-lifts open December-April

This is the main artistic and cultural area of Alta Pusteria, and one of the main such areas in the Alto Adige zone. In addition to this vocation, it is a notable ski resort that is well connected with the various skiing areas at the foot of the Baranci Mountains. San Candido (elev. 1,175m) combines its own charm with the allure of the Dolomites. This lively town, with 2,500 bed spaces, has numerous things to do. One of the draw cards is the range of hotels, able to meet just about all requirements, some of which are housed in notable buildings. Although there are a mere 8km of ski runs above the town, San Candido's skiing area, facing north on the first slopes of the Dolomiti di Sesto, is certainly worth trying.

From only 4km away, the large Versciaco cable car takes you to Mt Elmo and then, via other links, to Croda Rossa. The skiing area here, known as Baranci (part of the Alta Pusteria del Dolomiti Superski ski pass, covering a total of 52km of runs), lies beneath the jagged peaks of the Dolomiti di Sesto (Rocca dei Baranci and Punta Tre Scarperi). The main lift is a quad chairlift, followed by a ski-lift which takes you to over 1,600m. At the top, there are also a another two lifts.

The most notable runs are a red route and a blue one leading down into the valley (2.4km) and ending with a final, straight downhill section that arrives

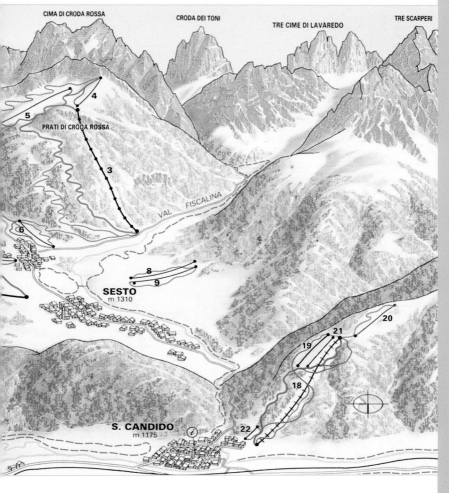

above the town. Perhaps the most attractive features of the Baranci area are the proximity to the town of the runs, the training slope and the so-called "ski kindergarten". Indeed, the entire Alta Pusteria is very well organized for children.

The mountain refuges have a definite Tyrolean feel. For cross-country skiing there are 70km of trails in the area (200km in total in the Alta Pusteria area, see Dobbiaco).

Bruneck/Brunico-Olang/Valdaora
ski-lifts open November-April

The Pusteria valley, one of the few valleys that runs east-west, flows into the Isarco valley, north of Bressanone, marking the northern border of the Dolomites. Along the valley floor, the farmsteads, castles and old towns lie amid cultivated fields, meadows and delightful expanses of conifer trees. Not long after the beginning of the Badia valley at San Lorenzo di Sebato

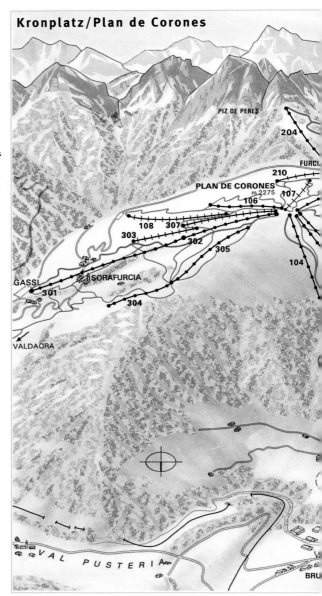

SKI RUNS
Brunico
Downhill skiing
14km
blue **1** red **2** black **2**
Cross-country skiing
at Riscone 10km of easy trails
covered by artificial snow
spraying
Valdaora
Downhill skiing
18km
blue **15** red **2**
Snowboarding
1 Half pipe

LIFTS
Brunico
Cable cars **5**
101 Kronplatz I 957-1863
102 Kronplatz II 1863-2271
103 Kronplatz 2000 957-2271
104 Gipfelbahn 1732-2273
106 Belvedere 2005-2273
Chairlifts **2**
107 Sonne 2067-2273
108 Marchner 1556-2112
Ski-lifts **1**
105 Korer 980-1084
San Vigilio di Marebbe
Cable cars **5**
201 Ruis 1748-2273
203 Skitrans-Bronta
       1183-1221
204 Pre da Peres 1738-2015
205 Miara 1221-1468
208 Col Toron 1468-1804
Chairlifts **4**
202 Piz de Plaies 1024-1620
206 Pedagà 1184-1299
210 Costa 1738-1861
211 Rara 1678-1816
Ski-lifts **1**
207 Cianross 1207-1288
Valdaora
Cable cars **4**
301 Olang I 1164-2072
302 Olang II 2072-2273
304 Alpen I 1635-1819
305 Alpen II 1819-2168
Chairlifts **2**
303 Arndt 1666-2088
307 Plateau 2025-2273
Ski-lifts **1**
–   Panorama 1130-1284

is Plan de Corones, a white natural dome with gentle slopes, woods and various ski runs.

Brunico, lying just below the skiing area, is the capital of the Pusteria microcosm. The town, enhanced by a lively pedestrian zone, is an important tourist center. It lies on a flat area at the bottom of the wide, open bowl at the opening of the Tures valley. The Plan de Corones ski-lifts are located in the Riscone district, on a small plateau

with various hotels. The second major center from which you can reach Plan de Corones is Valdaora, about 10km to the east at the start of the small Furcia valley. The third and no less important center is San Vigilio di Marebbe (see entry).

The lifts from the town leave from nearby Sorafurcia. The Plan de Corones skiing area has some hotels and numerous family-run bars and restaurants, creating a typical Dolomite

The Pramstall ski run

feel. This is the hub for an area that includes various, magnificently located villages lying on the sun-drenched slopes halfway up the right slop of Pusteria (Terento and Falzes), at the bottom of the valley (Chienes, San Lorenzo di Sebato, Perca and Monguelfo), on the steep northern side (the Anterselva valley and Casies) and at the beginning of the Badia valley (San Martino and Antermoia). There are numerous, different options for accommodation.

Plan de Corones is definitely the most technologically advanced skiing area in Italy: over 80% of the nearly 30 lifts are ergonomic and high capacity. The use of artificial snow spraying is also advanced, covering all of the ski runs. The dome on which Plan de Corones sits is the ideal location for a large array of ski-lifts that can be combined in varying ways. The upper part, above the trees, is one big, groomed skiing area with a relatively gentle gradient, enjoyable troughs and rises. In addition, the landscape has made it possible to make four trails leading down to the valley, all from 5-7km long with a vertical drop between 1,000 and 1,300m. The hardest section is the Brunico area, followed by Valdaora and San Vigilio. A gondola lift departs from Riscone. Once you are at the top, you can choose which slope to head down. The majority of trails are enjoyable, smooth red and blue runs that are ideal for fast turns. The Markner run is particularly enjoyable. The main run is Olang, a taxing red run that heads down for 3,300m to the parking lot. On

the north-facing slope, above Brunico, the snow is either powdery or firm. Here you can try the black Sylvester run, a 5km route winding through the wood with a truly notable vertical drop (about 1,300m), or its twin, Hernegg, which has even steeper sections. The feeling is fantastic as you seem to be flying above Brunico. If you want to just keep doing the first section, then you can use the second section of the Kronplatz II or Gipflebahn cable car. Once you are back at the top, you can relax on the Belvedere and Sole runs and then, for lunch, you can try one of the many mountain refuges halfway up. On the San Vigilio side, near the Furcia Pass, you can try the wide Furcia 9 or Furcia 12 runs.

The setting for this geological dome is extraordinary. From the flat summit, at 2,275m, you might wish to enjoy yourself by attempting to identify the following mountains: to the north lies the Alpine watershed with the Zillertaler Alpen and the Vedrette di Ries; while on the other side are the Dolomites; beyond the Badia valley you can see the top of Sasso di Putia; further away, Sella, Marmolada, Tofane and Pelmo. The flat summit of Plan de Corones makes this an ideal place for children. Croniworld is a large area with various facilities, including a castle with a snow maze and, next to it, the Dinosaur wood where children can ski amid these giant reptiles. There is also Cimo Club, a baby care center. Even the Kron restaurant, at the summit, has a section for children with special assistants.

The other ski-lifts in the area are at Antermoia, Anterselva, Tesido and Santa Maddalena Casies and there is a training slope at Valdaora di Sopra. In terms of cross-country skiing, (200km in total) you should head to two valleys where this sport reigns supreme: Anterselva and Casies (42km). Plan de Corones is also fairly popular among snowboarders.

Sankt Kassian/San Cassiano

ski-lifts open December-April
San Cassiano lies in a fabulous valley overlooked by some of the most beautiful mountains found in the Dolomites, including Conturines, La Varella and Lagazuoi. This is the most alluring town in Alta Badia, with renowned restaurants, famous hotels and beauty spas. Yet, its real charm lies in what might be termed its human dimension – it is quiet, small and still has a genuine mountain village atmosphere.

San Cassiano, overlooked from above by ancient *viles* (groups of *masi* or farmhouses), is a true gem. The town is well linked to all of the 130km of ski runs in the entire Alta Badia area (see Corvara and La Villa). The local skiing area is Piz Sorega, which is part of the Piz la Villa e Col Alto system. To reach the slopes you need to take the Piz Sorega eight-person gondola lift. This leads to the 2.1km red route with the same name, which is one of the best known in the area.

At the top, near the La Para ski run, is the snowboard park, which is, unsurprisingly, exclusively for snowboarders. Indeed, Alta Badia is a true breeding ground for champion snowboarders. The town is also known for the classical Armentarola ski tour. From the parking lot, shuttle taxis take you up to the Falzarego Pass, where you take the vertiginous Lagazuoi cable car. From the summit (nearly 2,800m), you enter a magical world characterized by typical Dolomite landscapes, where the traditional, idyllic and calm images are touched with a degree of harshness, severity and a smattering of adventure. For 7km as you descend Armentarola, you do not even see another road, ski run or lift. You are enclosed by snow and cliffs, in a cocktail of wind, sky, sun and nature. As such, the appearance of the Scotoni mountain refuge, about two-thirds of the way down, comes as something of a surprise. This normally turns to hunger as the aromas wafting from this wooden chalet are of meat and homemade cheese being cooked on a large open grill. From here, you continue on to Capanna Alpina and then along a flat ski path. On this section, people are often pulled along by snowmobiles or, better, by horses until they reach the Armentarola ski-lift and then the lower Piz Sorega cable station.

The Armentarola zone, with its open spaces and numerous woods, is a superb location for cross-country skiing, with 30km of trails. You can also enjoy being pulled along on a horse-drawn sled.

A splendid view of Sassongher and of the Sella massif

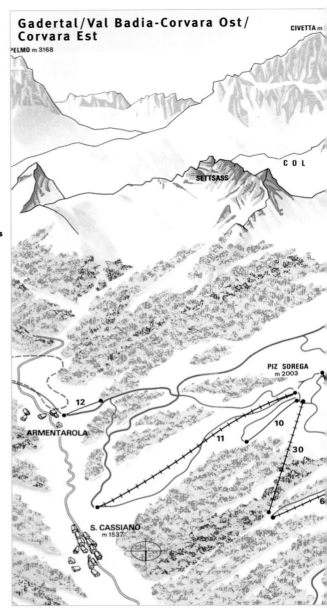

Gadertal/Val Badia-Corvara Ost/ Corvara Est

PELMO m 3168

CIVETTA m

COL

SETTSASS

PIZ SOREGA m 2003

12

10

11

30

ARMENTAROLA

6

S. CASSIANO m 1537

SKI RUNS

Information concerning all the skiing areas

Downhill skiing
130km, including 50 covered by artificial snow spraying
blue **63** red **26** black **4**

Cross-country skiing
40km of trails of varying difficulty

Snowboarding
1 Snow park

LIFTS

Corvara and Campolongo Pass

Gondola lifts **1**
19 Boè 1500-2200

Chairlifts **11**
1   Col Alto 1558-1988
2   Braia Fraida 1900-2030
15 Pralongià 1700-2050
21 Arlara 1685-2015
23 Costoratta 1850-2067
24 Cherz II 1852-2086
25 Vizza 1765-2088
28 Masarei 1761-2138
29 Costes da l'Ega 1537-1602
31 Cherz I 1840-2084
34 Borest 1500-1535

Ski-lifts **7**
13 Capanna Nera 1590-1750
14 Pralongià I 1750-1810
16 Pralongià II 1930-2120
17 Crep de Mont 1710-1870
18 Abrusè 1540-1640
26 Marentas 1758-2036
27 Incisa 1913-2120

Badia (La Villa-San Cassiano)

Cable cars **1**
–   Lagazuoi 2105-2778

Gondola lifts **2**
5   Piz la Villa 1427-2077
11 Piz Sorega 1553-2003

Chairlifts **8**
3   Roby 1903-2043
4   Pre dai Corf 1900-2060
6   Bamby 1792-2077
7   La Brancia 1900-2060
8   Biok 1900-2070
9   Ciampai 1903-2018
30 La Fraina 1799-2009
–   Braia Fraida 2044-2055

Ski-lifts **3**
10 Codes 1923-2003
12 Armentarola 1620-1700
22 La Para 1900-2003

Corvara/Corvara in Badia-Kollfuschg/Colfosco

ski-lifts open December-April

The Alta Badia phenomenon is created by an amazing combination of Nordic efficiency, Ladin warmth, hospitality and professionalism, tradition and technology. To top things off, everything is set in the marvelous and diverse landscape of the Dolomites. In the Alps, the name Alta Badia is a synonym for "complete holiday quality", combining great skiing, high-class cuisine and wellness. There is plenty of accommodation and related facilities. The valley itself is a side valley of Pusteria, carved by the Gadera stream. It ends at Corvara, where the roads winds up to the Campolongo Pass. The town (elev. 1,568m) is full of tourist resorts and well-positioned ski-lifts that blend in to

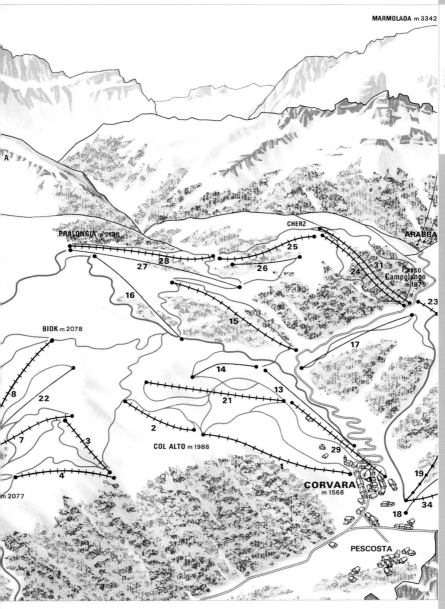

MARMOLADA m 3342

PRALONGIA m 2138

CHERZ

ARABBA

25

27   28

26

24   31

Passo
Campolongo
m 1875

16

23

BIOK m 2078

15

17

14

8

22

21

13

2

7

3

COL ALTO m 1988

4

29

m 2077

1

CORVARA
m 1568

19

18

34

PESCOSTA

the landscape. It lies in a Dolomite basin dominated by Sassongher, which is itself set against the Sella massif. The road up to the Gardena Pass climbs up in the shadow of the Sella massif. Colfosco is practically a satellite of Corvara, lying at the bottom of the pass. Here, the scene is a contrast between the wild, shadowy mountain (north slope of Sella) and the sun-drenched slopes below the light-colored rocks of Sassongher, dotted with *masi*. Colfosco has plenty of hotels and a good skiing infrastructure, but it has not lost its Ladin appeal. Its church, with Sella as a backdrop, is one of the classic images of the Dolomites. A network of lifts covers all of the slopes, making Alta Badia (and Corvara) the hub of the Sella Ronda area. The Badia valley is a frontrunner when it comes to the

Corvara West/Corvara Ovest

MARMOLADA
m 3342

CHERZ

ARABBA

Passo
Campolongo
m 1875

25

24

26

31

20

23

CREP DE
m 22

SKI RUNS

Information concerning all the
skiing areas

Downhill skiing
130km, including 50
covered by artificial snow
spraying
blue **63** red **26** black **4**

Cross-country skiing
40km of trails of varying
difficulty

Snowboarding
1 Snow park

LIFTS

Corvara and Campolongo Pass

Gondola lifts **1**

19   Boè 1500-2200

Chairlifts **8**

1   Col Alto 1558-1988
15   Pralongià 1700-2050
20   Vallon 2200-2530
23   Costoratta 1850-2067
24   Cherz II 1852-2086
25   Vizza 1765-2088
29   Costes da l'Ega 1537-1602
31   Cherz I 1840-2084

Ski-lifts **5**

13   Capanna Nera 1590-1750
14   Pralongià I 1750-1810
17   Crep de Mont 1710-1870
18   Abrusè 1540-1640
26   Marentas 1758-2036

Colfosco and Gardena Pass

Cable cars **1**

–   Lagazuoi 2105-2778

Gondola lifts **4**

39   Plans 1663-1836
40   Frara 1836-2220
45   Col Pradat 1700-2020
46   Colfosco 1545-1800

Chairlifts **5**

34   Borest 1500-1536
36   Sodlisia 1535-1655
42   Val Setus 2149-2280
43   Cir 2128-2292
50   Forcelles 1890-2200

Ski-lifts **3**

37   Pezzei 1645-1680
38   Belvedere 1675-1840
49   Stella Alpina 1800-1935

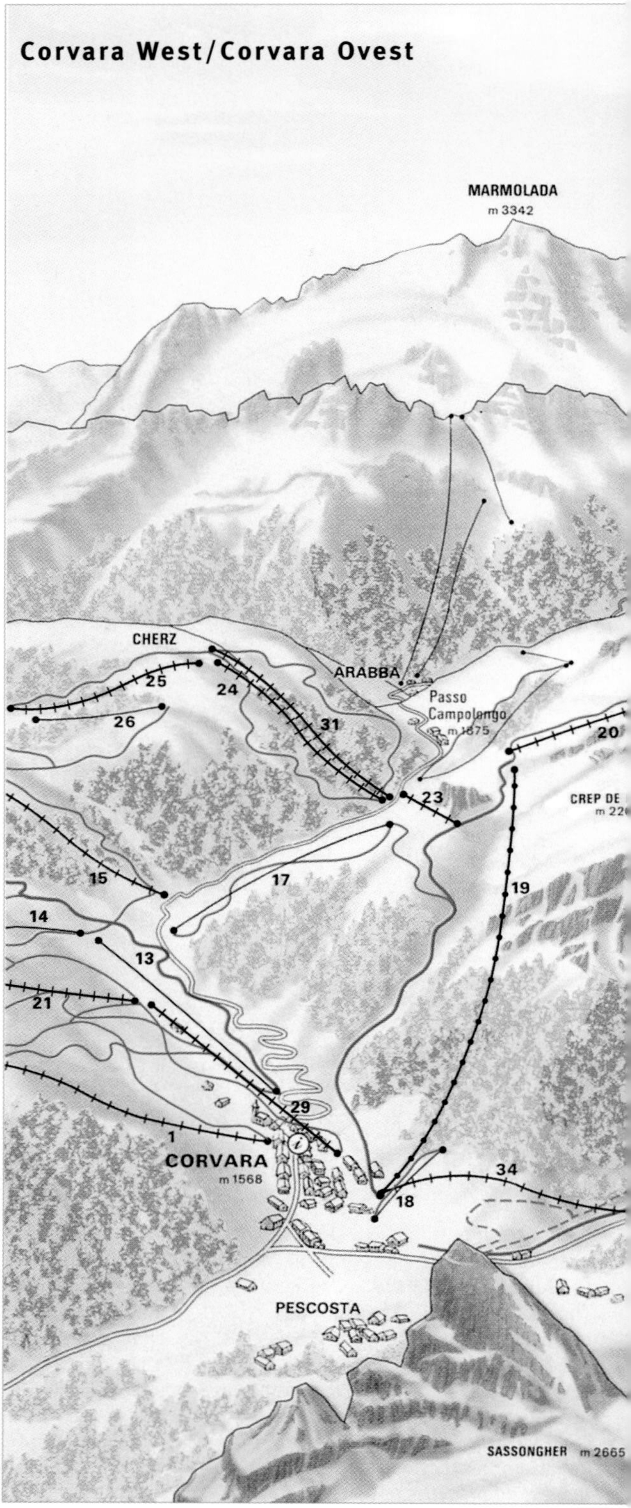

15

17

19

14

13

21

29

1

CORVARA
m 1568

34

18

PESCOSTA

SASSONGHER   m 2665

A panoramic view of the Sella massif seen from the Pralongià plateau

are, though, dotted with some cozy and lively mountain refuges. The most interesting routes are those that head to Corvara, San Cassiano and La Villa (see entry), with vertical drops of 400-600m. On Corvara, the Col Alto runs are never monotonous (blue and red). The other section is on the Sella massif and has a cable car to reach a much-loved route: the Piz Boè, a long and enjoyable snow-covered highway. The only dangers are the humped wall at the beginning that is always in shadow and the final section, often icy and sloping against the grain.

There are some more thrilling runs, at high altitude, on Vallon, especially the black route with plenty of changes in gradient and powdery snow. Here, by taking a chairlift and the Boè cable car, you can reach 2,550m, the highest skiing point in Alta Badia. From back near the upper cable station, by keeping right, you head onto red ski runs to the Campolongo Pass. Alternatively, you can take the Boè back to Corvara, which has about a 1,000m vertical drop over 4.5km.

The third section of the Corvara ski runs once again starts from the lower Boè cable station, which is an important hub. Chairlifts take you up to Colfosco and then, cable cars to the Gardena Pass, where the imposing bastions of the Sella massif dominate the landscape. The north face looms like a vertical wall: nearly 1,500m of rocks that then slope down for nearly 5km into the small valley of the Pisciadu stream, cutting the small side valley in which Colfosco stands. This massive extension of mountain is broken by some deep valleys. The main one is the Mezdì valley and, in winter, this offers the most sensational off-piste skiing in the Dolomites with a 45 degree gradient and a 1,500m vertical drop (to be done with a guide; accessible via the Sass Pordoi cable car from the Fassa valley). The Colfosco basin, by contrast, is one large, gentle skiing slope characterized by a web of lifts and wide-open runs. This area is all about skiing (you can reach the front door of nearly all the hotels on your skis) and the most celebrated runs are near Sassongher in the Stella Alpina valley. These runs are served by

concept of skiing from valley to valley. In addition, it was one of the first skiing areas in the Alps to take a long-term view of development that combines the need for balance and managerial dynamism without forgetting about the areas roots and the environment. In short this means 130km of ski runs (Dolomiti Superski ski pass), partially covered by an artificial snow spraying program, ski-lifts that are constantly being updated and, to top things off, a network of baby care centers.

The Corvara-Colfosco system is well connected both to the interesting villages of Alta Badia and the nearby Arabba and Val Gardena (a total of, at least, 450km of ski runs). This skiing area has two parts: one to the east and one to the west of Corvara. The first, vast area lies between 1,450 and 2,150m, and consists of a succession of small raised areas, mounds, clearings and plateaus lying between the San Cassiano valley, the famous Col di Lana Mountain, the Campolongo Pass, the Corvara basin and La Villa. The area is served by the ski-lifts of Piz Sorega-Piz La Villa, (see La Villa), Col Alto, Pralongià and Cherz. A feature of this section is high altitude lifts with wonderful, panoramic views. This is a relaxing place to ski as the runs are neither difficult nor long. They

cable cars. It is worth trying the red Forcelles route, served by a quad chairlift. For lovers of cross-country skiing, Alta Badia has the Armentarola center at San Cassiano, and a 15km circuit between Corvara and Colfosco.

Sella Ronda
opening of ski-lifts variable
This is the Ladins' mountain, acting as the ideal and physical center point for these minorities that live in the Val Gardena, Fassa, Livinallongo and Badia areas. These major Dolomite valleys seem almost to rotate around the Sella massif, creating one of the most thrilling, sought after and famed skiing experiences in the world.
This is Sella Ronda or the Quattro Passi tour (Sella, Pordoi, Campolongo and Gardena), which is part of the Dolomiti Superski ski pass. The main route of the Quattro Passi tour (literally, four passes tour) is never more than a red trail, allowing a wide range of skiers to "travel" from valley to valley and from town to town.
For most people, it takes 5 hours, which amounts to a whole day if you add in stops to admire the view, rest and, of course, get something to eat. The experience is like watching a film, taken from numerous different angles, of the loveliest peaks in the Dolomites. You go over passes that have become famous among cyclists, ski under sheer mountain walls scaled in epic mountaineering feats and pass areas that saw some major and bloody fighting in World War I. Step by step, the architecture changes, as do the accents and even the language.
The allure of Sella Ronda comes not from the technical challenge but because it is an in-depth journey into the nature and culture of four valleys and three provinces, namely Bolzano, Trento and Belluno.
The total distance, whether you head around clockwise or anticlockwise, is about 15-20km on lifts and 25km on skis, with a total vertical drop across the entire trail of 8,000m. The route markings are clear and plentiful, with green arrows for the anticlockwise route and orange ones for the other way. There is no single starting point so you can choose to

start from the Fassa valley (from Campitello or Canazei), which is the easiest option if you are in the Fiemme valley, from Arabba (or even Malga Ciapela, ideal for skiers staying at Agordino or in the Zoldo valley), from Alta Badia (the best option if you are staying in the Pusteria valley or at Cortina), or from Val Gardena (which is also the closest point if you are

A panoramic view of Sella.

arriving directly from the highway). This description takes the Fassa valley as the starting point and heads anticlockwise. Take the cable car from Campitello up the Rodella hill. The view is stunning from the beginning, and remains so throughout. The first stretch is a long red run of 4.5km that takes you to Pian Frataces along the road that heads up to the Sella Pass (fear not, small bridges and underpasses ensure you don't have to physically cross the road). Then you take the Lupo Bianco gondola lift to the upper Canazei skiing area, namely Belvedere, beneath Sass Becè. Next comes a chairlift. After admiring the Sella massif and the impressive Sass Pordoi cable car, you head down for 6km to Arabba. From 2,430m, the slope becomes quite steep, but still remains a red route; eventually you reach some chairlifts. From here, you can take the gondola lift or, if you

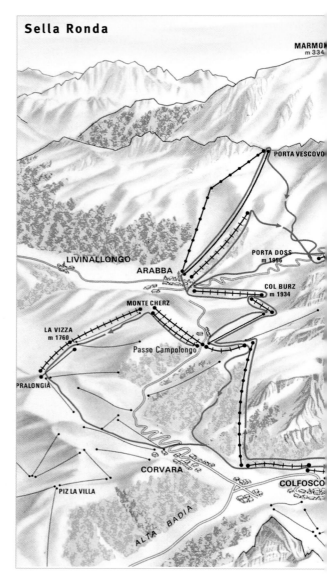

Sella Ronda

MARMO
m 334

PORTA VESCOVO

PORTA DOSS
m 195

LIVINALLONGO

ARABBA

COL BURZ
m 1934

MONTE CHERZ

LA VIZZA
m 1760

Passo Campolongo

PRALONGIA

CORVARA

COLFOSCO

PIZ LA VILLA

ALTA BADIA

prefer, head straight to Arabba. After crossing the town, you take a fast chairlift up to 2,093m at Bec de Roces and then you head down a medium hard trail to the Campolongo Pass. If you wish, by taking the Cherz charlift on the right, you can extend the route as much as you wish by enjoying some of the ski runs in the Alta Badia skiing area. The marked route, though, takes you to the Boè gondola lift down the valley, allowing you to enjoy half of the Boè ski run. The next stretch takes you to the Gardena Pass: two chairlifts,

then two gondola lifts and another chairlift. Then you start to ski again on the Dantercepies or the Cir. After passing between the hotels in Selva, you reach the Ciampinoi gondola lift, which takes you to another lovely red run down to Plan de Gralba. A further two, large chairlifts and you reach Città dei Sassi, an area of erratic rocks at the foot of the Sasso Lungo Mountain Pass. Once you reach the Sella Pass, you can take the chairlift up to the Rodella hill or ski down to Canazei along the red Bosco trail.

The clockwise options has equally long skiing stretches but, for example, from the Rodella hill, except for the first section on the Sella Pass, to Selva, you have to follow runs that are largely straight and offer less interest in terms of actual skiing. Then you need to take a chairlift and ski across to take the long route back up the Dantercepies. The next descent, on Corvara and Colfosco, is enjoyable at the beginning, but the rest is essentially of panoramic interest as the skiing is fairly straight-forward. From

Corvara to Arabba, you take the Boè gondola lift and then enjoy some more skiing on a red route (plus the necessary chairlifts) that is quite steep but not long. Going clockwise, you have to head up to Porta Vescovo, from where, before heading left to catch the lift to Pordoi, you could enjoy a run down into the valley if you feel like some extra skiing. From Pordoi or Sass Becè, the route is a fun zigzag through the wood on the Lupo Bianco trail. Next, you head on to Canazei or up to the Rodella hill via two lifts.

Sella Ronda is, though, not the only "thematic" skiing zone that can be explored entirely on foot. In Veneto, you can try the Percorso della Grande Guerra (Great War Trail). From the Falzarego Pass – Lagazuoi area, you head down into Alta Badia and Armentarola, explore the Alta Badia skiing area, pass by Arabba, Porta Vescovo and Malga Ciapela and head up Marmolada. Then, you can enjoy the Bellunese descent before taking the ski bus from Malga Ciapela – perhaps you can add in a run down the Serrai di Sottoguda to Alleghe.

Next, you head up Civetta and come down on Selva di Cadore. A ski-bus takes you to the Fedare chairlift and then you go down Cortina's Cinque Torri ski runs (near the starting point). In addition, by using the links to Val Gardena, you can even create your own itineraries, heading from one side to the other, all under the Dolomiti Superski ski pass (you need to plan your accommodation). You could, for example, go from Castelrotto-Alpe di Siusi to near Cortina. From Pedraces (and in the future, perhaps, from

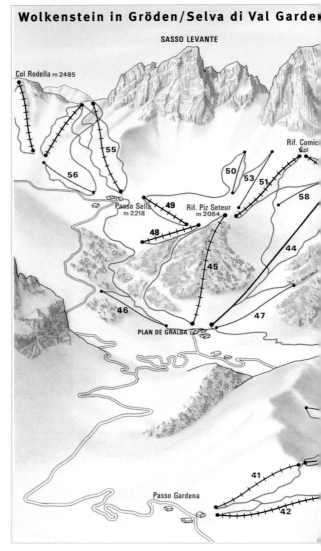

SKI RUNS
Information concerning all the skiing areas
Downhill skiing
175km, including 170 covered by artificial snow spraying
blue **18** red **29** black **6**
Cross-country skiing
62km of trails of varying difficulty
Snowboarding
1 Snow park
3 Half pipes

LIFTS
Cable cars **1**
44　Piz Sella 1804-2248
Gondola lifts **4**
14　Col Raiser 1500-2103
17　Saslong 1417-1968
29　Ciampinoi 1569-2254
30　Dantercepies 1657-2297
Chairlifts **13**
18　Sochers-Ciampinoi 1954-2250
22　Piza Pranseies 2033-2225
31　Costabella
33　Fungeia 1570-1590
41　Cir 2128-2292
42　Val Setus 2110-2280
45　Piz Seteur 1789-2063
48　Sole 1973-2063
49　Città dei Sassi 2030-2235
51　Comici I 2006-2157
52　Comici II 2153-2243
55　Sasso Levante 2187-2428
84　Ciampinoi 1588-2173
Ski-lifts **18**
16　Plan da Tieja 1460-1490
19　Sochers 1958-2136
32　Nives 1558-1585
34　Larciunei 1585-1625
35　Cadepunt 1586-1624
36　Biancaneve 1585-1623
37　Risaccia I and II 1631-1732
38　Freina 1565-1672
39　Terza Punta 1570-1642
40　Mickey Mouse 1950-2075
43　Panorama 2130-2225
46　Pudra 1806-1941
47　Senoner 1780-1866
50　Gran Paradiso 2000-2204
53　Sotsaslong 2029-2226
56　Passo Sella 2178-2247
58　Dolomiti 2070-2237

Brunico) to the Marmolada, Falzarego-Cortina, or even the Fassa valley. Or the other way around.

Selva di Val Gardena/Wolkenstein in Gröden

ski-lifts open December-April
Selva di Val Gardena is a giant of the ski industry, with ski runs and lifts at every corner, and a modern infrastructure with shops, bars, restaurants, hotels and other types of accommodation that spread across the valley floor. Of the three Ladin towns in Val Gardena, one of the major skiing

zones in Europe in the heart of Sella Ronda and Dolomiti Superski, Selva is probably the one with the most notable winter sport soul. Here, everything is geared towards a perfect skiing vacation, with top class organization, hotels that are, often, located practically on the slopes, almost allowing you to ski back to your lodgings, and other accommodation with that genuine high mountain feel. In total, Val Gardena (see also Ortisei and Santa Cristina) has nearly 18,000 bed spaces, of which 7,900 are in Selva (elev. 1,563m). Yet

SKI

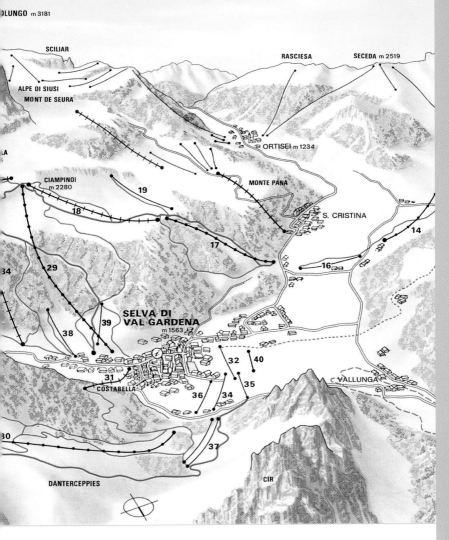

The ski run at Selva di Val Gardena leads right to the village

this does not mean everything is a mad crush of people and, often, one need only move off the main road to find true calm and charming scenes. One of the most memorable features of the area is the truly Dolomite landscape of the area, set amid Rasciesa and Odle on one side, and Alpe di Siusi and Sasso Lungo-Sasso Piatto on the other. Selva seems to enclose itself against the bastion of the Sella massif: to the left is the opening of the Vallunga ridge, penetrating wild zone towards Gardenaccia and Puez; the north facing side has the tall trees of Ciampinoi, which has some important ski-lifts; while the south facing side is dotted with isolated villages and districts. Sasso Lungo dominates the landscape with its light-colored, pointed rocks and fir trees. This majestic mountain looms above Plan de Gralba like a giant needle in a sea of white. Selva di Val Gardena is the hub of 175km of ski runs (about 10% are classed as difficult, 60% moderate, and 30% easy; nearly all are covered by snow canons) in the valley and a point on the Sella Ronda ski tour (see entry).

The poles are: the Dantercepies zone, served by a long gondola lift towards the Gardena Pass and Alta Badia; Plan de Gralba, beneath Sasso Lungo and connected to the Sella Pass and the Fassa valley; and Ciampinoi, accessible by the most central lift (cable car) or the chairlift in the upper part of the town. All of the poles are interconnected and also linked with other chairlifts, ski runs and connecting routes, ski-buses and the small underground train (Val Gardena Ronda Express).

Ciampinoi, 2,254m, has some notable vertical drops (nearly 800m) and, in the upper reaches, has enjoyable and easy runs with good snow. The gem, though, is the black run that is technically challenging and heads down the slope in a manner reminiscent of the more traditional ski runs in this area. It is a classic run that drops onto Selva after a series of big curves. The start is also the drop off point for the Sass Long black run. The Campinoi 2 red trail is also well worth tackling, especially since the underfoot conditions are always good. The area leading to the Gardena Pass and Alta Badia lies beneath the jagged crests of Cir. Here, you find the long Dantercepies ski runs, with constant gradients, and the parallel Cir ski run (starting below the pylons of the cable car), a lively red run with many changes in direction and some small walls. In fact, it is an official downhill run used for international competitions. Aside from the blue route back to the cable car, you can try the other, short but enjoyable runs that are wide open and offer spectacular views, such as, those of Plan de Gralba (many chairlifts and a large cable car up to Piz Sella, 2,284m) that is linked directly to Ciampinoi and Mt Pana.

There is a clear border between the pastures and the vertical rocks on Sasso Lungo. Indeed, it almost looks like nature built a wall here and, from the top of the ski runs, it almost seems as if you can lean against this wall. From this area, the Città dei Sassi "maze", a zone of erratic rocks in bizarre shapes, takes you to the Sella Pass-Rodella hill area. There is also a series of calm, sun-drenched ski-lifts radiating out of Selva, connecting the hotels with the main cable stations. This is also the case for the ski-lifts at the bottom of the Cir ski run and the base of Ciampinoi.

The U-shaped Vallunga is practically a canyon with a perfectly flat base covered in woods and dotted with some delightful clearings. It is also the setting for the best cross-country trails you can find in Val Gardena. There are simple circuits that are 3km long and more difficult ones that are 6 and 12km long. The tougher routes lead to Pra da Ri (1,800m) in the Parco Regionale Puez-Odle.

Schlern Hochgebiet/Altopiano dello Sciliar-Seiser Alm/Alpe di Siusi

ski-lifts open December-March

This natural balcony is located at 1,000m and lies between the Isarco valley and the rocky cliffs of the magnificent Sciliar. It is also the wonderful, sunny setting for Fiè allo Sciliar, Siusi and Castelrotto, three typical Tyrolean settlements characterized by old, solid houses decorated with wrought iron.

The plateau itself is dominated by the bulky, yet beautiful mass of Sciliar, the symbol of Alto Adige.

The bizarre gorges of the Santner and Euringer pinnacles and the steep vertical walls contrast sharply with the gentle landscape of the plateau, covered with cultivated fields, pastures and woods. The outline of Sciliar changes as you shift position, with the Euringer and Santner pinnacles seemingly becoming "one" with the mountain at times. From the settlements, a series of steep

A snowboarder in action

mounds hides Alpe di Siusi, which can practically be considered as a second section of this tourist area. This mythical alp, at the edge of the Parco Regionale dello Sciliar, is to be found a 1,000m higher, protected by Sciliar and the Denti di Terrarossa, to the south, and Sasso Lungo-Sasso Piatto to the east. To the north, it slopes down into Val Gardena and, to the west, it becomes part of the Sciliar plateau. This is the true "white" heart of Fiè allo Sciliar, Siusi and Castelrotto. Nonetheless, this is not only a place for skiing, whether downhill or cross country, but also for "living" the mountain life in winter, including just relaxing and escaping from other aspects of modern life. There are no cars on Alpe di Siusi, but this creates no problems as there is a network of hotels and mount refuge-hotels.

The towns themselves are very well organized, with 6,000 bed spaces spread between charming hotels, historic buildings and other hotels with wellness centers where, among other options, you might even try a "straw bath".

The Siusi gondola lift ensures you do not have to take a car or ski-bus and opens up new options for the towns on the Sciliar plateau, making Alpe di Siusi even more appealing. The relatively low altitude and the geographic layout mean the plateau has no real ski runs. For this reason, aside from Castelrotto (where there are a few cross-country skiing trails) and the small Marinzen area (with a chairlift and two ski-lifts going up to 1,500 m), the stations on the plateau focus on Alpe di Siusi, which is part of the Val Gardena-Alpe di Siusi section of the Dolomiti Superski ski pass. You can reach this area by the gondola lift that, from Siusi (or Ortisei, see

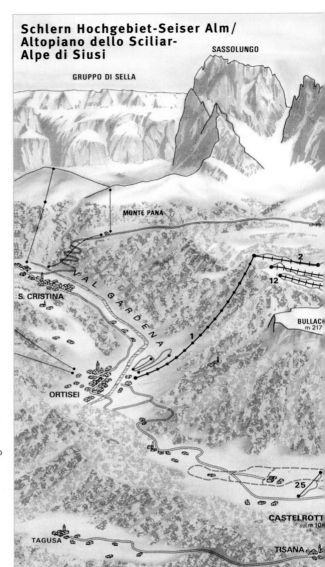

Schlern Hochgebiet-Seiser Alm/ Altopiano dello Sciliar- Alpe di Siusi

SASSOLUNGO

GRUPPO DI SELLA

MONTE PANA

S. CRISTINA

VAL GARDENA

ORTISEI

BULLACC m 217

12

2

1

25

CASTELROTT m 10

TAGUSA

TISANA

SKI RUNS
Downhill skiing
70km with artificial snow
spraying
blue **17** red **3**
Cross-country skiing
60km of trails of varying
difficulty
Snowboarding
1 Snow park

LIFTS
Alpe di Siusi
Gondola lifts **2**
1   Ortisei-Alpe di Siusi
    1219-2005
23 Siusi-Alpe di Siusi
    1000-1850
Chairlifts **15**
2   Al Sole 1858-1997
3   Monte Piz 1776-1914
4   Bullaccia 1860-2115
5   Panorama 1848-2009
6   Spitzbühl 1719-1939
7   Florian 1685-2097
11 Sanon 1850-1910
12 Leo Demetz 1915-2035
13 Mezdì 1776-1845
14 Steger Dellai 1818-1952
15 Euro 1828-1925
18 Bamby 1905-1966
19 Paradiso 1925-2130
21 Punta d'Oro I 1843-2210
22 Laurin 1779-2027
Ski-lifts **4**
10 Ludy 1824-1885
16 Eurotel 1823-1880
17 Strega 2030-2117
20 Floralpina 1705-1933
Castelrotto
Chairlifts **1**
8   Marinzen 1054-1481
Ski-lifts **2**
25 Santner 1051-1095
26 Guns 1085-1261

entry) rises nearly 1,000m.
The skiing area is ideal for people who love what can be termed "stress free" slopes. In addition, Alpe di Siusi is an ideal location for children as it has snow playgrounds and special ski schools.
The ski runs are located in a charming setting and tend to be gently undulating, making them generally easy, wide and sunny. They are also good for snowboarders.
The recent addition of the Floralpina ski-lifts, which make it possible to

reach 2,210m in conjunction with Punta d'Oro lift, means there are 50km of lifts. The best ski runs are those facing north. The Spiztbühl, Punta d'Oro and Florian runs offer something of a challenge to better skiers; while Laurin is an enormous, ideal training slope. The slopes are also gentle on the Bullaccia side and a touch steeper on the Piz side (where the cable car from Ortisei arrives).
In this area, the mountain refuges and chalets are often reachable on foot or cross-country skis and are well worth

the effort for the food, setting and atmosphere.

Alpe di Siusi has 60km of cross-country circuits and can easily be included in Europe's "Top Five". In many ways, it seems like the plateaux have been specifically designed for this discipline: undulating terrain, no excessive changes in level, plenty of natural snow, stunning views of the Dolomites and the perfect amount of sun. There are 11 marked routes, with Giogo being the toughest.

Sankt Ulrich in Gröden/ Ortisei

ski-lifts open December-April
Heading back up Val Gardena, near Chiusa, you come to the Isarco side-valley. After this, for the first time, Sasso Lungo "lets" you see the outline, on your right, of the village of Ortisei. Lying on sun-drenched slopes, this is the "capital" of the valley and home to a famed art institute (Kunstschule St Ulrich - Scuola d'Arte di Ortisei) that is the cradle of the wood sculpting craft that is such an

integral part of the surrounding area. This is an important ski and winter sport resort precisely because it is a true village (and not a tourist construction) with coffee houses, small squares, shops and a delightful pedestrian area.

In addition, the superb location and the relatively low altitude (about 1,200m) ensures the climate is mild and sunny. Some major hotels, other family-run ones and some vacation houses are, nonetheless, a clear indication of the importance of tourism (5,700 bed spaces). There are even some prestigious hotels with wellness centers.

Skiing is an age-old tradition here, but the town is less associated with the sport than Santa Cristina or Selva because the only ski runs right by the town are training slopes (Furdenan and

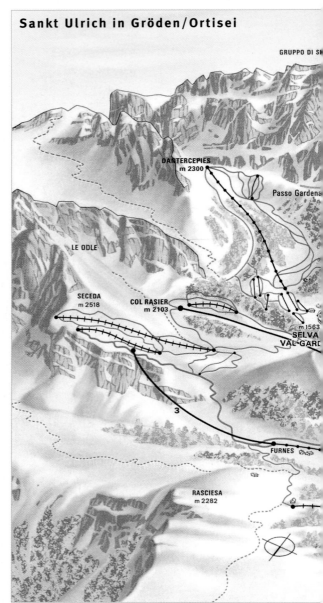

Sankt Ulrich in Gröden/Ortisei

GRUPPO DI SI

DANTERCEPIES
m 2300

Passo Gardena

LE ODLE

SECEDA
m 2518

COL RASIER
m 2103

m 1563
SELVA
VAL GARD

3

FURNES

RASCIESA
m 2282

SKI RUNS
Information concerning all the skiing areas
Downhill skiing
175km, including 17 covered by artificial snow spraying
blue **18** red **29** black **6**
Cross-country skiing
62km of trails of varying difficulty
Snowboarding
1 Snow park
3 Half pipes

LIFTS
Cable cars **1**
3   Seceda II 1736-2450
Gondola lifts **2**
1   Ortisei-Alpe di Siusi
      1219-2005
2   Seceda I 1236-1736
Chairlifts **1**
4   Rasciesa 1275-2093
Ski-lifts **2**
5   Furdenan 1220-1400
6   Palmer 1180-1280

Palmer, no longer than 900m) and the long Nogler del Seceda run. The latter is mainly used as a route back to town, even though it could be considered a worthwhile run by itself since it is 7km long and has some great curves.

There are two skiing areas accessible from Ortisei: the above mentioned Seceda (see Santa Cristina), reachable by a gondola lift followed by a cable car, and Alpe di Siusi (see entry), a part of the Val Gardena-Alpe di Siusi section of the Dolomiti Superski ski pass. The latter can also be reached by a gondola lift, which can also be used on the way back. In terms of cross-country skiing, there is only 1km in town, so it is better to head to Alpe di Siusi or the Pinei Pass, on the way to Castelrotto, where you can enjoy a 4km trail with some panoramic views.

TRENTINO

The substantial improvement in capacity, comfort and safety of the lifts, the careful grooming of the ski runs, the planned use of artificial snow and the development of the related service industry have made Trentino a major player among the pantheon of Italian skiing zones. Here, the mountains are viewed through a modern lens, integrating classic skiing with alternative sports, wellness, the environment, cuisine and local folklore. Of course, this does not forget that for many a holiday in a mountain chalet is also a journey in search of local values and highlights. The various ski resorts in Trentino are divided into two main groups: Dolomiti Superski (www.dolomitisuperski.com) and Skirama Dolomiti (www.skirama.it), which has 140 lifts and 360km of ski runs, making it one of the largest skiing areas in the Dolomites.

Canazei-Campitello di Fassa

ski-lifts open from December to April
Canazei and Campitello di Fassa lie beneath the imposing walls of the Sella massif and within sight of the inspiring Gran Vernel and Marmolada peaks. This is a major skiing area in the eastern Alps, with over 170 hotels. Set amid the best known Dolomites, Canazei is central for Trent, Bolzano and Cortina d'Ampezzo. The location helps to explain why this has been a main Alpine and tourist center since the early 20th century.

SKI RUNS
Downhill skiing
60km, including 45 covered by artificial snow spraying
blue **13** red **21** black **2**
Cross-country skiing
17km of easy to moderate trails

LIFTS
Pecol-Belvedere del Pordoi
Cable cars **1**
102 Pecol-Col dei Rossi 1932-2302
Gondola lifts **2**
101 Canazei-Pecol 1450-1932
105 Pian Frataces-Gherdecia 1726-2202
Chairlifts **4**
104 Toè 1932-2268
106 Kristiania 2150-2391
107 Sass Becè 2147-2423
108 Belvedere 2151-2349
Ski-lifts **1**
123 Gonzaga 2117-2199
Valley floor
Cable cars **1**
131 Alba Ciampac 1502-2160
Chairlifts **2**
132 Ciampac-Sella Brunech 2142-2441
136 Roseal 2180-2506
Ski-lifts **3**
133 Ciampac-Delle Baite 2150-2205
134 Sasso di Rocca 2201-2370
162 Canazei Avisio 1436-1470
Campitello-Col Rodella-Sella Pass
Cable cars **1**
141 Campitello-Col Rodella 1411-2395
Gondola lifts **1**
155 Pradel-Rodella 1724-2228
Chairlifts **1**
151 Salei 2125-2356
152 Rodella des Alpes 2224-2336

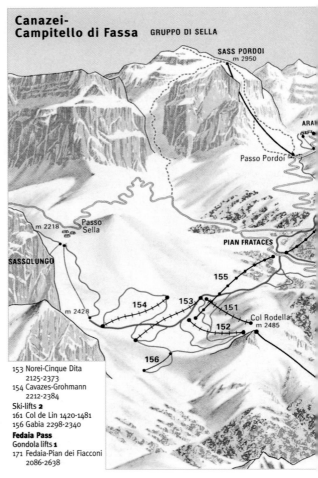

Canazei-Campitello di Fassa GRUPPO DI SELLA

SASS PORDOI m 2950

ARA

Passo Pordoi

m 2218 Passo Sella

PIAN FRATACES

SASSOLUNGO

155

m 2428 154 153 151

152 Col Rodella m 2485

156

153 Norei-Cinque Dita 2125-2373
154 Cavazes-Grohmann 2212-2384
Ski-lifts **2**
161 Col de Lin 1420-1481
156 Gabia 2298-2340
Fedaia Pass
Gondola lifts **1**
171 Fedaia-Pian dei Fiacconi 2086-2638

The lively town is spread out along the main roads lined with many different hotels, houses, rooms-to-rent and sports shops. The clusters of buildings around Via Pareda and Via Dolomiti are delightful, although they remain hidden from people who simply rush by without stopping and exploring. Barns, other rustic structures and rural houses line Vicolo Debertol, Via Antermont and Via Col da Ronch as well as characterizing the Gries district. By heading along Corso dell'Avisio, you get a magnificent view of the so-called "Queen of the Dolomites", namely Marmolada.

After Alba, a hamlet of Canazei lying beneath Colac, the road climbs and winds through snow-covered fields to the Fedaia Pass, leaving behind on the left the charming village of Penia. To the side, you can see the tiny villages of Vera, Lorenz and Insam, which form a lovely picture against the gentle Contrin valley, contrasting with the ruggedness of Gran Vernel and Marmolada.

Campitello di Fassa and Canazei are the hubs of the large, connected skiing area covering the valleys that surround the Sella massif. They are also the only places in Trentino from which you can access the Sella Ronda skiing area directly. All of this is still within the Fassa-Carezza section of the Dolomiti Superski ski pass, although, to make the most of the vast and diverse skiing options, it is normally better to get the general Dolomiti Superski pass, especially since it is often an interesting option to cross over

into Val Gardena or to go to Arraba. You can reach the Rodella hill and the Sella Pass-Val Gardena zone via a large cable car from Campitello di Fassa; from Canazei, take the gondola lift to Belvedere, from where you can reach the Pordoi Pass and Arabba. If you wish, you can drive up to the Plan Frataces-Lupo Bianco junction (Sella Ronda) and then head off in the direction of your choosing on the lifts. The other Canazei zone, on the opposite face, is Ciampac, which can be reached by the cable car from Alba. Ciampac is also connected to Buffaure di Pozza. It has a notable black trail: 2.8km long, 670m vertical drop, a gradient ranging from 28 to 49 degrees, and smooth and compact snow as it is north-facing.

The upper section has a few ski runs crossing open fields, with the highest part of this section being 2,500m; for children, there is the Tananai miniclub. A lift at the Fedaia Pass provides access to the lovely 2.2km Pian dei Fiacconi red trail, starting at 2,638m and dropping to 2,086m. The Rodella hill is an amazing viewpoint at about 2,500m; from here (to get back to Campitello you need to take the cable car) it almost seems as if you can touch Sasso Lungo and Sasso Piatto. On the other side, you can admire the rocky, snow-covered bastions of the Sella massif. It is worth stopping at the old Friedrich August mountain refuge, with a terrace from which you can gaze in admiration at the Duron valley and the walls of Sasso Piatto.

The wide-open ski runs of the Rodella hill-Sella Pass zone lie between 2,500m and 2,200m, and the snow is always soft and good. This area, too, has various high-capacity chairlifts, such as at Norei Cinque Dita.

Unfortunately, for a number of years, the Forcella del Sasso Lungo gondola lift has been taken down in winter, although this remains a challenging ski-mountaineering test only to be undertaken with settled snow.

From the Rodella hill-Sella Pass zone it is an easy descent to Plan de Gralba and the Val Gardena ski runs. If you wish to stay in the Fassa valley, head down from Rodella hill on the 3-Tre (4km of red trails) to Lupo Bianco and then Belvedere. By going right at the entrance to the wood on the 3-Tre trail, you find a romantic ski run, Bosco, that seems to be from a previous age. This is the only trail leading back to Canazei and has a certain magic, especially as it ends on a quiet street in the old center, Via Rio Antermont, near the lovely little church of San Floriano. It is a 10-minute walk back to the lifts (Belvedere gondola lift).

Belvedere, accessible from Canazei, is an amphitheatre of ski runs (25km) generally between 1,900m and 2,450m. Lying beneath Sass Becè, it is directly linked to Arabba and popular because of the high-capacity chairlifts. At the top, the vertical drop is sharp with some moguls, but lower down, the slope flattens into open areas covered in velvety snow. The views from the mountain refuges are spectacular: to the west rise Sasso Lungo and Sasso Piatto, with the unmistakable outline of Forcella del Sassolungo; to the southwest, you can make out the Fassa and Fiemme valleys, enclosed by endless peaks. If you want to take on the slopes and valleys of the Sella massif, you can make use of the Sass Pordoi cable car, which is like an escalator up to a lunar plateau. From the Maria mountain refuge (2,950m), you can enjoy stunning sunsets as the snow, peaks and people's faces take on pinkish hues. The view is 360°.

Sass Pordoi is also the starting point for the most thrilling off-piste skiing in the Dolomites. An hour of walking takes you to the edge of the Mezdì valley, which drops down to Colfosco in the Badia valley. Another, more direct route, runs down the large Lasties valley and ends on the road to the Sella Pass. Another route, which is well known and marked by the trails of other skiers (but a guide is recommended), heads down from Forcella Pordoi and ends at the lifts down the valley. The start is like a drop into a void, with the first 20-30m being very narrow and enclosed by rocks. Then, the slope opens up and the sun seems to gush down, although the gradient remains steep with a vertical drop of 730m. If you are looking for cross-country skiing, there is a good center at Canazei with small, simple circuits and a longer one (8.3km) going to Mazzin. There are also some short but taxing options at higher altitudes at Ciampac and Pian Trevisan.

Vigo di Fassa-Pozza di Fassa

ski-lifts open from December to April
Heading towards Vigo di Fassa, the area is dominated by Catinaccio, the mountain associated with the *Enrosadira* phenomenon, which is the time, just before dusk, when the sun's rays reflect off the rocky Dolomites, giving everything in a crimson-orange tinge. It is evident that the Fassa valley is a major Italian mountain tourism center, with even the smallest places, like Soraga, offering accommodation for tourists.

At Vigo, where the "Great Road of the Dolomites" heads across the Costalunga Pass, the Ladin heart of the valley emerges. Indeed, Vigo di Fassa is not merely a tourist resort, but also the cultural center of the valley. It is home to the Ladin Cultural Institute, which administers the Museo Ladin de Fascia located in nearby Pozza with branches in Moena, Pera and Penia. You can also see the first *vila* buildings, consisting of barns and decorated homes, which are a reminder of the *pitores* (decorators) tradition in Fassa. Vigo lies slightly above the road and, despite being a "small capital" and having numerous hotels, it is calmer and quieter than Canazei and Moena. It is practically joined to Pozza di Fassa, where the charming San Nicolò valley starts.

The skiing areas, connected to those of Pera di Fassa, have good facilities.

High altitude paragliding

Three areas are centered on Vigo and Pozza di Fassa and all three are part of the Fassa-Carezza section of the Dolomiti Superski ski pass, although you can also get just a local pass. The areas are: the ski-lifts of the Costalunga Pass, in the Alto Adige zone of Nova Levante-Carezza, with about 30km of trails; the Catinaccio skiing area, linked to Vigo-Pera di Fassa (12km); and the Buffaure skiing area (13,5km), linked directly to Pozza di Fassa and connected via two chairlifts to Canazei's Ciampac area (10km).

Finally, there are Catinaccio and Buffaure. The Catinaccio zone, located between 1,300m and 2,100m, has various high-capacity chairlifts and can reached from either Pera (chairlift) or Vigo (cable car). It has some delightful sections, such as the Gardeccia bowl and the Ciampedìe plateau. From there you can see Larsec and Catinaccio – the centerpiece of the Dolomites. The skiing highlight is the Tomba black trail (1km long, 300m vertical drop) with a gradient reaching about 59 degrees and some interesting moguls and turns. There are also amazing outings that take you through the magnificent woods that abound in the zone.

The Buffaure zone, reachable via the connection from Ciampac, is equally inviting with various chairlifts that take you up to the higher altitudes. From the top, while enjoying the panoramic view, look for the snow-capped peaks of Monzoni and, further in the distance, Catinaccio with the Torri del Vaiolet.

A good place to relax and replenish your reserves is the Cuz mountain chalet, located at 2,213m, overlooking

SKI RUNS

Downhill skiing
100km, including 90
covered by artificial snow
spraying
blue **18** red **15** black **4**
Cross-country skiing
16km of easy to moderate
trails
Snowboarding
1 Snow park

LIFTS
Bellamonte-Alpe di Lusia
Gondola lifts **1**
1   Lusia-Valbona 1370-1820
Cable cars **1**
2   Valbona-Le Cune
     1820-2206
Chairlifts **5**
3   Piavac 1764-2225
5   Campo-Le Cune 1855-2214
6   Lastè 1855-2340
7   Castelir-Le Fassane
     1549-1743
8   Le Fassane-La Morea
     1747-1969
Ski-lifts **1**
4   Valbona 1820-1850

San Pellegrino Pass
Cable cars **1**
16   Col Margherita 1874-2513
Chairlifts **5**
8   Campigal 1870-1978
10   Costabella 1924-2175
12   Gigante 1910-2266
13   Cima Uomo 2170-2394
15   Del Passo 1873-1955
Ski-lifts **5**
9   Capanna Margherita
     1891-1995
11   Paradiso I and II
     2100-2324
14   Chiesetta I and II
     1910-2028

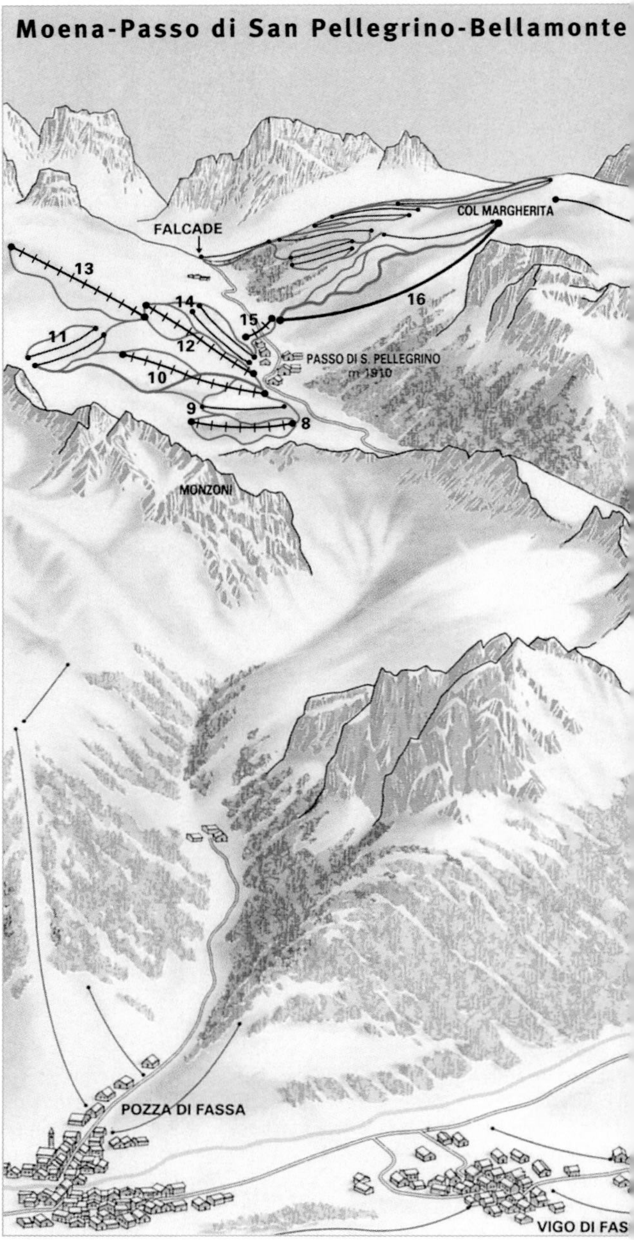

the small San Nicolò valley. The run down the valley, after an wondrous but only moderately difficult start, becomes an unending, solitary and enjoyable descent through the San Nicolò valley.

A little before the Buffaure cableway, you can test your technique on the taxing Aloch ski run, a red/black trail that drops from 1,630m to 1,320m over a distance of 1,100m. This is the so-called Ski Stadium Fassa – a floodlit route designed for training and competitions with a gradient topping 50 degrees. At Pozza-Pera di Fassa, you can try the floodlit but small cross-country track and the Marcialonga trail.

Moena-Passo di San Pellegrino-Bellamonte

ski-lifts open from December to April
Known as the fairy of the Dolomites, Moena stands at the start of the Fassa valley and the opening of the San Pellegrino valley. In terms of tourism, this place is chosen by those looking not only for great skiing but also for good hotels, a lively atmosphere, places to stroll around and a few spots to spend the evening.

Moena still has its Ladin heart. The Làtemar system is close, and to the east and northeast, things are dominated by Monzoni. The skiing area linked to the town is called Skiarea Tre Valli del Dolomiti Superski

107

and has 100km of trails divided into two sections: Alpe di Lusia-Bellamonte and San Pellegrino Pass-Falcade. In addition, given the proximity, many skiers spend time in the Fassa valley (Fassa-Carezza ski pass), which has a total of 9 areas and 147km of trails (200km, if you include the adjoining areas). As such, if you like to try a different place every day, it is best to get the general Dolomiti Superski pass. A highlight of Tre Valli is the so-called *Skitour dell'amore* (ski tour of love), a romantic route offering delightful views and taking in the whole area. The two secondary areas of Tre Valli are linked by a ski-bus or a ski run that heads down from the pass to the lower station of Alpe di Lusia cableway and then on to Moena.

Alpe di Lusia lies on a rounded mountain at an altitude where little grows; the bird's eye view of Catinaccio, Làtemar and Pale di San Martino is spectacular. On one side, the trails wind towards Moena; on the

other, towards Bellamonte (in the Travignolo valley, accessible via road from Predazzo). The black Fiamme Oro I trail is a severe test for the legs, with an average gradient of 32 degrees, a maximum gradient of 49 degrees and a vertical drop of 1,000m if you also count the consecutive Fiamme Oro II. The snow is always excellent. On the other side, you can also test yourself on equally steep slopes, like the Direttissima le Cune, before enjoying a relaxing 6km descent to Bellamonte through lovely woods on large snow "highways" (only blue trails) dotted with mountain refuges.

The Alpine and Nordic scenery of the San Pellegrino Pass, 1,918m, is ideal for cross-country skiing. The Alochet center has 3 trails covering 16km, including the red Campo d'Orso. Yet, there is also good downhill skiing. The main trails start from the Col Margherita Pass, a natural viewpoint at over 2,500m that can be reached

SKI RUNS
San Martino di Castrozza
Downhill skiing
45km, including 40 covered by artificial snow spraying
blue **11** red **9** black **2**
Cross-country skiing
9km of trails
Rolle Pass
Downhill skiing
15km, including 10 covered by artificial snow spraying
blue **6** red **3** black **1**
Cross-country skiing
5km of trails

LIFTS
San Martino di Castrozza
Gondola lifts **2**
8   Tognola 1420-2151
19 Col Verde 1502-1965
Cable cars **1**
20 Rosetta 1965-2639
Chairlifts **9**
9   Scandola 1899-2060
10 Rododendro 1955-2175
11 Conca 1933-2205
14 Ces 1471-1609
15 Punta Ces 1609-2250
16 Valboneta 1605-1750
18 Coston 1603-1880
26 Valcigolera
27 Cima Tognola 2017-2383
Ski-lifts **4**
12 Cigolera 1975-2195
13 Baby 2161-2188
24 Prà Nasse 1473-1495
–   Passo Cereda
Rolle Pass
Chairlifts **4**
2   Castellazzo 1987-2164
5   Paradiso 1890-2209

6   Cimon 1960-2025
7   Ferrari 1868-2015
Ski-lifts **1**
1   Rolle 1904-2008

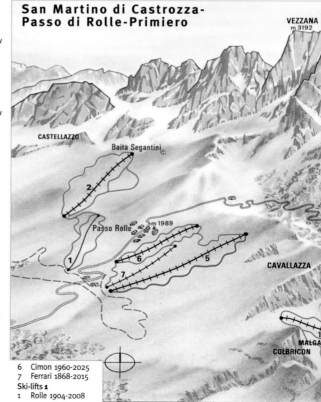

San Martino di Castrozza-
Passo di Rolle-Primiero

VEZZANA
m 3192

CASTELLAZZO

Baita Segantini

2

Passo Rolle   m 1989

1   6   5

7

CAVALLAZZA

MALGA
COLBRICON

by cable car or other lifts from Falcade. As you gaze at the scenery, note Monzoni, Torri del Vaiolet, Pale di San Martino, Marmolada, Pelmo, Civetta and Agner. The most famed trail here is a 3km black route that is quite steep without ever becoming impossible – this is definitely one of the "must do" runs in the Moena and Tre Valli area. On the other side of the pass, across the road, you can ski down various wide, sun-drenched trails (red and blue) that run over gentle fields beneath the Uomo peak (Costabella quad chairlift and other lifts).

San Martino di Castrozza-Passo di Rolle-Primiero

ski-lifts open from December to April
The Pale Mountains dominate San Martino di Castrozza and mark the most remarkable part of the Primiero valley, creating a classic Dolomite scene. Here you can see the almost surreal Cimon della Pala peak (3,184m).

This is the Cismon valley, at the southern edge of the Dolomites, where various geological and natural features meet in the Parco Regionale Paneveggio-Pale di San Martino. Here, you have the volcanic and granite Colbricon Mountains, the edges of the Lagorai to the west and the Dolomites, in all their most amazing shapes, to the east. In the middle lie the gently rolling pastures, meadows and age-old fir forests. Located at the border of the Travignolo valley (separated by the Rolle Pass), Feltrino and Agordino, San Martino di Castrozza (in the Siror municipal district) is the tourist heart of the Primiero area. The historic capital of the zone is Fiera di Primiero, offering plenty of accommodation. San Martino di Castrozza has an unusual charm and atmosphere. It is also the center for the surrounding towns and villages located at the base the mountains: Fiera di Primiero (elev. 717m), Siror, Tonadico, Mezzano and Imer. Here,

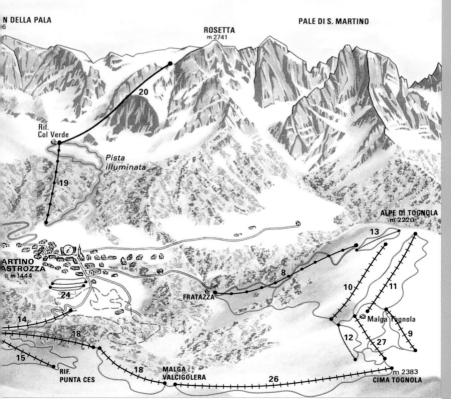

hotels and related facilities are located harmoniously amid the beautiful yet stark architecture of the old centers. Although the zone does not have record-breaking facilities, the San Martino skiing area is still very rewarding and should not be overlooked. The lifts cover over 60km of trails, ranging from an altitude of 1,420m to 2,383m, 90% of which can be covered by artificial snow. There are two main slopes: the primary one, like a viewpoint for the Pale, is to the west; the other one, the Verde hill, is actually on the Pale, although the views are probably better than the skiing. The main slope is the so-called *Carosello delle Malghe*: 45km of trails, from Alpe Tognola to Malga Ces. It is accessible in two ways: by the sizeable Tognola cable car, down the

Parco da Sciare (a park to ski) route. The first stop is the Prà delle Nasse ecological area, where you might see roe-deer. From there, you climb to Punta Ces and, in the distance, you can see the Colbricon frozen lakes, a favored haunt of the golden eagle. Heading down the Direttissima, with a touch of luck, you will see chamois deer intently seeking out any tufts of grass. After passing the rustic Malga Valcigolera, the route continues on to the amazing Tognola peak viewpoint (2,383m). A ski-bus then takes you to the other side to continue the tour. You then take a cable car up to the Col Verde mountain refuge and then, via another cable car, to the Rosetta Peak (2,639m). Up there, the only "trails" are off-piste routes to be done by the select few who have the correct

The Direttissima ski run at San Martino di Castrozza; the Pale Mountains are in the background

valley, and the Ces chairlift from the edge of the town. Variety, in terms of skill-required and slope exposure, is the key here. Generations of skiers have learnt the trade on the steep walls of Tognola 1 (nearly 3km). The Direttissima and Cristiania black trails are technically challenging, but well groomed; the Colbricon, Sole, Tognola peak and Record routes are ideal for riding the curves.
The ski runs of San Martino di Castrozza are in the Parco Regionale Paneveggio-Pale di San Martino and, as such, skiing is an ideal way for exploring the area by following the *Un*

experience and knowledge. This is really a place to go for the magnificent view of the large Pale plateau (10km long and 5km wide, although it does not seem so from the bottom), which runs from Sass Maor to Cimon della Pala, with the Marmolada in the background. There are only two ski runs on the Verde hill (those at the cable car), both leading back to the town. These runs are lit with special lights, making a nighttime ski a lovely experience.
From the Rolle Pass skiing area you get a stunning view of Cimon della Pala. One of the first to open and last

to close each season, it has 15km of ski runs (from 1,900 to 2,200m), accessible by various chairlifts. Some of the north-facing trails are thrilling, especially the black Paradiso 1 and the red Fiamme Gialle.

From the Segantini chalet, a gentle, snow-covered road (used only by hikers and skiers) leads along the Venegia valley in the heart of the Paneveggio forest, dotted with pastures and majestic fir trees. San Martino di Castrozza also has good facilities for children (babyland at Palazzetto dello Sport or Kinderheim at Alpe Tognola, with specialized staff) and cross-country skiers. For the latter, aside from 9km of trails around the town and the 5km at the Rolle Pass, you can try the Lake Calaita zone (7km) and the more technically demanding Cereda Pass (15km).

Cavalese

ski-lifts open from December to April
If you arrive in the Fiemme valley from Egna or the San Lugano hill, it does not seem like you have entered a Dolomite valley. The southern-facing slopes are wide open and sun-drenched, with various towns and villages dotted around. The northern-facing ones are steep, wooded and in shadow, an outpost of the great Lagorai range, which is not part of the Dolomites. To the north, the main mountain is Làtemar, although it is hidden from view for now; to the east, in the distance, is Pale di San Martino. This is the setting for Cavalese, sitting on the sunny slopes of the Fiemme valley in a pleasant landscape that is more hilly than mountainous. This is, in a way, a gateway to the magnificent Dolomites.

The feel, as you enter Cavalese, is of a small but lively town. It is the tourist, cultural, historical and political capital of the Fiemme valley, as well as a skiing and sports center. From the center, a high-capacity cable car takes you straight up to the Alpe Cermis skiing area (there is another, intermediary cableway station at the bottom of the valley, with plenty of parking). Aside from the hotels (110 across the whole Fiemme valley)

and shops selling souvenirs, local products and handcrafted wooden items, the most eye-catching aspects are the views of the old town (such as, from the Unterberger pedestrian walkway) and, especially, the refined buildings. Although Cavalese, Tesero and Predazzo are the main accommodation centers, the smaller towns and villages in the valley (Capriana, Carano, Castello-Molina di Fiemme, Daiano, Panchià, Valfloriana and Ziano di Fiemme) have holidays houses and apartments to rent and, particularly at Ziano and Molina, some good hotels.

The Fiemme valley has the largest skiing area in the Dolomites near the Brennero highway. 100km of ski runs divided into 5 zones, all covered by the Fiemme-Obereggen ski pass (Dolomiti Superski): Alpe Cermis, Ski Center Làtemar (Pampeago-Predazzo-Obereggen, see also Obereggen and Predazzo), Oclini Pass-Lavazè Pass, Bellamonte-Alpe di Lusia and the Rolle Pass. In truth, only the first two are truly in the Fiemme valley.

Oclini has only a few ski-lifts and a single chairlift to take you up the slopes of Corno Nero. Lavazè, where downhill skiing has practically ceased, is a paradise for cross-country skiing. Bellamonte and the Rolle Pass are also directly linked to other major towns in neighboring valleys, such as Moena and San Martino di Castrozza (see relevant sections). Cermis, 25km of ski runs, is on the north-facing slope of the valley and is already part of the Lagorai range, although it does allow you an amazing view of the Dolomites. The best viewpoint is the Paion mountain refuge (2,250m), at the top of the second, consecutive quad chairlift. Paion is the starting point for the Olimpia black trail, a jewel of the Dolomites. You descend keeping to the left: the start has a steep wall (there are flatter, less direct alternatives) followed by a fast and varied section leading to the Costabella plateau, practically the heart of the area, with mountain refuges and plenty of sun. It is also the start if the true Olimpia II, which cuts thrillingly through the forest as far as Doss dei Laresi. The total distance is

4,700m and a vertical drop of about 1,000m. The snow is always wonderful and although it is a taxing route, the gradient is never worrying. The Via del Bosco is an unusual, flat trail (6°) that takes you back to the town. Along the way, there are figures of animals, information panels and an interactive quiz about nature to explain the woods. Cermis has plenty of modern facilities: there are SOS stations along the ski runs, and a series of cameras with an option for having your run filmed and then downloading it onto your own computer.

The Fiemme valley is one of the best known places in Europe for cross-country skiing. Aside from the Marcialonga trail (shared with the Fassa valley), you can try the beautiful, almost Scandinavian area at the Lavazè Pass. This is a true capital for this discipline, with over 50km of trails ranging in altitude from 1,750m to 2,100m, thus ensuring good snow coverage. Some are also challenging, heading through woods and glades, and past inviting mountain refuges. Cross-country skiing is truly important here and some hotels have formed a consortium to target this market, offering places where you can hire not only the latest skis, but also the gear and clothes.

Tesero-Predazzo
ski-lifts open from December to April
A little beyond Cavalese, Tesero is a true Trentino town with solid houses, typical entrance halls, small alleys and lovely courtyards. From Tesero the road climbs to Pampeago, one of three poles of the Ski Center Làtemar

SPORTABILI ONLUS
Predazzo Via dei Lagorai 113
tel. 0462501999 www.sportabili.org
getting there
By car: A22 Highway, Egna-Ora exit, follow the SS48 road to Predazzo (36km)
By train: Ora, Bolzano and Trento stations; bus connections from Ora, Bolzano and Trento

This association was formed in order to make sport a chance for enjoyment, autonomy and integration for disabled people. It offers a model for people who wish to use sport to further the cause of everyone's right to enjoy recreational or leisure time. Sportabili places itself as a bridge between disabled and not disabled people, overcoming the division between these two worlds through sport. In winter, the major focus of this association is, of course, the ski courses held in the charming and beautiful setting of the Fiemme valley. Throughout the rest of the year, there are various intriguing options: horse-riding, rock-climbing, archery, swimming, cycle tours, nature trails, rafting, hydrospeeding (rafting with a water sled) and tennis. Each of these sports is play, as needed, with appropriate additional equipment.
The ski courses, both downhill and cross-country, are aimed at people with motor, sensory and intellective disabilities, and are held by teachers from the Alta Val di Fiemme and Lago di Tesero ski schools. The venues are the Bellamonte-Lusia skiing area and the Lago di Tesero cross-country skiing center. Some of the equipment used includes monoskis (for disabilities to the lower limbs), biskis and dualkis (for disabilities to the upper and lower limbs), and sleds for cross-country skiing for people with physical disabilities. Sportabili also provides for visually impaired people to be accompanied from the hotel to the slopes and back as well as helping to organize the stay, ensuring good access and proving a hotel booking service.

(with Obereggen and Predazzo). Predazzo is the last town in the Fiemme valley before it becomes the Fassa valley. It rises at 1,018m at the confluence of the Avisio and Travignolo (the valley climbs up to the Rolle Pass) and is enclosed by steep, wooded slopes concealing the major mountains to which this town is like a gateway. It is a busy and well-known tourist center for mountaineering and other sports, with plenty of hotels and holiday houses. About 6km away, in the Travignolo valley, Bellamonte (elev. 1,372m) is an Alpine settlement of refurbished barns, chalets and a few hotels. It is one of the two poles of the Alpe di Lusia skiing area. The gondola lift to the Ski Center Làtemar is located a little outside Predazzo, heading to Moena, near the ski jumping stadium used for international competitions. This lift, with plenty of parking, is the easiest way to reach the skiing area, although there is no ski run to get back to the cable station, meaning one has to take the cable car back down. The other way to the slopes is via the road, from Tesero to Pampeago, although it is best avoided when it is snowing and on Sundays or holidays. The skiing area has about 40km of ski runs between 1,500m and 2,500m, and includes the Predazzo and Pampeago slopes and the Obereggen one in Alto Adige. Sprawled over the rounded ridges of the Làtemar, this is one of the most modern skiing areas in the Dolomites. The ski runs are impeccably groomed, with artificial snow covering 90% of the trails. The "kindergarten on the snow" is also superbly organized. There are no queues since the Ski Center Làtemar was the first, along with Plan de Corones, to introduce high-capacity lifts. In terms of the trails, you should definitely try the Agnello with its taxing variants heading to Pampeago and the Cinque Nazioni to Gardonè, which has numerous changes in gradient and direction. Yet, the most interesting ski run is reached by one of the two ski-lifts: the Pala di Santa black route (only for experts). The upper section, a large expanse that is always covered in powdery snow, is actually a ridge leading to the summit at 2,415m

(the highest point in the skiing area). But, do not be fooled, the trail soon becomes narrow and steep. The snow is always compact, although the trail sometimes seems to be counter-slope, making things more trying.

In terms of cross-country skiing, Predazzo is also part of the Marcialonga trail. There are also interesting routes between the town and Ziano di Fiemme (12.5km, plus other simple circuits). The Centro Fondo Lago di Tesero is often used for international and world cup events.

Madonna di Campiglio

ski-lifts open from December to April
The granite colossuses of Adamello and Presanella herald the sloping shapes of the Dolomites. Indeed, to the east of the bowl in which Madonna di Campiglio sits, in the upper Rendena valley, the Brenta Mountains suddenly rise up, dominating the landscape with their jagged forms created by the peaks and gorges rising out of the pines, pastures and white scree. This is the first "island" of real Dolomite rocks after the so-called Rectic Alps (which include Adamello and Presanella, visible to the west). This setting creates the postcard perfect backdrop for Madonna di Campiglio.

For over 50 years, this resort has hosted one of the classic stops on the World Cup circuit, the 3-Tre. It is also one of the places to go for all winter sport lovers, yet its reputation is not merely because it is continually modernizing the facilities, but also because it managed to reverse a dangerous trend (almost too many houses were "second houses", with nearly 40,000 people for New Year) by focusing on rationalizing what was already there. To this end, a 2km tunnel was created to remove "transit traffic" from the old center, large parking lots were built and Piazzetta Righi and Via Dolomiti di Brenta were turned into pedestrian zones. The figures for the skiing area are certainly impressive (60km of ski runs, which become nearly 120km if you include the 30km of the Folgarida-Marilleva area – reachable without removing your skis – and the 27km of

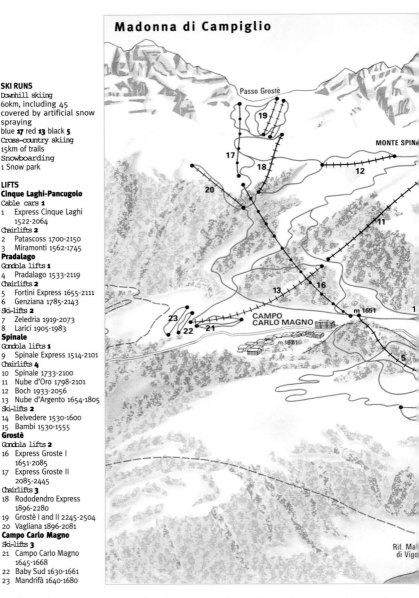

Madonna di Campiglio

SKI RUNS
Downhill skiing
60km, including 45
covered by artificial snow
spraying
blue **17** red **13** black **5**
Cross-country skiing
15km of trails
Snowboarding
1 Snow park

LIFTS
Cinque Laghi-Pancugolo
Cable cars **1**
1   Express Cinque Laghi
     1522-2064
Chairlifts **2**
2   Patascoss 1700-2150
3   Miramonti 1562-1745
Pradalago
Gondola lifts **1**
4   Pradalago 1533-2119
Chairlifts **2**
5   Fortini Express 1655-2111
6   Genziana 1785-2143
Ski-lifts **2**
7   Zeledria 1919-2073
8   Larici 1905-1983
Spinale
Gondola lifts **1**
9   Spinale Express 1514-2101
Chairlifts **4**
10   Spinale 1733-2100
11   Nube d'Oro 1798-2101
12   Boch 1933-2056
13   Nube d'Argento 1654-1805
Ski-lifts **2**
14   Belvedere 1530-1600
15   Bambi 1530-1555
Grostè
Gondola lifts **2**
16   Express Groste I
     1651-2085
17   Express Groste II
     2085-2445
Chairlifts **3**
18   Rododendro Express
     1896-2280
19   Grostè I and II 2245-2504
20   Vagliana 1896-2081
Campo Carlo Magno
Ski-lifts **3**
21   Campo Carlo Magno
     1645-1668
22   Baby Sud 1630-1661
23   Mandrifà 1640-1680

Pinzolo) but the real attraction lies in the nature of Madonna di Campiglio's ski runs: panoramic, winding, open and clearly marked. The zone receives more snow than anywhere else in the central and eastern section of the Alps and, although there are high-powered artificial snow machines should the need arise, you often ski through fir trees and chalets immersed in snow. In addition, the town lies at 1,550m, making it an integral part of the skiing area and ensuring you can always ski

back. The various connecting trails, with bridges, tunnels and little roads make it easy to move around.
The ski runs lie on two opposing sides of the bowl: to the west, the Pradalago-Cinque Laghi area and the more central Canalone Miramonti; to the east, the Spinale-Grostè area, at the foot of the Brenta Dolomites. Both sides have high-capacity gondola lifts. The Spinale one, aside from taking you to the famed black route, which might be wide and smooth, but has

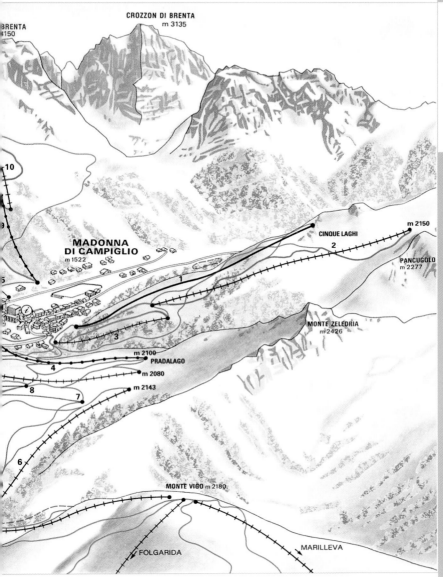

CROZZON DI BRENTA
m 3135

BRENTA
150

10

m 2150

CINQUE LAGHI
2

PANCUGOLO
m 2277

MADONNA
DI CAMPIGLIO
m 1522

1

MONTE ZELEDRIA
m 2426

3

m 2100
PRADALAGO

4   m 2080

8   m 2143

7

6

MONTE VIGO m 2180

FOLGARIDA

MARILLEVA

breathtaking drops (80°), allows you to reach the enjoyable red trails served by the Nube d'Oro chairlift and the simple, open areas of Campo Carlo Magno.
By taking the 6-person cable car in two sections on Grostè (one of the longest in the world), you come to the undulating "highway" where everyone feels like a champion (chairlifts at higher altitudes). These are the Grostè ski runs and are the highest section of the skiing area (2,504m), right by the only opening in the imposing bastion

of the Brenta Mountains.
The spectacular series of Dolomite mountains, Tosa, Brenta Alta and Crozzon, is even better from the opposing slope, especially from the 3-Tre red trail, which becomes the Canalone Miramonti black trail (used in competitions; reachable from the town via the Funivia Express Cinque Laghi), or the gentle slopes of Pradalago (gondola lift). From Pradalago there is another seemingly unending black trail, the Amazzonia (vertical drop

470m). Next to Pradalago, the Genziana Express covered chairlift has made it much easier to reach Folgarida and Marilleva, as well as some interesting red trails. One of the developments underway is a route to the Spinale zone, which will create ever more options.

In terms of cross-country skiing, there are the Campo Carlo

The views of the Dolomites are often magnificent on the ski runs

Magno trails (about 15km). In addition, Madonna di Campiglio is one of the European capitals for snowboarding. It is a setting for regular competitions (world cup and championship) and has a 50,000m² area with a snow park, half pipe and other specialized facilities. The best slopes for boarding are those on Grostè because of the snow coverage and the moderate gradients. It is also the site of the large Ursus snow park. In addition, providing they take the correct precautions, snowboarders can find good fresh snow and vertical drops not found in many places in Trentino-Alto Adige.

Folgarida-Marilleva

ski-lifts open from December to April
Folgarida, lying at the beginning of the Meledrio valley, which runs up to Campo Carlo Magno, and Marilleva, on the north-facing slopes of Val di Sole, are two successful examples of what could be termed a "complete Italian skiing experience".

These towns consist predominantly of holiday flats (especially Marilleva) and hotels (Folgarida has 2,400 bed spaces and a capacity of 5,700 in houses) and are a favored destination of those who love to be able to walk out the front door and start skiing without having the hassle of lifts or ski-buses. The location ensures excellent snow and there is also a connection to the famous resort of Madonna di Campiglio (see entry). Folgarida, at about 1,300m, is almost

an "upper level" of Dimaro. The main section of Marilleva, namely Marilleva 1400, stands above Mezzana, which is the departure point for the gondola lift. There is other accommodation a little outside Mezzana at Marilleva 900. The latter has the advantage, especially for those not arriving by car, of being on the Trento-Malè train line.

The commercial dynamism of Val di Sole ensures a range of promotions for ski passes (with the Skirama Adamello-Brenta, potentially with extension to Tonale, Pejo, the Paganella plateau and Folgaria-Lavarone) and a variety of different holiday packages.

The skiing area has about 50km of runs on Mts Spolverino and Vigo, with wonderful views of the Brenta Mountains. The most notable features are the variety, the range of difficulty, the artificial snow spraying and the advanced lifts. Generally speaking, these are very modern, with 4- or 6-person chairlifts, gondola lifts and cable cars (and some 15 person ones, like at Marilleva). Cable cars from both edges of Folgarida converge on Mt Spolverino, where there are other lifts, including chairlifts at higher altitudes. Other chairlifts and ski runs of average difficulty make it quick to get across to Mt Vigo, 2,180m, which is the focal point for the lifts from Marilleva (gondola lifts and chairlift). From Mt Vigo, a lovely 2km red trail with a sustained gradient heads down to the Malghette area, which is linked to Madonna di

Campiglio (single ski pass) via the Genziana Express chairlift.

The best-known ski runs in Val di Sole are famed for their changes in gradient and rhythm. The king of these is the Folgarida black route, which has a final section from the Ottava chairlift that is floodlit. The route cuts through the wood, has a notable wall and a vertical drop of 554m (or nearly 800m if you start from the Spolverino peak, along the Provetti, 1,300m long). The 1,850m Marilleva black route is no less interesting. The masses, though, prefer the easy descent down Mt Vigo and from Doss della Pesa. Like Madonna di Campiglio, Folgarida has specialized ski schools and a half pipe.

In terms of cross-country skiing, there are various centers at Pellizzano, Ossana, Commezzadura and Vermiglio (with the option of a new, continuous trail of 22km from Volpai to Velon). In total, Val di Sole (including the Rabbi valley and Cogolo) has 70km of cross-country routes.

Pejo

ski-lifts open from December to April
At Pejo you can combine the fun of skiing with the chance to admire some grand and majestic mountains. This is a quiet tourist resort but it has good facilities. It lies in a side branch of Val di Sole, known simply as *Valletta* (literally, little valley), that runs to the Cevedale Mountains in the heart of the Parco Nazionale dello Stelvio.

This is not an enormous skiing area, but the runs (15km in total) on the imposing Mt Viòz (3,643m), starting from as high as 2,360m, are truly varied, interesting and definitely worth trying. The vertical drop is 750m and one of the runs continues 5km down the valley. There are also two notable black trails. The two major lifts are the cable car and, further up, the quad chairlift. It is worth noting that the free ski-bus connects Pejo to Marilleva and the Tonale. If you prefer narrower skis, there is the Cogolo cross-country center, at about 1,200m, and, with such majestic mountains, ski-mountaineering is a real option (even on Cevedale or Viòz).

Fai della Paganella-Andalo-Molveno

ski-lifts open from December to April
This is a plateau cloaked in woods and enclosed by two of the major mountain groups in Trentino. Andalo, Fai della Paganella and Molveno are the main skiing areas, although Molveno is also a summer destination, largely because of its wonderful lake, and was once favored by a jet-setting crowd. Yet, the most striking feature of the zone, lying to the west, is the outline of the Brenta Mountains. This might be the lesser known side to view these mountains from, but the silhouette remains stunning. On the other side of the zone, to the east, the relatively gentle slopes painted with the white stripes of the ski runs conceal the harsh mass of the symbol of Trentino: Mt Paganella (2,125m) standing sheer over the Adige valley.

Andalo, located on a watershed between the Noce and Sarca basins, is characterized by pleasant tourist structures (60 hotels) and its 12 *masi* (farmhouses). The immediate impression is of a large, well-organized tourist resort. Fai della Paganella, standing on a natural balcony overlooking the Adige valley, is slightly less touristy. All together, the resorts on the plateau have an impressive amount of accommodation, with 15,000 beds, including over 6,000 in hotels. A key factor for this zone is good road access: it is a mere 18km from the San Michele all'Adige exit on the A22 Brennero highway.

Each of the towns on the plateau has its own identity, but in skiing terms, they combine to form the Paganella skiing area (nearly 50km of runs). The hubs are Andalo and Fai della Paganella, both with high-capacity lifts. From Andalo, a chairlift takes you to Prati di Gaggia and there is a high-powered detachable lift from the center; from Fai you can take a quad chairlift. The skiing area is well-organized and efficient, capable of managing 24,000 people an hour. Despite the relatively few lifts, there are 20 ski runs, tending to be long, open and surrounded by woods (except on the Paganella peak, where the tall trees give way to dwarf pines and the odd pasture or meadow). Nearly all of the trails are of moderate difficulty, except for Andalo's famed black route, namely Olimpica. Two remarkable features are the continuous slope, creating a vertical drop from 2,125m to 1,028m, and the distance from summit to valley (5km). The ski runs practically radiate out from the

by a comfortable chairlift. Molveno also has a lift that takes you up the Brenta, between the Pradel mountain refuge and Montanara (1,366/1,525m), to a blue route. This, though, is not included in the Paganella ski pass and is generally more favored by excursionists than dowhhill skiers. There is some cross-country skiing on the plateau around Lake Andalo (a

Fai della Paganella-Andalo-Molveno

Paganella peak, heading either towards Fai or Andalo. The view from the top, at the La Roda mountain refuge, is extraordinary and it is obvious why this spot is known as the terrace of Trentino. Another of the main routes, which includes the Olimpica trail, runs from the summit to the town of Andalo, while the third axis is centered on Prati di Gaggia, a lively plateau at 1,333m with a training slope served

3km floodlit circuit, another of 5km). There is also a plan to create other trails near Andalo at Lava.

Monte Bondone
ski-lifts open from December to April
Skiing on this natural viewpoint overlooking the Adige valley, Paganella and the Brenta Mountains gives you the sense of, literally, being above everything. The ski runs (20km over 70

118

ha) are challenging. The Gran Pista ski run starts from the Palon summit (2,090m) and heads to Mezavia (1,175m). This continuous route has a vertical drop of over 800m (900m if you add in the first stretch from Palon to Fortino) and, in a survey carried out by a local paper, it was voted as Trentino's favorite ski run. To get back up the mountain, you

trails (over 37km, varying levels) in the Viotte basin, which is a small capital of this sport.

Folgaria-Lavarone

ski-lifts open from December to April
Folgaria, on the gentle slopes of Becco di Filadonna and Cornetto, and Lavarone are situated amid rolling plateaus, snow-covered meadows and

can take the Rocce Rosse high-speed detachable quad. The other ski runs are also rewarding (located between Vaneze, 1,300m, and Palon, 2,090m) and served by various double and triple chairlifts. Generally, they are moderately difficult.

On Monte Bondone, there is also a place where children are looked after, a snow park and a giant half pipe. There are also good cross-country skiing

pastures, dwarf-pines and fir trees. The area is covered by a single brand, Skitour dei Forti (literally, the ski tour of the forts, the name is a reminder of the 7 Austro-Hungarian forts in the territory).

There are 70km of ski runs divided between two hubs, Folgaria-Serrada (the main one) and Lavarone. The lifts and ski runs have been modernized at a remarkable rate, with the newest ones being Ortesino and Costa-Moreta. There are 7 quad chairlifts that make moving around on the slopes even easier. This reasonably large area allows you to ski various slopes in a setting that is safe yet thrilling. The majority of ski runs are red and surprisingly long (sometimes 5km). You might take the main lifts from Folgaria-Francolini, then ski down to Fondo Grande. From there, head back up to the Dosso della Somme fort and then ski some more, this time down to Serrada, perhaps along Pragrant or Slalom Toll (two technically taxing variants). Head back in the opposite direction, then up to the Sommo Alto fort. This route includes the tough section of the black Martinella Nord trail. A blue route connects with Fondo Piccolo, where there are four parallel lifts, serving different ski runs,

SKI RUNS
Folgaria
Downhill skiing
52km covered by artificial snow spraying
blue **12** red **9** black **2**
Cross-country skiing
45km of trails
Lavarone
Downhill skiing
18km covered by artificial snow spraying
blue **4** red **5** black **1**
Cross-country skiing
42km of trails of varying difficulty

LIFTS
Folgaria, Francolin area
Chairlifts **1**
2   Francolin 1230-1541
Ski-lifts **1**
3   Cubl 1220-1272
Fondo Grande-Fondo Piccolo
Chairlifts **7**
5   Salizzona 1344-1635
6   Martinella 1340-1607
7   Malga Ortesino 1290-1585
8   Cima Spill 1464-1630
9   Trugalait 1470-1620
10   Cencio Rosso 1560-1660
11   Cargaore 1485-1630
Ski-lifts **2**
4   Campo Scuola I 1344-1388
12   Baby 1485-1510
Sled trails **1**
13   Slittinovia 1485-1500
Costa-Monte Cornetto
Chairlifts **2**
14   Dosso della Madonna
     1238-1303
18   Costa Moreta 1240-1450
Skilift **2**
15   Maso Baby 1240-1270
16   Maso Spilzi 12601378
Sled trails **1**
17   Slittinovia Costa 1240-1265
Serrada-Martinella
Chairlifts **1**
19   Martinella-Serrada
     1260-1604
Passo Coe and Forte Cherle
Chairlifts **1**
–   Frate Fiorentini 1450-1852
Ski-lifts **5**
20   Passo Coe I 1600-1655
21   Passo Coe II 1605-1700
–   Forte Cherle Baby
     1440-1480
–   Forte Cherle II 1410-1480
–   Baby
Folgaria-Monte Cornetto
Gondola lifts **1**
1   Paradiso 1183-1636
     (only in summer)

Lavarone
Chairlifts **4**
–   Tablat 1195-1380
–   Soneck 1333-1381
–   Ust 1180-1385
–   Malga Laghetto 1185-1555
Ski-lifts **2**
–   Rivetta Baby 1350-1388
–   Malga Rivetta 1350-1511
Conveyor belt lift **2**
–   Penner Skiweg

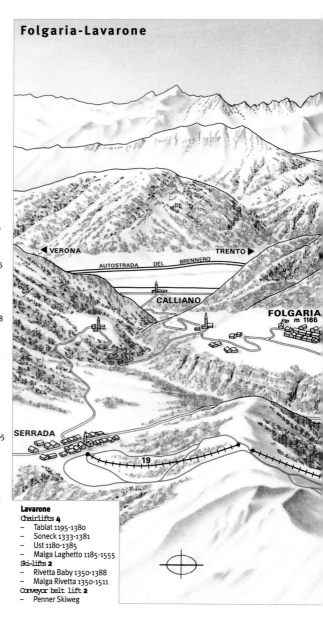

Folgaria-Lavarone

◄ VERONA   TRENTO ►
AUTOSTRADA   DEL   BRENNERO
CALLIANO
FOLGARIA
m 1166
SERRADA
19

and the Coe Pass lift. The return to Folgaria is a long, panoramic and gentle run.

The Lavarone area is smaller (only 18km of runs) but busy. The highlight is probably the black route, which can be accessed by the Tablat quad lift. A strength of this center is the way the beginners' slopes and blue trails spread out around the villages. The Coe Pass has an area for snowboarders and some famed cross-country circuits. The Forti plateau is, indeed, a cross-country paradise, with its undulating layout. The main centers are Forte Cherle, at Folgaria, and Millegrobbe on the Lavarone-Luserna plateau, accessible using an electronic ski pass (like for downhill skiing) that can also be used at other centers in Trentino, from Tesero to Vermiglio.

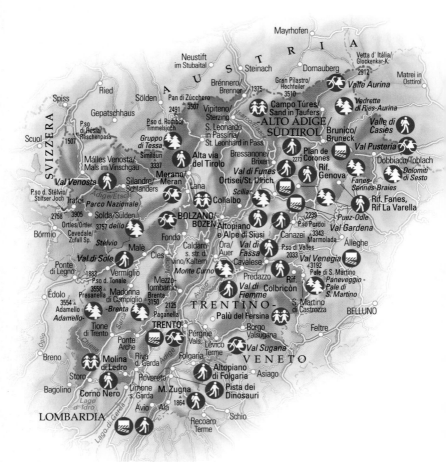

With its exceptional environmental heritage, Trentino-Alto Adige is the ideal place for sports enthusiasts and anyone who loves the outdoor life. Whatever the season, this region offers countless opportunities to absorb its beautiful landscape. Some of the options for exploring the zone are more relaxing activities, such as hiking or horseback riding, but others are more strenuous activities, such as rafting or canyoning. Of course, there is a vast range of other activities from skiing and biking to water sports, and all kinds of possibilities for naturalists.

- 🌲 PARKS
- 👪 CHILDREN
- 🚶 WALKS
- 🚴 BIKING ROUTES
- 🎞 CINEMA
- 🏃 SPORT

Itineraries

In this charming, still pristine and unspoiled landscape, where encounters with local species of fauna are not unusual, sports enthusiasts can also benefit from a sophisticated, modern logistics network, which will help them to maximize their leisure time to the full.

Highlights

- Unforgettable views of the magnificent rock walls of the Dolomites
- The clear, sparkling waters of Alpine lakes
- Breathtaking views of valleys full of flowers
- The lovely, unspoiled Alpine landscape

Inside

PARCO NAZIONALE DELLO STELVIO/NATIONALPARK STILFSER JOCH

PROVINCES OF BOLZANO, BRESCIA, SONDRIO, TRENT

AREA: 134,620 HECTARES. ORTLES-CEVEDALE MOUNTAIN MASSIF AND SIDE VALLEYS.

HEADQUARTERS: PIAZZA MUNICIPIO 1, GLORENZA (BOLZANO), TEL. 0473830430

VIA ROMA 65, COGOLO DI PEIO (TRENT) TEL. 0463746121

WEBSITE: WWW.STELVIOPARK.IT

VISITORS' CENTERS: CENTRO VISITE AQUAPRAD (PRATO ALLO STELVIO, BOLZANO), TEL. 0473618212. OPEN CHRISTMAS TO LATE OCTOBER, TUESDAY TO FRIDAY 9-12 AND 14.30-18; SATURDAY, SUNDAY AND HOLIDAYS 14.30-18.

CENTRO VISITE CULTURAMARTELL (MARTELLO, BOLZANO), TEL. 0473745027. OPEN MAY TO OCTOBER, TUESDAY TO FRIDAY 9-12 AND 14.30-18; SATURDAY, SUNDAY AND HOLIDAYS 14.30-18.

VISITORS' CENTERS: CENTRO VISITE NATURATRAFOI (STELVIO, BOLZANO), TEL. 0473612031. OPEN MAY TO OCTOBER, TUESDAY TO FRIDAY 9-12 AND 14.30-18; SATURDAY, SUNDAY AND HOLIDAYS 14.30-18.

VISITORS' CENTERS: CENTRO VISITE LAHNER SÄGE (ULTIMO, BOLZANO), TEL. 0473798123. OPEN CHRISTMAS TO LATE OCTOBER, TUESDAY TO FRIDAY 9-12 AND 14.30-18; SATURDAY, SUNDAY AND HOLIDAYS 14.30-18.

VISITORS' CENTERS: CENTRO VISITE DI RABBI (RABBI, TRENT), TEL. 0463985190. OPEN CHRISTMAS, AT WEEKENDS IN WINTER AND FOR A PERIOD IN SUMMER 9-12 AND 15-18; JULY AND AUGUST 8-19.

VISITORS' CENTERS: CENTRO VISITE DI PEJO (COGOLO DI PEJO, TRENT), TEL. 0463754186. OPEN EVERY DAY 9-12 AND 15-18; JULY AND AUGUST 8-19.

VISITORS' CENTERS: CENTRO VISITE STABLET (RABBI, TRENT), TEL. 0463985190 OPEN EVERY DAY FROM JUNE TO SEPTEMBER 10-16.

PARK GATES: LACES/LATSCH (BOLZANO), FOR THE SS38 ROAD. PEJO AND RABBI (TRENT), A22 HIGHWAY, SAN MICHELE DELL'ADIGE-MEZZOCORONA EXIT, FOR THE SS12, 42 AND 43 ROADS.

The Parco Nazionale dello Stelvio is part of one of the largest reserves in Italy. The northern border extends to the Engadina National Park in Switzerland, while the southern one touches Lombardy's Parco Adamello-Brenta, which is connected, in turn, to the Parco Naturale Adamello-Brenta in Trentino. This creates one of the largest protected areas in Europe (over 260,000 ha), with the Parco dello Stelvio right at the heart, in all senses. The mountainous nature of this zone is evident, with roughly 70% being above 2,000m.

The center of the park is the mountainous mass of Ortles-Cevedale. This massif is home to nearly 100 glaciers, including the largest in Italy (Forni, 20km²), and 25 valleys running off in all directions. The main valleys are the Pejo and Viso, heading south, the Rabbi to the east and, to the north, the Solda, Trafoi and Martello . The park is a haven of pristine nature where the green of the fields and larch and fir forests contrast with the white of the peaks and the bright blue of the lakes. The wealth of the park, aside from the great diversity of plants

THE MASI

The masi (literally, homesteads; the singular is maso) blend into the landscape perfectly and are a typical type of peasant dwelling found in the Trentino-Alto Adige region. They consist of a barn/stables section and a residential area. In the past, and still today, they are grouped together to form small urban agglomerations in the valleys and on the slopes of the mountains. Their simplicity, though, is only superficial. The architecture takes into account the need for excellent winter insulation and protection from rain, cold (no openings facing north or the prevailing winds) and snow (the roofs slope at about 25°).

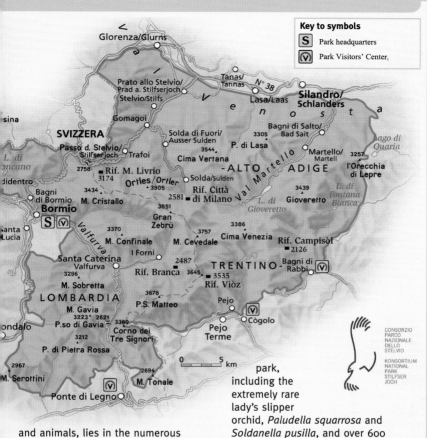

Key to symbols

ⓈPark headquarters

Ⓥ Park Visitors' Center,

Glorenza/Glurns

Prato allo Stelvio/
Prad a. Stilfserjoch
Stelvio/Stilfs

Tanas/
Tannas   N° 38

Lasa/Laas   Silandro/
Schlanders

Gomagoi

sina

SVIZZERA

Solda di Fuori/
Ausser Sulden   3305

Bagni di Salto/
Bad Sait

Lago di
Quaria

Passo d. Stelvio/
Stilfserjoch   Trafoi

P. di Lasa

3544

Cima Vertana

Martello/
Martell   3257

l'Orecchia
di Lepre

L. di
ncano

2758   Rif. M. Livrio
3174
Ortles/Ortler
3905

Solda/Sulden

ALTO ADIGE

Val Martello

didentro

Bagni
di Bormio   3434
M. Cristallo

Rif. Città
2581 di Milano

3439

L. di
Fontana
Bianca

Bormio   ⓈⓋ

Gran
Zebrù   3851

L. di
Gioveretto

Gioveretto

anta
Lucia

Valfurva

3370
M. Confinale
I Forni

3757
M. Cevedale

3386
Cima Venezia

Rif. Campisòl
2126

Santa Caterina
Valfurva   3296

Rif. Branca   2487
3645

TRENTINO   Bagni di
Rabbi   Ⓥ

M. Sobretta

3535

LOMBARDIA   3678

Rif. Viòz

P.S. Matteo

Pejo

M. Gavia
3223 2621
P.so di Gavia   3360

Corno dei
Tre Signori   3212

Pejo   Ⓥ
Cògolo

ondalo

Pejo
Terme

P. di Pietra Rossa

2967

0   5 km

M. Serottini   2694

M. Tonale

Ⓥ

Ponte di Legno

CONSORZIO
PARCO
NAZIONALE
DELLO
STELVIO

KONSORTIUM
NATIONAL
PARK
STILFSER
JOCH

and animals, lies in the numerous
landscapes where you can see
glaciers, Alpine pastures, forests,
farmed fields, farmstead settlements
and villages. The park covers an
enormous range of altitudes, from
650m at Laces in the Venosta valley
to 3,905m at the summit of Ortles,
and thus numerous different plant
species. Despite this, the woods are
dominated by firs: spruces, especially
in the valleys of Trentino and Alto
Adige, larch and Swiss stone pines.
The latter, along with dwarf mountain
pines, can be found as high as
2,300m. As you go higher, up to
3,500m, the vegetation consists of
"specialized" species, such as the
glacier crowfoot, that can resist the
harsh climate and especially the cold,
snow and ice.
The variety of terrains and
environments (including peat-bogs,
high-altitude pastures and snow-
covered valleys) means that over 1,200
plant species can be found in the

park,
including the
extremely rare
lady's slipper
orchid, *Paludella squarrosa* and
Soldanella pusilla, and over 600
other vegetal species (mushrooms,
moss and lichen).
All of the typical Alpine animals can
be found in the park. The chamois,
numbering over 4,500, is the most
common small hoofed-animal. The
present deer population, descendants
of animals from the Engadina park, is
the largest in Italy with nearly 2,500
animals. The best places to try and
spot them are the Venosta valley
forests. If you are looking for roe
deer, the best option is the valleys
of Trentino. The ibex was reintroduced
to the park as part of project begun
in 1968 and now there are a few
hundred animals, which can be seen
as far north as the border with the
Engadina park. In terms of other
mammals, the most widespread is
the marmot, although there are
numerous foxes, small rodents and
martens, such as the stoat and the
beech marten. The symbol of the park
is the golden eagle, of which there

are at least 10 recorded nesting pairs. The sizeable beak, the predatory look, the powerful talons and a wingspan of over 2m have always fascinated man. In the park, they are often seen circling high above the Martello or Rabbi valleys. Other birds-of-prey in the park include the goshawk, sparrowhawk, eagle owl and pygmy owl. In total, there are about 130 species of bird in the park, many of which nest there, including the Alpine grouses (wood, black, hazel and snow grouses), five species of woodpecker, nutcrackers, Greek partridges, ring ouzels, and treecreepers and other passerines. In recent times, the bearded vulture

At high altitudes, small lakes often form in areas once shaped by glaciers. An example of this is the small lakes of Scorluzzo, in a basin on the Lombard side of the Stelvio Pass

has been spotted, despite not being seen in the Alps for over a century. The reason for this wonderful development is that, in the 1980s, a program was launched to reintroduce this impressive bird that can fly hundreds of kilometers a day.

SENTIERI VIVI®

The Parco Nazionale dello Stelvio is crisscrossed by over 1,500km of trails, many of which were created by Italian and Austro-Hungarian troops during World War I. This network is well sign-posted and there are many inviting mountain refuges, making it a pleasure to explore some of the most famous cliffs, such as the north face of Ortles (3,029m), and largest glaciers in Italy, such as the Forni glacier (2,487m). For experienced mountaineers, the Ortles-Cevedale groups has some climbs and crossings that pass through some stunning areas, such as the classic crossing of the Tredici peak, which winds its way from the Cevedale peak (3,769m) to Pizzo Tresero (3,594m). In addition, there are 15 'theme' itineraries with plenty of observation points exploring the unusual geological and historical features and the various plant and animal life in the park (Percorso Geologico, Percorso delle Segherie, Percorso del Latte e dei Masi, Scalinata dei Larici Monumentali, etc.).

Yet, the most unexpected aspect of the park is the Sentieri Vivi® initiative, which is a system that makes substantial use of information technology to enable tourists to uncover, in a simple and personalized manner, the natural beauty and culture of a territory. The Sentieri Vivi® system consists of totem computers with touch screens, disk drives, printers and a palm pilot.

The totem is activated by touch and then displays a series of options to explore the flora, fauna, geology, folklore and much more, as well as showing a virtual tour of the trail. The totems are found beneath carefully chosen trees and at relevant tourist offices.

Once a choice has been made, a visitor can make use of a 'palmareamico' (palm pilot friend), which is equipped with GPS and uses video and audio to explain the major points of interest and unusual features of the chosen trail. At the end of an excursion, you can get a 'postcard printed' containing the route, time taken, the change in altitude and the best photos. You can, also, get a poster made and sent to your home.

PARCO NATURALE PROVINCIALE ADAMELLO-BRENTA

PROVINCE OF TRENT

AREA: 61.864 HECTARES. VALLEYS, SLOPES AND MOUNTAINS IN THE CENTRAL ALPS.

HEADQUARTERS: VIA NAZIONALE 12, STREMBO (TRENT), TEL. 0465806666

WEBSITE: WWW.PARCOADAMELLOBRENTA.TN.IT.

VISITORS' CENTERS: CENTRO VISITE AT LAGO DI TOVEL, TEL. 0463451033

This is the largest park in Trentino and Alto-Adige and covers one of the most charming and pristine sections of the Dolomites, including zones populated with many herds of chamois. Enchanting landscapes and a wealth of flowers and animals are the key characteristics of this protected section of the Ladin Alps that encompasses two mountain areas: to the west, the Adamello-Presanella massif, with some notable glacial features; to the east, the Brenta mountains, a mass of peaks, gorges and pinnacles. The spruce is the most commonly found fir tree, but it is more of a backdrop for the Alpine grizzly bear (*Ursus arctos*), which is an endangered species protected by the Life Ursus project and is the symbol of the park. The most beautiful section is the Genova valley, dotted with enormous rocks that creating deafening and lovely waterfalls that are as beautiful as any in the Alps: these are the 'steps' that lead to the majestic glaciers of Vedretta, Lobbia and Mandron. It is well worth heading to the Orti della Regina (vegetable gardens of the queen), above Campo Carlo Magno, to explore the numerous botanical treasures once loved by Princess Sissi. The Giardino Botanico

Rio Bianco (botanical gardens), near the ancient Stenico castle, and some delightful landscapes, such as the Fumo valley or the glaciers of Adamello, make the park a 'must see' for nature lovers. Visitors should consider buying the Parco Card, which allows you to combine visiting the park with tasting local products and visiting the province's museums. The Progetto Qualità Parco project has been initiated to increase environmental awareness and to involve local tourist operators in

THE GRIZZLY BEAR

In the depths of the woods in the most inaccessible parts of the park, the last 2 or 3 remaining grizzly bears (Ursus arctos) of the Alps live. It is the symbol of the park and the true king of the Alps. Hunting the bear was stopped in 1939, but it now suffers from the aggressive encroachment of man's settlements, surviving as best it can. To help it, we need to create 'refuges' where even felling trees is not allowed. In order to bring new blood to the area, bears from Slovenia and Croatia are being introduced.

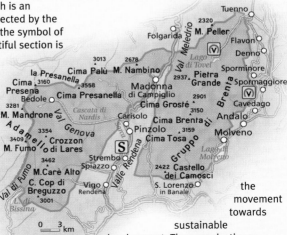

the movement towards sustainable development. The organizations involved in the project are aware of the environmental impact of tourism and so are working to safeguard against pollution and respect nature while maintaining high-quality service.

PARCO NATURALE PROVINCIALE PANEVEGGIO-PALE DI SAN MARTINO

PROVINCE OF TRENT (CONVENTION WITH TCI)

AREA: 19,711 HECTARES. VALLEYS, SLOPES AND MOUNTAINS IN EASTERN TRENTINO.

HEADQUARTERS: VILLA WELSPERG, VIA CASTELPIETRA 2 (TONADICO, TRENT)

TEL. 043964854

WEBSITE: WWW.PARCOPAN.ORG

VISITORS' CENTERS: CENTRO VISITE PRÀ DE MADEGO AND CASA DEL SENTIERO ETNOGRAFICO (CAORIA, TRENT), TEL. 043964854; CENTRO VISITE PANEVEGGIO, MAIN ROAD TO ROLLE (PREDAZZO, TRENT) TEL. 0462576283; CENTRO VISITE SAN MARTINO DI CASTROZZA, TEL. 0439768859;

the deer and it is also an indication of the renewed ecological balance of the area. There are nearly 1,000 deer in the park, along with over 650 roe deer, 800 chamois and a new program to reintroduce the ibex. There are various marked trails in the park.

The Parco Naturale di Paneveggio-Pale di San Martino lies in eastern Trentino across a pristine area including some of the Fiemme and Fassa valleys and Primiero. Within its borders lies one of the largest Alpine forests, namely Paneveggio, and the mythical Pale di San Martino dolomitic mountains. This integral environment is characterized by the deep green of age-old forests and the light green of the pastures. All this green is counteracted by the pink of the Pale di San Martino Mountains, the deep red of the rocks of Lagorài and the azure of the lakes. The forest, mainly red firs, is also called the 'forest of violins' as many past musicians, including Stradivari, came here to find the firs with the 'best resonance' since such wood was ideal for making the body of this instrument.

The head of Venegia valley has a wild beauty and great botanical wealth. It sits in a wide, glacial depression in the north of the park. This is where the Travignolo river starts and it is the setting for some rare plants endemic to the Dolomites: *Campanula morettiana*, *Primula auricola*, *Primula tyrolensis*. The symbol of the park is

The first is the Sentiero Vanoi ethnographic trail that goes from Caorìa (845m) to Malga Miesnotta, at nearly 2,000. Created as a 'museum' walk, it explores interesting aspects of mountain culture. The second trail is Sentiero Marciò, which is one of the many routes through the Paneveggio forest, starting from the local visitors' center. The third one is Sentiero Venegia valley. This takes in both the plant-life and the landscape along the Travignolo, starting from Malga Venegia. After two hours of walking, you are rewarded with a stunning view of the Pale di San Martino.

Val Venegia with the Pale di San Martino

PARCO NATURALE PROVINCIALE DOLOMITI DI SESTO/NATURPARK SEXTNER DOLOMITEN

PROVINCE OF BOLZANO

AREA: 11,635 HECTARES. PLATEAUS AND DOLOMITIC ROCK.

HEADQUARTERS: NATURAL PARKS OFFICE, VIA C. BATTISTI 21, BOLZANO
TEL. 0471417770

WEBSITE: WWW.PROVINZ.BZ.IT/NATUR

VISITORS' CENTERS: CENTRO CULTURALE GRAND HOTEL DOBBIACO (DOBBIACO, BOLZANO) TEL. 0474973017.

The square silhouette of the Tre Cime of Lavaredo, the serrated Undici Cime, Croda dei Baranci, the rocky Punta dei Tre Scarperi and Mt Popera are well known to climbers, all with summits around or over 3,000m and within this park on the northeastern edge of the Dolomites. Yet, one should also note the 'lower' aspects of the park: the Landro valley with its lake, and the lovely Fiscalina and Campo di Dentro valleys, which are like gateways to the area. The area is dominated by the spruce, often near larch up to about 1,900m. Gravel and rock-covered slopes account for about two-thirds of the park, creating good conditions for such species as dwarf pines, which are particularly abundant and impenetrable in Fiscalina valley. The two 'wonders' of the park are the yellow poppy and the snow-grouse. Some of the rocky outcrops are used by golden eagles as nesting sites. Over 50 other bird species also nest in the zone, including the wood grouse and the black grouse.

PARCO NATURALE PROVINCIALE FANES-SENNES-BRAIES/NATURPARK FANES-SENNES-PRAGS

PROVINCE OF BOLZANO

AREA: 25,680 HECTARES. PLATEAUS AND THE DOLOMITIC ROCK.

HEADQUARTERS: NATURAL PARKS OFFICE, VIA C. BATTISTI 21, BOLZANO, TEL. 0471414300

WEBSITE: WWW.PROVINZ.BZ.IT/NATUR

VISITORS' CENTERS: CENTRO VISITE SAN VIGILIO DI MAREBBE, TEL. 0471506120.

The most unusual section of the park is known by the lovely and intriguing name of 'Parliament of the Marmots'. This is not, though, some unusual government building or meeting place, but an open green field bordered by a semicircle of step-like rocks where dozens of marmots congregate every day. The other major animals in the park are the various herbivores, such as the roe deer, normal deer, chamois and ibex.
The park covers the northernmost section of the Dolomites and, together with the nearby Dolomiti di Sesto and Dolomiti Ampezzane parks, it forms

The Parco di Fanes-Sennes-Braies offers various walking itineraries

50 FEROCIOUS GRAMS

The pygmy owl (Glaucidium passerinum) might be small, but it is truly one of the most efficient and ferocious birds-of-prey you might see in Italy. Despite being a mere 16cm long and weighing little more than 50g, it can still catch small rodents and warbler birds that are nearly a match for it in terms of size. Two white superciliary lines (sometimes called eyebrows) above yellow eyes give the bird a menacing look that fits well with its nature as an efficient hunter. It is predominantly found in conifer woods, where its uses the nest-holes created by the pied or three-toed woodpecker for its own eggs.

the largest protected area in the eastern Alps. Within the park there are various distinct areas: the Braies Dolomites, reaching their peak at 3,148m with La Croda Rossa, and the zone of the great plateaus of Sennes, Fanes and Fosses. Typical karst phenomena, such as furrowed fields, sink holes, wells and blind valleys, highlight the harsh isolation of these areas, dotted with small, azure lakes that form where the land is less permeable. This unforgiving landscape favors specialized bird species, like the snow-grouse and the black grouse, which tend to conglomerate around the dwarf pines and rhododendron bushes.

There are, though, some of the more common animals, namely the marmot, roe deer and chamois.

The cliffs supporting the plateaus might be covered in red firs or Swiss stone pines and larch, but the actual flat areas are nearly without trees. Instead, they are host, especially in the right season, to splendid flowers: buttercups, orchids, crocuses and pasque-flowers. These, though, can be seen as a mere prelude to

rarer (and tougher) plants that can survive amid rocks at great heights, perhaps in the gravel depressions (Alpine poppies) or rock cracks (*Potentilla caulescens* or *Artemisia nitida*).

There are various marked trails. The first one is called *Sulle orme degli orsi* (on the track of bears). This walking itinerary takes six hours, starting and ending at La Villa. It takes you to the ancient cave (elev. 2,800m) housing the skeleton of a cave bear, an animal that died out in the late Quaternary era (50 to 30 million years ago). For further information: La Villa tourist association, tel. 0471 847037.

The second trail is *Al chiaro di luna* (moonlight trail). This easy night trail takes 3 to 4 hours on foot, starting and ending at Pederü. For further information: San Vigilio tourist association, tel. 0474501037.

The third trail is *Danzando intorno al vulcano* (dancing around a volcano). This takes 4 hours on foot, starting and ending at La Valle. It explores the geological history of Armentara and Prati della Croce. For further information: Pedraces tourist association, tel. 0471839695.

PARCO NATURALE PROVINCIALE GRUPPO DI TESSA/NATURPARK TEXELGRUPPE

PROVINCE OF BOLZANO

AREA: 33,430 HECTARES. A CRYSTALLINE MASSIF IN THE CENTRAL ALPS.

HEADQUARTERS: NATURAL PARKS OFFICE, VIA C. BATTISTI 21, BOLZANO, TEL. 0471414300

WEBSITE: WWW.PROVINZ.BZ.IT/NATUR

VISITORS' CENTERS: CENTRO VISITA GRUPPO TESSA (NATURNO, BOLZANO), TEL. 0473668201.

It is known as the 'screaming lake' because the sound of its waves crashing on the shores announce the arrival of bad weather. Lake Fagles is one of the many mysteries of the larger Parco Naturale dell'Alto Adige. The others are hidden in the history of this crystalline rock that was created in the early Paleozoic era (580 million years ago). These mountains are on the northern side of the Merano basin and continue to the Austrian border, bordered by Passiria valley to the east and Venosta valley to the south. Glaciers shaped these lovely series of ridges. The Sopranes lakes are the most beautiful remnant of this and a favored hiking destination. Here, you can explore 10 glacial lakes lying between 2,000 and 2,500m amid splendid natural sculptures and Alpine tundra. The lower slopes in Venosta valley are covered with unusual furrows known as *waale*. These drainage channels carry the cold glacial water to the mountain fields and helped to create a productive farming zone, which is dotted with durmast woods (lower down) and needle-tree forests (higher up), notably the larch wood in Senales valley and the Swiss stone pone forest in the upper Passiria valley. Forest is only found at the edges of the park since much of it is found at high and extremely high altitudes. In these extremes, tundra and rock vegetation thrives. You can also find stoats and the shy Alpine hare. The range of flowers includes the splendid *Soldanella montana*, rock jasmine, Alpine mugwort and purple saxifrage. These impenetrable spots are also home to some larger animals, like the chamois and ibex, which are true symbols of the mountains, along with the golden eagles that nest here.

A TINY KING

The goldcrest (Regulus regulus) is a bird in the kinglet family and, like its royal name, it has yellowy-gold feathers crowning its head that is particularly obvious when it is alarmed. Its Latin name means "little king". The little part of the name is also undeniable: at a mere 9cm long, it is the smallest European bird. Aside from the golden crown, it is like a small, olive-green ball of feathers and wings with short tail-feathers. Its kingdom is the conifer forest, especially when there are plenty of red firs, In its realm, it flits around, searching through the needles and twigs for blackflies, spiders and other little insects.

PARCO NATURALE PROVINCIALE MONTE CORNO/NATURPARK TRUDNER HORN

PROVINCE OF BOLZANO

AREA: 6.660 HECTARES. PORPHYRY AND DOLOMITIC RIDGE.

HEADQUARTERS: NATURAL PARKS OFFICE, VIA C. BATTISTI 21, BOLZANO, TEL. 0471414300

WEBSITE: WWW.PROVINZ.BZ.IT/NATUR

VISITORS' CENTERS: CENTRO VISITA MONTE CORNO (TRODENA, BOLZANO), TEL. 0471869247.

The park has some flora and fauna that is unique in Alto Adige. 90% of the park is covered in forest, hence the nickname 'Park of the Woods'. You can find all the various types of slopes typical of the southern Alps: the red fir woods around the harsh ridge of the Mt Corno ridge; the fields dotted with larch trees between Trodena and Anterivo that come alive with flowers in spring; the woods of beech and silver fir with an undergrowth of wood sorrel, woodruff, wood anemone and liverwort; Scotch pinewoods; arid fields; and the coppice woods. The latter, especially, are filled with durmast, hop hornbeam and manna-ash. This is the northernmost reaches of such woods, growing at heights of 1,000m. Shrubs and bushes bring color, in all seasons, to the sun-drenched slopes of the Adige valley. These are generally found slightly higher than the vineyards and fruit orchards, and include: the yellow flowers of the cornel tree, the white ones of the mahaleb, the deep blue fruit of the snowy mespil and the red bark of the ruscus. In this world of color, the 'classic' representative of the animal world is the green lizard. Amid the rocks you might spot the rare Greek partridge or, in the mixed woods, a nesting hazel grouse. The favorable climate aids numerous smaller birds, such as the nightingale, hoopoe, ortolan and bunting. The watercourses and peat bogs are home to various amphibians, water snakes and beetles. The park includes the porphyry and dolomitic ridges between the Adige valley, to the west, Cembra valley to the southwest and the San Lugano saddle to the north.

PARCO NATURALE PROVINCIALE PUEZ-ODLE/ NATURPARK PUEZ-GEISLER

PROVINCE OF BOLZANO

AREA: 10,196 HECTARES. DOLOMITIC PLATEAUX AND MOUNTAINS.

HEADQUARTERS: NATURAL PARKS OFFICE, VIA C. BATTISTI 21, BOLZANO, TEL. 0471414300

WEBSITE: WWW.PROVINZ.BZ.IT/NATUR

VISITORS' CENTERS: CENTRO VISITA MONTE CORNO (TRODENA, BOLZANO), TEL. 0471869247.

Odle, in the Funes valley

The northern border is the Erbe pass and the southern one the Gardena pass. Called the 'building yard of the Dolomites', it consists of plateaus, pastures, eroded peaks, ravines and forests. Geologists will be able to identify the types of calcareous-dolomitic sedimentation: the formations at Bellerophon in Funes valley; the layers of La Valle and San Cassiano, rich in marine fossils, such as the ray-shaped *Daonella*; the Sciliar dolomite, shaping the slopes to the north (Odle di Eores, Sasso Putia, Odle di Funes); the Raibl formation; the layers of Werfen; and much more. Above the conifers and bushes (Swiss stone and dwarf pine) lie meadows of flowers (in spring, *Soldanella montana*, bird's-eye primrose, crocuses; in summer, rock jasmine, monkshood and gentian). Above these, on the gravel and rock walls, you find edelweiss, mountain rampion and potentilla. Roe deer enjoy the pastures and chamois, the dwarf pines. There is other wildlife: the eagle owl is often seen in Vallunga; black grouses mate in the clearings of the upper woods; and beetles and butterflies bring color to the pastures.

PARCO NATURALE PROVINCIALE VEDRETTE DI RIES-AURINA/NATURPARK RIESENFERNER-AHRN

Province of Bolzano

Area: 31.505 hectares. Crystalline mountains of the Pusteresi Alps.

Headquarters: Natural Parks Office, Via C. Battisti 21, Bolzano, tel. 0471414300

Website: www.provinz.bz.it/natur

Visitors' Centers: Centro Visita Vedrette di Ries-Aurina (Campo Tures, Bolzano) tel. 0474677546.

The Vedrette di Ries are mountains of stone and glass because of the numerous glaciers and glacier-related phenomena, such as the moraine, erratic shapes, circles and lakes. At over 2,500m, you can find the Swiss stone pine (*Pinus cembra*), with its roots digging into the rock. The major Alpine animals might also be spotted: roe deer, marmot, chamois, ibex, deer, hares and pine martens. The birds that might be spotted include the Alpine chough, jay, and various species of tit, buzzard and goshawk. There are also black and wood grouses

The park has various marked trails that one can wander along: 1) To the Tauri pass. This follows the historical Krimmler Tauern route (route marker 14), which was used over the years by people from southern Europe to reach Salzburg. It begins at Casere (Aurina valley, 1,595m) and climbs to 2,633m at the pass, which lies beneath the Vetta d'Italia (literally, 'peak of Italy'). 2) Meetings. This guided tour takes about 6 hours, starting and ending at Anterselva di Mezzo. It includes a climb to Malga Grente (2,002m), a spot from which you get a lovely view of the Anterselva valley and the Vedrette di Ries. At the *malga*, they make hay and breed animals.

You can also explore the geological history of Armentara and the Prati della Croce. (For further information: Pedraces Tourist Association, tel. 0471839695).

PARCO NATURALE PROVINCIALE SCILIAR/NATURPARK SCHLERN

Province of Bolzano

Area: 5,850 hectares. Dolomitic mountains.

Headquarters: Natural Parks Office, Via C. Battisti 21, Bolzano, tel. 0471414300

Website: www.provinz.bz.it/natur

Visitors' Centers: Centro Visita Steger Säge (Bagni di Lavina Bianca, Tires, Bolzano), tel. 0471642196.

The silhouette of Sciliar (2563m), flanked by the Punta Santner and Punta Euringer peaks, is one of the symbols of Alto Adige.

The parks covers the whole limestone massif and the nearby Alpe di Siusi (6,817 ha), an area of exceptional natural interest. A 'step-like' shapes lends this protected environment a sense of enormity: the porphyry rocky base in the Fiè zone and at Castelrotto; the gentle volcanic and tufa plateaus, covered in grass, at Alpe di Siusi; the bastion-like summit of Sciliar, with its rugged, eroded sections. On the Siusi, Fiè and Tires side of Sciliar, the vegetation is typically Alpine with woods of various types of conifers and various forests, normally dominated by red firs. The high clay content at Alpe di Siusi means the pastures tend to be wet, even swamp-like, allowing bird's eye primrose and rot-grass to grow next to moss, sedge-grass, cotton-grass and rushes.

The scree and the higher rocky areas are rich in rare species, like the *Campanula morettiana* and the delightful *Physoplexis comosa*. In the park, you might see chamois, golden eagles, ravens and choughs.

The Sciliar massif dominates the pastures at Alpe di Siusi

CASTELLO DI TURES / BURG TAUFERS

Campo Tures/Sand in Taufers (Bolzano)
Tel. 0474678076

WEB: WWW.TURES-AURINA.COM

OPEN: MID-JUNE TO EARLY SEPTEMBER (THE CASTLE IS OPEN FROM EARLY JANUARY TO LATE OCTOBER AND, AT OTHER TIMES, BY BOOKING).

OPENING TIMES: WEDNESDAY AT 21.00, SERATA DEGLI SPIRITI (EVENING OF THE SPIRITS)

ADMISSION: ROUGHLY € 7

GETTING THERE

BY CAR: A22 BRENNERO HIGHWAY, BRESSANONE-BRIXEN EXIT, THEN THE SS49-E68 ROAD, THEN THE SS244 ROAD TO BRUNICO, FOLLOW THE SIGNS FOR CAMPO TURES (79KM FROM BOLZANO).

Castello di Taufers dates from the early 13th century, when the main tower was built. The keep and lower residential area were added at a later date. The square tower was built in the 15th century, as were the two bastions, the walkway and the drawbridges. The southwest wing was completed roughly a century after this. The best kept rooms are the Sala dei Giudizi (Judgment Room), the library and the so-called Stanza delle Streghe (witches' room), which derives its name from a legend about Margarete von Taufers, a noble lady who closed herself in the room for seven years before throwing herself from the window in desperation at the death of her beloved. It is said that the ghost of the hapless Margarete still haunts the castle. In summer, an unusual event challenges children aged 6 to 12 to overcome their fear during the Serata degli Spiriti (evening of the spirits): accompanied by two fairies, the children dress as ghosts and explore the armory, execution chamber and the dungeons while being told stories and legends.

TRENINO DEL RENON / DIE RITTNERBAHN

Collalbo/Klobenstein (Bolzano)
Tel. 800846047

WEB: WWW.SUEDTIROL-IT.COM/RENON/FERROVIA.HTM
WWW.SII.BZ.IT/IT/FUNIVIE-TRENO.PHP

OPEN: ALL YEAR

ADMISSION: CABLE CAR RETURN € 3,50, CABLE CAR + SMALL TRAIN RETURN € 7

GETTING THERE

BY CAR: A22 BRENNERO HIGHWAY, BOLZANO NORD EXIT, HEAD TOWARDS RENON (FINAL CROSSROADS PRIOR TO BOLZANO) AND THEN COLLALBO (CA 15KM).

The Renon railway line dates from the Austro-Hungarian empire, but it has been modernized and made more efficient. This is a convenient and ecological means of transport that allows one to undertake a lovely outing from Collalbo to Maria Assunta. This narrow gauge train covers a route of about 6km through woods and fields. The first stop, leaving from Collalbo, is Colle/Rappersbühl, which is the starting point for an itinerary going to the pyramids of earth. This is followed by other places that are also departure points for various outings, for example, Stella/Lichtenstern (the highest point) and Costalovara, with its little lake. Here, you can see one of the oldest houses in Renon, now home to the interesting Museo dell'Apicoltura (bee-keeping museum). Next you come to Soprabolzano and, then, the picturesque village of Maria Assunta. This trip can be combined with taking the cable car that connects Bolzano and Soprabolzano. At the ticket office and from the tourist offices, you can purchase all types of tickets, while on board you can only buy singles.

DAS MINENMUSEUM GRUA VA HARDOMBL

PALÙ DEL FERSINA (TRENT)
TEL. 0461550053

OPEN: IN MAY AND OCTOBER, SATURDAY, SUNDAY AND HOLIDAYS; IN JUNE AND SEPTEMBER, TUESDAY, THURSDAY, SATURDAY, SUNDAY AND HOLIDAYS; IN JULY AND AUGUST, EVERY DAY EXCEPT MONDAY

OPENING TIMES: GUIDED TOURS
10, 10.45, 11.30, 13.30, 14.15, 15, 15.45, 16.30, 17.15

ADMISSION: FULL-PRICE € 5, REDUCED (6-12 YEARS OLD) IS € 3.50

GETTING THERE

BY CAR: A22 BRENNERO HIGHWAY, TRENTO EXIT, SS ROAD TO PERGINE VALSUGANA, SANT'ORSOLA TERME, PALÙ DEL FERSINA; THE MINE IS NEAR THE PATH TO LAKE ERDEMOLO (CA 5KM FROM THE CENTER OF PALÙ).

The Fersina valley, known as the Mocheni valley by its German-speaking inhabitants, has been known to man since prehistory as a site of minerals and smelting. Today, the mineral-bearing cores are empty and the excavations are merely a reminder of the past. Yet, one can get a sense of the former importance of this sector by visiting the Grua va Hardombl mine, in use from the 1500s to the previous century.
Inside, you can see equipment and tools, original finds, minerals and other objects. During the visit, you have to wear the gear provided (hard hat and raincoat) and you must be accompanied by a guide. The maximum number in a group is 12. Entrance is at fixed times and booking is advisable. The entrance to the mine is at 1,700m and about 2km from the parking lot where you have to leave the car.
As such, it is best to wear suitable mountain clothes. A shuttle bus links the mine to the center of Palù, but this is only for groups of more than 20 on Sundays and holidays in July and August (book at least 5 days in advance).
The shuttle stops about 300m from the entrance.

MUSEO DELLE PALAFITTE/ PFAHLBAUTENMUSEUM

MOLINA DI LEDRO (TRENT), VIA LUNGOLAGO
TEL. 0464508182

OPEN: CLOSED DECEMBER, JANUARY, FEBRUARY

OPENING TIMES: MAR-JUNE 9-13 AND 14-17, CLOSED MONDAY; JULY-AUGUST 10-18; SEPTEMBER-NOVEMBER 9-13 AND 14-17, CLOSED MONDAY

ADMISSION: FULL-PRICE € 2.50, REDUCED € 1.50, FAMILIES € 5, 'SUMMER ACTIVITY' € 4-8

GETTING THERE

BY CAR: A22 HIGHWAY, ROVERETO SUD - LAGO DI GARDA NORD EXIT, HEAD TO LAGO DI GARDA - TORBOLE - RIVA DEL GARDA AND THEN LEDRO VALLEY; FROM THE OPPOSITE SHORE OF LAKE GARDA, ENTER RIVA DEL GARDA AND FOLLOW THE SIGNS FOR LAKE LEDRO.

The Museo delle Palafitte of Lake Ledro (Pile-dwellings of Lake Ledro) is located at the site of an archaeological dig of the Bronze Age settlement first uncovered in 1929. Aside from the reconstruction of a complete pile dwelling, the museum has a substantial collection of objects (ceramic cases, bronze objects, bone tools) and an area exploring the theme of imitation archaeology. In summer, the museum runs various initiatives for individuals and families, allowing visitors to immerse themselves in a prehistoric environment by, perhaps, exploring the complex process of smelting bronze, attempting to create fire or working natural fibers.
One of the most entertaining activities is the 'Merenda Preistorica' (prehistoric tea-time), in which you have to grind, knead and cook simple bread. You can also try archery with an ancient bow and arrows and take part in a Bàcmor (Stone Age canoe) competition.

High Altitude Cinema

Trentino-Alto Adige is a pristine natural world that cinema has used to great effect, starting with the mountaineering courage of Luis Trenker in the 1930s. This is a region that is historically divided into two parts, Italian and German, and yet closely linked in terms of the environment and culture. This is an area of stunning natural beauty with majestic peaks and glaciers, extensive valleys, thick woods, and crystal clear rivers, streams and lakes. Finally, there are the two regional capitals, Trent and Bolzano, with their wealth of monuments and art.

Mountaineers and Vampires on the peaks in Trent and Alto Adige

Luis Trenker explored the glory not only of Val Gardena but the entire region. He was born in 1892 at Ortisei/Sankt Ulrich and was a noted mountaineer, actor and director who, from the 1930s to 50s, used the stupendous scenery of Trentino and Alto Adige for his spectacular "mountain films". These films exalted the natural athleticism of the actors and audaciously filmed at great altitudes. Although the films have a certain depth through the recurring idea of leading a healthy and sporting life, Trenker also endows them with his sincere love for the mountains.
This aspect is reinforced by his ability to capture genuine emotion thanks to, above all, the mesmerizing and vertiginous locations. The landscape is the ideal backdrop not only for the action but also for the introspection, combined with an intense need for spirituality, which is so much a part of these high altitude stories. In 25 films, Trenker immortalized in every way imaginable the mountains of this region. Here, we will limit ourselves to the best-known ones and, more precisely, those filmed in these valleys and on these peaks, always in both Italian and German. *Mountains of Fire* (1931) is set in Alto Adige during World War I and marked Trenker's debut as an actor-director. The story is about a soldier from Alto Adige who is in the Austrian army, leading him to fight an old friend, the captain of the Italian Alpine soldiers. The two were once mountaineering buddies and their relationship

miraculously survives the war in this patriotic celebration of friendship between men and the powerful attraction of the mountain. *The Rebel* is from 1932. In the time of Napoleon's occupation of these parts, a student returns from Jena to find his small town half destroyed and his mother and sister murdered. He kills an enemy official, escapes and, with the help of his fiancée, organizes an anti-French insurrection. The film caught the imagination of the Americans to such a degree that not only did they co-finance it, but they also created a remake, with the same title and Trenker once again as the protagonist. Both versions give plenty of space to the mountains of Alto Adige around Val Gardena/Grödnertal and the surrounding valleys as well as displaying unquestionable technical and filmmaking skill in the mountain battle scenes. *The Prodigal Son* (1934), set in Ortisei, Alpe di Siusi/Seiser Alm and New York, tells of a mountain-dweller from Bavaria who, after saving the life of an American millionaire during a climb, is invited by the girl's father to visit the Big Apple. The impact of the metropolis of the mountain-man

is enormous and convinces him to return to his beloved mountains. The film is a simple and direct eulogy for the pureness of nature compared to the city. It has some stunning scenes, such as the one where the mountain peaks dissolve into the skyscrapers of New York. Lake Garda and the mountains are the setting for some scenes in *Prigioniero della montagna* (1955). In this film, Trenker tells the story of a boatman who has to escape into the mountains following a false accusation. Starting from Valsugana in the north, he heads to Pieve Tesino and Fiera di Primiero, before arriving in the San Martino di Castrozza zone with the extraordinary Pale peaks. Near here, in Venegia valley, the main set for Rachid Benhadj's *Mirka* (2000) was created. This French-Algerian writer tells the dramatic story of a 10 year-old child who was the result of an ethnic rape. The boy heads to a mountain village to find his mother. He finds a place to stay with an old, world-weary woman, but overcoming the distrust and xenophobia of the valley residents will not be easy. The mountain refuges, woods and silhouettes of the mountains are the backdrop for this unusual moral story against racism starring Gérard Depardieu and Vanessa Redgrave. From Canazei, we move via the Sella Pass towards Val Gardena, in Alto Adige. Amid unique and fascinating mountains, we head down to Ortisei, homeland of Giorgio Moroder, a composer who has won Oscars for three of his soundtracks, for *Midnight Express* (1977) by Alan Parker, *Flashdance* (1983) by Adrian Lyne and *Top Gun* (1986) by Tony Scott. From Ortisei we move into the Castelrotto/Kastelruth zone and, once again, Alpe di Siusi/Seiser Alm. In 1967, this sun-drenched plateau hosted Roman Polanski's crew for the macabre

comedy *The Fearless Vampire Killers!* The snow and glaciers of Alto Adige served as exterior shots in this film about Professor Abronsius and his assistants' (played by Polanksi) journey to Transylvania to study vampirism. The lovely Sharon Tate also appears in the film. Heading north from Ponte Gardena, we come to Bressanone/Brixen and then Brunico/Bruneck. This lovely town at the mouth of Pusteria valley/Pustertal was the birthplace of Nanni Moretti, one of the most inventive Italian directors – autonomous in both thought and filmmaking (director, screenwriter, producer, actor). His strengths are the irony with which he can describe the absurdities of society and his unique way of conveying the characters of people. For over 20 years his films have been making people think and laugh. Already well known in Italy, the film *Caro Diario (Dear Diary)* finally brought him international recognition.

Mountain cinema festival

In spring every year, Trent has hosted, for more than 50 years, the first and richest mountain film festival. It is characterized by its eco-friendly aims and the spectacular nature of the films that come from the world over. Over the 50 years of the Filmfestival di Trento, there has been an evolution, visible through the films shown, in the techniques and philosophies of mountaineering and the problems related to 'the mountain', namely, the environment, the territory and the impact of man on these aspects. The Filmfestival explores this theme through films and also through conferences, meetings and other events, such as exhibitions, photography competitions and material from the publishing industry. For further information: Festival Offices, Via S.Croce 67 at the Centro Santa Chiara, Trent; tel. 0461986120; www.mountainfilmfestival.trento.it

Whatever the season, this land is like an open-air gym immersed in nature with the charming backdrop of the delightful mountains. Moreover, this is a zone where you can easily enjoy the beauty, with stunning panoramas and enchanting glimpses of rare beauty. It is an ideal family spot. On foot, by bike, on horseback, with skis or using snowshoes, this region has endless possibilities for sport. There is even sailing, windsurfing and a host of other water sports (swimming, rafting, canyoning, kayaking, water-skiing, and so on). In addition to this 'traditional' range of options, there are some other, now fairly well known, options that offer real thrills, like paragliding or climbing.

For walkers

Walking is one of those sports without limits, even the limit of age. As you head up towards the Alpine pastures, nature comes ever closer. From the valleys, you can cross through woods and onto wide-open fields where the delightful tasting food in the refuges is a worthwhile reward for the effort of getting there. Some of the best (but not only) places for walking are the Venosta and Casies valleys and Alpe di Siusi. For those who are a little more advanced, there is a substantial network of paths and trails of varying distances, some even covering numerous stages. A few of these even cross the national border or require an overnight stay in one of the mountain refuges. This guidebook has a special section for these walks and includes some useful technical information. Perhaps the highlight is the Alta Via del Tirolo, which goes from Zillertal in Austria to Merano.

On horseback

There are many cycle paths that allow you to explore the territory, both in the towns and outside. These routes can also be used by horse-riding enthusiasts, after all, this is certainly the most rewarding sport for people who love to be in close contact with nature and animals. It is an ideal way to explore the beauty of the landscape of a region characterized by pristine nature.

Sailing

In summer, the numerous lakes that are dotted around the region are ideal destinations for sunbathing and swimming. In addition to this, these spots are great venues for lovers of sailing and windsurfing. The rivers and streams are ideal for paddleboat rafting, which is a thrilling sport where the only real requirement for starting is knowing how to swim. There are numerous exciting waterways to take on, but if you are an

adrenalin junkie, then perhaps you should try hang-gliding or paragliding, both of which are ideal sports for these conditions.

Thrilling rapids

Rivers and streams, whirlpools and tubes abound on the exciting runs down the

PanoramaPass–Val di Fassa

PanoramaPass, passed on the ski pass concept, allows you to use all of the 'ski-lifts' open during the summer in the Fassa valley. This initiative makes is possible to learn about and explore the Dolomites in a convenient way. You can take a lift up to a higher altitude and then walk along one of the paths, which vary in difficult and length, or merely relax and enjoy the panorama from one of the many mountain refuges. You can buy two types of PanoramaPass: one allows you to use it for any four days in a seven day period; the other, for any 6 days in a 13 day period. People who stay in one of the hotels or lodges linked to the Azienda per il Turismo della Val di Fassa (tourism association) receive one additional free day on the pass.

river in dinghies. This is canyoning, a relatively new sport that is especially popular in Alto Garda and the Ledro valley.

In Val di Sole, the Noce river is ideal for rafting and kayaking. A helmet and life jacket are essential for this thrilling sport where you bounce between the different river currents.

hut) where he could stay. When the cereal crops gave way to orchards, the irrigation system changed to spraying and many *Waale* fell into disuse. Some were maintained along with the paths, which now make an ideal route for a stroll through the woods and fields. There are also places where you can get something to eat and drink on the way.

BICIGRILL IN TRENTINO

The bicigrill are service stations for cyclists where you can get something to eat and drink, use the bathroom or take advantage of some shade in which to fill your flask or relax. In addition, local products are on sale and there are some basic services available if you need to carry out emergency repairs. You can also buy some bicycle spare parts, sports clothing, maps and informative material about the local routes. At present, there are two bicigrill in Trentino: at Novaledo (between Levico and Borgo Valsugana) and at Nomi (between Trent and Rovereto).

On the snow

Hundreds of kilometers of downhill skiing: large networks of ski-lifts leading to exciting and diverse ski runs. These slopes really do meet everyone's needs, including snowboarders, who revel in the snow parks. Cross-country skiing is equally interesting, with kilometers and kilometers of well groomed circuits.

The charming, silent landscapes are ideal for snow-shoe excursions. The advances in technology ensure agility whether walking up or downhill. Skis and sealskin are the favored equipment of ski-mountaineers. This discipline requires good skiing ability, knowledge of the mountains and fitness. Other options in this zone are sledding, hockey and ice-skating.

Walking along the Waale

The first record of the *Waale*, canals built to carry water from the side valleys to the villages and fields of Venosta valley, is from 1165. A *Waaler* was the man who maintained and operated the canals. To carry out this role, he went along the *Waalweg* (Waal path) every day. If the route to be taken was especially long, then there was a *Waalerhütte* (Waaler's

Nordic Walking

Nordic Walking is a new concept that strives to increase enjoyment and favors pristine nature. Specifically designed poles are used to ensure that 90% of the muscles in the body are used. The Trentino Nordic Walking Club has everything needed for an excursion: accommodation, trails, transport, luggage transfer and technical support. The accommodation is organized by indicating specific hotels equipped with everything necessary, from information to related activities, like hiking, *wandern* and theme outings. In addition, many Nordic Fitness parks have been created, with itineraries of varying difficulty and length: at Scena above Merano, in the Funes valley, at Alpe di Siusi and the Plan de Corones zone. Trentino's Nordic Walking parks, in Val di Sole, the Fiemme valley, the Folgaria plateau and Garda Trentino, offer a range of options, of varying difficulty and vertical change, starting form the valley floor. (For further information: www.trentino.to/mountainfitness, www.montagnaconamore.it, www.valdifiemme.info, www.valdisole.net, www.gardatrentino.it).

Breathtaking views

If you could mark the central point of the Alps, the mythical spot where the winds meet, then it would have to cover two provinces that, aside from obvious geographical elements, are mountainous in culture and tradition. Trentino and Alto Adige are, in many ways, the heart of the Alps. First, in geographical terms. The landscape is key: the walls and peaks in this zone are worth seeing in any season. There are numerous facilities and structures in the high mountains and these are often easy to reach, in many cases using ski-lifts that function throughout the year. Many of these structures are more like small hotels than traditional mountain refuges, making it possible for just about any type of hiker to explore the mountains and, even, the local food and wine. The Trento valley separates the Baldo, Brenta and Adamello massifs from the opposite slopes, where the plateaus are framed by the Lagorai Mountains and the Dolomites. The Rendena valley, Val di Sole and Val di Non are wide, creating plenty of space for villages and fields, but on the other side of the Adige, the Fiemme valley and Valsugana are somewhat more rugged. Further to the north, at Bolzano, the Isarco flows into the Adige after starting its journey in the high mountains. In Venosta valley, the glacial streams provide water for the rows of apple trees that, seen from the trails, form bizarre shapes. In the areas where the climate is milder, vineyards abound. Towards the east, the charming worlds of Badia valley, Val Gardena and Pusteria valley are the central valleys in a mountainous environment where the houses in the villages and the language are closer to those in the northern Alps than those you come across, just a little downstream, on the road from Trento. Two provinces and two cultures united by a passion for these valleys and the grand, pristine environment.

Monte Zugna

Mt Zugna rises a few kilometers outside of Rovereto and climbs to 1,864m. This itinerary explores the remnants of fortifications erected in World War One when Mt Zugna saw heavy fighting.

The route

The trail begins 200m beyond the open area around the Rifugio Malga Zugna (mountain refuge) (1,616m) and the astronomical observatory.
The asphalt road continues until a small chapel near which a boom across the road blocks access for cars. Here, the road becomes unpaved and a signpost has indications for the various trails. This trail continues along wide bends, heading higher in a gentle manner until it reaches the plateau known as Piazzale della Pace (Square of Peace), where there is an old war fort. An information panel gives more details about the history and uses of the

buildings. After the final structure on the right (the former field hospital), the track becomes single. Continue straight on. To the right, the hill seems flat but is not. Head on up past another signpost towards the summit of Mt Zugna. The path now becomes quite steep as it heads across a gravel section and then across the grass on a field dotted with bushes, Eventually, you come to the top, marked by a cross. Here, you can admire what remains of the defensive ramparts and some tunnels dug into the rock. From here, it only takes a few minutes to reach the small hill beyond the summit, from where you get a wonderful view of the mountain, and the rocky pass that precedes the summit. You can get there by going around the fencing of the antenna and heading down a tricky little path (red signs) that requires careful attention, but leads to the tunnels dug into the rock. From here, by keeping right,

THE ASTRONOMICAL OBSERVATORY

There is an astronomical observatory of Mt Zugna, in a zone where light and atmospheric pollution are practically absent. This first-class structure has a telescope with a diameter of half a meter. The center is used for a number of international studies and it is also the setting for various evenings and events of a more didactic and informatory nature. One of the weekly summer events is Astrogastro, combining the exploration of a starry sky with the tasting of typical cuisine from the nearby Malga Zugna (a traditional homestead).

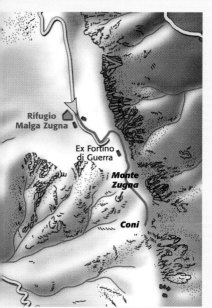

Rifugio
Malga Zugna

Ex Fortino
di Guerra

Monte
Zugna

Coni

Cipriana valley. From here, the route becomes more gentle and, from the base of Mt Selvata, you can make you way easily back towards the pass. There, an obelisk, a small church and a cemetery are a reminder of the bloody battles that led to this area being called the *Thermopylae of Italy*.

How to reach the start
From Trent, head south along the SS12 road to Rovereto. Near the castle, take the asphalt road (about 12km) that takes you right up to the area by Rifugio Coni Zugna (mountain refuge).

START
THE PARKING LOT AT THE RIFUGIO CONI ZUGNA (MOUNTAIN REFUGE)

FINISH: PEAK OF MT ZUGNA

VERTICAL CHANGE: 250M

TIME: 40 MIN TO THE SUMMIT. 1 HOUR VIA THE MOUNTAIN PASS.

DIFFICULTY: THE SECTION TO THE PASS IS STEEP AND REQUIRES CAUTION

BEST TIME OF YEAR: ALL YEAR

MARKINGS: ROUTE MARKINGS ON ROCKS AND TREES, STAKES WITH DIRECTIONS

MOUNTAIN REFUGES
RIFUGIO MALGA ZUGNA

ELEVATION: 1,616M

DISTRICT/ZONE: MT ZUGNA

OPEN: JUNE TO SEPTEMBER, SUNDAYS AND BY BOOKING

BEDS: 44

TEL. 0464917959

you head back down the bends through the bushes you passed in the final section of the ascent.

Possible extensions
If you want to carry on following the traces of the Great War, you can continue on past the summit of Mt Zugna and, by heading south, you come to the Buole Pass (1,462m), from where you get a spectacular view of the Carega Mountains and the San Valentino valley. Beyond the long gully, spotted with tunnels created by the military, is the beginning of the

The summit of Mt Zugna

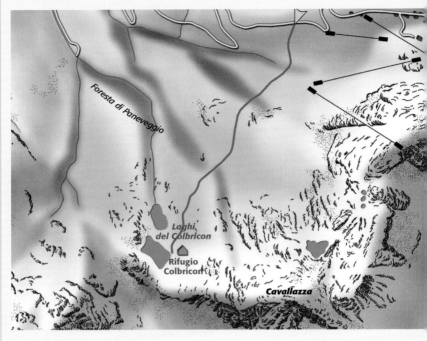

Rifugio Colbricon

The Rolle Pass, near Lake Forte Buso, lies between the Lagorai Mountains and Castellaz, connecting the San Martino di Castrozza area to Travignolo valley. A simple walk beneath the Pale di San Martino leads to the Colbricon lakes in the center of the regional nature park that has one of the largest fir forests in the Alps.

The route

From the Rolle Pass (or Malga Rolle), head off the road in a southerly direction and, after a short downhill stretch, you come to the lower cable station. From here, take trail no. 348. It is largely flat, running through the Paneveggio forest to reach Colbricon's Lake Alto, which has a refuge with the same name on the eastern shore. From here, you can admire the basin and Lake Basso, which is a few dozen meters below. The Colbricon lakes are named after the peak that rises above them with its rocky northeastern face, reaching 2,603m. The mountain refuge is well-known, being the first stopover point on the Sentiero Translagorai, which is a mountain route that crosses the area from Valsugana to the Fiemme valley. On the opposite shore of the lake you can see what remains of an Austrian barracks, a reminder that this area saw plenty of fighting in World War I.

How to reach the start

From the Egna-Ora exit on the A22 highway, take the SS48 road to Cavalese and Predazzo. At the latter, take the SS50 road into Travignolo valley. Beyond Lake Forte Buso, on the left shore, head right and up the winding road to the Rolle Pass, where there is parking.

START
THE MALGA ROLLE PARKING LOT

FINISH
RIFUGIO COLBRICON

VERTICAL CHANGE
— 60 M

TIME
45 MINUTES

DIFFICULTY
NONE

BEST TIME OF YEAR
MAY TO OCTOBER

MARKINGS
PAINTED MARKINGS ON ROCKS

Rifugio Colbricon and the adjacent Lake Alto, at the end of the route

TO THE SMALL AUSTRIAN BARRACKS ON THE
OPPOSITE SHORE OF THE LAKE

NOTES

THE FINAL SECTION OF THE TRAIL
CAN BE A CIRCULAR ROUTE ALONG THE RIDGE
OF MT CAVALLAZZA. HOWEVER,
THE VERTICAL CHANGE IS ROUGHLY
400M AND THE ROUTE IS ONLY
RECOMMENDED FOR EXPERT HIKERS.

MOUNTAIN REFUGES

RIFUGIO COLBRICON

ELEVATION: 1,927M

DISTRICT/ZONE: COLBRICON LAKES

OPEN: JUNE-SEPTEMBER

TEL. 0439768942

The Dinosaur Trail

The Lavini di Marco, in the Adige valley
to the south of Rovereto, is a giant
mound of enormous rocks that slope
sharply down to the valley. Here, over
200 million years ago, dinosaurs lefts
traces of their movements.

The route

The walk starts downhill on the tarred
road as far as the first bend, where you
head left onto an unpaved road. After a
few m you come to a wooden
information panel displaying the
morphology and trails of the valley.
Continue along the mule-track, stopping
at the information panels, until you

reach, after a slightly uphill, a stake
with directions. The route heading
down on the right goes to a gully where
you can see the first dinosaur prints.
Next, head back to the forestry road,
where you head right until you come to
the next sign: on the left, a gravel path
heads quite sharply up to a wooden
terrace from which you can make out

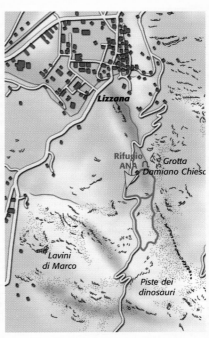

143

The Damiano Chiesa cavern

that cuts through a wooded area as far as the Damiano Chiesa cavern before returning to its starting point.

The Sentiero della Pace crosses the whole of Trentino, working its way along what was the frontline between Italian and Austrian troops in the Great War. You can see trenches, ammunition walkways and some old military fortifications.

How to reach the start

From Rovereto, head south towards the Sacrario di Castel Dante (memorial), located on a raised area overlooking the town. After this, continue upwards until the road ends, near Rifugio ANA.

other, larger tracks. The depth and width of the impressions suggest that the large animals where 5-6m long and weighed 1-2t. At the height of the Jurassic period, this zone was covered by an enormous expanse of water broken by long banks of sand, in which the animal tracks were made.

Heading up to the left once more (or by going back to the mule-track and then right until the next sign), you can follow a circular route along the Sentiero della Pace (Peace Trail)

Start
The parking lot at the end of the tarred road

Finish
The starting point

Vertical change
150 m

Time 1h30

Difficulty
None

Best time of year
March to November

Markings
Signs and information panels

The footprints on the left of the forestry road

Rifugio Fanes and Rifugio La Varella

The Parco Naturale Fanes-Sennes-Braies is one of the largest in Alto Adige. It lies between Badia and Pusteria valley, beneath the Cristallo massif. It covers areas of great environmental diversity, including woods, Alpine pastures and rocky plateaus with towering dolomitic cliffs.

The route

From Rifugio Pederù (mountain refuge)(1,540m) wooden signs clearly indicate the route to Rifugio Fanes and Rifugio La Varella.

A typical maso in front of the mountains in Parco Fanes

The spurs of Conturines La Varella

The route up can either follow the military mule-track or Sentiero 7 (trail 7), that works its way through tight bends along the side of Furcia dai Fers (2,523m). These bends take you up the first uphill section and into Valun de Fanes, which has some wonderful flowers. The next stretch is fairly flat, mixing rocky patches with areas of relatively short trees, including some fine Swiss stone pines. Once you have rejoined the mule-track, you come to the colorful Lake Picodel (1,819m), famed for its green water and the thick surrounding forest. You continue along the main road (with some stunning views, especially along the section where the road rises once more), enjoying the panorama that takes in the Piz de Sant Antone Mountains (2,655m). A slightly inclined stretch leads passed a typical Alpine summer pasture and to a fork that, heading left, takes you to Rifugio Fanes (2,060m). From the same fork, by heading right, you head along the route of a stream until Rifugio La Varella (2,042m) at Alpe di Fanes Piccola. The area, crossed by various brooks and dotted with ponds, is enclosed in a rocky amphitheater that includes the peaks of Sasso delle Dieci (3,026m), the Sasso della Croce Mountains, Piz La Varella (3,055m) and the Conturines (3,064m). Continue along Sentiero 7/12 until you come to a small bridge where, by heading left, you came to Lake Verde with its inviting shores. After returning to the bridge, you continue to Rifugio Fanes.

Possible extensions

From Rifugio Fanes, it takes about 30 minutes to reach the lovely Lake Limo. On Sentiero 10, after a fairly steep section

THE STUBE

In Alto Adige, the characteristic architectonic forms of the stube (farmsteads) reveal a spontaneous and varied taste that is, nonetheless, almost always centered on the, which is, quite literally, the area in the house that is the heart of all family life in Alto Adige. Once, the Stube was the only heated room in the house, thus becoming a refuge for all members of the clan and, consequently, the focal point for the socializing that helped to overcome the particular difficulties of life in these parts.
Days used to be spent working barren land, with extreme temperatures for much of the year. The first concrete examples of the Stube can be traced to 1200, although these were not in country houses but noble residences. From the 16th century on, this model of living was also adopted by the people living in the mountains.

that is made easier with gentle bends, you come to a panoramic, grassy plateau. From the back of this area, you can look down on the complex of houses and homesteads of Alpe di Fanes Piccola. Another 10 minutes and you can reach the shores of Lake Limo (2,159m), which varies in depth depending on the season. From the mountain refuge, you will need about 30 minutes to get there and the vertical change is nearly 60m.

How to reach the start
From Bressanone, head towards Brunico on the SS49 road and then into Badia valley and towards San Vigilio di Marebbe. From here, you can reach

SENTIERO 7/12 AND 10
EXTRA SECTIONS
TO LAKE LIMO
MOUNTAIN REFUGES
RIFUGIO FANES
ELEVATION: 2,060M
DISTRICT/ZONE: ALPE DI FANES PICCOLA
OPEN: JUNE-OCTOBER AND DECEMBER-MAY
TEL. 0474501097-
0474501097
RIFUGIO LA VARELLA
ELEVATION: 2,042 M
DISTRICT/ZONE: ALPE DI FANES PICCOLA
OPEN: JUNE-OCTOBER AND MARCH-APRIL
TEL. 0474501079

Along the route

Rifugio Pederù via a 12km scenic road (toll) through the thick Scotch pine wood lying at the base of the cliffs of Rudo valley.

START
RIFUGIO PEDERÙ
FINISH
RIFUGIO FANES AND RIFUGIO LA VARELLA
VERTICAL CHANGE
510 M
TIME: 2H
DIFFICULTY
NONE
BEST TIME OF YEAR
JUNE TO OCTOBER
MARKINGS
WOODEN SIGNS, ALTA VIA NO. 1,

Corno Nero
Not far outside the dolomitic area, under the silhouette of the Sella Mountains and the Ladin valleys, the Lavazè Pass is an exceptional starting point for various hikes through the surrounding, grassy slopes. The *malghe* (Alpine huts) offer wonderful opportunities to savor the local cuisine.

The route
Probably the most taxing (and most beautiful) ascent is the one up Corno Nero (2,439m). From the parking lot of the hotel with the same name, a sign indicates the direction to take, towards a bench amid some fields, not far away. From here, the trail becomes clearer and leads to a second route marker. The trail is clearly signed, with a marker

147

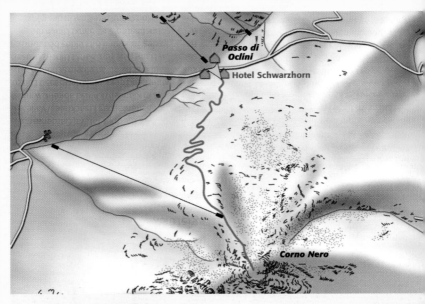

Passo di Oclini

Hotel Schwarzhorn

Corno Nero

with a red and white flag. You walk along the crag, passing through patches of wood and other, shorter vegetation, dominated by rhododendrons. The path is relatively sharply uphill until you come to a stony downhill (ski run). Head right, leaving the path and going to a small, wooden lodge. Once you have passed this, on your left, you continue to the cable station. The panorama opens up, revealing the pass below and the facing Corno Bianco (2,317m). Here, you take Sentiero 582 along the ridge, at this point without vegetation, heading up until you are only slightly below the summit, amid the porphyry rocks on the northwest face. Note that on some of the more exposed sections you need to take care and use your hands. At the end of this part, by heading left, you come to the summit, marked by a wooden cross.

The view is southeast, taking in Varena and Cavalese, as well as the Fiemme valley and the Làtemar Mountains. To get back down, you can go on a circular route that takes you back to the starting point. From the summit, follow the signs that, to the right (looking over the Fiemme valley), start from the area between the two summit

The basin at the foot of the mountain

crosses. There are some taxing stretches over a steep, rocky landscape. You then reach some large fields and a grass-covered saddle with what remains of a mountain chalet. Here, you leave the ridge and head down the rocky left face (white-red route marker) until you reach a small road near a brook. There, you head back up, in a northerly direction, on Sentiero 4. This stretch takes about an hour and then you are back at the Lavazè Pass.

Possible extensions

This suggestion can be seen more as an alternative than an extension. From the end of the tarred road, you head right across a pasture on the slopes of Corno Bianco (2,317m). As you climb, you head left until you reach an area of

How to reach the start

From Cavalese, head north until you reach Varena. From there, heading in the same direction, you climb through the wooded Gambis valley until you reach the Lavazè Pass. Here, you turn left and upwards until you reach the grassy plateau of the Oclini Pass, where you will find a parking lot.

START
THE PARKING LOT AT THE CORNO NERO HOTEL
FINISH: THE PEAK OF CORNO NERO
VERTICAL CHANGE
440M
TIME: 1H45
DIFFICULTY
SOME STRETCHES REQUIRE CARE AND SOME

Corno Nero from the Oclini Pass

dwarf pines and a stake.
From here, follows the signs for Weisshorn (Corno Bianco), to the left. Once out of the bush, you head up through a rocky area to the ridge, which is not too far above. Then, as you continue west, you can admire the enormous erosion furrow on the opposite face of the mountain.
Next you head down into the wood, towards Malga Gurndin (mountain hut, 1,952m). To get back to the Oclini Pass, from the hut head along the slope on the mule-track between the pastures.

MOUNTAIN EXPERIENCE
BEST TIME OF YEAR
JUNE TO OCTOBER
MARKINGS
WHITE-RED MARKS ON THE ROCKS AND TREES, STAKES WITH DIRECTIONS
EXTRA SECTIONS
AT CORNO BIANCO, A CIRCULAR ROUTE THAT LEADS TO MALGA GURNDIN. FROM HERE, YOU CAN ALSO REACH THE PASS BY TAKING, THROUGH THE PASTURES, AN UNPAVED ROAD THAT SLOPES DOWN (ALTHOUGH SEEMS FLAT) AND IS IDEAL FOR FAMILIES AND CYCLING.

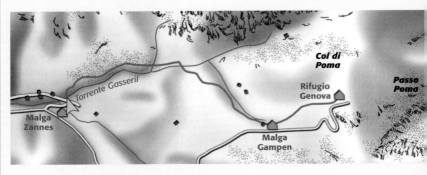

Rifugio Genova

In the lush green Funes valley, a hike leads to Rifugio Genova, near the Poma Pass. This is a good way to explore the lovely Parco Naturale Puez-Odle, a wooded zone between the Sass de Putia massif and the Odle peaks, which Reinhold Messner, born in the valley, climbed in his youth.

The route

From the parking lot at the Info Zannes information point (1,685m), various signs indicate the different trails. Follow the indications for Malga Gampen and Rifugio Genova. After taking some time to admire the steep, dolomitic cliffs of Odle (*aghi* in the Ladin language), you head towards the center of the park of Sentiero 33, which starts from behind the small wooden lodge with a bar. You head into a thick wood of conifers along a wide mule-track along the Kasserill stream. After passing a bridge on your right, you continue until a large clearing in a pastoral setting with a small chalet and a wooden fence. At this point, you cross the stream via a bridge and then head

uphill through open fields. From here, you can see the Odle Mountains, with a particularly good view of the Furchetta and Sass Rigais peak (both at 3,025m), which are characterized by tower-like shapes. Next, you head gently uphill until you reach an almost flat grassy area. This is the setting for Malga Gampen (2,062m), which is the end point for many walkers. To continue, you follow a slightly inclined section until you reach a point with various signs. Here, you head left and up the slopes of Odle di Eores. By now, Rifugio Genova (2,297m) is in sight and you continue by heading right along the trail that works its way through fields of flowers.

It is worth climbing a little beyond the mountain refuge, towards the Poma Pass (2,340m), so that you can see the summit of Sass de Putia and the mountains of the Parco di Fanes-Sennes-Braies, which overlook the Longiarù valley.

Possible extensions

On the climb to Sass de Putia, which reaches 2,875m, you are rewarded with a vast and stunning view of the peaks in

Corno Nero

the Parco Naturale Puez-Odle and the main mountains in the Dolomites. From Rifugio Genova, head along Sentiero 4 towards the bulk of Sass de Putia. You walk along an incline on a clearly visible trail that winds through pastures. A series of steep bends then lead into the gully, the bottom of which soon become rocky. To reach the summit you need to tackle a rocky stretch with ropes (already in place). This final section should only be done by experienced climbers. For others, the best bet is to head for the other summit, to the left, known as Piccolo Sass de Putia.

How to reach the start

From Bolzano, take the A22 highway towards Bressanone. At the Chiusa-Val Gardena exit, follow the signs for the

The section of path that borders on the rural properties

TREKKING DELLE LEGGENDE

The greatest treasures of Trentino are the extraordinarily beautiful mountains between the Fiemme, San Martino, Primiero, Vanoi and Fassa valleys, including Lagorai, Pale di San Martino, Marmolada, Piz Pordoi, Torri del Sella, Catinaccio and Làtemar. All of these are part of the Trekking delle Leggende project. This is a path through the breathtaking natural scenery of the Dolomites: nine stages covering 200 km of trails that uncover the mythology of the Dolomites. Trekking delle Leggende can involve one or more of the stages and can be undertaken with or without an Alpine guide.
Whatever form you do it in, it has everything you need for such excursions: accommodation, trails, transport, baggage transfer and technical support.
The projects means there are now maps, which can even be downloaded onto palmtops, and marked trails. In terms of the hotels, the ones that are highlighted are those that offer hikers what they need, from information to packed lunches.

Funes valley and San Pietro. From the latter, a road leads to the parking lot at Malga Zannes.

START: FROM THE PARKING LOT AT THE INFO ZANNES POINT

FINISH
RIFUGIO GENOVA

VERTICAL CHANGE: 612M

TIME: 1H50

DIFFICULTY: NONE

BEST TIME OF YEAR
JUNE TO SEPTEMBER

MARKING
WOODEN SIGNS, SENTIERO 33, ALTA VIA 2

POSSIBLE EXTENSION
TO SASS DE PUTIA, ABOUT 2 HOURS

MOUNTAIN REFUGES
RIFUGIO GENOVA

ELEVATION: 2,297M

DISTRICT/ZONE: POMA PASS

OPEN: JULY-SEPTEMBER

TEL. 0472840132

RIFUGIO MALGA GAMPEN

ELEVATION: 2,062M

DISTRICT/ZONE: POMA PASS

OPEN: JUNE-OCTOBER,

IN WINTER, A SIMPLE RESTAURANT
TEL. 0472840001

PUSTERIA VALLEY (SAN CANDIDO-LIENZ)

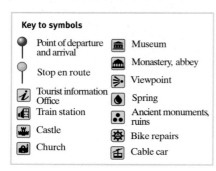

Key to symbols

Point of departure and arrival		Museum
Stop en route		Monastery, abbey
Tourist information Office		Viewpoint
Train station		Spring
Castle		Ancient monuments, ruins
Church		Bike repairs
		Cable car

ROUTE (CA 45KM): SAN CANDIDO - VERSCIACO - SILLIAN - ABFALTERSBACH – MITTELWALD - AUE - GALLIZENKLAMM - LIENZ. YOU CAN ALSO START FROM THE DOBBIACO TRAIN STATION AND, FOLLOWING THE 2.5KM CYCLE PATH, REACH SAN CANDIDO.

DIFFICULTY: ALL LEVELS. VERTICAL CHANGE OF 500M OVER 44KM ON GENERALLY GOOD ROADS.

BIKE + TRAIN: FOR TIMETABLES AND PRICES FOR TRAINS FROM LIENZ AND TO SAN CANDIDO WWW.DOLOMITI.IT/ITA/ZONE/PUSTERIA/IT6.HTM

BIKE SERVICE: PAPIN SPORT, M.H. HUEBER 1, SAN CANDIDO; TEL. 0474913450. CAN ALSO OFFER ASSISTANCE ON THE ROUTE.

TROJER MARTIN, VIA DUCA TASSILO (NEAR THE CHURCH), SAN CANDIDO; TEL. 0474913216.

TOURIST INFORMATION

ASSOCIAZIONE TURISTICA, PIAZZA MAGISTRATO 1, SAN CANDIDO; TEL. 0474913149; WWW.SANCANDIDO.INFO/

AZIENDA DI SOGGIORNO E TURISMO DI BOLZANO, PIAZZA WALTHER, 8 BOLZANO; TEL. 0471307000; WWW.BOLZANO-BOZEN.IT

A classic cycle-tourism route that can be done by all levels but offers the thrill of cycling in the mountains. The route starts along the cycle path from San Candido/Innichen,

in the heart of Pusteria valley, and follows the Drava river. You cross the Italian-Austrian border to get to Lienz, a small Tyrol town, heading through the charming setting of the Dolomites.

The route is 44km long, but not taxing. Indeed it is known as the Strada di Famiglia (family road).

The starting point is 500m higher than the finish. From Lienz, and other towns along the way, you can take the train to return to the starting point.

The start is the main square in San Candido and, by following the signs for the border (Confine di Stato), you reach Versciaco/Vierschach after 4km. Pass under the main road and the railway line, before continuing along the left bank of the Drava. The road is, at times, unpaved but always smooth. Continue to the border.

Immediately after the border, head left and across the Drava towards Sillian, the first village you come to in the Tyrol. Note the typical architecture of the zone. 13km after the start, you come to Sillian. Continue for a further 4km, until you cross the main road, and then follow the Drava.

Upon reaching Abfaltersbach, if you need, there is an assistance point for cyclists near the sawmill.

The landscape is delightful: green fields and soaring mountains.

Continue cycling, slightly downhill, until you reach Thal, where there is another assistance point at the Gasthof Aue (guesthouse). You are now 14km from the end and the remaining road is a gentle downhill that leads to Gallizenklamm and then, a further 4km away, to the train station in Lienz, a charming Tyrol town.

VALLE AURINA (GAIS-SAN GIACOMO)

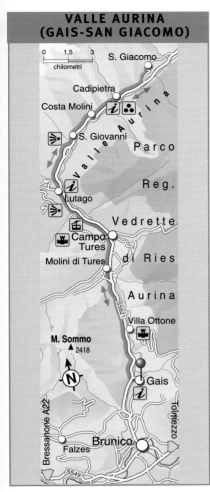

ROUTE (25KM OR 50 THERE AND BACK):
GAIS - VILLA OTTONE – MOLINI DI TURES –
CAMPO TURES – LUTAGO – SAN GIOVANNI –
CADIPIETRA – SAN GIACOMO. ON CYCLE PATHS.
YOU CAN, IF YOU WISH, RETURN TO GAIS BY BUS
(LEAVE EVERY 30 MINUTES).

DIFFICULTY: THE SETTING AND THE CALMNESS
MAKE THIS AN IDEAL RIDE FOR FAMILIES WITH
CHILDREN.

BIKE SERVICE: RAINER BIKE, VIA TALFRIEDEN
12, GAIS; TEL. 0474504526.

HOFER HUBERT, VIA AURINA 106,
CADIPIETRA; TEL. 0474652126.

TOURIST INFORMATION

CONSORZIO TURISTICO VALLI DI TURES E
AURINA, VIA AURINA 95, CADIPIETRA; TEL.
0474652081; WWW.TURES-AURINA.COM

ASSOCIAZIONE TURISTICA VALLE AURINA,
VIA AURINA 22, LUTAGO; TEL. 0474671257.

WWW.AHRNTAL.IT

ASSOCIAZIONE TURISTICA
VIA JOSEF JUNGMANN 8, CAMPO TURES;
TEL. 0474678076.

ASSOCIAZIONE TURISTICA GAIS-VILLA OTTONE,
VIA ULRICH VON TAUFERS 5, GAIS; TEL.
0474504220. WWW.GAIS.UTTENHEIM.COM

The route follows the cycle path running through the Aurina valley and heads to San Giacomo, a village engulfed by nature. The cycle starts from Gais, lying on a vast plateau a few kilometers from Brunico/Bruneck, where the clearly marked cycle path starts. It crosses the Tures valley and then into the Aurina valley. After a few hundred meters, you come to an artificial lake. Continue towards Villa Ottone and, as you close in on the town, you can see, through the green of the many trees, Canova castle. A further 10km, slightly uphill, takes you to Campo Tures/Sand in Taufers, the main town in the valley of the same name. Note the imposing castle. The backdrop for the cycle is an amphitheater of mountains and you can start to sense the Tyrol. Once you have passed Campo Tures, the view changes notably. The valley narrows and the route starts following the Aurino stream, through woods of fir, pines and larch, as well as vast pastures. At one point, the thick vegetation cuts off the view, but unexpectedly, high to the left, you can see the majestic Sasso Nero glacier. The route now starts heading slightly west, following the base of the Palù massif to Lutago, set in a green basin. After this village, the road continues northeast and you come to the only tough uphill on the route, which lasts a few hundred meters. Before reaching the Speikboden ski-lifts, the route heads back down and to the other side of the stream. After crossing the main road and entering another wood, but still along the stream, you continue along a relatively flat stretch. You pass San Martino/St. Martin and, a kilometer further on, San Giovanni/St. Johann in Ahrn. Next you pass through the Cadipietra/Steinhaus district and then, after 3km, you come to the small, charming village of San Giacomo. To return, you have to follow the same route back, which is now an enjoyable descent.

VALLE DELL'ADIGE (MERANO-BOLZANO)

ROUTE (38KM): MERANO – LANA – NALLES – ANDRIANO – FRANGARTO – BOLZANO. ASPHALT ROAD WITH UNPAVED SECTIONS.

DIFFICULTY: ASIDE FROM A FEW, SHORT UPHILL SECTIONS, THE ROUTE HAS NO PARTICULAR CLIMBS AND IS IDEAL FOR FAMILY OR GROUP CYCLING.

BIKE + TRAIN: YOU CAN RETURN TO THE START USING THE BOLZANO-MERANO LINE.

BIKE SERVICE: BIKE POINT MERAN, VIA PORTICI 337, MERANO; TEL. 0473237733.

JOSEF STAFFLER, VIA FELDGATTER 2, LANA; TEL. 0473562592. WWW.STAFFLERBIKE.IT

VELO SPORTLER, VIA DEI PORTICI 1, BOLZANO; TEL. 0471977719.

TOURIST INFORMATION

CONSORZIO TURISTICO MERANER LAND, VIA PALADE 95, MERANO; TEL. 0473200443.

WWW.MERANERLAND.COM

CONSORZIO TURISTICO BOLZANO VIGNETI E DOLOMITI, VIA PILLHOF 1, FRANGARTO; TEL. 0471633488. WWW.SUEDTIROLS-SUEDEN.INFO

AZIENDA DI SOGGIORNO E TURISMO DI BOLZANO, PIAZZA WALTHER 8, BOLZANO;

TEL. 0471307000. WWW.BOLZANO-BOZEN.IT

ALP BIKE - CICLOTREKKING, VIA FLAVON 101, BOLZANO; TEL. 3475203472-3498836578. WWW.ALPBIKE.IT

THIS SPORTS ASSOCIATION FOCUSSES ON CYCLE OUTINGS FAVORING MOUNTAIN BIKES WITH GUIDES THAT ARE NATIONAL MASTERS.

VARIOUS COURSES, INCLUDING ORIENTEERING, FOR CHILDREN AND ADULTS.

This route along the Adige river goes from Alto Adige to Veneto, passing Trentino. It includes a cycle path that, from the Lake Resia, runs down through Venosta valley and into the more open Adige valley. This is a classic cycle-tourism route and, combined with the train, is easy to do. From the center of Merano/Meran, follow the left bank for the Passirio river and then head left across the overpass and on to Marlengo/Marling and Lana. From Lana, follow the Strada del Vino (wine route) to Nalles/Nals and Andriano, and then, after 2km, to Lana di Sotto/Niederlana. After Via Brandis/Waalweg, the route becomes a gentle pedal through apple orchards. At the junction with the road to Gargazzone, keep on straight to Nalles without going through the town center. After a few more kilometers, you come to Andriano, and, at the junction that leads to Terlano/Terlan, head right and then immediately left. A slightly uphill takes you to a road that runs along the edge of the mountains. After a downhill stretch and beyond the hamlet of Unterrain, you reach the SS42 road that leads up to Caldaro/Kaltern. Head across the main road until you reach the section joining the cycle path from Bolzano/Bozen with the one along the Strada del Vino from Caldaro. By turning right onto the latter, you head up to Appiano along the Strada del Vino/Eppan an der Weinstrasse. Next you come to Caldaro and then to Termeno on the Strada del Vino/Tramin an der Weinstrasse (beyond Bolzano). If you continue straight downhill, you cross the Adige and the railway line. If you head right, you come to the 'confluence' with the path from Bolzano that follows the

A lane amid the fruit orchards

VALLE DELL'ADIGE (BOLZANO-TRENT)

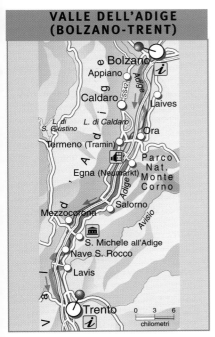

Bolzano, Piazza Walther 8, Bolzano; tel. 0471307000. www.bolzano-bozen.it

Consorzio Turistico Bolzano Vigneti e Dolomiti, Via Pillhof 1, Frangarto; tel. 0471633488. www.suedtirols-sueden.info

Ufficio Turismo Trentino, Via Manci 2, Trent; tel. 0461216000; www.apt.trento.it

The descent towards Trent along the Adige valley is a route that is rich in meaning: Trent is a historical stop along the north-south route and, as such, has always played an important role in connecting Mediterranean and Middle-European cultures. The cycle path, as it leaves Bolzano/Bozen, follows a bank between the Isarco and Adige rivers, which join further downstream. After crossing a bridge that takes you onto the right bank of the Adige, continue until Laives/Leifers. Another bridges takes you back to the other side of the river, where you head through apple and pear orchards. Near Ora/Auer, you have to go under the railway line and, by keeping right, you come to Termeno/Tramin. From Termeno, you cycle along the road to the Egna-Termeno train station, where you head left to cross the highway and the Adige. After a bridge, you come to Egna/Neumarkt, where you might want to admire the lovely porticoes in the pedestrian zone. After this, you head back onto the cycle path by the river. Aside from the lush vegetation of the Parco Naturale Monte Corno, on the left, note the bell tower of Salorno/Salurn in the distance. A few kilometers further along, you leave Alto Adige and enter Trentino. Keep following the cycle path, which has numerous places to stop, and after a wide bend in the river, you reach the Mezzocorona zone, at the mouth of Val di Non. After a further 1.5km on the cycle path, you cross the village of Grumo, where you need to head to San Michele all'Adige. At Nave San Rocco, you cross the Adige once more and then remain on the left bank as far as Trent. The sizeable flood plain of the Avisio river, which flows into the Adige, means that, once in sight of Lavis, you need to head back up the river to cross it at the first bridge. Once you have done this, you need to resume cycling in the correct direction after passing under the railway line and the highway. Trent is a few kilometers away.

Isarco river; by going left, you reach the center after about 20 minutes. The return can be done on the train or, if you wish, you can lengthen the route by doing a stretch of the cycle path (see the Bolzano-Trent route on the next page).

Route (63km): Bolzano - Termeno - San Michele all'Adige - Nave San Rocco - Lavis - Trent. On asphalt cycle paths (except for brief stretches). The starting point is the path that, from the Talvera river, runs down to where it joins with the cycle path of the Isarco; then you head right and keep going until you reach the Adige.

Difficulty: An easy route that, largely, follows the riverbanks.

Bike + Train: To return to the starting point, you need to take the train from to Bolzano.

Bike service: Velo Sportler, Via dei Portici 1, Bolzano; tel. 0471977719.

Theresia Vescoli, Piazza Principale 18, Ora; tel. 0471811233.

Tuttobici, Via Rosmini 103, Lavis; tel. 0461241999.

Cicli Giovanni Baldo, Corso 3 Novembre 70, Trent; tel. 0461915406.

Tourist information
Azienda di Soggiorno e Turismo di

VALSUGANA-CIRCULAR ROUTE OF SELLA VALLEY

ROUTE (29KM): BARCO - OLTREBRENTA – RONCEGNO TRAIN STATION - BORGO VALSUGANA - SAN GIORGIO - MALGA COSTA - BARCO. ASPHALT AND UNPAVED ROADS.

DIFFICULTY: A ROAD OF MEDIUM DIFFICULTY THAT REQUIRES ABOUT 3 HOURS OF ACTUAL CYCLING. THE ROUTE WINDS THROUGH A SECTION IN THE MID-MOUNTAINS AND THE VERTICAL CHANGE IS ABOUT 650M IN TOTAL.

BIKE + TRAIN: A SECTION FOLLOWS THE TRENT-BASSANO DEL GRAPPA RAILWAY LINE, PASSING THE STATIONS IN LEVICO TERME, NOVALEDO, RONCEGNO AND BORGO VALSUGANA.

BIKE SERVICE: PEPE CICLI E MOTOCICLI VIALE CITTÀ DI PRATO 29, BORGO VALSUGANA; TEL. 0461754268.

DEBORTOLI CICLI E ARTICOLI SPORTIVI; CORSO AUSUGUM 20, BORGO VALSUGANA; TEL. 0461752275.

CETTO CICLI, CORSO CENTRALE, LEVICO TERME; TEL. 0461701314.

TOURIST INFORMATION

AZIENDA PER IL TURISMO VALSUGANA VACANZE, VIALE V. EMANUELE 3; NUMERO VERDE 800018925; WWW.VALSUGANA.INFO

APT LAGORAI VALSUGANA ORIENTALE E TESINO, VIA DANTE 10, CASTELLO TESINO; TEL. 0461593322; WWW.LAGORAI.TN.IT/
IAT BORGO VALSUGANA, PIAZZA DEGASPERI, BORGO VALSUGANA; TEL. 0461752393.

ASSOCIAZIONE ARTE SELLA, TEL. 3392099226; WWW.ARTESELLA.IT

This is an ideal part of Trentino to experience and enjoy nature directly. Unpaved roads and paths lead to the calm waters of the Levico and Caldonazzo lakes, the woods and alpine grazing areas on the giant plateaus. Valsugana is an outdoor paradise. The tour through Sella valley runs from the valley floor, between Valsugana and Novaledo, to the mountain ridge running from Pizzo di Levico (1,908m) to Dodici Cime (2,336m), winding through woods and grazing land.

The starting point is near the church in Barco. Head straight until you come to an intersection, where you head left towards Lago Morto. After crossing the bridge over the Brenta river, continue straight and before the level-crossing, take the first road to the right, which follows the river bank. Continue on to the train station in Novaledo. At the level crossing, turn tight and, after reaching a four-way intersection, head left into Oltrebrenta. About 100m later, the unpaved road starts.

After reaching the train station in Roncegno-Marter, continue on, over the level crossing and then right onto the road to Fontana di Sotto. At the traffic lights in the center of Borgo Valsugana, you need to turn right to Sella valley. Follow this asphalt road to San Giorgio. Continue on to Hotel Legno, Hotel Val Paradiso and then Malga Costa (an unpaved road). From there, keep cycling until a fork, where you need to go left. You pass a pasture, go over a fence and follow the signs SAT "Barco di Levico - 203". Next comes a mule-track that, after a section through a wood, reaches a small hill with a good view. Continue along the bottom, following the trail through the grass, passing the odd rural building, until you reach an unpaved road. Head left and, after 350m, you come to a road over the brook. At this point, the real descent to Barco di Levico starts, following a bumpy route that borders on a field with some rural buildings. After passing a crag, you head down into a small, isolated valley and then to the gravel quarries. Once you have gone by the gully, you come to outskirts of Barco, marked by an isolated farmstead, and the end of the trail.

THE PLATEAUS IN TRENTINO - ANELLO DI LAVARONE

ROUTE (20KM): BERTOLDI - COST PASS - CAMINI – BELVEDERE FORT - MASI DI SOTTO - LAKE LAVARONE - MT RUST INTERSECTION - CARBONARE - BERTOLDI. 18.8KM ON UNPAVED ROAD, 1.2 ON ASPHALT. YOU CAN EASILY REACH THE START FROM FOLGARIA (10.5 KM) TOWARDS CARBONARE, WHERE YOU CONTINUE IN THE DIRECTION OF VIRTI AND THE SLAGHENAUFI CEMETERY.

DIFFICULTY: THE ROUTE IS QUITE SHORT, BUT IT IS NEARLY ALL ON UNPAVED ROADS AND PATHS. IN TOTAL, THERE ARE 4.5KM OF UPHILL, ALTHOUGH MUCH OF THE ROUTE IS UP AND DOWN, WITH MANY CHANGES IN DEGREE OF SLOPE AND SOME SHORT BUT TOUGH SECTIONS.

BIKE SERVICE:
MODA SPORT, VIA MAFFEI, COSTA DI FOLGARIA; TEL. 0464721321.

TOURIST INFORMATION

AZIENDA PER IL TURISMO FOLGARIA, LAVARONE, LUSERNA, VIA ROMA 67, FOLGARIA; TEL. 0464721133.

GIONGHI 73, LAVARONE; TEL. 0464783226.
WWW.MONTAGNACONAMORE.IT

This lovely route follows paths based on old military roads and forestry roads and trails that cross the Folgaria, Lavarone and Luserna plateaux along the former Austro-Hungarian border. This is the area of the challenging "100 km dei Forti" mountain bike race and is a wonderful zone for mountain biking in summer and spring.
To tackle the entire route, one needs to be in excellent shape, but it can be divided into three different circuits that wind along the plateaux of Folgaria (44km long; 1,055m of veritical change), Lavarone (20km; 360m) and Luserna (27km; 575m).

The Lavarone ring (the least taxing) starts from Bertoldi. Leave the car at the Slaghenaufi parking lot, near the military cemetery. The first section is up a forestry road. After about 400m, you come to an fork: keep right and then follow the main route, ignoring the deviations to the right. After about 1.5km, you join the "100 km" route and then you meet the Cost Pass road (asphalt), before taking the unpaved road down to Camini, which is recognizable by a large clearing in the wood. After a stretch with a lovely view of Astico valley, you come to an asphalt road, where you head left to the Belvedere fort. Following the "100 km" route, you pass Masi di Sotto, cycling by the typical stonewall that marks the edge

Lake Lavarone

of this property. Next, you go by Lake Lavarone and the Mt Rust intersection, where a 500m long ascent with a 9% slope starts. After this, there is a downhill section and, near the ski lifts, you leave the main route for the path that heads below these lifts. Here, you need to be careful to not lose your way (watch out for the lifts!).The last part is really beautiful and runs through a shady section of a wood.
You head down to Carbonare (asphalt), where you keep right, ignoring the "100 km" signs. Once at the intersection, cross the main roadand continue to the first fork, where you find the "100 km", indicating right, once more. Follows these to return to Bertoldi and the Slaghenaufi parking lot.

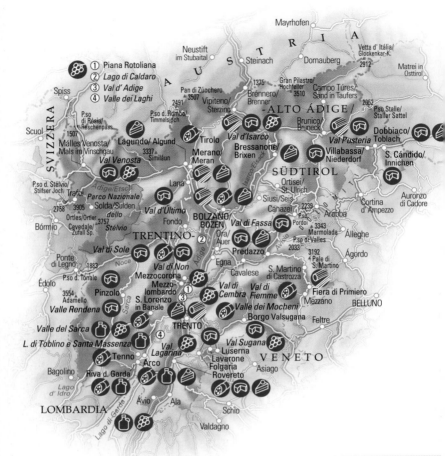

① Piana Rotoliana
② Lago di Caldaro
③ Val d' Adige
④ Valle dei Laghi

 PASTA	OIL
HAMS AND SALAMI	WINE
CHEESE	CAKES

Trentino-Alto Adige, forms a borderland between Central Europe and the Mediterranean culture found to the south. The result, in terms of gastronomy, is a combination of Austro-Hungarian and Italian cuisine. Common characteristics of the food here are traditional flavors and fresh mountain ingredients. Some of the highlights are the excellent apples grown in the area, the cured meats (especially speck), and other products made in the *malghe*, the old mountain farms with adjoining cowsheds where the longstanding cheese-making tradition is still alive and well. In terms of

Food

sweetmeats, there are plenty of regional specialties. Like for the main course, the desserts and cakes reflect the demanding requirements of living in the mountains, where it was once essential that food had to be not only highly nutritious but also easy to conserve.

Highlights

- Delicious farm produce made in the *malghe* (mountain farms)
- The mountain taste of Tyrolean speck
- The wholesome flavor of Trentino apples
- The excellent wines made in the valleys of Trentino-Alto Adige

Inside

Genuine mountain flavors

The Trent and Bolzano area is situated around the Adige valley. The most familiar image of the area is of its celebrated mountains, the Dolomites. These are beautiful, justly famous, and the subject of many local legends. A common factor in this "double" region is the mountain flavors. After all, this region has a dual identity, where the Latin spirit of the Province of Trent lives side-by-side with the Germanic soul of Alto Adige. This dualism can also be seen in the region's cuisine. We find *pasta e fagioli* (bean and pasta soup), a typical winter dish in the mountains of Trent, on the same menu as *Knödeln*, large bread dumplings in various forms flavored with meat or vegetables. The same menu might have *manzo alla trentina*, beef cooked with milk, and *Gulash*, a spicy stew dating back to the Habsburgs. In addition, it could have *polenta* made with maize flour, or sometimes potatoes, and different kinds of bread made from rye flour. The wines are probably Marzemino and Teroldego, made on the wine farms in the lower part of the valley, or Traminer made with Rhineland grapes grown in the triangle between Caldaro, Merano and Bressanone. In any case, regardless of these contrasts, the cuisine comes from the mountain tradition, where the ingredients depend on an economy based on fruit grown in the valleys, on the vines and crops grown on hillside terraces, on the natural products of the woods, on game and trout from farms fed with mountain water, on the meadows used for grazing, (mainly cows, but also sheep and goats), on pigs and on dairy farms where the milk is turned into delicious cheeses.

The superb, undulating landscape of the Altopiano di Siusi

Local produce includes apples and soft fruits such as strawberries, raspberries and blueberries; cheese, such as Grana Trentino and the strong-smelling Puzzone di Moena; salamis and cured meats, such as speck. Certain provinces are associated with specific products, but there are also many lesser-known products, creating a good excuse for studying the area more closely. For example, the '*Carne Salada*' (salt beef), typical of Valsugana, is usually served with beans according to a traditional recipe; or *Graukäse*, a cheese from the Pusteria valley, with its typical gray rind and strong flavor. Then there are other specialties with very limited production, such as the olive oil made near Lake Garda, the most northerly olive oil produced in Italy, which enhances the taste of fish caught in the lake; or the traditional Viennese-style cake-making tradition, with *Strudel*, one of the attractions of the pretty holiday resorts of Alto Adige.

The restaurants deserve a special mention. For starters, the venues are charming, ranging from restaurants in towns and cities, like those in the medieval center of Trent or below the worldly porticoes of Bolzano, to the small villages where romantics may choose between the *masi* (farmhouses) dotted in the meadows or little hotels tucked away in the woods. The professional skills of the restaurateurs also deserve the highest praise: they are faithful to tradition or apply innovative touches to traditional recipes. It is difficult to say whether it is preferable to visit the area in summer or in winter. There is such a wide choice of areas to explore here and tourism is one of the main drivers of the regional economy. Food and wine tourism in Trentino-Alto Adige is now officially one of the main tourist attractions and is currently the key feature of the region being promoted. This is demonstrated in initiatives such as the Strade del Vino and others like the "Osteria Tipica Trentina" club, as well as many events throughout the region, which combine culture with the pleasures of the table.

PASTA

Pasta, whether it is homemade or the industrial variety, is not as common in Trentino-Alto Adige as it is in other regions of Italy. Polenta, and, more particularly, gnocchi, compensate for this, especially *canederli* and *strangolapreti*, which is made using stale bread. There are many regional variations on the theme of gnocchi, including *gnocchi di ricotta*, flavored with more salted, smoked ricotta cheese, and *gnocchetti di spinaci* tossed in melted butter and sage, which originally come from the German culinary tradition. Finally, the gnocchi from the Pusterla valley are called *Schlutzkrapfen*, and are stuffed with spinach and cheese.

Canederli Trentini

In Trentino, *canederli* are large gnocchi made with stale bread and milk, sausage, bacon, Grana Trentino, egg, parsley, garlic, pepper and nutmeg. They are boiled in water or meat stock and then served either in the cooking stock or drained and tossed in butter with a sprinkling of grated Grana Trentino. *Canederli al Formaggio* or *Gnoches dà Formai* are a version of the typical Trentino gnocchi made with bread and, especially, cheese.

Gratini

This kind of pasta is used in the typical soups of Trentino. *Gratini* are made from a mixture of breadcrumbs, egg, nutmeg, cheese and salt. They look rather like large, irregular grains of rice and are boiled in meat stock before being served.

Knödel

Also called *canederli*, these large round gnocchi are made with white bread, milk, flour, egg and parsley. They are typical of the Province of Bolzano and are flavored in various ways with liver, salami, speck, spinach, nettles, beet, *crauti*, cheese and buckwheat. They are boiled in meat stock and served with the cooking stock.

Nocken

These long gnocchi typical of the Province of Bolzano are made with white bread, milk, flour, egg, parsley and one of the following ingredients, which give character and flavor: spinach, nettles, *crauti*, beet, cheese, buck wheat, and so on. They are normally served with melted butter and grated cheese.

Schlutzkrapfen

A typical dish of the Pusteria valley (Province of Bolzano), *Schlutzkrapfen* is a semi-circular filled pasta. The pasta itself is made with rye flour, a little wheat flour, egg and olive oil. First the pasta, which is quite firm, is rolled out into a thin layer. Circles of pasta are then cut out, filled with a mixture made of ricotta and spinach, flavored with chopped onion and nutmeg, and folded into half-moon shapes. *Schlutzkrapfen* are served with melted butter and a sprinkling of grated grana cheese.

Schwarzplentene Spatzeln

These small gnocchi are made with buckwheat flour, cheese and melted butter. In the Province of Bolzano, a special sieve is used to make these small gnocchi.

Schlutzkrapfen, filled with spinach and ricotta

Strangolapreti

These typical green gnocchi from Trentino are made with stale bread, milk, spinach (or other green vegetables similar to spinach, Swiss chard or nettles), egg, Grana Trentino, white flour, onion, salt, pepper and nutmeg. Once they have been boiled, they are served with melted butter, sage, and a generous helping of grated Grana Trentino cheese.

Tirtlan

This filled pasta typical of the Isarco valley (Province of Bolzano), is filled with spinach, ricotta, *crauti* and jam. The pasta is made with mashed potatoes, rye flour, wheat flour, onion, butter and milk.

BOZEN/BOLZANO

Pasta Fresca Gastronomia
Via Därer 9, tel. 0471201489
This pasta house only makes fresh pasta by hand. The typical shapes of pasta made here include *Schultzkrapfen* made with rye-flour pasta and *canederli*.

Meran/Merano
Pastashop
Via Portici 29, Tel. 0473270973
This pasta house makes fresh, handmade and slow-dried pasta. It is produced in various shapes, including the typical *canederli* flavored with spinach, speck, cheese, rocket, walnuts and mushrooms. It also makes various kinds of colored pasta with rocket, walnuts, chives, basil, *radicchio*, salmon, squid ink, lemons, oranges, spinach, chili pepper, nettles and tomatoes. You can also buy products from other artisan producers: honey, olive oil, balsamic vinegar, jams and fruit infusions.

TRENT/TRENTO

Pastificio Dal Lago
Via G. Mazzini 45, Via Esterle 14
Tel. 0461230557
This fresh pasta house chooses the mills from which it orders its flour with great care. It makes a wide range of pasta shapes and, in addition to pasta from other regions of Italy, *gnocchi*, *strangolapreti* and rolls of fresh pasta containing mushrooms or spinach. It also makes pasta with unusual fillings and is always open to new suggestions from its clients.

Fiera di Primiero
Pastificio Primiero
Via Garibaldi 19, tel. 043964413
This pasta workshop specializes in making fresh, pasteurized pasta using durum wheat and semolina. In terms of types, it makes traditional Italian pasta shapes, some local varieties and an interesting range of colored pasta: pasta made with tomato and spinach, blueberries, cocoa and beet.

Spinatspätzle, originally a typical German recipe, normally served with melted butter

Trentino-Alto Adige takes a pride in its long tradition of processing and maturing meat. In the case of speck IGP, production of this specialty in the South Tyrol dates back to the 14th century. As well as using meat from typical mountain species (such as roe-deer, chamois and red deer), the local charcuterie industry also employs refining and maturing techniques which rely a great deal on smoking. The smoke released by birch, juniper or beech gives salamis and cured meats an unmistakable aroma of resinous wood. These aromatic hints are further accentuated by the use of berries, spices and herbs in the curing process. It is during this process that producers have the chance to add their own creative touches to their products. Mother Nature sees to the rest, assisted by the favorable climate in the valleys and on the plateaus of the Alpine Chain and the Dolomites. 'Carne Salada', Luganega (sausage) and speck are eaten raw with the typical local rye bread, whereas Hauswurst, Probusto and Ciuighe are cooked first, served with polenta (made either with maize flour or potatoes) and washed down with one of the excellent local wines.

Carne di Cavallo Affumicata

This cured horsemeat is made around Rovereto (Province of Trent). All the processing is done by hand, using cuts from the haunch (rump or topside) or from the front of the carcass, which are processed in seasoned brine, and then smoked and matured. When cut, it is a deep red color and should be eaten thinly sliced, as it is, with whole meal or rye bread and butter, or with olive oil, lemon-juice and chives. It is also excellent eaten with fresh cheeses made from cow's or goat's milk.

Carne Salada

This specialty is made mainly in the hilly area around Riva del Garda, Arco and Tenno (Province of Trent). It is basically rump of beef which is left to marinate for about twelve days in a mixture of rock salt, bay leaves, black pepper, juniper berries, garlic and rosemary. It is eaten raw, in thin slices or it is basted with a little oil and vinegar and grilled. "Carne Salada" di Capra or Pecora is similar but made from mutton or goat's meat and comes especially from the Fiemme valley. Cuts of meat from the leg or back are left to marinate in a mixture of salt, pepper, garlic, Alpine yarrow, thyme and juniper, to which white wine is later added. After it has matured, it is red in color and has a taste reminiscent of speck.

Ciuighe

This is dressed meat produced in the area of Banale (Province of Trent), made with a mixture of the less valuable cuts of pork and beef (cheek, pork belly). When the meat has been lightly smoked, turnips, pepper and garlic are added. They should be eaten within a month and preferably cooked.

Hauswurst

This is homemade salami with a medium-rough grain made in small towns in Alto Adige. Pieces of beef and pork are finely

FOOD

Juniper berries, bay leaves, rosemary and various spices enhance the flavors of many of the cured meats and salamis of the Trentino Alto Adige

chopped and then seasoned with salt, pepper, garlic, pimento and mild paprika, after which the mixture is stuffed into pieces of pig's intestine. These small salamis (about 150g) should be eaten while they are still fresh, boiled, and served with crauti. Meraner Hauswurst, which is the local version made around Merano, is similar to the previous one but tends to be denser because water is added. The mixture is then made into sausages which are hung up to dry at a temperature of about 60°C/140°F, and are then cooked at 75°C/167°F.

Kaminwurzen
These small, smoked salamis are typical of the Province of Bolzano. Their aroma is dominated by smells of garlic, which is one of the ingredients, and the juniper used in the smoking process.

Lucanica Mòchena
This sausage is made in various versions in the Mocheni valley behind Pergine Valsugana (Province of Trent). Lucanica di Cavallo is dressed meat consisting of top-quality horsemeat and pork, seasoned with pepper, pimento and garlic. It is matured and eaten raw. Its cousin, the Lucanica Piccante is matured, dressed meat made of pure pork, seasoned with black pepper, chili pepper and garlic and is also

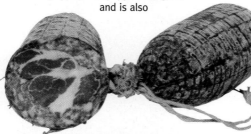

Lucanica, a sausage native to the Valle dei Mòcheni

eaten raw. The Lucanica Stagionata is a high-quality dressed meat made only with pork, seasoned with pepper and garlic, which is matured and then eaten raw. There is also a smoked version.

Luganega Trentina
Hand-made all over Trentino, the Luganega is a lean sausage made of top-quality pork and about 10% beef. Once the bones have been removed, fat is added and the mixture is minced to a rough grain, seasoned with salt, pepper and chopped or powdered garlic, stuffed into natural gut and made into sausages about 15cm long. The Luganega is then transferred to a ventilated room with a constant temperature for 30 days, and is matured for a maximum of 4 months in a cool maturing environment.

Mortandela Affumicata della Valle di Non
This hand-made salami looks rather like a large, flat rissole. It is made with minced pork meat, including the lungs, heart and throat of the pig, with a variable quantity of fat, to which salt and other seasonings are added. After the smoking process it turns brown.

Pancetta Affumicata
This lean bacon can be found all over the region. First it is cut into 2-3kg pieces, then it is rubbed with salt and pepper and left to rest for about a week under weights. Finally, it is smoked over a fire of juniper twigs. It is eaten both raw and cooked, and is used in various traditional dishes (*zuppa di crauti, canederli*).

Probusto
Probusto is a small sausage from the area of Rovereto (Province of Trent), made with pork, seasoned with pepper, mild paprika, pimento and mace. The sausages are smoked and then steamed. They are either boiled or cooked over the grill.

Prosciutto del Contadino/ Bauernschinken
The best cuts of pork meat are used to make this ham, which is common throughout the region. First the meat is dry-salted, then soaked in brine and then left to mature for 2-3 weeks. Finally, the ham is beaten, smoked and cooked.

Speck cotto/Südtiroler Bauernschinken
This is the typical ham of Alto Adige. The meat of the haunch of the pig is removed from the bone, dry-salted and spices are rubbed into the surface. It is then cooked in the oven and left to mature for 20 days.

Pancetta affumicata (smoked bacon) is one of the cured meats most commonly used in the cuisine of the Trentino

Speck dell'Alto Adige IGP/ Südtiroler Speck

The best known of all Alto Adige charcuterie, this cured meat, invented from the need to preserve meat, is first mentioned in the 1500s. The preparation, following a strict tradition, uses cuts of pork loin or haunch, which are sprinkled with a mixture of salt, pepper, juniper berries, paprika and bay leaves. The meat is then soaked in brine for about 2 weeks, after which it is smoked over a fire of juniper wood and matured for at least 4 months. The finished product weighs about 4.5kg and, when sliced, is a deep red color with white veining. Another common version of speck found throughout the region is made with meat trimmed from the leg of pork, which is smoked and processed in a dry seasoning bath of pepper, juniper berries and other spices. The product is then matured in a curing cellar for 100-120 days for the semi-mature type but takes a minimum of 6 months to reach full maturity.

BOZEN/BOLZANO

Antica Salumeria Masè
Via Goethe 15,
Tel. 0471978685
The cured meat and salamis sold here, produced in the Rendena valley, include speck, and small salamis made with venison, wild boar, chamois, and roe-deer. Local cheeses and other typical local products are also on sale here.

Antica Salumeria Masè
Via Goethe 15,
Tel. 0471978685
The products are made in the Rendena valley: salamis with deer, wild boar, chamois and roe-deer meat. Local cheeses and products are also sold.

Delicatessen Seibstock
Via Portici 15,
Tel. 0471324072
This traditional shop under the portico has a vast range of cured meat and salamis produced by small artisan butchers in Alto Adige. There is also a wide choice of regional specialties.

BRIXEN/BRESSANON

Schanung
Via Plose 14, Tel. 0472837748
Founded in 1887, this butcher's still uses the original recipes: speck, hams, smoked shin and filet of pork, and small salamis made of venison, chamois, wild boar and beef.

BRUNECK/BRUNICO

Karl Bernardi
Via Centrale 36,
Tel. 0474555472
www.bernardi-karl.it
In addition to the delicatessen and the butchery, there is a tasting room, which is also used for presenting the products made and sold here. Try their würstel (frankfurters) and speck.

EPPAN AN DER WEINSTRASSE/ APPIANO SULLA STRADA DEL VINO

Macelleria Franz Windegger
San Michele/Sankt Michael,
Via Johan G. Plazer 1,
Tel. 0471662153
www.windegger.info
The cured meat and salamis are made on site using traditional methods, and include prosciutto cotto, speck IGP, Kaminwurzen, Wurzen and manzo affumicato (smoked beef).

MÜHLBACH/RIO DI PUSTERIA

Macelleria Franz Pichler
Via Lanz 12,
Tel. 0472849721
The cured meats, speck and sausages made with garlic, game and chamois are all made, smoked and matured at a maso in the Pusteria valley.

VÖLS AM SCHLERN/ FIÈ ALLO SCILIAR

Macelleria Pramstrahler

Piazza Chiesa 15,
Tel. 0471725038
Purely traditional curing methods are
used here to make the typical cured
meats and salamis of Alto Adige:
speck, prosciutto di manzo (cured
smoked beef) flavored with juniper and
mountain herbs, prosciutto di cervo
(cured venison), cured meats and
salamis made with chamois and roe-
deer meat and raw salamis.

TRENT/TRENTO

Macelleria Ravagni

Piazza Duomo 43, Tel. 0461980061
Here you will find meat produced on

To guarantee the quality of the product, the
Consorzio di Tutela places a special brand mark
on the cheese

Trentino farms, fresh Lucanica, sausages
and other cured meats and salamis.
Postal

Via Carducci 30, Tel. 0461984636
This pork butcher's produces traditional
local cured meats and salamis: Lucanica,
cotechino (pork meat sausage), würstel
(frankfurters), "Carne Salada" and speck.

CAMPITELLO DI FASSA

Bottega della Carne

Piazza Centrale 4, Tel. 0462750401

To preserve the aroma of speck, it should
be stored in a cool place, wrapped in parchment
paper

This shop specializes in smoked Tyrolean
food and salamis made with pork and
game. It has a good range of freshly
made gastronomic specialties.

FOLGARIA

Macelleria Cappelletti

Via Emilio Coppi 1,
Tel. 0464721109
The recipe for making speck has been
handed down for generations and their
homemade raw salamis and würstel are
also made according to traditonal recipes.

MOENA

Felicetti

Via Nazionale 11, Tel. 0462573347
www.felicettispeck.it
This pork butcher's specializes in making
speck, in three different versions,
according to how long it has been
matured. They also make würstel, stinchi
affumicati (smoked shin of pork) and
sausages made with venison and the
meat of roe-deer.

RABBI

Macelleria Zanon

San Bernardo 169,
Tel. 0463985385
Here they make speck made in the
traditional Trentino way, which involves a
lighter smoking process than its Alto
Adige cousin. They also make excellent
coppa, lucanica, pancetta, salamis and
meat from locally reared animals, which
they slaughter themselves.

ROVERETO

Salumeria Giuliani

Via Rialto 34, Tel. 0464421334
Probusto is the specialty of this pork
butcher's, which also makes cotechino,
sausages, sausage meat and würstel.

CHEESE

One region, two souls; an incomparably beautiful setting for two cultures. One of Venetian influence, the other Central European. Some of the most magnificent mountains in the world cover about 90% of the region. The Alpine landscape is incised with valleys, home to people whose origins go back many centuries. The Venetian culture lives alongside that of the South Tyrol (now Alto Adige): they have different customs, which reverberate through their everyday lives and affect what they eat. But the local gastronomy crosses the mountains, spreading from one valley to another, sometimes remaining the same, and sometimes being subjected to diverse interpretations. Living in the mountains, people are brought together, farming in the Alpine pastures, moving the herds up to the Alpine pastures in summer and taking them down again for the winter, and making cheese in the Alpine dairies. Another unifying factor is the lifestyle geared to economy and saving, which has resulted in many different ways of preserving food: the meat is salted and milk is turned into fresh, matured or smoked cheese. Polenta is served with harder cheeses, such as Puzzone di Moena, Spressa or Vezzena in Trentino, and Graukäse in Alto Adige.

Algunder

Algunder is produced in the Burgraviato area (Province of Bolzano). Algunder Bauernkäse Halbfett, or Formaggio Contadino Semigrasso di Lagundo, is a round table cheese (6kg) made from low fat milk, with a body with evenly distributed eyes, and a mild flavor. It is matured for 60 days. Algunder Butterkäse, also called Formaggio di Lagundo, is made with whole milk and cream. The cheese (5kg) is cuboid in shape, with a strong taste, and the body has small eyes. It is matured for 60 days. Algunder Ziegenkäse, or Formaggio

The milk and cheese varieties made here conserve the smell and fragrance of the hay: pungent when freshly-mown and sweet when dry.

di Capra di Lagundo, is a round table cheese (1kg) made with goat's milk, with a strong flavor. It is matured for 30 days.

Asiago DOP

This famous cheese, named after the capital of the Sette Comuni plateau, in the Alto Vicentino (Veneto), has a production area which stretches as far as the valleys on the edge of the Province of Trent.

Canestrato

Produced in the area of Rovereto (Province of Trent), this round cheese (3-3.5kg) is made with whole cow's milk. The body is compact, semi-cooked and pale, with small, irregularly distributed eyes. It has a wrinkly rind and a flavor ranging from strong to spicy. It is fit for the table after 90 days and suitable for grating after 6 months.

Casolet

Also known as Casolèt dell'Adamello, they have been making this cheese in Val di Sole (Province of Trent) for hundreds of years. This round cheese (1-3kg) is made with whole cow's milk. The body is raw, tender and pale, with unevenly distributed small eyes. It is fit for eating after 20-30 days.

Dolomiti

Produced mainly around Predazzo (Province of Trent), this round soft cheese (3 kg) is made with whole cow's milk. The body is raw, tender and pale, with irregularly distributed small or small-medium eyes.

Fontal

This round cheese (10-12kg) made of whole cow's milk was invented in the 1950s in Val di Non. The body is raw, pale, compact but soft, with irregular, sparse, medium-large eyes.
The Trent version can be distinguished from Alto Adige version because of the unusual taste of the milk produced in the mountains.

Formaggio Affumicato/ Räucherkäse

This cheese is made from low fat milk. The body is soft with small, irregularly distributed eyes. It has a mild taste, and a characteristic flavor, which it acquires during the final processing. After it has matured, it is smoked for several days over a fire of resinous wood.

In the Trentino, the variety of cheeses conveys the spirit of enterprise of the many milk co-operatives

Formaggio Alta Pusteria/ Hochpustertaler

This cheese is typical of the towns of Dobbiaco and Villabassa (Province of Bolzano). It is a matured cheese and comes in two versions: made with low fat milk (max 35% fat) and whole milk (min 45% fat). This round cheese (12kg) has a distinctive taste.

Formaggio Aschbach Magro/ Aschbacher Magerkäse

Produced in the area of Burgraviato (Province of Bolzano). It is a round table cheese (5kg) with a mild flavor and has a body with regularly distributed eyes. It is matured for 30 days.

Formaggio d'Alpeggio/Alpkäse

This cheese is mainly produced in the northwestern part of the Province of Bolzano, especially in the *malghe* of the Venosta, Ultimo and the Isarco valleys. The body is medium-hard and it is made with raw cow's milk. The cheese is round and weighs between 4.5kg and 8kg. The body is smooth, the color varies from pale yellow to ivory, and the eyes are small and regularly distributed. The flavor depends on how long it is matured: mild when it is matured for a short time and strong when it reaches full maturity (60 days).

Formaggio Fresco Aromatizzato/ Zieger

This cheese is made with skimmed milk using a natural acid coagulation process and is small and conical (150g). The body is crumbly with a mild after-taste, and is sometimes flavored with pepper and herbs.

Formaggio Originale Dobbiaco/ Toblacher Stangenkäse

This cheese is typically produced around Dobbiaco and Villabassa. A table cheese made with low fat cow's milk. Rectangular in shape (5.5kg), it is matured for 45 days.

Grana Padano Trentino DOP

The word "Trentino" marked all over the edge of the cheese guarantees that the cheese was produced locally but also that it was made observing fairly stringent standards in terms of the diet of the dairy cows used for producing the milk (only fresh grass, hay and cattle feed consisting of cereals and leguminous plants). It is made with low fat milk, has a hard body, a flaky consistency and a distinctive taste.

Graukäse

Made particularly in the Pusteria and the Isarco valleys (Province of Bolzano), this cheese is made from skimmed cow's milk with the occasional addition of pepper or aromatic herbs. According to the old-fashioned method, only raw milk is used. The rind is thin and grayish in color. The body is friable and granular, and slightly oily. It has a pronounced, rather acidic taste.

Inticina

The name refers to the old Latin name of San Candido (Province of Bolzano), which is the center of production. The taste of this round, soft cheese (12kg) varies from mild to strong, depending on how long it has been matured (up to 3 months).

Montagna

This typical round cheese (9-12 kg) of Borgo Valsugana (Province of Trent) is a hard, semi-cooked cheese made with whole cow's milk. It has a distinctive yet delicate flavor.

Monte Baldo/ Monte Baldo Primo Fiore

This is a typical round Trentino cheese with a wonderful taste and aroma, made from low fat cow's milk. The body is medium-hard, semi-cooked, and is an intense straw color in summer and a pale straw color in winter, with evenly distributed eyes. It is matured for between 7 months and 4 years. The Primo Fiore label is only applied to *Malga* cheeses made when the herds are grazing the Alpine pastures and the grass is full of aromatic plants.

Nostrano

Nostrano is a Trentino medium-hard round cheese made from whole cow's milk. The body is semi-cooked, pale with small-medium, irregularly distributed eyes. This round cheese (9-12kg) is matured for at least 2 months. Nostrano is a by-product of Grana Trentino since it is made with the whole milk from the morning milking left over from making the other cheese. It is mainly produced in Val di Non. Nostrano de Casel is a round cheese (6-9kg) made according to an ancient recipe. It is a medium-hard,

semi-cooked, pale cheese with sparse, medium-size, irregularly distributed eyes. It is usually matured for between 3 months and a year (or more). Part of the cream is skimmed off to assist the maturing process and to make butter. With a few regional variations, this cheese is made throughout the valleys of Trentino. Nostrano di Malga is made with either whole or skim cow's milk, in a similar way to the previous cheese but in Alpine pastures. About 90 *malghe* in Trentino still produce this cheese. Nostrano di Primiero is a locally produced, prestigious cheese, made in an area which has a particularly dynamic dairy industry based on the many active *malghe* around Primiero.

Ortler

This typical cheese of the Venosta valley (Province of Bolzano) is made with skim milk, and comes in wheels weighing 3kg. It has a reddish rind, a soft body with small, irregularly distributed eyes and an aromatic, spicy taste. It is matured for 60-80 days.

Pustertaler Bergkäse

Produced in the Pusteria valley (Province of Bolzano), especially around Brunico, this round cheese (9kg) with a reddish rind is made from low fat milk. The body is firm with variable eyes. It has an intensely aromatic flavor and a walnut-like smell. It is matured for 60-80 days.

Puzzone di Moena

Its Ladin name, Spetz Tsaorì, means 'cheese with a strong flavor'. This round cheese (9-12kg), made with whole cow's milk, is typical of the Fassa valley (Province of Trent). The body is medium-hard, semi-cooked, soft and pale with sparse, small-medium eyes. It is matured for between 60 days and 8 months. When fully mature, the rind is ochre-yellow, smooth and slightly oily, since the surface is treated with warm, sometimes salted water. This process encourages anaerobic fermentation inside the cheese, giving it a distinct taste and a strong aroma.

A dairy production house of Grana Trentino cheese: the curds are placed in the molds

Spressa delle Giudicarie DOP

This round cheese weighing 7-10kg is one of Trentino's traditional mountain cheeses, a legacy of the time when local farmers used to skim off as much cream from the milk as possible to make butter.

Spressa cheese is the result of the habit of skimming the cream off the milk to make butter

It is typical of the southwestern part of the Trentino mountains, around Pinzolo and the Rendena and Chiese valleys. It has a dark, lumpy rind and a very low-fat content. It is a compact, pale cheese with sparse, small-medium eyes. It is matured for at least 3 and sometimes more than 6 months. It has a strong fragrance and a slightly bitter taste.

Sextner Almkäse

This is a typical round table cheese (7kg) of the Pusteria valley (Province of Bolzano), made with at least 50% fat. The body has regularly distributed eyes. The strength of the taste and smell are linked to how long it is matured.

Stelvio/Stilfser

Typical of the Venosta valley (Province of Bolzano), this is a soft cheese with irregularly distributed, small or medium-size eyes that is made with milk from cows grazing on Alpine pastures. It is round (9-10kg) and slightly concave with a typical reddish rind. The mature cheese (after 60-90 days of aging) has an aromatic, intense flavor.

Vezzena

One of Trentino's most ancient and traditional cheeses, it is produced on the Vezzena, Lavarone, Folgarìa and Luserna plateaus (Province of Trent). Before the Great War, it was practically the only cheese used to season food, and was grated over soups and used to flavor *canederli* and other mountain dishes. Over time, it lost ground to grana, which is now the most common cheese to season food. It is a round (8-10kg), semi-fat cheese, with a medium-hard body and a few sparse eyes. The Mezzano type is matured for 4 months; the Vecchio for more than 1 year and the Stravecchio for more than 2 years. It has a lively taste which grows in intensity to a spicy peak. It can be eaten as is or grated.

BOZEN/BOLZANO

Milkon Alto Adige
Via Campiglio 13/A, Tel. 0471451111
The largest dairy in Alto Adige, it sells cheese made on the premises as well as yogurt, milk, cream, butter and ricotta. Book beforehand for a guided tour.

BRUNECK/BRUNICO
Dariz Delikatess
Via Stuck 2, Tel. 0474410177
This cheese-shop is about 30 years old. It selects cheeses made with cow's and goat's milk from *malghe* on small farms.

INNICHEN/SAN CANDIDO
Sennereigenossenschaft Innichen
Via Castello 1, Tel. 0474913317
The dairy opened in 1875 and is famous for its mountain, herb and semi-fat cheeses.

SEXTEN/SESTO
Holzer Alimentari e Vino
Moos, Via Heideck 2, Tel. 0474710599
It sells a broad range of cheeses, some matured in grape-pressings and rosé Moscato, as well as speck made from the pigs reared by the owners.

TOBLACH/DOBBIACO
Sennerei Genossenschaft Toblach
Viale S. Giovanni 25, Tel. 0474972045
Founded back in 1882, today, this shop has an impressive cheese-counter with various types of Originale Dobbiaco, Fontal, grana, and cheeses from the Pusteria valley, butter and milk.

TRENT/TRENTO

Gastronomia Mattei
Via Mazzini 46 Tel. 0461238053
This shop has a selection of local cheeses such as Spressa and Puzzone di Moena. It also sells typical salamis and cured meats.

La Gastronomia
Via Mantova 28, Tel. 0461235217
In the old town center, a veritable 'food boutique' with a host of typical local foods: cheeses from Lavarone, goat's-milk cheeses, sausages, mortandela (a type of salami) and dried meat from the Valsugana.

Consorzio Produttori Latte Trento e Borgo
Via Campotrentino 9, Tel. 0461820722
A member of the Consorzio Trentingrana, it sells cheese made on the premises as well as cheeses made by other local consortiums.

CAMPITELLO DI FASSA

Caseificio Sociale Campitello
Via Pent de Sera 11, Tel. 0462750301
This dairy, a member of the Consorzio Formaggi Trentini, sells its own products as well as cheeses made by other members of the consortium, including Nostrano Val di Fassa.

CAVALESE

Caseificio Sociale Val di Fiemme
Bivio, Via Nazionale 8, Tel. 0462340284
All the products made at this dairy are on sale here: Fontal, goat's-milk cheeses, Grana Trentino, Nostrano, milk, butter and yogurt.

FOLGARIA

Caseificio Sociale Folgaria e Costa
Costa, Via Maffei 269, Tel. 0464720763
A dairy with a marvelous cheese-counter, including Vezzena, Asiago, Grana Trentino and soft cheeses flavored with herbs or walnuts.

MEZZANO

Caseificio Sociale Comprensoriale
Primiero, Via Roma 179, Tel. 043962941
www.caseificioprimiero.co
This dairy has been doing business for 20 years, and has a vast range of local cheeses: fresh, matured and *malga*-made Primiero, Asiago Pressato, Latteria, Trentingrana and Dolomiti.

PREDAZZO

Caseificio Sociale di Predazzo e Moena
Via Fiamme Gialle 48, Tel. 0462501287
www.puzzonedimoena.com
Make a note of this address if you want to buy the much-prized Puzzone di Moena. Other products include Dolomiti, Fontal, Grana Trentino and Nostrano.

ROVERETO

Finarolli Alimentari
Via Mercerie 7/9, Tel. 0464434319
This shop has been doing business for more than a century. It has a wonderful array of Italian cheeses to choose from. In terms of local cheeses, look for the Casolèt and Puzzone di Moena.

Nowadays, it's hard to find Vezzena cheese, which is only made in a few malghe (Alpine dairies) between the Valsugana and the Vallagarina

TAIO

Trentingrana
Segno, Via Cooperazione 4
Tel. 0463469256
www.trentingrana.it
The Consorzio Trentingrana has transferred some of its activities to Taio. A major step in this process was to convert a local dairy into a maturation warehouse. In addition, a shop was added so that you can buy interesting dairy products, including Trentingrana, Spressa, Vezzena, Puzzone di Moena, milk and butter.

VILLA LAGARINA

Caseificio Pinzolo-Fiavè-Rovereto
Via Pesenti 2, Tel. 0464413513
They produce classic local cheeses, including good Grana Trentino, Asiago Pressato and Asiago d'Allevo and Fontal.

FOOD

The cultivation of olives in Trentino-Alto Adige is limited to the Sarca river valley, which benefits from the fact that it flows into Lake Garda. Not only does it have fairly high minimum temperatures but also low maximum temperatures throughout the year. In a region like Trentino-Alto Adige, olives can only grow in the areas with a mild climate, near the lake (actually, near the lakes, since there are other lakes in the valley) but they must be planted on hillside terraces or on hillsides protected from the wind, since the valley floor gets severe frosts in winter. The DOP Interregionale Garda label specifically mentions Trentino and names ten towns, starting with Riva del Garda, Nago-Torbole and Arco. Here, olive-trees are cultivated alongside oleanders and palm-trees, giving rise to what can be described as cash-crop farming. Further along the valley, they begin to thin out. Then, at Lake Toblino and Lake Santa Massenza olive-trees suddenly dominate the landscape again (together with castles and old farmhouses dotted among the vineyards). The types of olive grown here are the Garda (varietal Casaliva), Frantoio, Pendolino and Leccino. These varietals represent at least 80% of the olives grown in the area. Each year, the two olive-presses in the area produce 80,000-120,000kg of green olive oil with traces of gold. It has a pungent, delicately fruity taste with hints of herbs. It is particularly recommended with fresh-water fish from lakes or rivers, either boiled or grilled, but also with an Alpine specialty called "Carne Salada" (salted meat), which is best eaten thinly sliced and sprinkled with some lemon-juice and, of course, olive oil.

TRENT/TRENTO

ARCO
Frantoio Ivo Bertamini
Vignole, Via Mazzini 12, Tel. 0464517229
One of the few producers who also sells the delicate extra-virgin olive oil of Lake Garda. The oil is also used in cosmetics.

RIVA DEL GARDA
Associazione Agraria Riva del Garda
Via Lutti 10, Tel. 0464552133
www.agririva.it
This olive oil producer has a lovely spot, north of the lake, between the enormous expanse of water and the hillside. You can also buy Lake Garda extra-virgin olive oil on site.

THE BREAD-BAKING TRADITION OF TRENTINO

One thing you should definitely try with olive oil is the local bread. The variety of bread in this region deserves a chapter to itself in the context of Italian bread production. In the Province of Bolzano alone, they make more than 100 different kinds. This is the kingdom of brown bread, a scrumptious concoction of perfumes and natural ingredients which comes in many different, interesting shapes. Because the Alpine climate doesn't suit wheat, the farmers grow rye, millet, oats and barley. These cereals are used extensively to make bread. Here, bakers like to enhance the already distinctive flavor of the less common cereals with strong, characteristic aromas. When they prepare the dough, using natural rising agents, they add different kinds of seeds such as fennel, cumin, pumpkin, flax, poppy, sesame and sunflower. They also use various herbs, and all kinds of dried fruit: pears, apples, walnuts, hazelnuts, and so on. Once upon a time, bread was kept in the attic, so that it would develop new aromas while it was drying. It was then used in many regional recipes, to make various kinds of canederli, the Trentino version of strangolapreti, and croutons to garnish delicious soups. Many local recipes use bread for making cakes and pastries. The many types of traditional bread made in the region include Bauernpaarl, which contains rye flour, clover, cumin and fennel seed, Bechipanzalini, which is typical of the Province of Trent, Brezel, which is traditionally eaten with salami, cured meats and beer, and schiacciatina, a type of focaccia made throughout the region.

WINE

Record quality, a record number of varieties

The valley of the Adige river, where the vineyards of Trentino and Alto Adige are situated, has been a winemaking area for a very long time, with a tradition that goes back many centuries. Today, this is reflected in the variety and excellent quality of its wines. In fact, the area was famous for its wines in Roman times, when vineyards covered a much greater area than at present, owing to the different climatic conditions at that time. Then, during the Middle Ages, wine-production became the monopoly of the monasteries in Bavaria and Swabia, which established branches south of the Brenner Pass, maintaining the exclusive rights over the grapes until the Napoleonic period. The Istituto Agrario di San Michele all'Adige was founded in 1874. This farming institute was very influential during the more recent history of wine-production in an area where the growing of vines in mountain areas has become increasingly specialized. The wine-production sector, which is extremely important in the regional economy, involves about 9,000 hectares in the Province of Trent and 3,800 hectares in the Province of Bolzano. Here, the fact that the environment is ideal for vine-growing means that farmers can concentrate their efforts on producing the highest possible quality, and such a variety of wines is difficult to find elsewhere. The region is the fourth-largest producer of fine wines in the national scenario, but first in terms of the percentage of DOC wines grown on its territory. On the subject of DOC, the largest area of DOC wines is Valdadige (Adige valley), a title shared with the Veneto region, whereas, at a provincial level, bottles are marked with Alto Adige and Trentino labels. Of the last two, the former includes all the wines grown in the Adige valley (more than 30 wines!), which are divided into geographical sub-zones, including the famous wines of Santa Maddalena and Merano hill. The only exception, Lago di Caldaro DOC, is from a single area. The second label includes such DOC wines as Casteller, Teroldego Rotaliano and Trento, the latter having the exclusive rights on using the *metodo classico* (classic method) for making spumante. Many grape varietals are grown here: the vines dating back to the earliest times have been joined by other varietals from north of the Alps, both from Germany—these play an important part in the regional scenario—and France. The main method of training vines here, which is typical of the region, is the single or double pergola method, when the vines are trained along overhead trellises.

The vineyards of Trentino

The wine-growing area of the Province of Trent is an extraordinarily varied area, most of it in the valley of the Adige river, stretching from the border with the Veneto to the border with Alto Adige, marked by the place where the valley narrows at Salorno.
There are two offshoots at the beginning

The vineyards of Alto Adige

FOOD

173

of Valsugana and the Cembra valley, and there is another quite separate area of production in the valley of the Sarca river, north of Lake Garda. The vineyards constitute a mosaic of grape varietals, where traditional varietals, like Marzemino and Teroldego, grow alongside foreign varietals, like the Pinot and Cabernet vines, introduced in the late 19th century, or Chardonnay, planted here in the 20th century by the Istituto Agrario Provinciale di San Michele all'Adige to give new life to the white wines of the area.

The vineyards of Alto Adige

In Alto Adige, the vines form a spectacular landscape. Vineyards are planted on hillsides and on the lower slopes of the valley stretching from Salorno to Merano, on the sunny slopes of the Venosta valley as far as Silandro, and between Bolzano and Bressanone on either side of the Isarco river. Significantly, almost all the vineyards in this area produce wines with DOC labels. The Province of Bolzano, as a whole, lies in the production area of Alto Adige DOC, which includes various wines which, today, are made from specific grape varietals or come from a specific geographical sub-zone. The range of wines produced here is considerable, especially the traditional red Schiava grapes, which have played a major role in the winemaking of Alto Adige since medieval times. The latest generation of wines includes Pinot Nero and Cabernet, which are increasingly aged in barriques.

Casteller DOC

This wine is produced in the Lagarina valley, on hills up to an altitude of 600m. Made with the typical red grapes of the region, this wine (minimum alcohol content of 10.5%) tends to be a ruby red of varying intensity, with a light, pleasant bouquet and a dry or semi-sweet taste. It is ideal with soups and boiled meats, although the rosé version is best with starters and mild cheeses. There is also a Superiore version, which is aged for up to 2 years and has a minimum alcohol content of 11.5%.

Gewürztraminer/Traminer Aromatico

This wine is excellent with fish and shellfish and light meals, with a minimum alcohol content of 11.5%. It has a straw-yellow, golden color, a slightly to intensely aromatic bouquet and a full, dry, pleasantly aromatic taste.

Kalterersee/Lago di Caldaro DOC or Kalterer/Caldaro

Made with Schiava grapes, this table wine has a light to medium ruby red color. It has a delicate bouquet and a smooth, harmonious taste, with almond-like undertones, and a minimum alcohol content of 10.5%. It is classified into 3 categories: Scelto, with a minimum alcohol

content of 11.5%; Classico, if it is produced in a certain area; and Classico Superiore if it undergoes further processing (both carry the Alto Adige-Südtiroler label). The Scelto variety is recommended with white meats, and can be aged for up to 2 years.

Marzemino

Marzemino, a historic Trentino DOC wine, is made from the grape of the same name. Marzemino is mentioned in Mozart's opera, Don Giovanni. It is mainly cultivated in the area of the Lagarina valley, where it grows particularly well. It has a bright ruby red color, a full, rounded bouquet, with hints of almond and violet, a full, dry taste with an almond-like after-taste, and should be drunk young. It is particularly recommended with duck, kid, medium-hard cheeses, hot cured meats and salamis served with polenta. The best variety is the Riserva, aged for 2 years and with a minimum alcohol content of 11.5%.

Nosiola

This light, white wine is made with the grape of the same name, and should be drunk young with delicately-flavored dishes. Straw yellow in color, it has a delicate bouquet and a dry, slightly bitter taste. Minimum alcohol content 10.5%.

Pinot Nero/Blauburgunder

Made with the grape of the same name, this table wine is aged for up to 2 years and has a minimum alcohol content of 11.5%. Ruby red in color, with hints of orange in older wines, it has a heavenly bouquet and a dry, smooth, rounded taste, with a bitter after-taste. The Riserva, which must be aged for 2 years, is recommended with red meats and game. There are two white versions recommended as an aperitif or a table wine: Spumante Brut, lightly sweet, and the dry Extra Brut.

Südtirol Sankt Magdalener/Alto Adige Santa Maddalena DOC

This is a table wine, with a minimum alcohol content of 11.5%, made with various sub-varietals of Schiava grapes. The color varies from ruby red to deep garnet, with a winey, heavenly bouquet reminiscent of violets after a short period of aging. It has a rounded, smooth taste with hints of almond. The wine is aged for more than 3 years. It is classified as Classico/Klassisch, if produced in the older winemaking area

FOOD

BEER FROM THE FIEMME VALLEY

The reputation of the Trentino beer from the Fiemme valley (Province of Trent), known as Birra di Fiemme, dates as far back as the 19th century. It is slightly fizzy, a touch cloudy and straw yellow in color.

Wine Categories

Three labels define Italian wines according to quality. IGT (Typical Geographic Indication) guarantees vine cultivation according to certain regulations. DOC (Controlled Origin Denomination) indicates conformity to regulations on area of origin, and production and maturation procedures. The top label is DOCG (Guaranteed and Controlled Origin Denomination); there are around 20 DOCG wines in Italy, 6 in Tuscany. VDT is for table wine with an alcohol content of at least 10%.

around Santa Maddalena, and Vigna/Gewächs (Wachstum), accompanied by the name of the place where it was made.

Südtiroler Terlaner/Alto Adige Terlano

This pale, straw-yellow wine is ideal with fish. It has a delicate, fruity bouquet and a dry, slightly acidic taste. It has a minimum alcohol content of 11.5%. It is classified as Classico/Klassisch, if produced in the older wine area, or Vigna/Gewächs (Wachstum), accompanied by the name of the place where it was made.

Teroldego Rotaliano DOC

This is one of the symbols of wine-production in this area. It is mainly produced in the Piana Rotaliana area, where the landscape is dominated by expanses of pergola vineyards and protected by the surrounding mountains. The wine is a deep ruby red, with hints of violet, an intense bouquet of fruit and flowers, and a dry, flavorsome, smooth taste, with a hint of almond. There are two types: Superiore, with a minimum alcohol content of 12%, and Riserva, aged for 2 years, with a minimum alcohol content of 12% (both are excellent with roasted meats). It is also recommended with game, kid, polenta and hard cheeses. The rosé version is recommended with more delicate dishes, such as starters, soups and medium-hard cheeses.

Vin Santo

This dessert wine is made exclusively from the indigenous grape varietal Nosiola, which is mainly grown in the Valle dei Laghi area. When the grapes are picked late in the season, bunches in which the grapes are wide apart are selected, spread on trays and stored, usually in the attic. Assisted by the constant ventilation from the Ora wind which blows from Lake Garda (see page 57), the grapes are left to dry for five or six months. Then they are pressed and the must is put in oak vats to ferment for between 6 and 8 months. Vin Santo is a lovely golden yellow tending towards amber, smelling slightly of dates, with the sweet, smooth taste typical of wine made from *passito* (dried) grapes. Highly recommended with the typical sweets and cakes of Trentino and blue cheeses. It is aged for 3 years, or for 5 in the case of the Riserva.

WINE LEGEND

Wines are listed with symbols which indicate their type

● red
○ white
◑ rosé
◐ sweet or dessert

BOZEN/BOLZANO

Cantina di Bolzano
Piazza Gries 2, Tel. 0471270909
www.kellereibozen.com

●   Alto Adige Santa Maddalena Classico Huck Am Bach DOC
●   Alto Adige Santa Maddalena Classico DOC Sellerei St. Magdalena
○   Alto Adige Traminer Aromatico Kleinstein DOC Sellerei St. Magdalena

EPPAN AN DER WEINSTRASSE/ APPIANO SULLA STRADA DEL VINO
Stroblhof
Via Pigano 25, Tel. 0471662250
www.stroblhof.it

○ Alto Adige Gewürztraminer DOC
Pigeno
● Alto Adige Lago di Caldaro
Scelto DOC Burgleiten

KALTERN AN DER WEINSTRASSE/ CALDARO SULLA TRADA DEL VINO
Cantina Ritterhof
Via Strada del Vino 1, Tel. 0471963298
www.ritterhof.it
○ Alto Adige DOC Gewürztraminer
Aromatico Gral
○ Alto Adige DOC Gewürztraminer
Ritterhof
● Alto Adige DOC Lago di Caldaro
Scelto Ritterhof
Prima&Nuova/Erste&Neue
Via della Cantine 5/10, Tel. 0471963122
www.erste-neue.it
● Alto Adige DOC Santa
Maddalena Gröbnerhof
● Alto Adige DOC Lago di Caldaro
Scelto Puntay
● Alto Adige DOC Lago di Caldaro
Scelto Leuchtenburg
○ Alto Adige Traminer Aromatico
Puntay

TRENT/TRENTO

Cavit
Via Ponte di Ravina 31, Tel. 0461381711
www.cavit.it

● Teroldego Rotaliano DOC Maso
Cervara
● Teroldego Rotaliano DOC
Bottega Vinai
○ Trentino DOC Nosiola Bottega
Vinai
● Trentino Superiore DOC
Marzemino d'Isera Vaioni

ROVERETO
Conti Bossi Fedrigotti
Via Unione 43, Tel. 0464439250
www.bossifedrigotti.com
● Trentino Superiore DOC
Marzemino Selezione
Campo Bove
● Trentino DOC Marzemino
○ Vigneti delle Dolomiti I.G.T.
Traminer Aromatico
● Vigneti delle Dolomiti I.G.T.
Teroldego
● Vigneti delle Dolomiti I.G.T.
Teroldego Trecento

SAN MICHELE DELL'ADIGE
Zeni Roberto
Grumo, Via Stretta 2,
Tel. 0461650456
www.zeni.tn.it
● Teroldego Rotaliano DOC Pini
● Teroldego Rotaliano DOC
Vigneto Lealbere
○ Trentino DOC Nosiola Vigneto
Maso Nero

FOOD

SPUMANTE FERRARI

This is one of Italy's best-known sparkling wines and is made exclusively with grapes grown in Trentino. The metodo classico production process for spumante is a combination of technology and tradition. The grapes are only lightly pressed and yeast is added to the must to assist fermentation and maintain the original aroma of the grape. Usually, the wine starts as a blend of various superior wines, a mixture known as the cuvée. The wine ferments again in the bottle thanks to the addition of the liqueur de tirage, a cane sugar, yeast and wine

solution, which triggers second fermentation. The wine continues to "work" in the bottle for at least 2 more years. Then it is enhanced by adding the liqueur d'éxpedition, a high sugar-content syrup added to metodo classico spumante wine prior to the final corking, which adds other aromas and perfumes. Ferrari spumante comes in various versions matured for different periods of time: 10 years for Giulio Ferrari Riserva del Fondatore, 5 years for Brute Perlé Rosé, 4 years for Brut Perlé and 3 for Rosé.
www.cantineferrari.it

LIQUEURS

Trentino-Alto Adige is one of the areas where grappa is produced. This is so for two main reasons: the fact that excellent wine is produced here, resulting in large quantities of aromatic grape-pressings, and the local metal-working tradition, which specializes in the manufacture of stills. Distillates of fruit (blueberries, pears, apricots, and so on) are also made here, to satisfy the Central European passion for them. There are also liqueurs made with herbs, a true Alpine tradition.

Amaro Valle di Ledro

This liqueur made in Trentino has a low alcohol content (20%) and is an infusion of medicinal herbs: gentian, gentianella, lady's mantle, Chinese rhubarb, Alpine avens, bitter oranges and liquorice.

Genziana/Enzianschnaps

This alcoholic drink is made all over the region and is obtained from infusing the roots of the great yellow gentian (*Gentiana lutea*). It is greatly appreciated for its tonic and digestive properties. In the Rendera valley (Province of Trent) it is distilled using a still called the 'Tullio Zadra bain-marie'. Alcohol content: 40-45%.

Ginepro or Gin Distillato/ Kranewitter

This alcoholic drink is made from juniper berries and is well known all over the region for its tonic properties. In Trentino, these distillates are made using a still known as the 'Tullio Zadra bain-marie' method. Alcohol content: 40-45%.

Grappa di Mirtillo con Frutti/ Schwarzbeerschnaps

This liqueur is made in Alto Adige with grappa, blueberry juice, sugar, natural flavorings and water. It is very aromatic and drunk as a digestif.

Grappa di Vinaccia/Treber

This distillate from Alto Adige is made with the fermented grape-pressings of local grapes. Traditional copper stills are still used.

Grappa Giovane – Metodo Tullio Zadra/ Junger Grappa – Methode Tullio Zadra

This grappa with an alcohol content of 40-45% is made from fresh Trentino grape-pressings using the 'Tullio Zadra bain-marie' method.

Imperatoria/Kaiserswurz

This brandy, made from the aromatic roots of masterwort, is typical of the Rendera valley (Province of Trent). The 'Tullio Zadra' distilling method is common all over the Province of Trent. Alcohol content: 40-45%.

Liquore al Mugo/Latschenschnaps

This typical liqueur of Alto Adige is made

by soaking the fresh buds of the dwarf pine in grappa for at least 40 days.

Nocino/Nusseler

This famous Alto Adige liqueur is made by flavoring alcohol or grappa with green walnuts, spices and sugar.

Picco Rosso

This liqueur made from raspberries and strawberries has a high alcohol content (61%), and is typical of the Ledro valley (Province of Trent). It is bright red in color and has an aromatic perfume and flavor. No extra sugar is added.

Stomatico Foletto

This liqueur is characteristic of the Ledro valley (Province of Trent) and is made by infusing medicinal herbs: gentian, gentianella, lady's mantle, Chinese rhubarb and bitter oranges. In the last century, 'Tintura Stomatica Foletto' was well known as a digestif and a laxative.

CAKES

Trentino-Alto Adige is a region with a dual ethnic identity and this also applies to the cakes and desserts made here. Salorno, where the Adige valley narrows, is an administrative boundary and, in many ways, also a gastronomic boundary. On one side of it lies the culinary tradition of the Veneto, albeit altered to suit the mountain palate, while, on the other, lies a cuisine based on the Austrian model, further divided into the peasant cooking of the Ladin people and the refined dishes once prepared at the courts of the Habsburgs. In many cases, the ingredients are similar: milk and cream, chestnuts and apples, plums and apricots, walnuts and forest fruits. Their respective vocations for making wine are also similar: Moscato wine is made on both sides of the "divide". The most obvious distinction between the two areas, for climatic reasons, is the kind of flour they use. The flour in Trentino is white or yellow while, in Alto Adige, it tends to be dark, especially the rye flour. However, the decisive factor differentiating the two areas is a historical one. Despite the fact that they shared the yoke of Habsburg dominion for a long time, the two provinces absorbed the culture in different ways. From Bolzano to Bressanone, the cakes and desserts are based on Viennese principles: the *Sachertorte*, *Krapfen* (doughnuts) and those sweet pancakes, which go under the name of *Kaiserschmarren*. From Trent to Rovereto, along with *Strudel* and *Zelten*, we find the *Pinza* and the *Torta di Fregolotti*, of Venetian origin. The final word goes to the ice cream made by the master ice cream makers of the Zoldo valley.

Basini de Trent

These small round biscuits from Trent are made with eggs, sugar and sweet almonds, according to a 16th-century recipe.

Bomboloni di Carnevale/ Faschingskrapfen

These are typical ring-shaped doughnuts from Alto Adige that are filled with various sorts of jams or creams.

Brazedèl

This ring-shaped, plaited cake is amber and straw yellow in color. The name refers to the fact that Trentino women used to carry them on their arms!

Buzòla or Ciambella Dolce

Aniseed liqueur or grappa is added to the mixture, giving this typical Trentino doughnut a special taste and fragrance.

Cròfani

This sugar-dusted Trentino fritter is fairly flat, and as long as a teaspoon, with a walnut in the middle.

Dorf Tiroler

Traditional crunchy cakes from Alto Adige made with egg whites whipped with sugar and lemon-juice, containing flakes of chocolate and almonds.

Frittella alla Marmellata/ Polsterzipfl

This typical Alto Adige fritter is usually square or triangular, and filled with jam. The mixture is made with boiled potatoes, wheat flour, eggs, milk, baking powder and sugar.

Frittella di Mele/Apfelkiechl

These apple fritters are typical in the Province of Bolzano. Slices of apple are dipped in a batter made with flour, milk, salt, sugar and rum. They should be served hot, dusted with icing sugar.

Apples are also used to make fritters, garnished with fresh cream and redcurrant- juice

Hausgemachtes trentinisches Speiseeis

The centuries-old Trentino ice-cream-making tradition is based on ingredients found locally: milk, first of all, sugar derived from apples and fruit.

Germzopf

This typical cake from the Province of Bolzano is plaited before being baked in the oven. When the dough has risen, sultanas are added. Before baking, the top is brushed with white of egg and scattered with rough grains of sugar.

Krapfen (doughnuts) are wonderfully light and are made with various fillings

Grostoli or Crostoli

These light, very fragile golden fritters are made in Trentino during the carnival period or for some of the village festivals.

Hollermulla

Red gelatine produced in Alto Adige, which is obtained by boiling elderberries in water and sugar.

Kiechl

These typical round cakes from the Province of Bolzano contain sultanas. Once the cake mixture has risen, the top is garnished with jam and icing sugar.

Krapfen

These large doughnuts come from the Alto Adige culinary tradition. They have various fillings: jam, poppy seed, spinach and so on. The basic mixture consists of wheat flour, butter, sugar, milk, cream and eggs. Once they have been fried, Krapfen should be eaten while they are still warm, dusted with icing sugar.

Mohnmingilan

These little round fritters are typical of the Isarco valley (Province of Bolzano). The basic mixture consists of boiled potatoes, eggs, poppy seed and cinnamon, and they are dipped in a batter of flour, eggs, rum, sugar and milk. Before serving, they are dusted with icing sugar.

Pinza

This sweet focaccia from Trentino has a quite distinctive taste.

THE APPLES OF TRENTINO

The tradition of growing apples in the valleys of Trentino goes back a very long time. It was first documented in the 17th century. The orchards of Val di Non, in particular, grow apples with the "Mela della Val di Non DOP" label, which are used in many traditional recipes. Another famous area for apple production is Val di Sole which, in addition to having some of the most beautiful, unspoiled scenery in the region, is home, along with Val di Non, to the Melinda apple, the quality of which is guaranteed by the organic farming methods used here.

The farmers are involved at every stage of production, controlling the crop step by step. The award of the Protected Denomination of Origin label in 2003 was confirmation of the ongoing commitment of the farmers to ensuring that the product remains a high-quality, healthy food. In 1997, Consorzio Melinda opened mondoMelinda, a visitors' center, to enable the public to learn more about Melinda apples. Visitors can watch films and CD-ROMs, visit the apple orchards and processing rooms, and learn about apples, farming methods, and the processing phases in the cooperatives prior to sale.

For further information: www.melinda.it

Strudel di mele (apple strudel), the pride of Alto Adige pastry-making

Strauben

These spiral-shaped fritters from Alto Adige are made from a batter of flour, melted butter and milk. They are dusted with icing sugar and served with red blueberries.

Strauli or Straboli

This typical wheat dessert from Trentino resembles a golden fritter.

Strudel

This pastry roll is the flagship of Alto Adige pastry making. The pastry itself may be shortcrust or plain pastry (made with water, flour, oil and salt). The most common filling is made with apples from Alto Adige, sultanas, sugar, breadcrumbs and spices, especially cinnamon, although various flavorings, pine nuts and walnuts may also be added. Individual bakers have added their own touches, such as leaving the sultanas to soak in grappa or rum. As for the pastry, there is a third possibility: pastry made in the old way (with flour, butter, water, eggs and salt), shortcrust pastry and puff pastry. There are countless variations on the filling, all of them sweet: cherries, apricots, pears, grapes, ricotta or poppy seeds. It may be served with milk, coffee or a dessert wine.

Torta di Fregolotti

This very common dessert has many variations throughout the region. The traditional recipe contains the following ingredients: white flour, sugar, butter, cinnamon and lemon zest. A recent version of the recipe adds almonds and grappa.

Tortoleti coi Purioni

These fritters from Trentino are flavored with dried mint leaves.

Vinschger Schneemilch

This white, creamy dessert from Alto Adige is usually served chilled in a glass. The ingredients are white bread, milk, whipped cream, walnuts, sultanas, rum and cinnamon.

Zelten or Celteno

Also called Pane di Frutta, this dessert is common throughout the region. In Trentino, it is usually eaten at Christmas, often washed down with a glass of Vin Santo. The mixture is made with rye flour and generous portions of figs, chopped apples, grated almonds and walnuts, candied peel, pine-nuts, sultanas, sugar and orange-juice. There are many local variations.

There are many recipes for this traditional Trentino cake called Celteno or Zelten.

Zwetschgen- und Marillenknödel

These sweet *canederli* are typical of Alto Adige. They are made with grated boiled potatoes, with a fruit filling of apricots or plums and sugar. After they have been boiled, breadcrumbs, sugar and cocoa powder or cinnamon are sprinkled over the top.

BOLZANO/BOZEN

Klaus
Via Vintler 2,
Tel. 0471972193
Along with the more traditional sweets, such as the ubiquitous Strudel and Zelten, he also makes chestnut cakes and hearts.

Peter
Piazza delle Erbe 20,
Tel. 0471978086
This cake-shop on one of the town's main squares produces excellent sweets and cakes, including the Christmas Zelten.

FOOD

ALGUND/LAGUNDO
Überbacher
Via P. Thalguter 2,
Tel. 0473448451
A huge choice of Tyrolean and Viennese cakes and sweets, including Zelten, Krapfen and Strudel.

BRIXEN/BRESSANONE
Pupp
Via Mercato Vecchio 37,
Tel. 0472834736,
www.pupp.it
A classic venue in Viennese style: coffee, cappuccino, hot chocolate and fruit infusions are served with typical cakes made on the premises.
Tscholl
Via Rio Scaleres 54,
Tel. 0472838000
All the recipes used in this cake-shop are traditional: Christmas biscuits, honey cakes, crostoli with various fillings, Zelten and Strudel.

CORVARA IN BADIA
Dorigo
Strada Rutort 1,
Tel. 0471836288
This cake-shop produces the classics of the local cake-making tradition.

MERAN/MERANO
Cafè – Konditorei König
Corso della Libertà 168,
Tel. 0473237162
An elegant venue where you can sample the best of Alto Adige cake making: Strudel and excellent cakes that are imaginatively presented.
Konditorei – Confiserie Pöhl
Via Roma 27,
Tel. 0473234804
This venue serves traditional cakes and sweets: Zelten, Christmas biscuits, honey cakes and Merano apple cakes, Crostoli and Strudel.

TOBLACH/DOBBIACO
Konditorei Stern
Via Dolomiti 16/B, Tel. 0474972257
This charming venue has a whole range of Strudel but also typical Tyrolean, and almond and hazelnut cakes.

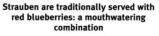

Strauben are traditionally served with red blueberries: a mouthwatering combination

TRENT/TRENTO

Bertelli
Via Oriola 29,
Tel. 0461984765
The pastry-making tradition here dates back 80 years. The perfect place to taste homemade cakes.

ARCO
Cristini
Via Mantova 14, Tel. 0464514535
A small, bright, charming venue; the vast range of products, including Strudel, is made in the bakery next-door.

PINZOLO
Bar Caffè Marconi
Via Marconi 13, Tel. 0465502022
This fine cake and pastry shop is well located in the center of the town, which has lovely views over the valley. The sweets and ice creams here are made by hand in the bakery next-door.
Fratelli Pasquini
Via Dolomiti di Brenta 13,
Tel. 0465440710
A small, central, elegant venue, which makes and sells high-quality sweets such as chocolates, pralines, and the typical sweets and traditional cakes of the valley.

PREDAZZO
Fior di Bosco
Via Garibaldi 7, Tel. 0462502474
This wood-furnished venue has a vast range of typical cakes and sweets (Strudel, Zelten, Crostoli), Panettone and cakes and biscuits for tea.

ROVERETO
Bar Meeting
Via Fiume 2,
Tel. 0464437677
This gelateria makes its own ice cream. The beautifully furnished venue has a vast assortment of local homemade sweets and cakes, including some in elegant gift-wrappings.

Food and Wine Festivals

MAY

⬎ **Third weekend in May**
FESTA DELLO SPECK
Bozen/Bolzano
*Information: tel. 0471307000
(www.bolzano-bozen.it)*
Held in the town center, these three days (Friday to Sunday) are devoted to the finest of Alto Adige cured meats, which are prepared in a thousand different ways. Folk music and traditional dancing provide a merry background to the food stalls where you can sample the local fare.

JULY

⬎ **Beginning of July**
MOSTRA DI CEMBRA
Cembra (Trent)
*Information: tel. 0461557028
(www.aptpinecembra.it)*
At Cembra, Trentino's capital for Müller Thurgau wine, in the charming setting of Palazzo Barbi, this exhibition is a showcase for Trentino's finest wines, and more than 100 foreign wine labels.

⬎ **End of July**
CAMMINAGRESTANA
Val di Gresta (Trent)
*Information: tel. 0464430363
(www.aptrovereto.it)*
A tasting marathon held in the splendid setting of the Gresta valley, where you can sample the produce of the season, visit farms and be entertained by music and other events.

AUGUST

⬎ **Mid-August**
FESTA DEL VINO
**Kaltern am See (Bozen)/
Caldaro al Lago**
*Tourist office: tel. 0471963169
(www.kaltern.com)*
This festival spans the four days over the public holiday of Ferragosto (August 15), and involves tastings of local wines and typical products, with concerts given by local bands and games for the kids.

SEPTEMBER

⬎ **Beginning of September, every 2 years (Next festival 2007)**
ALLA CORTE DI RE LAURINO
Bozen/Bolzano
*Information: tel. 0471307000
(www.bolzano-bozen.it)*
From Friday to Sunday, the town center becomes a huge stage for traditional local gastronomy. The festival includes a series of musical events.

⬎ **Beginning of September**
ALLA SCOPERTA DEL TEROLDEGO
Mezzocorona (Trent)
*Information: tel. 0461600392
(www.ideaviaggi.com)*
In the heart of the Piana Rotaliana, this festival is all about Teroldego Rotaliano DOC, and involves three days of wine-tastings accompanied by the best local food products. This event, like the other Trentino events listed, is part of the initiative called "Vacanze con gusto", which encourages people to get to know the culture, traditions and wonderful flavors of Trentino.

⬎ **Second half of September**
DESMONTEGADA DE LE CAORE
Cavalese (Trent)
*Information: tel. 0462341419
(www.fiemmeres.it)*
Set in the lovely Fiemme valley, the town of Cavalese is invaded by hundreds of goats, decorated with flowers and ornaments, making their way down from the Alpine pastures. The event emphasizes the strong links between the community and the cycles of Nature, in the form of stalls selling malga cheeses, livestock shows and tastings of local wines.

⬎ **Second half of September**
GRAN FESTA DEL DESMONTEGAR
Primiero (Trento)
*Information: tel. 0439762525
(www.primieroiniziative.it)*
This festival celebrates the return of the cows from the Alpine pastures. Decorated with necklaces of flowers, branches and decorated cowbells, they go through the villages of the upper Primiero valley, hailing the arrival of autumn.

OCTOBER

FESTA DELLA ZUCCA
Bozen/Bolzano
*Information: tel. 0471307000
(www.bolzano-bozen.it)*
Piazza Walther is awash with pumpkins of every conceivable shape and size, while stalls and restaurants offer a wide range of dishes based on this versatile vegetable.

⬎ **Mid-October**
POMARIA
Casez (Trent)
*Information: tel. 0463423002
(www.guidavacanze.it)*
Val di Non, that vast orchard surrounded by mountains, is the scene of a spectacle during the fruit harvest. The valley, with its castles and gorges, is in festive mood and the small Renaissance town of Casez hosts the events associated with the "Strada della Mela e dei Sapori delle Valli di Non e Sole" (the Apple Route and the Flavors of Val di Non and Val di Sole).

NOVEMBER

⬎ **Beginning of November**
SAGRA DELLA CIUÌGA
San Lorenzo in Banale (Trent)
*Information: tel. 0465702626
(www.comano.to)*
Held in the streets below the balconies of the stone-and-wood houses of Prusa, near San Lorenzo in Banale, this festival is dedicated to a typical cured meat called the ciuìga. An opportunity to immerse yourself in the atmosphere of days gone by and sample the local fare.

THE TYPICAL TAVERNS OF TRENTINO

"Osteria Tipica Trentina" is a trademark, conceived with the aim of safeguarding and exploiting the typical gastronomic and cultural specialties of the valleys of the region. It is a hallmark of undisputed quality and exceptional service. About 50 venues were found to meet the stringent requirements of the trademark. In fact, the restaurateurs who are participating in the scheme exclusively use produce made or grown in Trentino, whether you are talking about the water, the wine, the salamis and cured meats, the cheese, the flour or fruit, which are all certified in terms of quality and origin. Furthermore, all the recipes used in these venues are absolutely traditional.

www.trentino.to/osteriatipica

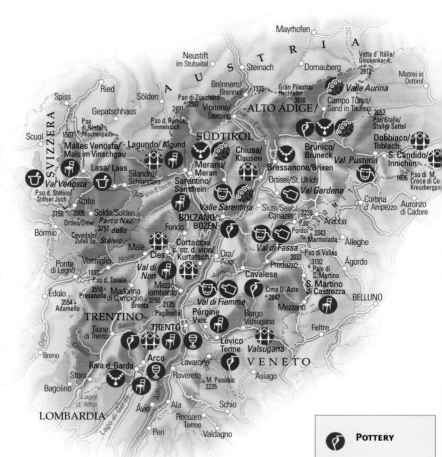

POTTERY	
WOOD	
MASKS	
GLASS	
FURNITURE	
WROUGHT IRON	
MARBLE	
FABRICS AND EMBROIDERY	
GOLDSMITHERY	

Mountain traditions pervade every aspect of the craft heritage of Trentino-Alto Adige. Starting by working the raw materials which could be procured locally by hand, regional craftsmen have attained extremely high levels of esthetic and artistic expression. This region is extraordinarily complex in cultural terms. As a result, the craftsmen may be German-speaking people with a culture very close to the Austrian culture of the Tyrol (now Alto Adige), people who speak Ladin with their own culture (in Val Gardena, and the Badia and Fassa valleys) or people of Italian language and culture (in Trentino). These strong ethnic differences have resulted in high-quality craft products with a very distinctive local character which can be admired and purchased in the many markets held in the towns and villages of the region.

Highlights

- The ancient tradition of woodcarving
- Old-fashioned stoves decorated with majolica tiles
- The creativeness and marvelous colors of local glassware
- The artistic skills of local metal craftsmen

Inside

ARTS AND CRAFTS

Even during a brief visit it is evident how the ancient craft traditions of the zone have influenced the decorations of the churches, castles and museums. The range of items is also impressive, going from the religious stone sculptures of the Romanesque period to the Gothic trusses, from the coffered ceilings in Renaissance style to the baroque wrought iron railings, and from the belts adorned with zinc studs to those made of embroidered leather. Trentino and Alto Adige contain an extraordinary cultural complexity with enclaves of German culture and language in the areas near Tyrol in Austria (in Alto Adige, the Fassa valley and Trentino), and of Ladin culture and language (Val Gardena, and the Badia and Fassa valleys). It is this ethnic diversity that has lead to placing substantial importance on local differences in artistic craft production, as can be seen with the typical local outfits.

Wood

In the past, at the various houses spread across the valleys, small wooden objects (in particular, animal-toys, figures for the Christmas nativity scene display, bottle tops decorated with grotesque figures and pipes) were made entirely by hand, although the actual production was carried out in a manner reminiscent of an assembly line: each member of the family would specialize in a part of the process, such as the hewing-out, finishing or coloring. This method resulted in strongly stylized shapes and designs, which have become a defining feature of this type of craft that, these days, tends to create only decorative and religious objects.
In Val Gardena, woodcarving was already being practiced by the mid-17th century. Some interesting

A typical country Stube

examples from these times are on display in the Museo di Ortisei. Most of these items were of a religious nature, favoring crucifixes and enormously creative nativity scene displays. In this area, as in other Alpine valleys, the inhabitants started processing wood to create tools to work the land and to be used in the home. They then moved on to making items with a commercial value, such as frames and wooden cases for grandfather clocks. In Val Gardena, these wood carvers soon started to make more intricate items, notably crucifixes, statues of saints, and items for the stations of the cross and the nativity scene displays. Today, this tradition lives on in the creation of polychrome wooden statues and is the most important craft tradition in Val Gardena, the Fiemme and Fassa valleys and numerous other villages in Alto Adige.

This 'chosen' craft is, though, flanked by the production of more useful objects. Here and there you can find the last wood-turners who have not been swallowed by big industry. They create a variety of objects, including cups, bowls, candlestick holders and old-fashioned toys. In the modern world, these wood craftsmen produce non-religious items as well as the more classic religious objects. The tradition is ancient but still very much alive, with the techniques having been passed down through the generations from ancient masters and, notably, by the art schools in Ortisei and Selva di Val Gardena. The extraordinary success of wines from Trentino and Alto Adige has ensured the continuation of the cooper profession (barrel maker and repairer). Indeed, this ancient trade is such an integral part of local life that the word for the trade, *bottaio* in Italian, can be found in many surnames from Alto Adige. Although the barrels are generally produced industrially, the lids are, in accordance with the dictates of local traditions, made by artisans and decorated and inscribed in such a way that each barrel becomes a unique piece.

Majolica stoves

In Alto Adige, the *Stube* is the room containing the stove and was often the only part of a peasant's house. Over time, the *Stube* become more than the physical center of the house and took on a symbolic and cultural value that positively influenced all of the elements of which it was comprised. Of these, the most characteristic is undoubtedly the large brick stove that, through the skill and sensitivity of the local ceramic artists, came to be a wonderful item of majolica decoration. There are some surviving pieces that tend to be monumental, with splendid decorations and of notable quality (both in esthetic and functional terms). These are like 'reference points' for modern production. The major stove workshops, which also create other ceramic objects, are located in Bolzano/Bozen and Brunico/Brunick. In these areas, their 'rediscovery' in recent times has given a substantial boost to artisan items. Here, the majority of potters still work the clay using traditional methods and then fire their objects in old-style wood kilns. They create terracotta bowls, vases, plates and cups as well as the majolica tiles for the stoves and other artistic ceramic objects.

Furniture

Wood has long been a key element in the economy of the Trentino and Alto Adige valleys. Often, it led to the creation of a series of activities in which the borders between necessity and decoration became blurred. In terms of these 'functional' productions, the main one is undoubtedly the rustic furniture that is made across Trentino, but especially in Val di Non, Pergine Valsugana, Trent and various villages on Lake Garda. Lagundo, Malles Venosta and Sarentino are the main production centers in Alto Adige, being known mainly for the furnishings they create for the traditional *Stube*. The typical elements of a *Stube* were the wood-covered walls, a comfortable corner-bench, a large and solid table and a brick stove with a wooden top, which was once used even as a bed. The combination of these elements created a welcoming and cozy room, an atmosphere of calmness and peace where the harmonious equilibrium between shape and material was witness to the artisans' skill and their ability to create a coherent style despite differing elements.

Peasant houses from the 1400s still have Gothic *Stube* and ceilings with finely carved beams. The way these houses were furnished is the inspiration for many items produced now: cupboards, chairs, benches, tables, the typical wall cupboards with wroughtiron locks and engraved chests that can bring a delightful, rustic touch to even the most modern rooms.

In the Ladin valleys, the creation of furniture is notable for the use of conifer wood decorated with finely carved friezes and lively floral decorations.

Metals

The passion and dedication of generations and generations of smiths in the forging and hammering of iron can be gauged from the artistic railings that still adorn many noble residences, separate the choir from the rest of the church and mark the age-old village

SHOPPING

taverns and inns. In this part of the world, the tradition of working wrought iron lives on, although it should not be confused with the various, banal items that are merely produced industrially using strips of metal and then assembled.

The difference between the two 'types' of metal is evident when one visits a forge where the red-hot metal is still worked using various small hammers that the smith, usually, makes as needed.

These types of workshop are dotted around the entire area, with the main centers being Trent, Valsugana and Cles, in Trentino, and Cortaccia, Dobbiaco, Lagundo, San Candido and Chiusa, in Alto Adige.

The items produced in these workshops often copy the masterpieces of past centuries, using decorative elements that are part of the regional artistic heritage, and traditional methods and techniques. Even copper working has age-old roots here. Archaeological finds show that copper was being worked in the Aurina valley as early as the Bronze Age. The highpoint for this valley was probably the Middle Ages and on. For nearly five centuries, the Predoi mines provided the material that, once processed, adorned noble residential buildings, such as those in Predoi and Cadipietra.

This lasted until the 19th century, when cheaper copper started to be imported from America, leading to the closure of the mine in 1893.

These days, this rich heritage of working metal (not only copper, but also pewter and brass) ensures that numerous collectors' pieces can be found in the many local antiques markets that bring life to numerous towns and villages in the region.

THE ANGEL OF BOLZANO

In 1950, Count Otmar Thun and his wife Lene decided to 'dedicate' their lives to ceramics, which had long been their passion. In the cellar of the Klebenstein castle, at the mouth of the Sarentina valley, they created a craft workshop and began to produce vases, bowls, jugs and other objects.

This was followed by the creation of the "praying angel" and the Thun brand became famous across the world. 1978 was a year of generational change: Peter Thun, the count's second child, entered the company, which remained faithful to the original philosophy of creating objects with unmis—takable character that are instantly recognizable as being Thun. By 1992 the production range had grown to include dinner and coffee services and every imaginable type of giftware. As such, production was moved to the industrial zone of Bolzano. In 2002, Thuniversum was opened. This is a modern museum and showroom that was created inside the company by the count's first son, Matteo Thun, an internationally acclaimed architect. This museum is a world of angels, small statues, decorations, and tiles for covering the traditional Tyrol stoves. There is also a section on the history of the company and the characteristics of production (with a factory outlet and shop, see p. 195).

Lace and fabrics

In contrast to the oft-heard rhetoric, which claims that poor craftsmen used to work to satisfy the desires of the rich, precious pillow lace from Alto Adige was, originally, created by well-off people (or nobles) with the sole purpose of warding off boredom. Following this example, the women of peasant families also took up this pastime, especially in the Aurina valley. The latter zone is where the true artisan production of these small masterpiece began. Today, the practice is centered on Merano/Meran and the Sarentina valley. Even today, the tools used to create pillow lace are simple and limited in number: an upholstered cushion, bobbins, pins, linen threads and paper patterns, which are nothing more than pieces of paper with the desired pattern on them. Once the paper pattern has been fixed to the upholstered cushion, the lace maker takes the bobbins and, using precise and fast movements, passes them from one hand to the other in such a way as to cross, knot, stretch and fix the threads until they form the desired pattern. Using this method, today as in the past, the pillow lace that is created that will be used for blouses, tablecloths and bed clothing. In Alto Adige, and especially in Brunico, the production of felt and loden items (mainly hats and slippers) still flourishes, as does the creation of handmade fabrics with traditional patterns. The latter are used for tablecloths, towels, curtains, cushions and furniture. One of the most characteristic types of craftwork in Alto Adige (and of clear Austrian origin) is embroidery of leather that is used for belts, shoes and wallets. It is done using peacock feathers that are cut into thin strips and then re-combined to create stylized patterns.

Stone and marble

The marble from the Lasa/Laas quarries in the Venosta valley is known for its whiteness and its ability to resist atmospheric and climatic elements. Although the Romans knew of this marble, the first documented use of it in a building is in the 15th century. At this stage, it started to be used for doorways,

Traditional pillow lace headwear

columns and ornamental sculptures, especially in churches and other religious buildings. It was favored for its 'duration' and brilliant whiteness, as well as its ability to resist bad weather and maintain is true 'whiteness' for a long period of time. Yet, for about four centuries, the quarrying of this stone remained sporadic. Real quarrying in the Venosta valley only began after 1850. At first, the quarrying was open-air, but later it moved underground. This systematization also resulted in an increase in the types available, ranging from statuary marble (absolutely white) to arabesque (with fantastic undulating veins of colors, from blue to grey) and an infinite number of options in-between, including brown, reddish, greenish and yellowy-pink. The availability of this precious material influenced local artisan and artistic work, leading to an increase in stone and marble working. To prevent this tradition from fading away, since 1982, increased emphasis has been placed on the local Professional Institute for Stone Sculptors. The aim is, through the teaching of traditional methods, including techniques for chiseling, or using a mallet and a small pick, to improve the ability and output of the students.

SHOPPING

Glass

Artisan glass-working in the Trentino and Alto Adige valleys makes use of the ease with which molten glass can be manipulated to create simple objects, including small glass designs in lead frames, mirrors, filigree or etched vases, hand-designed lampshades and Christmas tree decorations. The glass takes on distinctive and charming features that are blown, frosted, filigreed and etched or simply painted by hand. In Alto Adige a special technique is practiced. It is known as *vetro incamiciato* and involves placing layers of different colored glass on top of each other, often with the addition of a gold foil during the fusing phase. The use of this technique has led to the development of a substantial market for minute objects and artistic costume jewelry. Indeed, this sector is booming and the objects are being exported to various other countries across the world.

Jewelry

In the past in Trentino-Alto Adige, gold and precious stone working focused on creating religious objects and decorations for traditional outfits that,

MUSEO DEL LODEN DI VANDOIES

Loden is a completely natural fabric that is made with top quality sheep's wool using a process that has numerous phases and takes 50 days to complete. In olden times, 'milling' was used to turn woolen cloth into loden by crushing it along with the addition of unknown ingredients. The fabric obtained was then roughened using thistles, before being shaved and compressed. The history of loden is linked to the mountain areas and their need to protect themselves against the cold and snow. In this way, sheep's wool becomes extraordinarily strong, water resistant and warm. For centuries it was only used by shepherds, but in the 19th century it became fashionable in high society, largely due to Emperor Franz Joseph and the famed Ludwig of Baveria. This changed social standing of loden, though, inevitably led to a change in its nature: the emperor's wardrobe favored fabrics that were warm and waterproof, but also soft and refined. The result was the loden found today, an expensive and elegant fabric that is often enriched with various fine fibers, such as cashmere or mohair, which is made from more delicate wool. Now, loden is often worn when strolling around towns, walking in the mountains or, possibly, on hunting excursions. Today, loden is almost entirely associated with forest green, but in the past, that is before it was adopted by the upper classes, the typical color was that of untreated wool – grey. Next, red became dominant, followed by white, black and, now, green. The Museo Interattivo del Loden di Vandoies (see photo) explores the history of this fabric and the techniques currently used to make it.

worn at the most important events during the year, had to be carefully cured down to the last detail. The skills learned in this sector led to fertile conditions for the growth of a sector that, in terms of quantity, is the largest artisan field in the region. In addition, the forms used, unlike all other crafts in Trentino-Alto Adige, are totally new and not 'restrained' by traditional esthetic ideas. It is an area of enormous creativity. As such, today, there are wonderful combinations of gold with precious stone, pearls, silver, colored glass and steel. The jewelry created is truly refined in the workmanship and a testimony to the great capability and skills of the craftsmen, who are playing an increasingly prominent role in the bubbling world of Italian fashion.

Wax
The creation of wax objects using molds or through modeling and coloring is widespread across Alto Adige, but is little known beyond these borders. The works produced are often of such skill that they seem to be true full- or low-relief sculptures.
In the valleys of Alto Adige, this craft can be seen as one of the parts of the 'production line' for creating the items that typify the *Stube*. In their own way, they are as important as the carved wooden furniture and the objects and decorations made of leather and metal.
The craft of working wax has its origins in the traditions of Austria and Bavaria, and is intricately linked to bee keeping. Once upon a time, wax was formed into shapes that were largely of ceremonial or ritualistic value, such as votive offerings or gifts given for a wedding. Today, thanks partly to the demands of the market, this craft has evolved and now focuses mainly on decorative items, such as decorations for the Christmas tree or unusually shaped candles.

Masks
Our society eats up and digests everything, normally turning things into 'products' that were, for thousands of years, created for entirely different reasons. One major example of this is the carved wooden mask. They obviously have artistic and decorative worth, although they were not born of a craft. Instead, they are linked to more complicated, and sometimes more mysterious, aspects of Alpine culture. Still today, they are made to be used in actual ceremonies that are held from early December until carnival. People wear them along with extremely colorful traditional outfits to play the parts of various characters, some of which are grotesque, some tragic, some playful, some elegant and some refined. This production, which is totally non-commercial, is still alive in certain parts of the Fassa and Fiemme valleys, in Trentino, and many villages in the Pusteria and Sarentina valleys in Alto Adige.

BOZEN/BOLZANO

Ceramica Thun
Via Galvani 29,
Tel. 0471245111
Ceramics and giftware
August Mittelberger
Via Castel Firmiano 33,
Tel. 0471633374
Barrels
Atelier Kompatscher
Piazza Municipio 9
Tel. 0471973375
Jewelry

BRIXEN/BRESSANONE
Fill Peter & Co
Portici Maggiori 15, Tel. 0472834790
Jewelry

BRUNECK/BRUNICO
Josef Gabrielli
Via Centrale 8
Tel. 0474555301
Jewelry

MERAN/MERANO
Richard Winkler
Passeggiata d'Inverno 15
Tel. 0473235378
Jewelry

SANKT CHRISTINA IN GRÖDEN/ SANTA CRISTINA VALGARDENA
Hans Giovanni Malsiner
Strada Dursan 65
Tel. 0471793714
Wood sculptures

SANKT ULRICH IN GRÖDEN/ ORTISEI
Andreas Moroder
Strada Resciesa 53
Tel. 0471798110
Wood sculptures
Bruno Walpoth
Via Nevel 21
Tel. 0471798179
Wood sculptures
Giuseppe Rumerio
Strada Rumanon 12
Tel. 0471797206
Wood sculptures

WOLKENSTEIN IN GRÖDEN/ SELVA DI VALGARDENA
Aron Demetz
Strada Nives 20Tel. 0471794097
Wood sculptures
Otto Piazza
Strada Ruacia 14, Tel. 0471794526
Wood sculptures

TRENT/TRENTO

Galleria Trentino Art
Via Belenzani 43/45
Tel. 0461263721
Ceramics and giftware
Arrigo Degasperi
Via Fersina 6/1
Tel. 0461910637
Working different metals
Navarini
Ravina, Via Val Gola 22
Tel. 0461923330
Working copper

Linea Vetro
Via P.E. Chiocchetti
4/6, Tel. 0461826760
Artistic windows

ARCO
Artevetro
Via Linfano 18/H, Tel. 0464510212
Glass giftware

CAVALESE
Fiemme Antica
Via Trento 2, Tel. 0462342115
Ceramic stoves
Patrizia Borelli
Via Trento 13, Tel. 0462340384
Wood sculptures

FIERA DI PRIMIERO
Zeni Renzo & Silvano
Via Roma 156, Tel. 043967674
Wood sculptures

LEVICO TERME
Martelli Guido
Via Marconi 22, Tel. 0461702334
Ceramic giftware

MADONNA DI CAMPIGLIO
Campiglio Legno
Via Cima Tosa 64, Tel. 0465440055
Wood sculptures

RIVA DEL GARDA
Orafi Stein
Via Chiesa Vecchia 13,
Tel. 0464550242
Jewelry

ROVERETO
Linea Luce
Via Mercerie 13, Tel. 0464431171
Lamps

SAN MARTINO DI CASTROZZA
Falegnameria Orsingher Dino & Annalisa
Via Passo Rolle 8, Tel. 043968103
Decorated furniture

MARKETS

In Trentino-Alto Adige, the value of craft production is well entrenched in popular culture and the techniques used to produce items by hand are protected and improved by workshops and markets. Indeed, local life is made livelier by typical little markets where it is possible to find rare antiques as well as unique pieces that were crafted with loving attention to detail. Such markets are also a good opportunity to find the material and social expressions of the different cultures located in the area: Italian, Ladin and German. For centuries these differing cultures have lived side-by-side and their traditions have been passed down precisely through such events.

BOZEN/BOLZANO

Christkindlmarkt
From late November to 23 December
Piazza Walther and Piazza Municipio come to life as nearly a hundred sellers display their typical craft products: wooden, glass and ceramic objects, traditional materials, jackets and boiled wool slippers, felt hats, small figures of animals and decorations made of raffia, straw, bark and other natural materials. Music, singing, concerts, exhibitions and shows make the atmosphere even warmer.
For further information: tel. 0471307000
www.bolzano-bozen.it

Festa dei fiori
30 April and 1 May
Piazza Walther becomes a luxurious garden of geraniums, petunias, carnations, fuchsia, succulents, roses, valerian, small conifers and bushes. There are also plenty of vegetables: different types of lettuce, onions, peppers, fennel and basil. You might also find some citrus fruit and medicinal and other herbs.
For further information:
tel. 0471307000
www.bolzano-bozen.it

Giornate dell'Artigianato Artistico
September, every two years
(next in 2007)
For about 10 days, the artisans of Alto Adige leave their workshops to display their goods on Piazza Walther. There are often live displays of how these minor masterpieces are created. Turners and decorators of clay and ceramics, and wood carvers show off their skills. There is also a full musical program.
For further information: tel. 0471307000
www.bolzano-bozen.it

BRUNECK/BRUNICO
Mercato di Stegona
End of October
This is the oldest and most traditional market in Alto Adige, with a 1,000 years of history and the largest product market in the Tyrol. For three days, there are over 80 stands selling nearly everything: clothes, leather jackets, craft objects and so on. The large amusement park also brings more life to the event.
For further information: tel. 0474555722
www.bruneck.com

EPPAN AN DER WEINSTRASSE/ APPIANO SULLA STRADA DEL VINO
Esposizione di Presepi
From early December to 6 January
Held in the San Paolo district, various different types of nativity scenes are on display in the streets. It is lovely to walk along the lit streets and admire these works in this festival atmosphere. There are nativity scenes in every corner of the center: behind windows, in niches or in the corners of famous buildings. On the two Sundays prior to Christmas, there is also a nativity play.
For further information:
tel. 0471662206
www.eppan.net

GLURNS/GLORENZA
Sealamorkt
2 November
The Sealamorkt, that is the market of the souls, is an interesting market that, every year, brings to life the streets and piazzas of medieval Glorenza. There are numerous stands where you can buy fabrics, giftware, clothes and numerous other interesting items.
For further information: tel. 0473831209
www.comune.glorenza.bz.it

MERAN/MERANO
Meraner Advent

From late November to late December
About 70 stall owners set up their characteristic wooden kiosk-stalls along the river. At night, everyting is lit, creating a fantastical atmosphere. They sell decorations and ceramic objetcs, traditional fabrics, wooden statues, felt slippers, clothes made of boiled wool, games and other interesting items. You can aslo enjoy a ride through the streets in a carriage, passing through the lit old center with its many stalls, nativity scenes, wind concerts and choirs singing.
For further information: tel. 0473272000
www.meraninfo.it

SAND IN TAUFERS/CAMPO TURES
Mercatino di Natale

From late November to 31 December
The small Campo Tures market is the smallest in Alto Adige, but the quality makes up for the size. Aside from the traditional wooden kiosk-stands, there are numerous events for children and music by pop and folk groups.
For further information:
tel. 0474652081
www.tures-aurina.com

TRENT/TRENTO

Mercatino di Natale/Weihnachtsmarkt
From late November to 24 December
This small market takes place within the city walls, which become filled with the characteristic wooden kiosk-stalls. It is a wonderful opportunity to discover the true artisan tradition of Trentino. There are also local gastronomic specialities, a fascinating theme tour of the museums, concerts, shows and events for children. On the days before and after 13 December, there is the Fiera di Santa Lucia (Feast of St Lucy), where there are about 100 stalls selling desserts, cakes, items of clothing and toys.
For further information:
tel. 0461983880
www.apt.trento.it

ARCO
Mercatino Asburgico/Habsburger Markt
From late November to 24 December

Little wooden kiosk-stalls, normal stalls, lights, music and singing make this old village delightful. The small market is set up along a path running from the castle with an olive grove, through the public gardens and the arboretum, with its range and centuries-old plants, to the Alpenzoo, which has some wonderful examples of Alpine animals. The market runs during the weekend and you can buy a wide range of things: decorations and other local Christmas items, wooden sculptures, local craft objects, glass and ceramic vases, dolls and games. You can also take a ride in a carriage and look at the nativity scenes.
For further information: tel. 0464516161
www.gardatrentino.it

LEVICO TERME
Mercatino di Natale/Weihnachtsmarkt
From late November to early January
Set in the lovely Parco Secolare degli Asburgo, this little market has about 50 vendors in the traditional wooden kiosk-stalls. They sell local craft products, food specialities, toys and Christmas decorations. During the festive season, the park is also the setting for shows with folklore groups, fireworks, nativity scenes, rides in carriages and the feast of polenta (maize flour dish), in which people dress up in costumes give sweets to the children.
For further information: tel. 0461706101
www.valsugana.info

A splendid view of the traditional Christmas market at Bressanone

FASHION

Factory outlets are the new and modern way of shopping at discount prices. These centers are like 'virtual' villages that are built entirely for the practice of shopping, where the users can lose themselves in the multitude of shops and the playground like atmosphere. Side-by-side with boutiques, normally selling the top Italian brands of clothes, shoes and accessories, you find all the services and facilities needed to make the experience more comfortable: large parking lots, bars and places to get something to eat, ice-cream parlors with tables and benches to sit at, and areas specifically designed for younger children. In Trentino-Alto Adige you find both ends of the scale, with outlets filled with the major national and international brands, such as Vipiteno, and single-factory stores where you can get the quality and design excellence of Italian products at reduced rates, such as Thun.

BOZEN / BOLZANO

Thun Store
Via Galvani 29, Tel. 0471245111
www.thun.it
Local production of giftware and decorative objects, such as animals, Christmas items, watches and jewelry made of ceramic and porcelain. A large range of original knickknacks for kitchens and living rooms.

BRUNECK/BRUNICO

Franz Kunstweberei
Via M. Pacher 9, Tel. 0474555385
www.tessiturafranz.it
Local production of tablecloths, bedspreads and linen for the house made using age-old fabric-production methods. A large number of fabrics can be bought by the meter or in whatever bundles you desire. A big area is also dedicated to the sale of carpets, rugs, cushions, and fabric for furniture.

Tuchfabrik Moessmer
Via W. Von der Vogelweide 6
Tel. 0474533111, www.moessmer.it
Production and sale of outfits, overcoats and loden jackets made with wool and boiled wool. "Total look" clothing for men, women and children. There is also an outlet where you can pick up items at reduced prices.

JENESIEN/SAN GENESIO ATESINO

Kaufmann
Via Paese 3, Tel. 0471354595
www.kaufmannwalker.it
Production and sale of boiled wool materials: this process, typical of Austria and Alto Adige, involves washing the pure wool yarn at a high temperature so that the inside threads overlap to create a felt-like effect. The range of uses for this material includes jackets, sleeveless jackets, jumpers and jerseys, all exclusively made of boiled wool.

STERZING/VIPITENO

Timberlad Factory Outlet
SS12 del Brennero 46, Tel. 0472767670
Timberland outlet where you can get items at reduced prices. The majority of items are casual wear, but there are some more refined, elegant and comfortable pieces.

TRENT / TRENTO

Cereria Ronca
Mattarello, Via della Cooperazione 13
Tel. 0461946030
www.cereriaronca.it
Local production of waxes and candles to decorate the house as well as artistic and religious candles. The candle becomes a furnishing accessory, using the latest shapes and colors.

Dolomiten Sportswear
Via Piera 2/a Tesero, Tel. 0462813106
www.dolomiten-sp.it
Classic and sports wear from Dolomiten Sportswear in a vast range of sizes and shapes for men, women and children. There are also many of the major leisure and sportswear brands. A large range of loden jackets in all colors and fabrics.

AVIO

Pelletterie Anna Valli
Via del Lavoro 26, Tel. 0464684367
www.annavalli.it
An outlet where you can buy everyday and office items. Large array of bags, wallets, luggage, belts, gloves, office folders and leather diaries.

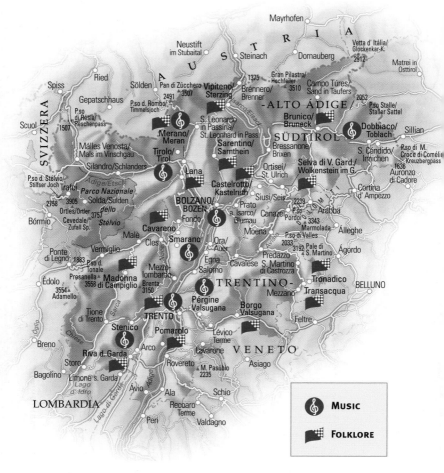

🎼	**MUSIC**
🏁	**FOLKLORE**

Trentino-Alto Adige is now and has long been home to all kinds of cultural and social identities. Interestingly, the ethnic complexity of the region has become a unifying rather than a divisive factor of this land, where the Italian culture of the Trent area lives side-by-side with the German language and the Habsburg traditions of the Bolzano area, not to mention the minority of Ladin speakers dotted around the Val Gardena area. The unusual folk events of the region have roots which are embedded in its cultural and social heritage, expressions of the various local cultures. In fact, old social traditions lie behind the charming historical re-enactments and pageants in period costume, and the events associated with the customs of the mountain tradition. The range of musical events which animate summer evenings, often held in splendid natural settings, is also worthy of mention.

Highlights

■ The colorful traditional outfits worn at local festivals

■ Concerts held in beautiful mountain settings

■ The excitement of the traditional palios (horse-races)

■ Re-live the past watching colorful processions in period costume

Inside

MUSIC

Together, the two provinces of Trent and Bolzano make up the autonomous, multi-ethnic and multilingual region of Trentino-Alto Adige. These provinces have different histories and traditions, yet they are tied by sharing some of the most beautiful land in the world and by the fact that, since ancient times, they have been lands of transit and 'meeting places' for the exchange of both commercial goods and elements of culture. They were on the chosen route for Middle European cultures that wished to reach the Italian peninsula and vice versa. In addition, the love of music has always been a key characteristic of the peoples of these splendid valleys. Indeed, it is no exaggeration to say that, throughout the year, in every town and village in Trentino-Alto Adige, even in the tiny villages perched on the slopes, music can be heard from people singing or playing instruments and from organs, bands, orchestras and soloists. In conjunction with the tourist industry, the musical calendar in Trentino-Alto Adige becomes particularly busy during summer.

BOZEN/BOLZANO

Bolzano Danza
July
A contemporary dance festival involving some of the best choreographers and dance companies in the world. There are also courses, other related experiences and a rich program of other events.
For further information:
tel. 0471307001, www.bolzano-bozen.it

Concerti di Ferragosto
August
Symphonic and chamber orchestras perform in concerts conducted by internationally renowned maestros.
For further information:
tel. 0471307001,www.bolzano-bozen.it

Musicastello
June and September
Across the whole of Alto-Adige, chamber and medieval music concerts are held in the wonderful castles of the region.
For further information:
tel. 0471307001,
www.bolzano-bozen.it

Nuovo Teatro Comunale
Piazza Verdi 40, tel. 0471304130
Located only a few hundred meters from the heart of the city, right behind the Duomo, the theater was designed by Marco Zanuso and opened in 1999. The best of the city's various wonderful venues, it hosts operas and concerts.

DORF TIROL/TIROLO
Serate a Castel Tirolo
From June to July
Concerts of medieval and Renaissance music in the majestic castle that gave

its name to the region.
For further information:
tel. 0471307001, www.bolzano-bozen.it

MERAN/MERANO
Settimane Musicali Meranesi
August and September
A festival for internationally acclaimed symphonic orchestras, soloists and conductors.
For further information:
tel. 0473272000, www.meraninfo.it

TOBLACH/DOBBIACO
Settimane Mahleriane
July
Concerts, art exhibitions and other events

The Damiano Chiesa refuge on Mt Altissimo di Nago during the Coro Anuna festival

DOBBIACO AND GUSTAV MAHLER

"It is marvelous here, come and visit us some Sunday, even if only to see this place! I'm sure that a painter would be able to get something from so much splendor". These are the words that Mahler wrote to the publisher Emil Hertzka in July 1910. This great composer (who was not highly regarded among his peers and was seen more as a conductor) spent the summer holidays of the final years of his life (1860-1911) in Dobbiaco in the lovely family house of Trenker at Carbonin Vecchia/Altschluderbach (coming from Villabassa, it is slightly before the town on the right). During those peaceful weeks, far away from the commitments of work and the obligations of social life in Vienna, Mahler wrote some of his final two symphonies (only a part of the last one remains) and of Lied von der Erde (The Song of the Earth), one of the major musical works of the 1900s.

At present, in Trenker's house (destined for refurbishment), the memory of those days are contained in displays cases in one of the drawing rooms and in the wooden house in the garden where the musician used to go to be alone so he could study and compose.

to celebrate the music of Gustav Mahler.
For further information:
tel. 0471307001,
www.bolzano-bozen.it

TRENT/TRENTO

Dolomiti di Pace
July and August
This festival combines meetings where journalists discuss peace with musical events on the same theme. Some of the most well-known locations from World War I are the setting: the Folgaria plateau, the Vezzena plateau, Dolomiti di Fassa, Lagorài, Lavarone, Luserna, Pale di San Martino, Presanella, Rovereto and the Vanoi valley. These places are all immersed in nature and connected by the Sentiero della Pace (see p. 143).
For further information:
tel. 0461405405,
www.trentino.to

Festival Internazionale W. A. Mozart
September and October
Every year, in Trent, Ala, Rovereto and Villa Lagarina they rediscover the character and legacy of this celebrated musician from Salzburg. The calendar of events also recalls the time when Mozart passed through and played in Trentino.

The works of this famous composer come to life in the various settings, halls and churches linked to his passed concerts as well as in some more modern venues. There is, in addition to the traditional repertoire, space for contemporary productions and experimenting with different languages. The numerous events of music by classical composers and Mozart, including wonderful symphonies and some pieces by lesser known contemporaries of Mozart, are led by established international musicians. There is also some theater and cinema.
For further information:
tel. 0464439988
www.festivalmozartrovereto.com

I Suoni delle Dolomiti
July and August
This is a high-altitude musical festival that brings artists from all over the world together in the lovely Trentino mountains. The event combines music, art, nature and, of course, the mountains. One of the parts of the program is the *Alba delle Dolomiti* (Sunrise in the Dolomites): as night becomes day, words and music infuse the delightful atmosphere of dawn.
For further information:
tel. 0461405405
www.isuonidelledolomiti.it

EVENTS

Musicans and the general public walking to a mountain refuge for a concert

Oriente e Occidente
September
A dance festival held in Trent and Rovereto where different cultural ideas of contemporary dance come together. Africa is the pumping heart of this event that is like a crossroads for contemporary dance trends. The African rhythms of both today and yesterday mix with the great classics of modernity, transforming the acrobatics of the dancing into a type of poetry.
For further information:
tel. 0464431660
www.orienteoccidente.it

Teatro Sociale di Trento
Via Oss Mazzurana 19,
tel. 0461213834
www.centrosantachiara.it
This famous building has been a true symbol for the people of Trent and inextricably tied to much of the happenings of the last two centuries. Opened in 1819, the theater hosts both classical and other concerts, opera and folklore seasons and the Trentinojazz festival.

Trentinojazz
From March to November
A substantial calendar of musical events and important initiatives in the world of jazz. The valley floor, slopes, piazzas in old villages, fields and summits become the backdrops for performances by internationally acclaimed artists. The places involved are: Ala, Arco, Denno, Drena, Fondo, Malé, Mori, Riva del Garda, Rovereto, Sanzeno, Torbole, Trent and Villa Lagarina.
For further information:
tel. 0461496915
www.trentinocultura.net

PERGINE VALSUGANA
Pergine Spettacolo Aperto
From June to August
This is like a link between musical research, including singing and dance, and theater research.
The actual shows are moments in which different genres, languages and cultures meet and "contaminate" each other, helping to create new understandings of the question of "contemporaneity". A film festival in July and August is also part of the program.
For further information:
tel. 0461530179,
www.perginepsa.it

SMARANO
Accademia Internazionale di Improvvisazione all'Organo e al Clavicordo
July and August
During these months, the village of Smarano, set on the slopes of Val di Non, becomes a landmark for lovers of classical and organ music. In this quiet mountain village, the Academy focuses on research and training as well as promoting free concerts.
For further information:
tel. 0463536573,
www.eccher.it

STENICO
Musica nei Castelli
July and August
Set in the lovely Castel Stenico, there is music from the Renaissance up to the present.
For further information:
tel. 0461496915
www.trentinocultura.net

FOLKLORE

Folklore in Trentino-Alto Adige has been strongly influenced by the fact that the region is a zone where different cultures meet and exist together, especially ones of Italian, Ladin and German origin. In addition to the traditional religious festivals, the Christmas markets and the religious processions, this region has various "knightly" festivals with dancing, music, tournaments and colorful parades in masks. Country and mountain life also have substantial traditions in this region. There are some wonderful and unusual feasts dotted throughout the peasants' year, linked to the seasons: the feast of thanksgiving for the harvest and the one connected to the return of the herds from the alpine pastures.

BOZEN / BOLZANO

BRUNECK/BRUNICO
Festa delle Pozze
End of April, every two years
This feast is held at the end of the skiing season on the Seewiese ski run, on the Brunico side of Plan de Corones. The event takes place on a Sunday and involves numerous skiers trying to get over a puddle of water that has formed on the ski run. Literally anything goes in trying to achieve this goal: skiing, snowboarding, sledding, cars without tires, beds, baths, sun beds and many more imaginative methods. The less adventurous can simply enjoy the music and taste the various local dishes and products.
For further information:
tel. 0474555722,
www.bruneck.com

KASTELRUTH/CASTELROTTO
Cavalcata Oswald Von Wolkenstein
Mid-June
An exciting and historical horse ride through the places where the poet and knight errant Oswald Von Wolkenstein spent his days. The four competitions can date their origins back to the Middle Ages. They are held one after the other in various places on the Sciliar plateau, over an area of about 40km². The teams that take part consist of 4 riders each and represent various districts in the province. The event starts in the morning at Mt Calvario di Castelrotto with a race around a circuit: the riders gallop around a circular track, showing off their ability by attempting to put their lances through a series of large rings hanging from trees. The second test, held at Matzlbödele di Siusi, is a relay race that involves extreme precision and ends with the four riders galloping side-by-side to the finish. The third event is an obstacle course for horses and test of skill around the small Lake Fiè. Finally, the teams have to complete a slalom gallop between tall poles that they must not touch, otherwise points are deducted. The final challenge takes places in front of the Presule castle. The event ends with the prize giving followed by tasting of *canederli* (a type of dumpling) and beer. The festival also has numerous medieval shows, music and food stalls that help to re-evoke the times of Oswald.
For further information:
tel. 0471706333,
www.castelrotto.com

LANA
Festa della Fioritura
First two weeks in April
This grand spring festival lasts for a fortnight and is held at Lana, a delightful town set amid fruit orchards and vineyards. It involves musical events with food stalls, outings (on foot or by bike) through the blossoming fruit orchards, guided tours of the castles in the zone, barbecues and torchlit processions, baking of bread in the town's ancient wood oven, and flea and other markets. It is also possible to visit the Museo della Frutticoltura (museum of cultivating fruit).
For further information:
tel. 0473200443
www.meranerland.com

MERAN/MERANO

Festa dell'uva

Third weekend in October

This feast (literally, the feast of the grape) lasts all weekend and is linked to the grape harvest.

On Saturday night, a concert takes place. On the Sunday, which is the main and most popular day of the festival, the town is filled with food stalls and stands selling local products, newly-harvested grapes, grape juice, wine, beer and traditional desserts and cakes. Various folk groups, in costumes typical of the Tyrol area (but differing from village to village and valley to valley), parade through the streets and piazzas. In the afternoon, there is a large flag-throwing parade with decorated floats. The latter are adorned with bunches of grapes and vine leaves to celebrate the harvest. All this is accompanied by various other forms of entertainment typically found at festivals as well as shows and plenty of delightfully smelling chestnuts being roasted under the porticoes.
For further information:
tel. 0473272000,
www.meraninfo.it

SARNTAL/SARENTINO

Sagra della Val Sarentino

First weekend in September and the following Monday

On the Saturday and Sunday, there is a parade with allegorical floats, shows by folklore groups, a fanfare on horseback,

St Nicholas surrounded by the Krampusse during the festival in Vipiteno

musical concerts and a torchlit procession. Food stalls and other stands are also plentiful. Most of the locals get into the spirit and wear traditional outfits. The men wear loden trousers held up by Kraxn (larges suspenders with stomachers of black leather) and the Sarnar Huet (a felt hat with a black strip; green for married men, red for bachelors). The women wear long black skirts with bodices, on top of which they wear the traditional flowery aprons, and a shawl with lace and fringing. They also wear the Bänderhuet, a gracious felt hat with two long silk ribbons on the back.

Sarentino has some excellent stud farms for Avelignese (ponies with white tails and manes) and the best ones are shown off to the public. On the Friday before the feast, the most beautiful ponies are given prizes and receive a star on their side, a symbol of quality. During the folklore parade on the Sunday afternoon, the ponies appear, along with their riders, the fanfare and the floats. A large livestock market is held on the Monday.
For further information:
tel. 0471623091,
www.sarntal.com

STERZING/VIPITENO

Corteo di San Nicolò

5 December

The ceremony marks the entrance of St Nicholas into the town wearing sumptuous bishop's clothing. The saint is accompanied by two Moor servants, his servant Ruprecht and a group of devils, the Krampusse, covered in black fur and wearing horrible masks. While St Nicholas and the servants give sweets to the children, the devils try to keep order and occasionally "dirty" some of the onlookers. Historically, the saint is seen as especially helping the poor and children. The veneration of this saint started in the German area in 1087.

The parade of St Nicholas is most likely to be linked to ancient, popular dramas, which are recorded in the Tyrol area as far back as the 15th and 16th centuries.
For further information:
tel. 0472765325 www.vipiteno.com

WOLKENSTEIN IN GRÖDEN/ SELVA DI VAL GARDENA

Val Gardena in Costume
Beginning of August
This festival is held alternatively here, in Ortisei and Santa Cristina Valgardena. It takes place on the

Characteristic female outfits from Val Gardena

Sunday, beginning in the morning with musical events, stands and food stalls. The main attraction of the festival takes places in the afternoon: a seemingly endless parade. This involves the splendid traditional costumes of the Ladin population in Val Gardena: embroidered white shirts, red and green waistcoats, large black felt hats of various shapes and decorated with rosettes, feathers, ribbons and flowers; red headgear with gold embroidery; leather belts; knee-length shorts; light-colored, long socks tied with red ribbons and bows. During the festival, men, women and children proudly wear traditional outfits to a backdrop of allegorical floats and musical bands.
For further information:
tel. 0471792277
www.valgardena.it

TRENT/TRENTO

Feste Vigiliane
Second half of June
This feast is held in honor of the patron saint, St Vigilius. There are 9 days of festivities surrounding the festival of the saint, which takes places on June 26. The city comes to life with parades in period costumes and outfits, religious processions, various games, challenges, shows and small markets where you can buy crafts and some delightful local products.
One of the traditional events is the Palio dell'Oca (goose competition), in which the districts of the city challenge each other on rafts on the Adige river. Another event on the river is the Pena della Tonca, which is a re-enactment of an ancient form of punishment known as dumping or dunking: in the past, people who took the Lord's name in vain were, quite literally, dumped into the river. The real highlight, though, is the Mascherada dei Ciusi e dei Gobj (masquerade of the Ciusi and Gobj), a pageant about an ancient challenge involving the people of Trent (known as the Gobj) and Feltre (the Ciusi). According to the legend, King Theodoric decided to fortify the walls of the city but he did not have enough manpower. So, to do this, he called in the help of people from the neighboring villages, including people from Feltre. During this period, there was a severe famine, leading the people of Feltre to rob the food stores of Trent. A battle ensued that is now 'replayed' in Piazza Fiera. In the re-enactment, 40 Gobj have to defend an enormous cauldron, in the center of the piazza, against the assault of 40 Ciusi. Victory goes to the side that best defends or attacks the cauldron. At the end of the competition, there is polenta for everyone.
For further information:
tel. 0461917111
www.festevigiliane.it

BORGO VALSUGANA

Palio del Brenta
Last weekend in August
This event recalls the ancient rivalry between two districts of Borgo Valsugana, the Farinoti and the

Semoloti, who lived on opposites sides of the river running through the town, namely the Brenta. The Farinoti were nobles and more well off; the Semoloti were poor peasants. The feast begins on the last Friday in August to the sounds of bugles and drums that call the inhabitants to take part in the historical pageant that was held in the streets of the ancient district. This is followed by the games of the Palio (competition), including a raft challenge on the river, which is lit by torches. On Saturday afternoon, there are the games for the children and then, in the evening, there is a slingshot and archery competition. Sunday sees the actual historical pageant (in appropriate costumes) followed by the *gioco della quintana*, a challenge on horseback.

At the end of the games, the winner receives the Palio (banner).

During the two days of festivities, visitors can also enjoy concerts and folklore events.
For further information:
tel. 0461753033
www.comune.
borgo-
valsugana.tn.it

CAVARENO
Festa della Charta della Regola
First weekend in August
The Charta della Regola
(charter of regulations) is an ancient document that was originally passed down orally and then penned in 1632. It contains the rules for the citizens, thus it is a sort of municipal statute. The festival is in honor of this document and tries to recreate the ways of the past. It starts on the Friday with some theater or a pop music concert.
On the Saturday, you get an idea of the ancient traditions and trades amid

the stalls in a notable antiques market. On the Sunday, the whole town dresses up like it is the Middle Ages and wanders around the streets of the medieval district. You can "see" artisans, traders, peasants, plebs and nobles. There are also some religious events: a mass with Gregorian chants and the procession of the Virgin Mary. In the evening, you can try some age-old recipes and a historical parade makes its way through the torchlit old center. Everything ends with more theater and some fireworks.
For further information:
tel. 0463850106
www.cavareno.com

MADONNA DI CAMPIGLIO
Carnevale Asburgico
During carnival
A mountain carnival lasting for more than a week. Madonna di Campiglio has a magical reputation that is filled with tradition, so it is fitting that this festival recalls the atmosphere of the time in which the Emperor Franz Joseph and his wife, the celebrated Princess Sissi, made this the setting for their fabulous summer court. The festival includes a parade of floats and people dressed in Habsburg-style costumes, various representations of the

An original type of headwear worn at one of the regional festivals

way of life of the Viennese royalty, a party in masks for children and a large period ball held in the famous Hofer hall of the Grand Hotel Des Alpes, where the royal couple used to stay. Throughout this eventful week, there are wonderful fireworks displays, lively and more formal dancing and food stalls selling local dishes and vin brulè.
For further information:
tel. 0465447501
www.carnevaleasburgico.com

POMAROLO
Comun Comunale
Beginning of June
This festival is held every year over a weekend at the beginning of June, although the municipality it is held in alternates among Aldeno, Cimone, Isera, Nogaredo, Nomi, Pomarolo and Villa Lagarina.

It includes various medieval-type events, such as parades in costumes, historical re-enactments and pageants, tournaments and games. The main games are the so-called *tiro della bora* (an unusual event in which various woodcutters compete at rolling logs, called *bore*, with a hoe), tug-of-war and a stilt race. After the games, the victorious municipality wins the *cassa delle regole* (crate of rules), a large wooden crate that contains the regulations which govern the relations between the different municipalities. In addition, it is the winning municipality that receives the honor of hosting the games the following year. Throughout the whole weekend, the municipality where the event is held comes alive with busy markets filled with stores selling a wide range of products, concerts of ancient music, traditional food and fireworks.
For further information:
tel. 0464430363, www.aptrovereto.it

RIVA DEL GARDA
Notte di Fiaba
Last weekend of August
Riva del Garda becomes a fabulous land. The atmosphere of a famous fable or fairy tale, which changes each year, is recreated in the streets through theatrical performances, giant papier-mâché figures, theme-workshops for children, storytelling and outdoor games. Famous tales like those of *Pinocchio*, *Snow White*, *The Wizard of Oz* and *Alice in Wonderland* come alive for adults and children as they immerse themselves in a world of fantasy. There are also theme displays, tasting of local food, concerts, an antiques and crafts market, and a giant fireworks display.
For further information:
tel. 0464560113, www.nottedifiaba.it

TONADICO
En Giro par i Filò
Mid-August
This event was created to recall and celebrate the old trades and peasant life in the area. During the week around 15 August, the stables, barns and cellars of the town come to life as artisans 'bring to life' age-old activities such as weaving on old wooden looms, creating chairs stuffed with straw and wooden sculptures. The center of the event is the *filò*, that is, evening gatherings in which the women worked the winders while the men husked the corn, played music and told stories. There are also folklore events, concerts and fireworks.
For further information:
tel. 043962407
www.sanmartino.com

TRANSACQUA
Palio de la Sloiza
Second half of August
The *sloiza* is a large wooden sleigh that was used to transport straw and firewood. Today, it is the symbol of this festival that is held in Transacqua every year. The event lasts three days and has various stages. At the start, the traditional trades of the area are represented: from mining to working in the fields, from craftwork to timber-related activities. On the final day, there is the Palio, which involves a series of competitions to test the strength and skills of the various villages in the area. Throughout the festival, in the old center, you can try food that is typical of the Primiero mountain area.
For further information: tel. 043962407
www.sanmartino.com

EVENTS

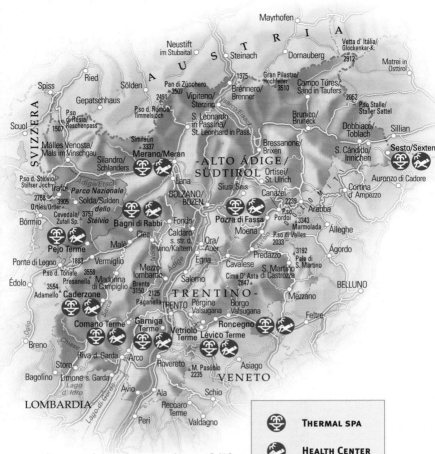

THERMAL SPA

HEALTH CENTER

Indisputably, the quality of life in Trentino-Alto Adige has few equals anywhere in Italy. In keeping with the overall regional context, the spa establishments and wellness centers here are of extremely high quality, equipped with cutting-edge technological facilities and housed in settings of incomparable beauty. Experience the thrill of a swim in a thermal pool at altitude, surrounded by meadows of flowers and cathedrals of rock, or the wide range of treatments to restore psychological and physical well-being. In addition to esthetic and body treatments, there are all kinds of opportunities in terms of sport, culture and entertainment. A holiday at a thermal spa in Trentino or Alto Adige

Wellness

is a chance to experience global wellness, including relaxation treatments and fun outdoors, where the charm of the natural setting combines with the highest level of hospitality and professional skills.

Highlights

- Relaxing hay baths at state-of-the-art wellness centers
- The beneficial properties of local raw materials, enhanced by the latest technologies
- Spas and wellness centers in Alpine settings with clean air, a mild climate, unspoiled scenery and products made using only natural ingredients

Inside

BAGNI DI RABBI ♈ 🏃

Terme di Rabbi

Fonti di Rabbi 162, Tel. 0463983000
www.termedirabbi.it
Closed in winter

The spa complex is situated at 1,195m above sea level, on the road leading up to the head of the Rabbi valley, in Trentino. Behind the traditional facade of the building is a state-of-the-art interior. In addition to the facilities for treatments involving drinking and bathing in the spring water, there is a pool fed by thermal spring water and used for "therapeutic

walks". The spa offers one of the most recently developed esthetic treatments: an anti-cellulite treatment involving injections of carbon dioxide taken from the spring water. The Grand Hotel Rabbi, across the road, is an integral part of the spa complex. This charming building has just undergone refurbishment that has turned it into a cutting edge hotel and wellness center. In addition to accommodation, the hotel has a wellness center (regeneration bath, Kneipp therapy, peat treatments) and a hydro-esthetic center that uses the Henri Chenot method.

CADERZONE ♈ 🏃

Terme Val Rendena Fonte S. Antonio

Via Damiano Chiesa 2, Tel. 0465806069
www.fontevalrendena.it
Open February-November and December-January

The spa is located in the picturesque town center in a palazzo of the noble Lodron-Bertelli family. The water comes from the S. Antonio spring, which breaks the earth's surface at an altitude of 970m, below the peaks in the Parco Naturale Adamello Brenta (Trent area). The spring water has a low mineral content with iron salts and some important trace elements, such as lithium and selenium. It is thus suitable for treatments involving drinking the water as well as those (e.g. hydro-massage with ozonized water) that help respiratory ailments and peripheral vascular diseases. The center also provides a continuous medical service with ear, nose and throat specialists and dermatologists. The adjoining wellness center offers a vast range of massages, esthetic treatments and the Thermae Veritas cosmetic line, a line of products made using water from the S. Antonio spring.

The Vita Nova Club
The hotels in the Vita Nova-Trentino Wellness project offer a high level of quality and diversity in all aspects, including accommodation and wellness centers. In the charming natural setting of Trentino, the project combines a wide range of hospitality carefully put together according to the concept of global wellness. This includes exclusive beauty and relaxation treatments at the project centers as well as facilities for exercise and enjoying life outdoors. It even extends to providing balanced meals made with good ingredients and the benefits of a holiday in harmony with the rhythms of nature. For further information: Vitanova-Trentino Wellness, Via Solteri 78, Trento; tel. 0461420603; www.vitanova.to

---

COMANO ♈ 🏃

Terme di Comano

Tel. 0465701277,www.termecomano.it
Open April-November and mid-December-mid-January

The treatment sessions are held in the spa complex, a modern building set among spruces on a bank of the Sarca river, in Trentino, in the middle of a huge park with a pond, footpaths, jogging routes, a bar and playgrounds for kids.

The complex includes a wellness center, seven specialist surgeries and departments for thermal treatments, and other facilities for massages, working out, and esthetic and anti-cellulite treatments. It also has a skin and cosmetic line, Comano Salus per Aquam, which is particularly effective for treating psoriasis and acne. Every year, many different events are held at the spa's conference center. The Grande Albergo Terme is party of the spa, although it can be regarded as a spa complex in its own right as it has facilities for various treatments (bathing, inhalation, drinking spring water) and hydromassage as well as a sun terrace. This spring water has a low mineral content and surfaces at a temperature of 28°C/82 °F. It contains bicarbonate, magnesium, calcium and a high percentage of fluorine.

GARNIGA TERME

Terme di Garniga
Via Bagni di Fieno 13, Tel. 0461842818
www.termedigarniga.it
Open May-October
Garniga is surrounded by a natural garden of Alpine plants such as gentian, arnica, St. John's Wort, thyme, dandelion, carline thistle and *Pusantilla anemone*, all known for their medicinal and therapeutic properties. This combination of medicinal plants, which is unique to Trentino, can be found in the Viotte basin on the slopes of Mt Bondone, at an altitude of approximately 1,000m and is used by the spa establishment for straw baths, a practice that has been handed down from the local farming tradition, and an effective treatment in the cure of rheumo-arthropathies. The well-being treatments available include physical therapy, massotherapy, massage, gymnastics and esthetic treatments.

LEVICO E VETRIOLO TERME

A large garden surrounds the spa complex at Lèvico Terme

Terme di Levico e Vetriolo
Viale Vittorio Emanuele
Tel. 0461706481
www.imperialhotel.it
Open April-October
The spa establishments of this complex in Trentino are situated at Levico and the village of Vetriolo Terme, 12km away, at an altitude of 1,500m. The heart of the complex is the Parco delle Terme, covering an area of more than 150,000m^2, which has a variety of tree species (magnolias, cedars, sequoias) worthy of a botanical garden. The park is the setting for the majestic Imperial Grand Hotel Terme, built at the end of the 19th century as the residence of the Austrian Imperial family, who used to stay here during the spa season. Recently restored, it

combines the charm of a historic, traditional building, ideal setting for congresses and other events, with a cutting edge hotel and spa. There are two pools and a gym as well as a wide range of treatments, saunas, and massages at the Principessa Sissi wellness center.

Not far away, in another park, is the Nuovo Palazzo delle Terme, a modern stone and glass building that was especially designed for mud, bathing, inhalatory and gynecological treatments and massotherapy.

The facilities at Vetriolo Terme, situated near the thermal spring, have recently been modernized and now offer thermal baths, inhalations and physical therapy.

The Terme di Levico has also invented a new line of cosmetics. The water here contains traces of iron salts and arsenic. The spring reaches the surface at a constant temperature of 9°C/48°F.

Imperial G. H. Terme 🐾
Via di Silva Domini 1,
Tel. 0461706104
www.imperialhotel.it
81 rooms, open April-October
Formerly a summer residence for the Austrian Imperial family and set in the charming park where the mineral springs are located, the hotel has retained the refined and elegant atmosphere which has always been its defining feature. Some of the notable aspects are the frescoes, antique furniture and dinner services. It has a gym and two pools (one indoor, one outdoor), and offers saunas, hydromassage, esthetic treatments, and manipulative and therapeutic treatments.

MERAN/MERANO 🧖 🐾

Terme di Merano
Piazza Terme 9,
Tel. 0473252000
www.termemerano.com
Open year-round
The fate of the South Tyrolean town of Merano was sealed in the early 19th century with the creation of the first spa establishment. Merano was also issued with a decree by the Habsburgs, regular visitors to the spa. The beautiful buildings in the old town center are imbued with the spirit of those times, especially the sumptuous Kurhaus, a place of leisure and a venue for grand events, facing the Lungo Passirio promenade. On the opposite bank is the spa establishment, fed by the S. Vigilio spring. The water is slightly radioactive, with a low mineral content and some

---

Adria 🐾
Via Glim 2,
Tel. 0473236687
www.hotel-adria.com
45 rooms, open March-November
This wellness center set in a splendid 19th-century palazzo immersed in an ancient park, offers manipulative, therapeutic and esthetic treatments, as well as treatments designed to restore psychological and physical well-being.

Castel Rundegg 🐾
Schennastr. 2,
Tel. 0473234100
www.rundegg.com
30 rooms, open year-round
The castle is an extremely pleasant place to stay. Next to it is a wellness center with a heated pool, a sauna, a Turkish bath, and individual whirlpools with aromatherapy. The center offers manipulative, therapeutic and esthetic treatments, as well as treatments designed to restore psychological and physical well-being.

G. H. Palace-Schloss Maur 🐾
Via Cavour-Straße 2/4,
Tel. 0473271000
www.palace.it
130 rooms, open year-round
Built in 1906 in a neo-classical style influenced by Art Nouveau, this wellness center is surrounded by a park with many different plant species. It offers manipulative, therapeutic and esthetic treatments, as well as treatments designed to restore psychological and physical well-being.

Villa Eden 🐾
Via Winkel 70,
Tel. 0473236583
www.villa-eden.com
47 rooms, open year-round
Set in the splendid natural setting of Merano, and built in the Art-Nouveau style in the middle of a large park, the building was converted into a wellness center with accommodation in 1976. Its guests can relax in its two pools or take advantage of the manipulative, therapeutic and esthetic treatments available, as well as treatments designed to restore psychological and physical well-being.

fluorine. The temperature is a constant 6.1°C/43°F. The complex is in a large park and has indoor and outdoor pools (including one with spring water and one for sport), the Spa & Vital center, a fitness center, saunas and vapor baths. There are facilities for looking after children and the hotel has most comforts. A pedestrian path leads to the town center.

The old Kurhaus at Merano, situated on the Passirio River

PEJO TERME

Terme di Pejo

Via delle Acque Acidule 3
Tel. 0463753226, www.termepejo.it
Open June-September and Christmas-Easter

This modern complex with its charming wooden facade has windows facing the woods and plenty of space devoted to recreation, including an auditorium often used as a cinema. It is located near some of the oldest springs in this area of Trentino. The water here is used for: treatments involving drinking spring water to help intestinal and kidney problems; inhalatory treatments for respiratory problems; bathing therapy for circulatory and dermatological ailments; and, the recent additions of anti-cellulite treatments and photo-therapy. You can take advantage of the health center with a pool fed with spring water (30°C/86°F), a gym and hydromassage; the wellness center with a Turkish bath (48°C/118°F) and a pool with massage jets; the esthetic center with UV-lamps and beauty-farm programs. The range of services includes massage for rehabilitation and relaxation. It also offers a range of cosmetics (Aqua) prepared with water from the various springs: Antica Fonte, (6.5°C/48°F) which has iron salts and a medium mineral content; Fonte Alpina, (6.5°C/48 °F), with a low mineral content; and Nuova Fonte, (6.5°C/48 °F) containing carbon dioxide and a medium mineral content.

The entrance to the Terme di Pejo spa complex

POZZA DI FASSA 🏺 🏃

Terme Dolomia
Tel. 0462762567
www.termedolomia.it
Open year-round
Set amid the splendid scenery of the Trento Dolomites, the spa establishment uses the ancient thermal spring-water at Alloch. This water has been known to man since ancient times because of its therapeutic properties. The water used in the resort is drawn directly from the spring. At the Club Terme Dolomia you will find the best that classical-style medicine and thermal treatments have

to offer. In addition, you can exercise and practice sport outdoors or take advantage of the vast range of beauty and relaxation programs. The thermal springs of Alloch, which contain sulfur, calcium, sulfates, magnesium and fluorine, gush out of the sedimentary rocks of Bellerophon (in the Monzoni range). The flow is constant, as is the compostion, which has remained unchanged with the passing of time. This water has various therapeutic applications, and is used in the treatment of gastro-intestinal problems, respiratory ailments, bad circulation and bone and joint disorders. It is also used in the treatment of constipation, obesity, allergies, varicose veins, stiff joints, skin disorders and fibroses. The thermal courses can also be integrated with examinations by specialists. A wellness center is attached to the spa establishment offering esthetic and relaxation treatments, and massages.

RONCEGNO 🏺 🏃

Casa della Salute Raphael
Piazza A. De Giovanni 4
Tel. 0461772000,
www.casaraphael.com
Open March-November
Treatments are available at the Casa di Salute Raphael, which is situated in a park with mineral springs, chestnuts and conifers. This hotel, built during the Belle Époque, has been completely modernized and is equipped for bathing therapy and inhalatory treatments based on the spring water, which

Roncegno, the Palace Hotel and the Casa della Salute Raphael (antique print)

contains a touch of arsenic and iron salts. The water surfaces at a constant temperature of 8.8°C/48°F at the nearby Vetriolo Terme spring.

In addition to the treatments mentioned above and those available at the wellness center, the spa offers a range of treatments based on the anthroposophical medicine invented by Rudolph Steiner. The latter came to the Levico, Vetriolo and Roncegno area in the 19th century and enthused about the exceptional quality of the mineral water. These treatments include phytotherapy, homeopathy and artistic therapies.

Casa di Salute Raphael 🏃
Piazza A. De Giovanni 4,
Tel. 0461772000
www.casaraphael.com
85 rooms, open March-November
This spa establishment was opened in 1989 in the Grand Hotel, which was built in the late 19th century and has retained its Art-Nouveau character.

It is surrounded by a large park and has a vegetable garden where most of the vegetables consumed on the premises are grown, as well as many medicinal herbs.

The wellness center offers a range of esthetic, thermal, manipulative and therapeutic treatments. In addition, there are therapies designed to restore psychological and physical well-being.

SEXTEN/SESTO ⚕ 🏃

Sport & Kurhotel Bad Moos
Moos/Moso, Fischleintalstr. 27
Tel. 0474713100, www.badmoos.it
Open June-November
The thermal springs are located in the upper Fiscalina valley (Alto Adige), at an altitude of 1,950m, below Croda Rossa. The water flows from the largest of these springs and contains sulfur, bicarbonate, calcium and sulfates. (4°C/39 °F). It is traditionally drunk as a diuretic, as well as being used for bathing therapy. The water has been exploited for therapeutic purposes since 1765, at first in an impromptu way, and later at a simple wooden spa establishment which, in the space of a few decades, was upgraded to the present, elegant stone building. Today, the spa establishment is part of Sport e Kurhotel Bad Moos, an elegant complex that combines charming accommodation with old wooden *Stuben*, and cutting edge facilities, such as the ozone pool, housed in a wooden building with huge windows. In addition to the hotel there is a residence and a charming annex.

The adjoining wellness center, Beauty Vital, offers massage, herb or straw baths, cosmetic treatments and integrated treatment packages.

Sesto's lovely setting in the upper Val Pusteria

THE A-Z OF WHAT YOU NEED TO KNOW

GETTING TO

By plane to Trentino-Alto Adige

BOLZANO/BOZEN – Bolzano Dolomiti Airport
www.abd-airport.it
Information, tickets and lost luggage:
tel. 0471255255
Telephone check-in: tel. 0471255266. This service is open every day from 6 to 21.45. You may check-in from 12 hours to 60 minutes prior to your flight. Requirements: valid booking, valid ticket, only hand luggage weighing less than 8 kg.

Getting there:
Car: A22 Brennero highway, Bolzano Sud exit, follow the signs. The airport is about 3km away.
Train: Bolzano/Bozen station.
Taxi: Radio Taxi Bolzano tel. 0471981111
Parking: There are 70 parking spaces in front of the airport, of which 20 are for a maximum of an hour. A further 30 spaces can be found on the road to the airport. Parking is free.

Car hire:
Travelcar tel. 0471252242-199180180
Hertz tel. 0471254266
Europcar tel. 0471252152
Maggiore tel. 0471971531

By train

The main line of the regional train network runs north-south across the area, connecting Trento and Bolzano before continuing on to Innsbruck. Various smaller lines then run off this towards Merano, San Candido (and then on to Salzburg) and Borgo Valsugana (continuing to Veneto). Bolzano is an important hub between northern and southern Europe and, as such, has an international train station with connections to Germany (various Eurocity trains link Munich to Verona, Venice, Milan, Rome and Naples).
For timetables and fares: Trenitalia, tel. 892021, every day from 7 to 21, only from Italy; telephonic ticket office 199166177, every day from 7 to 21; www.trenitalia.com.
Val Venosta railway, built mainly to serve local needs between Merano and Bolzano, is now used to link many national and international trains.
Information Office:
tel. 800846047
www.vinschgauerbahn.it
The Trentino Trasporti Spa company runs the line linking Trento to Malé and then Marilleva via Piana Rotaliana, Val di Non and Val di Sole.
Information Office:
tel. 0461821000,
www.ttspa.it

By car

The A22 Brennero highway connects Trento to Bolzano and then continues on to Innsbruck. Autostrade spa, Motorway information center: tel. 0643632121, 24 hours a day; Freephone 800269269-800279940; Bolzano Traffic Information tel. 0471200198 www.autostrade.it

TRANSPORT

Public Transport

BOLZANO – The cooperation of all the local public transport operators means that one can use, across all of Alto Adige, the buses, cable cars, and trains. www.sii.bz.it
The Servizio Trasporto Integrato dell'Alto Adige means you can use coaches, trains and interurban buses with a single ticket. Tickets can be bought from newsagents, ticket offices and on the buses themselves, for interurban journeys. A weekly ticket can be bought at the ticket offices and the tourist information offices.
Freephone: 800846047

THE CABLE CARS

The provincial fare system means that, aside from the normal and interurban buses, you can also use the Renon cableway, with the annexed Renon railway that links the upper cableway station with Collalbo, and the Mendola funicular. Here, there is the same provincial tariff system, with single tickets, multiple tickets and weekly (or longer) tickets. The *carta valore* (value card) is a 'universal' ticket that allows you to use all of the public transport in Alto Adige at a discount. For interurban routes or for the cable cars that leave from or arrive in a municipality that is part of the public transport network, tickets remain valid for 45 minutes for use on other forms of public transport.

RENON: CABLE CAR AND TRAIN

The cable car connecting Bolzano to Soprabolzano rises over 1,200m and is 4.56km long. From the upper cable station, a narrow gauge railway line, opened in 1907, goes to Collalbo via Costalovara. At the lower cable station it is possible to buy all the different types of tickets that are available. The carta valore (value card) and single tickets for the cable car and the train can be bought at the tourist offices in Soprabolzano and Collalbo. Single tickets can also be bought on the train from the conductor.

MENDOLA

The funicular cableway from Caldaro (S. Antonio) to Mendola rises over 850m at a gradient of 65 degrees. Single tickets can be bought from the automatic machines at both the upper and lower stations and from the funicular staff (ticket office at both stations).

THE SAN GENESIO CABLE CAR

The San Genesio cable car connects Bolzano and San Genesio. Single tickets can be bought from the cable station staff.

TRENT – The entire province is covered by Trentino Trasporti, which is responsible for public

Practical info

Radio information:
Isoradio FM 103,3
Viaradio FM 102,5

CLIMATE

The climate of Trentino-Alto Adige is predominantly alpine, being very cold in winter and enjoying a short, cool summer. As you climb higher, the temperature drops. During winter there are abundant snow falls. In the valleys, the climate is milder. Over an entire year, the change in temperature is notable, from -20 °C/-4 °F at Cima d'Italia in winter to 30 °C/86 °F in the Adige valley in summer. The Lake Garda and Merano basin areas enjoy microclimates not unlike Mediterranean climates, as can be guessed by the nature of the vegetation found in those parts. However, as you climb higher, the vegetation also changes, starting from broadleaf forests and cereal crops, through the fruit orchards and vineyards of the valley floor and then up into conifer forests on the slopes and, finally, moss, lichen, bare rocks, gravel and tundra.

TOURIST INFORMATION

Website der Region Trentino-Südtirol:
www.regione.taa.it

transport in Trent and Rovereto, trains from Trent to Malé and to Marilleva and interurban transport.
www.ttspa.it
CALL CENTER: 0461821000
Car hire:
TRAVELCAR tel. 0461263495
HERTZ tel. 0461421555
EUROPCAR tel. 0461390747

Fly Sky Shuttle

This is a transfer service, in operation from December to April, from the main northern Italian airports to the most famous skiing areas in Trent. Shuttle buses go from the Verona and Brescia airports to the Folgaria plateau, the Fassa and Fiemme valleys, the Paganella plateau and Val di Sole. There are two buses per day: the shuttles to the Paganella plateau and Val di Sole leave from Brescia airport in the early and late afternoon; the shuttles to the Fiemme

and Fassa valleys leave from Brescia airport at roughly the same time. Both shuttles (heading in both directions) stop at Rovereto Nord, where passengers going to Folgaria need to change shuttle. People going to Paganella (Andalo and Molveno) need to change at Rocchetta, which is at the start of Val di Non. If you are going to Madonna di Campiglio, then there is a transfer service: every Saturday, a shuttle goes from the Brescia and Verona airports to the ski resort. This service also operates on Sundays, in the same months, from the Milan airports: the coach leaves from Malpensa 2000 and then stops at Linate and Bergamo.
For timetable information and bookings:
www.trentinoviaggi.net;
call center 0461391111
(Monday-Saturday 9-18)

Inside

EMERGENCY NUMBERS

112	Military Police (Carabinieri)
113	State Police (Polizia)
115	Fire Department
117	Financial Police
118	Medical Emergencies
1515	Fire-watch
803116	Road Assistance

ANDALO

> 🛈 **APT Dolomiti di Brenta**
> *Piazza Dolomiti 1*
> *tel. 0461585836*
> *www.aptdolomitipaganella.com*

Hotels

Adler * ♿**
Piazza Centrale 2
tel. 0461585828
www.adlerhotel.it
70 rooms.
Credit cards: American Express, Visa
A building in the heart of the center with classic wooden balconies that is spacious and well-furnished. The restaurant serves regional specialities. Internet access, wellness center and sauna.

Olimpia * ♿ ★**
Via Paganella 17
tel. 0461585715
www.gottardi.it
41 rooms.
Credit cards: Bancomat, Diners Club, Mastercard, Visa
A quiet, comfortable hotel near the ski-lifts. Light wood furniture and rooms with balconies. Garden with games for children, free parking in the garage, sauna and restaurant.

Piccolo Hotel * A**
Via Pegorar 2
tel. 0461585710
www.piccolo.it
33 rooms.
Credit cards: American Express, Diners Club, Mastercard, Visa
In a quiet location, this cozy and welcoming hotel has a splendid view of the Brenta and Paganella mountains. Regional cuisine, Turkish baths and sauna, library with a fireplace and a small *Stube*.

Serena * ♿ ★**
Via Crosare 15
tel. 0461585727
www.hotelserena.it
38 rooms.
Credit cards: American Express, Diners Club, Mastercard, Visa
A hotel with a cozy mountain feel. Restaurant, Internet access and a *Stube*. The playground makes it an ideal place for families with children.

ARCO

Hotels

Al Frantoio * ♿**
Varignano, Via delle Grazie 22
tel. 0464518317
www.garnialfrantoio.it
37 rooms.
Credit cards: Bancomat, Mastercard, Visa
This hotel was once a spinning-mill and then an oil-press (note the mill-stone by the door and the old wooden-beam ceilings). It has Internet facilities and a fitness center with hydro-massage and a sauna.

Everest * ♿**
Viale Rovereto 91
tel. 0464519277
www.hoteleverest.it
55 rooms
Credit cards: American Express, Bancomat, Diners Club, Mastercard, Visa
A beautiful hotel in a panoramic setting; Internet and keep-fit facilities (pool and sauna), piano bar, bikes for use of the guests and a restaurant, open from April to October.

Pace * ★**
Via Vergolano 50
tel. 0464516398
www.hotelpace.net
42 rooms.
Credit cards: American Express, Bancomat, Diners Club, Mastercard, Visa
In a quiet location in the old town center, with jolly decor and furnishings and a restaurant.

Palace Hotel Città **♿ ★**
Viale Roma 10
tel. 0464531100
www.welcometogardalake.com
81 rooms.
Credit cards: American Express, Bancomat, Diners Club, Mastercard, Visa
Centrally located, this hotel offers a comprehensive range of facilities and comfort: restaurant, pool with hydro-massage and esthetic treatments (including a sauna).

Rural lodgings

Michelotti ♿
Bolognano, Via Soccesure 2
tel. 0464516272
www.agriturmichelotti.it
Open all year
Located in the Lower Valle del Sarca where the river broadens out before entering Lake Garda. The rooms have large balconies and rustic furnishings; pool, tennis courts, horse-riding and hiking.

Restaurants

Belvedere ǀ
Varignano, Via Serafini 2
tel. 0464516144
Open October-May
Credit cards: Visa
This trattoria, located in a 19th-century farm deep in the countryside, offers the typical cuisine of the area: cured meats and salamis, canederli, carne salada, strudel and apple cake. What's more, the olive oil is made on the farm.

Da Gianni ǁ ♿
Chiarano, Via S. Marcello 21
tel. 0464516464
www.dagianni.it
Open evening (Sunday only midday); closed Mondays
Credit cards: American Express, Diners Club, Mastercard, Visa
Located in an 18th-century building, this venue has a barrel-vaulted ceiling and a rustic ambience. Traditional cuisine and local wines. Also a hotel.

Lega ǀ ♿ ★
Via Vergolano 8 tel. 0464516205
www.ristoranteallalega.com
Closed Wednesday
Credit cards: American Express, Diners Club, Mastercard, Visa
A converted 16th-century building with frescoed rooms. Trentino cuisine and locally-produced olive oil. Good choice of local wines and distillates.

BAGNI DI RABBI

> 🛈 **APT delle valli di Sole, Pejo e Rabbi**
> *Malé, Via Marconi 7*
> *tel. 0463901280*
> *www.valdisole.net*

Hotels

G.H. Rabbi ***
tel. 0463983050
www.grandhotelrabbi.it
52 rooms.
Credit cards: Bancomat, Mastercard, Visa
Modern hotel opposite the spa complex, ideal for people who want a relaxing holiday and wellness facilities. The restaurant serving Trentino cuisine is next to the fitness center with a sauna.

Rural lodgings

Ruatti ♿
Pracorno 95, tel. 0463901070
Open mid June-mid September, Christmas and Easter
Located at the beginning of the Valle di Rabbi, the complex consists of two typical Alpine masi (farmhouses). One has rooms, the other is a restaurant. The cuisine is an interesting combination of vegetables, apples, cured meats, salamis, and meat produced on the farm.

BOZEN/BOLZANO

> ℹ **Azienda di Soggiorno e Turismo**
> *Piazza Walther 8*
> *tel. 0471307000*
> *www.bolzano-bozen.it*

Hotels

Alpi **** ★
Via Alto Adige 35
tel. 0471970535
www.alpi.sudtirol.com
111 rooms.
Credit cards: American Express, Diners Club, Mastercard, Visa
Not far from the town center, this hotel has a restaurant and access to a wellness center at the Albergo Stadt-Città, a stone's throw away.

Four Points Sheraton **** &
Via Buozzi 35
tel. 04711950012
www.4p-sheraton-bolzano.it
189 rooms.
This seven-storey glass and concrete building has made innovative use of plaster-board inside; sound-proofed rooms with full-length windows; bar of modern design, restaurant, pool, sauna, Internet and fitness facilities.

Luna-Mondschein **** &
Via Piave 15
tel. 0471975642
www.hotel-luna.it
78 rooms.
Credit cards: American Express, Diners Club, Mastercard, Visa
This charming 14th-century house has a lovely garden, used by the restaurant in summer to provide an outdoor service, and a traditional Stube.

Magdalenerhof *** &
Via Rencio 48/A
tel. 0471978267
www.magdalenerhof.it
39 rooms.
Credit cards: American Express, Diners Club, Mastercard, Visa
Set among the vineyards just outside town, this hotel with a typically Alto Adige flavor has a restaurant and a pool.

Parkhotel Laurin **** ★
Via Laurin 4, tel. 0471311000
www.laurin.it
96 rooms.
Credit cards: American Express, Diners Club, Visa
The building and the art-works here are original, and the old bar, with a fresco depicting the legend of King Laurino, adds to its charm. Pool, restaurant and Internet point.

Parkhotel Werth *** &
Via Maso della Pieve 19
tel. 0471250103
www.hotelwerth.com
57 rooms.
Credit cards: American Express, Diners Club, Mastercard, Visa
Quiet, rural location. Rooms have AC and hydro-massage. Sports facilities (pool, tennis courts, sauna), restaurant and Internet point.

Pircher ***
Via Merano 52, tel. 0471917513
www.hotelpircher.it
22 rooms.
Credit cards: American Express, Diners Club, Mastercard, Visa
This hotel has a south-facing terrace, a pool in the garden, AC and a restaurant.

Post Gries ***
Corso Libertà 117
tel. 0471279000
www.hotelpost.bz
100 rooms.
Credit cards: Bancomat, Mastercard, Visa
Only a few steps away from the center, this hotel offers a high standard of local cuisine and an Internet point.

Scala-Stiegl **** &
Via Brennero 11
tel. 0471976222
www.scalahot.com
65 rooms.
Credit cards: American Express, Diners Club, Visa
Built in the early 20th century, the hotel has an Internet point, a pool and, in summer, meals outside in its lovely shady garden; breakfast features home-made jams and sweet and savoury options.

Stadt-Città *** & ★
Piazza Walther 21
tel. 0471975221
www.hotelcitta.info
102 rooms.
Credit cards: American Express, Bancomat, Mastercard, Visa
This hotel in the heart of the city, on Piazza Walther, has a wide range of facilities including a piano bar, restaurant, Internet point and a wellness center with a sauna, a Turkish bath and a large hydro-massage pool.

Restaurants

Cavallino Bianco-Weisses Rössl ⫪
Via dei Bottai 6
tel. 0471973267
Closed Saturday evenings and Sundays
Credit cards: Bancomat
A historic venue with a reputation for typical local cuisine, including canederli allo speck in brodo and apple strudel.

Laurin ⫪⫪
Via Laurin 4, tel. 0471311000
www.laurin.it
Closed Sunday midday
Credit cards: American Express, Diners Club, Mastercard, Visa
Art Nouveau decor and local Alto Adige cuisine. Don't miss the bar which has live entertainment in the evening: jazz every Friday.

Moritzingerhof ⫪ ★
Via Merano 113,
tel. 0471932202
Closed Sunday evenings and Mondays
Credit cards: American Express, Diners Club, Mastercard, Visa, Bancomat
At this family-run venue, where special care is devoted to children, you can taste all the specialties of Alto Adige cuisine.

Rastbichler ⫪⫪
Via Cadorna 1,
tel. 0471261131
Closed Saturday midday and Sundays
Credit cards: American Express, Diners Club, Mastercard, Visa, Bancomat
A typical venue with a longstanding tradition; meals are served in the garden in summer; cuisine based on produce available in season.

Vögele ⫪
Via Goethe 3,
tel. 0471973938
www.voegele.it
Closed Sundays
Credit cards: Mastercard, Visa
Traditional all-wood decor, dining-rooms tastefully furnished; traditional cuisine, with home-made speck, canederli and gnocchi di ricotta.

At night

Bar Murphy's Pub
Via Parma 97

Havana Beach Club
Viale Druso 339

Kubo
Via Gobetti 4

Museums, Monuments and Churches

Museo Archeologico dell'Alto Adige
Via Museo 43,
tel. 0471320100
www.iceman.it
Opening times: Tuesdays-Sundays 10.00-13.00; Thursdays 10.00-19.00. Closed 1 January, 1 May, 25 December

Museo Civico
Via Cassa di Risparmio 14
tel. 0471974625
www.comune.bolzano.it/
museo_civico
Temporarily closed for
alterations. Scheduled
to re-open in 2008.

Museo della Scuola-
Schulmuseum
c/o Scuola Elementare Dante
Alighieri, Via Cassa di Risparmio
24, tel. 0471982805

Museo di Scienze Naturali
dell'Alto Adige
Via Bottai 1, tel. 0471412964
www.museonatura.it
Opening times: Tuesdays-
Sundays 10.00-18.00. Closed 1
January, 1 May, 25 December

Museo Mercantile
Via Argentieri 6/Via Portici 39
tel. 0471945709-0471945702
Opening times: Mondays-
Saturdays 10.00-12.30

BRIXEN/
BRESSANONE

☑ **Consorzio Turistico**
Valle Isarco
Bastioni Maggiori 26/A
tel. 0472802232
www.valleisarco.info
☑ **Associazione Turistica**
Bressanone
Via Stazione 9
tel. 0472836401
www.brixen.org

Hotels

Best Western Hotel Grüner
Baum **** ★
Via Stufles 11, el. 0472274100
www.bestwestern.it/
grunerbaum_bz
80 rooms.
Credit cards: American Express,
Bancomat, Diners Club,
Mastercard, Visa
The ideal place to relax and
enjoy the peaceful atmosphere.
It has a pool, a sauna, a
restaurant and fitness and
wellness facilities. Traditional
Alto Adige cuisine. The hotel
organizes hikes in the area
and sports events.

Dominik **** ⅃
Via Terzo di Sotto 13
tel. 0472830144
www.hoteldominik.com
36 rooms.
Credit cards: American Express,
Bancomat, Mastercard, Visa
This hotel, with its stunning
location, mountain views, indoor
pool and sauna, is a perfect
place to re-charge your
batteries.

Elephant ****
Via Rio Bianco 4
tel. 0472832750
www.hotelelephant.com
44 rooms.
Credit cards: Mastercard, Visa
This lovely hotel has a pool,
restaurant, sauna and tennis
courts; a really peaceful,
exclusive place to stay; Internet
point and, in the annex, there's
a sauna, a solarium and a gym.

Goldene Krone-
Vital Hotel **** ⅃
Via Fienili 4, tel. 0472835154
www.goldenekrone.com
48 rooms.
Credit cards: American Express,
Bancomat, Diners Club,
Mastercard, Visa
The aim of this hotel (a Vital
Hotel) is total wellness; the chef
uses only typical local produce.
Relax at the wellness center
which offers a sauna, Kneipp
treatments, massage and beauty
treatments.

Goldener Adler **** ⅃
Via Ponte Aquila 9
tel. 0472200621
www.goldener-adler.com
28 rooms.
Credit cards: Bancomat, Diners
Club, Mastercard, Visa
Formerly a 16th-century post
inn, in the pedestrian precinct of
the old town center, overlooking
the Isarco River; restaurant and
a sauna.

Senoner-Unterdrittel *** ⅃
Lungo Rienza 22
tel. 0472832525
www.hotelsenoner.it
21 rooms.
Credit cards: American Express,
Bancomat, Diners Club,
Mastercard, Visa
This venue dates back to the
late 15th century and has
retained its original facade;
restaurant with tables outside in
summer.

Restaurants

Elephant ⅠⅠⅠ ⅃
Via Rio Bianco 4
tel. 0472832750
www.hotelelephant.com
Open March-mid November and
December-6 January
Credit cards: Mastercard,
Bancomat
This old inn has two Stuben
and an elegant dining-room;
traditional and vegetarian
cuisine.

Fink ⅠⅠ
Via Portici Minori 4
tel. 0472834883
www.restaurant-fink.it
Closed Tuesday evenings and

Wednesdays
Credit cards: American Express,
Diners Club, Visa
This venue with its century-old
tradition keeps alive the Alto
Adige's most refined cuisine.

Oste Scuro-Finsterwirt ⅠⅠ
Vicolo del Duomo 3
tel. 0472835343
www.finsterwirt.com
Closed Sunday evenings and
Mondays
Credit cards: Mastercard, Visa,
Bancomat
Dating from the 13th-century,
this historic venue has period
decor and a fine collection of
early paintings and weapons.
Alto Adige cuisine and farm
cheeses.

Sunnegg ⅠⅠ ⅃ ★
Via Vigneti 67, tel. 0472834760
www.gasthof-sunnegg.it
Closed Wednesdays and
Thursday midday
Credit cards: American Express,
Diners Club, Visa
This Tyrolean-style maso is
surrounded by vineyards; meals
served on terrace in summer
with mountain views. Alto Adige
cuisine favors game and
seasonal produce, but includes
specialties like speck, canederli
and strudel. Also has some
rooms.

Museums, Monuments
and Churches

Museo della Farmacia
Bressanone
Via Ponte Aquila 4
tel. 0472209112
www.pharmazie.it
Tuesdays and Wednesdays
14.00-18.00; Saturdays
11.00-16.00. Guided tours by
prior arrangement for groups
Museo Diocesano
Piazza Vescovile 2
tel. 0472830505
www.dioezesanmuseum.bz.it/it/
home.htm
15 March-October: Tuesdays-
Sundays 10.00-17.00.
December-January: Mondays-
Sundays 14.00-17.00
(only Nativity collection).
Closed 24-25 December

BRUNECK/BRUNICO

☑ **Associazione turistica**
Brunico
Piazza Municipio 7
tel. 0474555722
www.bruneck.com
☑ **Consorzio turistico**
Crontour
Via M. Pacher 11/A
tel. 0474555447
www.kronplatz.com

Hotels

Andreas Hofer * ★**
Via Campo Tures 1
tel. 0474551469
www.andreashofer.it
48 rooms.
Credit cards: Bancomat,
Mastercard, Visa
Comfortable rooms and a fitness
center with a pool, sauna,
Turkish bath and massage are
some of the features of this
hotel, also known for its fine
cuisine.

Petrus **
Riscone/Reischach
Via Reinthal 11, tel. 0474548263
www.hotelpetrus.com
35 rooms.
Credit cards: Visa
A relaxing place to "fill up" with
fresh air and sunshine, with a
belvedere, a pool, a sauna and
a restaurant (BBQs in the
garden in summer).

Royal Hotel Hinterhuber **
Riscone/Reischach, Via Ried 1/A
tel. 0474541000
www.royal-hinterhuber.com
49 rooms.
Credit cards: American Express,
Mastercard, Visa
A spacious garden surrounds
this fine building with the air of
a stately home: good sports
facilities (pool, sauna, tennis
courts), an Internet point and a
restaurant.

Rudolf **
Riscone/Reischach
Via Riscone 33
tel. 0474570570
hotel-rudolf.com
37 rooms.
Credit cards: American Express,
Bancomat, Diners Club,
Mastercard, Visa
A refined ambience, with a
range of facilities for sport and
leisure; rooms have balconies
with views; pool, sauna, guided
hikes, wellness center and
beauty parlor; no restaurant
service in April or November.

Rural lodgings

Stienerhof
San Giorgio/Sankt Georgen
Via Pipen 25, tel. 0474550294
Open all year
Typical Alto Adige residence on
the edge of the forest; it
overlooks meadows which
stretch away towards the broad,
flat Valle di Tures.

Restaurants

Langgenhof ❙❙ &
Stegona/Stegen
Via S. Nicolò 11
tel. 0474553154

www.langgenhof.com
*Open evening only; closed
Sundays*
Credit cards: American Express,
Mastercard, Visa, Bancomat
A Tyrolean atmosphere,
including the Stube and the
winter garden, plus a shady
garden where meals are served
outside in summer. Traditional
Alto Adige cuisine and menus
based on what is available
locally; local wines predominate.
Tyrolean evenings with music.

Oberraut ❙
Anieto 1, tel. 0474559977
Closed Thursdays
Credit cards: American Express,
Mastercard, Visa, Bancomat
This maso on the slopes of the
mountain specializes in local
cuisine.

Museums, Monuments
and Churches

Museo Civico di Grafica ★
Via Bruder Willram 1
tel. 0474553292
www.stadtmuseum-bruneck.it
*January-June: Tuesdays-Fridays
15.00-18.00; Saturdays and
Sundays 10.00-12.00. July:
Tuesdays-Sundays 10.00-12.30,
15.30-18.30. August: Mondays-
Sundays 10.00-12.30, 15.30-
18.30. September-December:
Tuesdays-Fridays 15.00-18.00;
Saturdays and Sundays 10.00-
12.00*

CALDONAZZO
Hotels

Due Spade ** ★
Piazza Municipio 2
tel. 0461723113
www.albergoduespade.it
24 rooms.
Credit cards: Visa
This quiet, centrally located
hotel has some rooms in the
attic with exposed beams;
traditional furnishings, pool and
restaurant.

CAMPITELLO
DI FASSA

> 🄸 **APT della Val di Fassa**
> *Strêda de Dolèda 10*
> *tel. 0462609500*
> *www.fassa.com*

Hotels

Crepes de Sela * &**
Via Dolomiti 30
tel. 0462750538
21 rooms.
Credit cards: Bancomat,
Mastercard, Visa
300m from the cable-car, typical

Tyrolean-style ambience with
views of Sassolungo; Turkish
bath, hydro-massage, solarium
terrace, tropical shower with
cold mist, sauna and restaurant.
Crampon-warmer and mountain
bikes for use of guests.

Salvan * &**
Via Dolomiti 20
tel. 0462750307
www.hotelsalvan.com
35 rooms.
Credit cards: Bancomat, Diners
Club, Mastercard, Visa
Typical mountain-style venue
with fitness facilities; traditional
regional cuisine, lunch served
on the terrace. Also pool and
sauna.

Villa Campitello * & ★**
Via Roma 6, tel. 0462750002
www.villacampitello.com
25 rooms.
Credit cards: Bancomat,
Mastercard, Visa
Located near the ski facilities,
all rooms have balconies;
restaurant, sauna and Turkish
bath. In summer, hikes with an
Alpine Guide; mountain bikes
for hire against deposit.

Museums, Monuments
and Churches

Museo degli Sci
c/o stazione della funivia
tel. 0462750350
*December-April: Mondays-
Sundays 8-18.30*

CANAZEI
Hotels

Andreas * &**
Via Strada Dolomites 18
tel. 0462602106
www.andreas.it
32 rooms.
Credit cards: American Express,
Bancomat, Diners Club,
Mastercard, Visa
Located in the old town center,
this hotel has a fitness center, a
sauna and a restaurant serving
regional cuisine.

Astoria ** &**
Via Roma 92, tel. 0462601302
www.hotel-astoria.net
39 rooms.
Credit cards: American Express,
Bancomat, Diners Club,
Mastercard, Visa
This centrally-located hotel has
a restaurant, a large terrace and
a sauna. Some rooms have a
small sitting-room and a
balcony. It also has a beauty
parlor with a wide range of
treatments.

Cesa Tyrol * &**
Viale alla Cascata 2

tel. 0462601156
www.hotelcesatyrol.com
42 rooms.
Credit cards: American Express,
Diners Club, Mastercard, Visa
Set in a garden, the charming
rooms in this hotel have Alpine
decor. There is also a Turkish
bath, a sauna, aromatized
showers and Kneipp massage.
Bonuses here include an
excellent restaurant and views of
Gran Vernel and Catinaccio. There
is an adults' games room and
there are mountain bikes for hire.

Dolomites Inn * & **
Penia, Via Antersies 3
tel. 0462602212
www.dolomitesinn.com
27 rooms.
Credit cards: Bancomat
This sunny hotel in typical
Tyrolean style has a Stube and
rooms with balconies
overlooking the view; it also has
a restaurant, an Internet point, a
sauna, squash courts and
fitness facilities.

Restaurants

**De Tofi ⫟ & **
Via Roma 92, tel. 0462601302
www.hotel-astoria.net
Closed Mondays
Credit cards: American Express,
Mastercard, Visa, Bancomat
Typical Alpine restaurant, in a
hotel in the town center. Ladino
cuisine based on local produce,
partcularly cheeses, speck and
other cured meats, and
vegetables. Typical dishes
include carne salada with grana
trentino, canederli al puzzone di
Moena and fagottino di mele
renette.

CAVALESE

☑ **APT della Valle
di Fiemme**
Via Fratelli Bronzetti 60
tel. 0462241111
www.valdifiemme.info

Hotels

Bellavista ** & ★**
Via Pizzegoda 5
tel. 0462340205
www.hotelbellavista.biz
46 rooms.
Credit cards: American Express,
Bancomat, Diners Club,
Mastercard, Visa
In a panoramic position, one of
the city's historic hotels; a
restaurant, a sauna, a small
library, an Internet point and a
wine bar. It has a wellness
center, a beauty parlor and a
center based on homeopathic
medicine.

Corona * & **
Carano, Via Don Giovannelli 71
tel. 0462340246
www.hotelcorona.it
31 rooms.
Credit cards: Bancomat,
Mastercard, Visa
This 20th century hotel has
retained its typical Val di
Fiemme character: wood
predominates, some rooms have
balconies, others in attic.
Restaurant and sauna.

Restaurants

**Costa Salici ⫟⫟ & **
Via Costa dei Salici 10
tel. 0462340140
www.costasalici.com
Closed Mondays and Tuesday
midday except Christmas and
August
Credit cards: American Express,
Diners Club, Mastercard,Visa,
Bancomat
Trentino cuisine successfuly
combining a new interpretation
with the local tradition; meals
served outside in summer. Also
has some rooms.

El Molin ⫟⫟⫟ ★
Piazza C. Battisti 11
tel. 0462340074
www.valdifiemme.it
Open evening in winter; closed
Tuesdays
Credit cards: American Express,
Diners Club, Mastercard, Visa,
Bancomat
Set in a charming 17th-century
mill, two floors are connected by
a wooden staircase. Trentino
cuisine with a new slant; fine
assortment of cheeses from the
valley and the surrounding area;
home-grown vegetables and you
can visit the wine-cellar.

Museums, Monuments and Churches

**Museo Pinacoteca della
Magnifica Comunità Generale
di Fiemme**
Piazza Cesare Battisti 2
tel. 0462340365
www.magnificacomunitafiemme.it
Closed for restoration until 2012

COMANO TERME

☑ **APT Terme di Comano-
Dolomiti di Brenta**
Via C. Battisti 38/D
tel. 0465702626
www.comano.to

Hotels

Cattoni Plaza **
Ponte Arche, Via Battisti 19
tel. 0465701442
www.cattonihotelplaza.com
75 rooms.

Credit cards: American Express,
Bancomat, Mastercard, Visa
This hotel distinguishes itself for
its high standard of cuisine,
sports facilities (pool, tennis
courts) and leisure activities
(sauna).

G.H. Terme ** AC**
tel. 0465701421
www.termecomano.it
82 rooms.
Credit cards: American Express,
Bancomat, Diners Club,
Mastercard, Visa
Set in a century-old garden,
it has rooms with balconies and
some suites, hydro-massage,
spa treatments and a wellness
center with a pool, Turkish bath,
sauna, massage and beauty
treatments. The chef uses
typical local produce.

Park Hotel Villa Luti **
Campo Lomaso
Piazza Risorgimento 40
tel. 0465702061
www.villaluti.it
42 rooms.
Credit cards: American Express,
Bancomat, Diners Club,
Mastercard, Visa
Historic villa converted into a
hotel with frescoed reception
rooms and avenue of
hornbeams; also restaurant,
Internet point, and facilities for
leisure (tennis courts) beauty
treatments and relaxation
(sauna).

CORVARA IN BADIA/
CORVARA

☑ **Consorzio turistico Alta
badia**
Via Col Alt 36
tel. 0471836176
www.altabadia.org

Hotels

Cappella e Dependance ** & **
Colfosco/Kollfuschg
Strada Pecei 17, tel. 0471836183
www.hotelcappella.com
46 rooms.
Credit cards: Mastercard, Visa
An elegant reception area,
reading room, decor of rooms
varies (singles have French
beds) and luxurious suites
(some designed by Matteo
Thun); rightly defined as an "Art
hotel" since, apart from the
Renée gallery, the rooms and
halls are hung with signed
originals. Also an Eastern-style
wellness center, a restaurant, a
pool, sauna and tennis courts.

Colfosco-Kolfuschgerhof ** & **
Colfosco/Kollfuschg
Via Rönn 7, tel. 0471836188

www.kolfuschgerhof.com
40 rooms.
Credit cards: Mastercard, Visa
Stunning position with views of the Sella massif and the Val di Mesdì, this hotel has an Internet point, a beauty and health center, a pool, a sauna and a piano bar (evenings); locally grown/made raw ingredients used in the cuisine.

Sassongher ★★★★ &
Via Sassongher 45
tel. 0471836085
www.sassongher.it
53 rooms.
Credit cards: Bancomat, Mastercard, Visa
Hotel in a fabulous position, filled with Tyrolean antiques, old Stuben with complete range of facilities for sport and keeping fit (including massage and hydro-massage). Some rooms have majolica stoves. Also restaurant, pool and sauna.

Restaurants

La Stüa de Michil ⅲ &
Strada Col Alt 105
tel. 0471831000
www.hotel-laperla.it
Open December-March and mid June-mid September, only evenings; closed Mondays
Credit cards: American Express, Diners Club, Mastercard, Visa, Bancomat
Located just above the town, this wonderfully typical venue was once a Stube. Traditional local cuisine with a high standard of raw ingredients.

DEUTSCHNOFEN/ NOVA PONENTE

ⓘ Consorzio Turistico Catinaccio-Latemar
Ponte Nova di Sotto 9
tel. 0471610310
www.rosengarten-latemar.com
ⓘ Associazione Turistica Nova Ponente
Via Castello Thurn 1
tel. 0471616567
www.valdega.com

Hotels

Erica ★★★★ ★
Via Principale 17, tel. 0471616517
www.erica.it
30 rooms.
Credit cards: Bancomat, Mastercard, Visa
Situated at the edge of the forest and close to the ski facilities, this hotel has a wellness center, a restaurant serving regional dishes, a pool and a sauna.

Oberlehenhof ★★★ &
San Nicolò d'Ega/Sankt Nikolaus Eggen, tel. 0471615801
www.oberlehenhof.com
26 rooms.
Credit cards: American Express, Diners Club, Mastercard, Visa
The offering here includes: a trail for getting back into shape with a sauna, a fitness room and pool with hydro-massage; Stuben, a taverna and a restaurant; kids' playroom, Internet point and tennis courts.

Rural lodgings

Bachnerhof
Unterwinkl 2, tel. 0471615163
Open all year
Approached from Bolzano, Val d'Ega is a wild gorge carved out of the red rock, but it soon opens out giving views of Catinaccio and Latemar. You can stay on the plateau, with these same views at Monte San Pietro, at the Santuario della Madonna di Pietralba.

Ortnerhof
Obereggen 18, tel. 0471615722
www.ortnerhof.it
Open May-October and December-April
Credit cards: Bancomat, Mastercard, Visa
Below Monte Latemar, this hotel has every possible comfort: five-a-side football field, a restaurant, a wellness area, sauna, horse-riding and, in summer, a mini club for kids.

Museums, Monuments and Churches

Museo Territoriale di Nova Ponente &
Via Castello Thurn 1
tel. 0471617500

EPPAN AN DER WEINSTRASSE/ APPIANO SULLA STRADA DEL VINO

ⓘ Associazione Turistica Appiano sulla Strada del Vino
Piazza Municipio 1
tel. 0471662206
www.appiano.net

Hotels

Landgasthof Kreuzstein ★★★ &
Via Monte 60, tel. 0471664025
www.kreuzstein.com
12 rooms.
Credit cards: Mastercard, Visa
On the edge of the wood, this is a great starting point for outings on foot or by bike into the

various vineyards dotted around. There is also a restaurant and some apartments that are ideal for families or groups of friends.

Stroblhof ★★★★ &
San Michele/Sankt Michael Via Piganò 25
tel. 0471662250
www.stroblhof.it
34 rooms.
Credit cards: Mastercard, Visa
Situated in an old wine-making *maso*, it has rustic rooms, some on the terrace and some with balconies, and a wellness center offering various treatments, massages and beauty treatments. Pool, sauna and restaurant.

Weinegg ★★★★★ &
Cornaiano
Via Lamm 22
tel. 0471662511
www.weinegg.com
42 rooms.
Credit cards: Bancomat, Mastercard, Visa
A house in the vineyards with a Tyrolean *Stube*, a sitting room with a fireplace, wellness and beauty facilities; outdoor pool and tennis. Regional cuisine and wines made on site.

Rural Lodgings

Federerhof
San Michele/Sankt Michael Via Monticolo 29
tel. 0471662048
Open March-November
This *maso* in the hills around the Adige and not far from Lake Monticolo is a wonderful place to stay amid the greenery of meadows and woods.

Restaurants

Bellavista-Marklhof ⅱ
Cornaiano/Girlan
Via Belvedere 14
tel. 0471662407
www.eppan.com/marklof
Closed Sunday evenings and Mondays
Credit cards: American Express, Mastercard, Visa
This restaurant in a old *maso* is set amid vineyards and has a Tyrolean *Stube*. Traditional local cuisine, with excellent homemade ham.

Belvedere ⅱ
Via Mazzini 7, tel. 0543445127
www.belvedere-ristorante.com
Closed Wednesdays
Credit cards: American Express, Diners Club, Mastercard, Visa
Two cozy rooms with a coffered ceiling from the 1500s and a terrace-veranda used in summer. Regional cuisine with local hams and salamis.

Zur Rose ⃞ ⃟
San Michele/Sankt Michael
Via Innerhofer 2, tel. 0471662249
www.zur-rose.com
Closed Sundays and Monday
midday
Credit cards: American Express,
Diners Club, Mastercard, Visa
This restaurant in the center is
set in a typical 13th-century
house. The cuisine combines
tradition with local ideas.
Wonderful range of local
cheeses, excellent wine
(also available per glass)
and spirits lists.

FAI DELLA PAGANELLA
Hotels
Arcobaleno ***
Via C. Battisti, tel. 0461583306
www.hotelarcobaleno.it
37 rooms.
Credit cards: Bancomat, Visa
In a panoramic setting, not far
from the ski facilities, with a
restaurant and a sauna. Beauty
center and fitness facilities.

Negritella **
Via Tonidandel 29
tel. 0461583145
www.hotelnegritella.it
20 rooms.
A hotel with a splendid view
and fine cuisine with local
specialties.

Santellina *** ★
Santel, tel. 0461583120
www.hotelsantellina.com
40 rooms.
Credit cards: American Express,
Bancomat, Diners Club,
Mastercard, Visa
Surrounded by garden and pine-
woods, a few meters from the
chair-lift to la Paganella and the
ski-slopes, this Alpine-style
hotel serves Trentino cuisine
and typical cured meats and
salamis of the area.

FOLGARIA

> ⃞ **APT Altipiano**
> **di Folgaria**
> *Via Roma 67*
> *tel. 0464721133*
> *www.montagnaconamore.it*

Hotels
Villa Wilma ***
Via della Pace 12
tel. 0464721278
www.villawilma.it
24 rooms.
Credit cards: Bancomat, Visa
Tyrolean-style hotel in a quiet
location with great views, next

to the Paradiso cable-car;
Trentino cuisine.

FOLGARIDA

> ⃞ **APT Dolomiti**
> **di Brenta**
> *Andalo, Piazza Dolomiti 1*
> *tel. 0461585836*
> *www.aptdolomitipaganella.*
> *com*

Hotels
Alp Hotel Taller **** ⃟
Via del Roccolo 39
tel. 0463986234
www.hoteltaller.it
27 rooms.
Credit cards: Mastercard, Visa
Charming chalet with wooden
decor and rooms with balcony
facing the Val di Sole or the
Brenta Dolomites; in the
restaurant, traditional dishes are
served with local wines.
Program of excursions and wide
range of wellness and beauty
facilities (sauna).

Sun Valley ***
Via del Roccolo 1
tel. 0463986208
www.sunvalleyhotel.it
20 rooms.
Credit cards: Mastercard, Visa
Typical Alpine architecture,
relaxing setting; local cuisine.

GARNIGA TERME
Hotels
Miramonti ***
Via dei Bagni di Fieno 20
tel. 0461843243
www.hotelmiramontigarniga
terme.com
33 rooms.
Credit cards: American Express,
Bancomat, Diners Club,
Mastercard, Visa
Located near the hay-bath
complex, the hotel offers
relaxing accommodation;
angling and many hikes
and excursions.
A few km from the ski-slopes
of Monte Bondone.
Also restaurant.

GLURNS/GLORENZA

> ⃞ **Associazione turistica**
> **Alta Venosta Vacanze**
> *tel. 0473737073*
> *www.altavenosta-*
> *vacanze.it*

Hotels
Posta-Zur Post *** ⃟
Via Flora 15
tel. 0473831208
www.hotel-post-glurns.com

30 rooms.
Credit cards: American Express,
Bancomat, Mastercard, Visa
Formerly a 15th-century post
inn, this hotel has a charming
atmosphere; also sauna and
restaurant.

INNICHEN/ SAN CANDIDO

> ⃞ **Consorzio Turistico Alta**
> **Val Pusterla**
> *Piazza del Magistrato 1*
> *tel. 0474913156*
> *www.altapusterla.net*
> ⃞ **Associazione Turistica**
> **San Candido**
> *Piazza del Magistrato 1*
> *tel. 0474913149*
> *www.sancandido.info*

Hotels
Orso Grigio **** ⃟
Via Rainer 2
tel. 0474913115
www.orsohotel.it
23 rooms.
Credit cards: American Express,
Diners Club, Mastercard, Visa
This comfortable hotel housed
in an 18th-century building has
a restaurant with an impressive
wine-cellar and serves home-
made products for breakfast.
Sauna and special rates at the
municipal indoor swimming-
pool.

Sporthotel Tyrol *** ★
Via P.P. Rainer 12
tel. 0474913198
www.sporthoteltyrol.it
28 rooms.
Credit cards: Bancomat,
Mastercard, Visa
A comfortable, peaceful
ambience with a relaxation area
(pool, sauna) and a restaurant
serving regional cuisine.

Villa Stefania **** ⃟
Via Duca Tassilo 16
tel. 0474913588
www.villastefania.com
30 rooms.
Credit cards: Mastercard, Visa
This rural hotel has rooms
facing the mountains;
restaurant and charming
Teestube (tea-room)
with an "Imperial Austrian"
flavor. Wellness area with sauna,
Turkish bath and massage.
Free access to Acquafun
and free use of pool and tennis
courts.

Rural lodgings
Gadenhof
Via Elzenbach 1
tel. 0474913523
www.gadenhof.it

Open all year
A valley-dwelling set in the lovely meadows around San Candido amid the spectacular scenery of the Parco Naturale delle Dolomiti di Sesto, dominated by Cima Nove; guests have free access to the pool at San Candido.

Museums, Monuments and Churches

Dolomythos
Villa Wachtler, Via P.P. Rainer 11, tel. 0474913462
Open all year: Mondays-Saturdays 10-12, 15-19; 15 July-September: 10-12, 15-19

Museo della Collegiata
Via Atto 2
tel. 0474913149-0474913278
www.altapusteria.info

*15 June-15 October :
Thursdays-Saturdays 17.00-19.00; Sundays 10.00-11.00. 15 July-August: Tuesdays 10.00-11.00, 20.00-22.00; Wednesdays-Saturdays 10.00-11.00. Closed 16 October-14 June*

KALTERN AN DER WEINSTRASSE/ CALDARO SULLA STRADA DEL VINO

[i] **Associazione turistica Caldaro al Lago**
*Piazza Mercato 8
tel. 0471963169
www.kaltern.com*

Hotels

Goldener Stern *
Via Hofer 28, tel. 0471963153
www.goldener-stern.it
30 rooms.
Credit cards: Mastercard, Visa
This 18th-century Alpine house in the town center also has a restaurant with traditional cuisine.

Seeleiten **
*San Giuseppe al Lago/ St. Joseph am See
tel. 0471960200*
www.seeleiten.it
39 rooms.
Credit cards: American Express, Bancomat, Mastercard, Visa
In a beautiful location, this hotel has good facilities for sport and leisure (pool, sauna, tennis courts); also a restaurant and a wellness center.

Tannhof ** &
*Pianizza di Sopra/Oberplanitzing
tel. 0471669077*
www.tannhof.it
30 rooms.

This small house by a pine-wood is the starting-point for hikes and mountain-bike expeditions; rooms with balcony or in attic; solarium terrace, bowls, pool with whirlpool. Also a restaurant.

Rural lodgings

Eichhof
*San Nicolò/Sankt Nikolaus
Kalterer Höhe 10
tel. 0471962634*
Closed December-February
Comfortable accommodation in a maso surrounded by vineyards and orchards, on the slopes of Monte Penegal.

Siganatenhof &
*Via S. Maria 2A
tel. 0471962025*
www.siganatenhof.it
Open all year
Near Lago Caldaro, surrounded by expanses of meadows and fruit trees. It has an attic, a solarium terrace, wooden balconies with geraniums and typical Erker: an ideal holiday base for families with children.

Zur Traube
Pozzo/Pfuss 7, tel. 0471963369
Open Easter-October
Enjoy a holiday at the bottom of the valley among orchards and vineyards, staying in a country house with an open-air pool. The best view of this landscape, with Latemar and Catinaccio in the background, is from the road leading up to Passo di Mendola.

Restaurants

Castel Ringberg ⦀
*San Giuseppe al Lago/ Sankt Joseph am See
tel. 0471960010*
www.castel-ringberg.com
Closed Tuesdays
Credit cards: Visa, Bancomat
Accommodation in the romantic rooms of a mid-17th-century castle with its panoramic terrace; Alto Adige cuisine.

Ritterhof ⦀
*Via del Vino 1,
tel. 0471963330*
Closed Sunday evening and Mondays
Credit cards: American Express, Diners Club, Mastercard, Visa, Bancomat
Traditional building on the Wine Route with lovely views across the lake; traditional cuisine.

Museums, Monuments and Churches

Museo Provinciale del Vino
Via dell'Oro 1, tel. 0471963168
www.provincia.bz.it/volkskunde

---

*museen/Wm_it_o.htm
April-11 November: Tuesdays-Saturdays 9.30-12.00, 14.00-18.00; Sundays, Sundays 10.00-12.00*

KARERSEE/ CAREZZA AL LAGO

[i] **Consorzio turistico Alpe di Siusi-Altipiano dello Sciliar**
*Piazza Krausen 1
tel. 0471706333
www.castelrotto.com*
[i] **Associazione turistica Sciliar-Castelrotto**
*Via Catinaccio 2
tel. 0471704122
www.sciliar.com*
[i] **Associazione turistica Siusi all Sciliar**
*Siusi, Via Sciliar 16
tel. 0471707024w
ww.siusi.it*

Hotels

Simhild **
Via Bellavista 1, tel. 0471612169
www.simhild.com
9 rooms.
Small hotel with restaurant, ideal for a relaxing holiday.

KASTELRUTH/ CASTELROTTO

Hotels

Diana ** &**
Via S. Osvaldo 3, tel. 0471704070
www.hotel-diana.it
54 rooms.
Credit cards: Bancomat, Mastercard, Visa
Reception with wooden paneling, open fire and fine collection of Tyrolean antiques; also restaurant, Internet point, two pools with sauna, Turkish bath and solarium.

Posthotel Lamm ** &**
*Piazza Krausen 3
tel. 0471706343*
www.posthotellamm.it
58 rooms.
Credit cards: Bancomat, Mastercard, Visa
In the heart of the old town center, the hotel dates from the 15th century, with restaurant, pool and sauna; physical treatments available include hay baths, a Kneipp trail, Turkish bath and massage.

Rural lodgings

Binterhof &
Via Panidei 49, tel. 0471700071
www.binterhof.com
Splendid position, surrounded

by meadows, minutes from the town center and c. 20 minutes from Alpe di Siusi and the Val Gardena, a maso (farmhouse) with flowers on the balconies and Tyrolean decor. Evening entertainment and BBQs; bikes for use of guests, use of kitchen.

Patenerhof
San Valentino/
Sankt Valentin
Via Patener 11
tel. 0471706033
www.patenerhof.com
Open all year
Typical Alpine house set in meadows, with views towards the Dolomites and Sciliar, popular with hikers; mountain sports nearby and at nearby Alpe di Siusi. Evening entertainment and free shuttle service.

Restaurants

Sassegg 🍽
Via Sciliar 9
tel. 0471704290
www.sassegg.it
Closed Mondays and Tuesday midday
Credit cards: American Express, Diners Club, Mastercard, Visa, Bancomat
Guests can eat in the dining-room or on the terrace; in the kitchen, the smells and flavors of the dishes, mainly fish, are influenced by the use of local products. (Booking advisable).

LANA

> ☑ **Associazione turistica Lana**
> *Via Andrea Hofer 7/B*
> *tel. 0473561770*
> *www.lana.net*

Hotels

Poeder **** &
Via Gilmann 1
tel. 0473561258
www.hotel-poeder.com
47 rooms.
Credit cards: American Express, Diners Club, Mastercard, Visa
Friendly welcome, in the traditional Tyrolean style, offers a restaurant, pool, sauna and the opportunity to chill out in its garden full of flowers.

Vigilius Mountain Resort *****
Giogo di San Vigilio/
Vigiljoch
tel. 0473556600
www.vigilius.it
41 rooms.
Credit cards: American Express, Bancomat, Mastercard, Visa

Designed by highly-acclaimed architect Matteo Thun, at an altitude of 1,500m, it can only be reached by cable-car. Charming atmosphere, wellness facilities on three floors with pool, sauna and Alpine and Zen treatments; endless scope for hikes or mountain bike expeditions. Two restaurants, one a Stube serving Alto Adige specialties.

Völlanerhof **** &
Foiana/Völlan, Vicolo Wieser 30
tel. 0473568033
www.voellanerhof.com
47 rooms.
Credit cards: Mastercard, Visa
Set among the Merano vineyards, this complex has excellent sports facilities (pool and tennis courts), a beauty center, a fitness center and BBQs with entertainment and dancing in the evening. Also restaurant.

Rural Lodgings

Kammerhof
Via Feldgatter 19/1
tel. 0473564551
www.kammerhof.it
Open March-November
In sunny position surrounded by an orchard, with views of the mountains above Merano, a maso with a grill, bikes for hire, a small zoo and a kids' play area.

Leilichhof
Via Monte Luco 3/12
tel. 0473563065
Closed December-February
Apples are one of the symbols of the Alto Adige, from spring, when the white flowers bloom on the trees, to autumn, when the fruit matures, and is converted into the delicious strudel made locally. Here apples are grown using organic methods which respect the environment.

Mair am Turm
Foiana/Völlan, Vicolo
S. Maddalena 3
tel. 0473568009
www.garnifernblick.com
Closed December-February
A maso surrounded by orchards with scope for hiking, from the thickly wooded Val d'Ultimo to the Parco Nazionale dello Stelvio; at the end of the path leading up towards the glaciers is Rifugio Canziani (2,561m).

Restaurants

Kirchsteiger 🍽
Foiana/Völlan
Via Prevosto Wieser 5
tel. 0473568044
www.kirchsteiger.com

Closed Thursdays
Credit cards: Diners Club, Mastercard, Visa
Housed in a typical wooden Stube, this venue serving Alto Adige cuisine places great importance on local produce.

Museums, Monuments and Churches

Museo Sudtirolese della Frutticoltura
Casa Larchgut, passeggiata Brandis 4, tel. 0473564387
www.obstbaumuseum.it/
museum_infos_it.asp
Aprile-7 November: Tuesdays-Saturdays 10.00-12.00, 14.00-17.00; Sundays and holidays 14.00-18.00

LAVARONE

> ☑ **APT Altipiano di Folgaria**
> *Folgaria, Via Roma 67*
> *tel. 0464721133*
> *www.montagnaconamore.it*

Hotels

Caminetto ***
Bertoldi
tel. 0464783214
www.infotrentino.net/
hotelcaminetto
18 rooms.
Credit cards: American Express, Diners Club, Mastercard, Visa
Alpine-style hotel with flower garden; the kids' play area and the ski facilities nearby make this a great base for family holidays and skiers. Also pool and restaurant.

G.H. Astoria ****
Piazza Italia 1
tel. 0464783155
www.astorialavarone.com
49 rooms.
Credit cards: American Express, Bancomat, Mastercard, Visa
On the Lago di Lavarone, this hotel has a pool, a sauna, and a health and beauty center with a vast range of treatments; in the kitchen, local specialties are prepared using the typical products of the area.

Restaurants

Enoteca Ruz a &
Azzolini 1
tel. 0464783821
Closed Thursdays
Credit cards: American Express, Mastercard, Visa, Bancomat
On the town's main street, this rustic wine-bar serves local cuisine and sells local wines and grappas.

LEVICO TERME

Hotels

Eden *** ★
Viale Vittorio Emanuele III 14
tel. 0461706103
www.eden-hotel.com
39 rooms.
Credit cards: American Express, Diners Club, Mastercard, Visa
Late 19th-century palazzo with restaurant, an interesting excursion program and a fitness club (pool, sauna, remise en forme, anti-cellulite and relaxation treatments).

G.H. Bellavista *** & ★
Viale Vittorio Emanuele III 7
tel. 0461706136
www.ghbellavista.com
87 rooms.
Credit cards: American Express, Diners Club, Mastercard, Visa
Neo-classical palazzo serving regional cuisine, with heated pool and large terrace. Kids' play area, a relaxation center with sauna, various types of showers, a fitness and tecno-gym center, Internet point, mountain-bike storage and maintenance facilities.

Imperial G.H. Terme **** & ★
Via Silva Domini 1
tel. 0461706104
www.imperialhotel.it
81 rooms.
Credit cards: American Express, Bancomat, Mastercard, Visa
Formerly a summer residence of the Austrian Imperial family, with frescoed rooms and antique furnishings, set in a large garden; now provides excellent accommodation, physical treatments and beauty treatments. Also restaurant, pool and sauna.

Parc Hotel du Lac ** ★
Via al Lago 3, tel. 0461706590
www.dulachotel.com
54 rooms.
Credit cards: American Express, Bancomat, Diners Club, Mastercard, Visa
Between the lake and the vineyards, with a panoramic solarium terrace and a restaurant and pizzeria on the beach; rooms with terrace (almost all have lake views) and Internet point.

Restaurants

Scaranò ⁙
S.P. per Vetriolo 106
tel. 0461701733
Closed Sundays evening and Mondays (winter)
Credit cards: American Express, Diners Club, Mastercard, Visa

Set on the hillside, its picture windows overlook the Valsugana; local cuisine.

Boivin ⁙
Via Garibaldi 9
tel. 0461701670
www.boivin.it
Closed Mondays
Characteristic venue in an old wine-bar in the town center with a small veranda; serves Trentino cuisine with a creative touch.

MADONNA DI CAMPIGLIO

Hotels

Alpina *** & ★
Via Sfulmini 5
tel. 0465441075
www.alpina.it
27 rooms.
Credit cards: American Express, Bancomat, Mastercard, Visa
A relaxing place to stay with a very good restaurant (Trentina cuisine). Guests have free use of the sauna and there are mountain bikes for hire.

Bertelli **** &
Via Cima Tosa 80
tel. 0465441013
www.hotelbertelli.it
49 rooms.
Credit cards: American Express, Bancomat, Diners Club, Mastercard, Visa
Close to the ski facilities (the hotel offers skiing lessons and hire and maintenance of skiing equipment), in a fine position, chalet with a beauty center for face and body treatments; restaurant, swimming-pool, sauna and Internet.

Bio-Hotel Hermitage **** &
Via Castelletto 65
tel. 0465441558
www.chalethermitage.com
25 rooms.
Credit cards: Mastercard, Visa
Hotel built according to the tenets of bio-architecture, with a viewing terrace, a restaurant, a lounge with a majolica stove and wooden decor. For the guests: a pool, sauna and programs for physical wellness and relaxation.

Carlo Magno Zeledria Hotel **** &
Campo Carlo Magno
Via Cima Tosa 25
tel. 0465441010
www.hotelcarlomagno.com
120 rooms.
Credit cards: American Express, Diners Club, Mastercard, Visa
In a panoramic position, with

views of the Brenta Dolomites, opposite a golf course and 200m from the ski facilities, a hotel with a piano bar for winter entertainment, activities and a nursery for kids. The restaurant serves Trentino cuisine and there is a beauty area with a pool, a sauna and a Turkish bath.

Dolomiti Hotel Cozzio *** & ★
Via Cima Tosa 31
tel. 0465441083
www.cozzio.it
29 rooms.
Credit cards: Bancomat, Visa
This hotel reflects local tradition, from the rooms to the cuisine; also pool and sauna.

Restaurants

Alfiero ⁙⁙ & ★
Via Vallesinella 5
tel. 0465440117
www.alfiero.it
Open December-April and mid June-mid September
Credit cards: American Express, Diners Club, Visa
Occupies three adjoining rooms, all different; serves traditional Trentino cuisine with an innovative touch.

Sartini ⁙ ★
Via Cima Tosa 47
tel. 0465440122
Open December-April and July-September
Credit cards: American Express, Diners Club, Mastercard, Visa, Bancomat
This restaurant serves Trentino cuisine, even recipes which many have forgotten. Also a pizzeria with wood oven.

MALÉ

> ℹ **APT delle valli di Sole, Pejo e Rabbi**
> *Via Marconi 7*
> *tel. 0463901280*
> *www.valdisole.net*

Hotels

Henriette ***
Via Trento 36, tel. 0463902110
www.val-di-sole.com
43 rooms.
Credit cards: American Express, Bancomat, Mastercard, Visa
Wooden decor, pool and sauna, in a central, panoramic position, this hotel is a natural base for people visiting the Parco Naturale Adamello-Brenta and the Parco Nazionale dello Stelvio. The restaurant serves traditional cuisine, enhanced by local cheeses, cured meats and salamis.

Rauzi ★★★
Via Molini 27
tel. 0463901228
42 rooms.
Credit cards: Visa
In sight of the pine-woods and glaciers of Presanella, this typical mountain hotel has a restaurant and a sauna.

Restaurants
Conte Ramponi ⫴
Magras, Piazza S. Marco 38
tel. 0463901989
Closed Mondays in winter
Credit cards: American Express, Diners Club, Mastercard, Visa
Housed in the 15th-century palazzo of the Counts Ramponi, this venue has retained its old-world atmosphere and there is still an 18th-century Stube. Innovative Trentino cuisine and locally produced cheeses, cured meats and salamis.

Segosta ⫯ ♿
Via Trento 59
tel. 0463901390
www.segosta.com
Closed Monday evenings and Tuesdays (except in high season)
Credit cards: American Express, Diners Club, Mastercard, Visa, Bancomat
A restaurant which does justice to the Trentino tradition: from the wooden decor to the cuisine.

Museums, Monuments and Churches
Museo della Civiltà Solandra
Via Trento 40
15 June-15 September, Christmas and Easter holidays: Mondays-Saturdays 10.00-12.00, 16.00-19.00. In other periods by prior arrangement for groups

MALS IM VINSCHGAU/ MALLES VENOSTA

> ⓘ **Associazione turistica Alta Venosta Vacanze**
> *Via S. Benedetto 1*
> *tel. 0473737070*
> *www.altavenosta-vacanze.it*

Hotels
Garberhof ★★★★
Via Nazionale 25
tel. 0473831399
www.garberhof.com
40 rooms.
Credit cards: American Express, Bancomat, Mastercard, Visa
In a panoramic position, with view of Ortles, this hotel has areas where guests can relax,

with a pool, sauna, beauty and physical treatments; also a restaurant.

Greif ★★★ ♿
Via Gen. Verdoss 40/A
tel. 0473831429
www.hotel-greif.com
15 rooms.
Credit cards: American Express, Diners Club, Visa
Once the bishop's summer residence in the 16th century, this hotel with a sauna offers cuisine based on special diets with theme weeks devoted to healthy eating; the food is prepared using fresh local ingredients.

Rural lodgings
Montecin
Monteschino/Muntetschining 66
tel. 3355627210
www.montecin.com
The scenery here is majestic: Ortles and Palla Bianca, but also Castel Coira, both picturesque and dignified; Glorenza, one of the most characteristic towns in the region; the Abbazia di Monte Maria, a splash of white surrounded by pinewoods; Malles, with its Carolingian frescos depicting the Life of St Benedict. Accommodation in apartments with solid wooden furniture, kitchen and dining-room and panoramic terrace.

Rameishof
Prämajur 12, tel. 0473830282
www.thoeni.it
Closed November-mid December
Hospitality in a typical Alto Adige residence surrounded by meadows and pine-woods, on the road leading from Burgusio up the Valle Slingia towards Rifugio Rafass and the homonymous pass; it also has a gym and a sauna.

Restaurants
Aquila d'Oro ⫯
Clusio/Schleis,
tel. 0473831139
www.zum-goldnen.adler.com
Credit cards: American Express, Diners, Visa Mastercard, Bancomat
Today, this old farm building is a hotel. It incorporates an osteria which serves Alto Adige cuisine including home-made speck and sausages; trolley with range of olive oil and malga cheeses.

Moro ⫯
Burgùsio/Burgeis
tel. 0473831223
Closed Tuesdays and Wednesday midday
Rustic venue located in a small Stube and four small, charming

dining-rooms; Alto Adige cuisine with dishes geared to the produce in season, meat from home-reared animals, home-made desserts; also some accommodation.

Weisses Kreuz ⫯
Burgùsio/Burgeis
tel. 0473831307
www.weisseskreuz.it
Closed Thursdays
Credit cards: American Express, Mastercard, Visa, Bancomat
Rustic venue with wooden decor; traditional Alto Adige cuisine with good choice of typical local cheeses.

MERANO/MERAN

> ⓘ **Consorzio Turistico Meraner Land**
> *Via Palade 95*
> *tel. 0473200443*
> *www.meranerland.com*
> ⓘ **Associazione Turistica Merano**
> *Corso Libertà 45*
> *tel. 0473272000*
> *www.meraninfo.it*

Hotels
Castel Fragsburg ★★★★ ♿
Fragsburg
Via Fragsburg 3
tel. 0473244071
www.fragsburg.com
20 rooms.
Credit cards: Bancomat, Mastercard, Visa
16th-century hunting lodge on top of a hill set in garden with ancient trees; panoramic terrace and Art-Nouveau veranda with charming views. Also pool and sauna, restaurant with Alto Adige cuisine and wellness and beauty center.

Eremita-Einsiedler ★★★ ♿
Maia Alta/Obermais
Via Val di Nova 29
tel. 0473232191
www.einsiedler.com
37 rooms.
Credit cards: Mastercard, Visa
Set among apple orchards and green, undulating landscape, not far from the cable-car, this hotel has a pool, a sauna, tennis courts, and a restaurant serving traditional cuisine. Organized excursions and entertainment in summer.

G.H. Palace-Schloss Maur ★★★★★ ♿
Via Cavour 2/4, tel. 0473271000
www.palace.it
130 rooms.
Credit cards: American Express, Diners Club, Mastercard, Visa
One of the traditional, classic

hotels of Merano, still shrouded in the aristocratic atmosphere of days gone by. It has a restaurant, a sauna, a winter garden in the diet room and evening entertainment.

Isabella * &**
Via Piave 58
el. 0473234700
www.hotel-isabella.com
30 rooms.
Credit cards: Visa
Not far from the spa complex and the hippodrome, this hotel has a charming old wooden Stube and a restaurant.

Meranerhof ** &**
Via Manzoni 1, tel. 0473230230
www.meranerhof.com
70 rooms.
Credit cards: American Express, Diners Club, Mastercard, Visa
On the banks of the Passirio River, opposite the spa complex, this building in the Art-Nouveau style has a garden and a solarium terrace; also a restaurant (the local cheeses, salamis and cured meats are particularly good), a pool, an Internet point, a beauty center and a fitness center.

Westend * & ★**
Via Speckbacher 9
tel. 0473447654
www.westend.it
21 rooms.
Credit cards: American Express, Bancomat, Diners Club, Mastercard, Visa
Situated in a late 19th-century villa, in a garden overlooking the promenade along the Passirio River, this hotel has period furnishings; restaurant and Internet point

Rural lodgings

Sittnerhof
Via Verdi 60, tel. 0473221631
www.bauernhofurlaub.it
Open March-November
A fine country residence with a pool and five-a-side football field, the perfect base for hiking in the Parco Naturale Gruppo di Tessa or skiing at Merano 2000.

Restaurants

Artemis ❌ & ★
Via Verdi 72, tel. 0473446282
www.villativoli.it
Open mid March-mid November; closed Sunday evenings and Mondays
Credit cards: American Express, Mastercard, Visa
Elegant ambience with picture windows and local cuisine with à la carte specialties which change according to season.

Maria-Theresia ❌❌❌ &
Via Cavour 2/4, tel. 0473271000
www.palace.it
Open only evenings; closed 6 January-March
Credit cards: American Express, Diners Club, Mastercard, Visa
A lovely venue with a romantic atmosphere and a terrace facing the garden.

Sissi ❌❌❌
Via Galilei 44, tel. 0473231062
www.sissi.andreafenoglio.com
Closed Mondays
Credit cards: Mastercard, Visa, Bancomat
The restaurant serves traditional cuisine; extensive wine menu with about 400 labels, including about 70 of the local area's finest wines.

Weinstube Schloss Rametz ❌❌ &
Via Labers 4/A
tel. 0473212227
www.rametz.com
Closed Wednesdays
Credit cards: American Express, Diners Club, Mastercard, Visa
In the vicinity of Castello Rametz, as you would expect in a Weinstube, traditional local specialties are accompanied by a fine selection of wines, sparkling wines and distillates produced on the estate. Guided tours of the wine museum and the medieval wine-cellars of Castello Rametz, with tastings.

Museums, Monuments and Churches

Museo Civico di Merano
Via delle Corse 42/a
tel. 0473236015
www.comune.merano.bz.it/tuttocitta/cultura.asp
Tuesdays-Saturdays 10.00-17.00; Sundays 10.00-13.00

Museo della Donna - La Donna nel Corso del Tempo
Via Portici 68, tel. 0473231216
www.museia.org
February-October : Mondays-Fridays 10.00-12.00, 14.00-17.00; Saturdays 10.00-12.30. November-December: Fridays-Sunday 10.00-17.00

Museo Provinciale del Turismo-Touriseum
Via S. Valentino 51/A
tel. 0473270172
www.touriseum.it

MOENA
Hotels

Belvedere *
Via Dolomiti 14, tel. 0462573233
www.hotelbelvedere.biz
30 rooms

A typical mountain hotel with a Stube, rooms with Tyrolean decor and hand-made antique furniture. Its guests may enjoy the restaurant, a sauna, a Kneipp trail, hay baths and hydro-massage.

El Laresh * ★**
Via Even 4/C, tel. 0462574346
www.laresh.com
27 rooms.
Credit cards: Bancomat, Diners Club, Mastercard, Visa
In a verdant setting, this comfortable hotel has a restaurant serving traditional cuisine with tasty local products; also a sauna and sports facilities.

Laurino * & ★**
Via R. Loewy 15
tel. 0462573238
www.laurino.com
42 rooms.
Credit cards: Mastercard, Visa
The hotel offers entertainment and advice on walks and excursions; some rooms have Turkish bath or hydro-massage. The restaurant serves hypo-allergic diets and special diets for children. In winter, a ski-bus takes guests to the ski-slopes.

Restaurants

Foresta ❌❌ &
Via Nazionale 1
tel. 0462573260
www.hotelforesta.it
Closed Fridays in low season
Credit cards: American Express, Diners Club, Mastercard, Visa, Bancomat
Next to the pine-wood, this restaurant adjoins the hotel of the same name. The menu, based on locally-procured ingredients, is based on traditional recipes. The wine-cellar contains wines made by the more than 140 wine-producers in the region.

Malga Panna ❌❌❌ &
Via Costalunga 56
tel. 0462573489
www.malgapanna.it
Closed Mondays (except July and August)
Credit cards: American Express, Diners Club, Mastercard, Visa, Bancomat
Housed in a characteristic baita (Alpine house) with splendid views over the valley, this venue serves traditional cuisine.

Tyrol ❌❌
Piazza Italia, tel. 0462573760
www.posthotelmoena.it
Open December-April and June-September; closed Tuesdays in low season

Credit cards: American Express, Diners Club, Mastercard, Visa, Bancomat

Typical mountain venue, incorporated in a hotel, which serves Trentino and Ladin cuisine; home-grown vegetables.

MOLINA DI LEDRO

Museums, Monuments and Churches

Museo Tredentino di Scienze Naturali - Museo delle Palafitte ★
Via Lungolago
www.mtsn.tn.it
16 June-10 September: Tuesdays-Sundays 10.00-13.00, 14.00-18.00. 11 September-15 June: Tuesdays-Sundays 9.00-13.00, 14.00-17.00. Closed December-February

MOLVENO

Hotels

Dolomiti ★★★ &
Via Lungolago 18
tel. 0461586057
www.alledolomiti.com
36 rooms.
Credit cards: American Express, Diners Club, Mastercard, Visa
Perfect for a relaxing holiday in the soothing scenery surrounding the lake; heated pool, mountain bikes for use of the guests and a restaurant serving typical cuisine which is also happy to respect personal diets.

Restaurants

Al Caminetto ⑂ &
Via Lungolago 14/A
tel. 0461586949
www.residencealcaminetto.com
Open June-September and Christmas period
Credit cards: Bancomat, Mastercard, Visa
Set in a typical mountain house, this rustic venue has a large terrace; typical local cuisine with locally produced cheeses, salamis and cured meats.

MONTE BONDONE

☑ **APT Trento e Monte Bondone**
Trento, Via Manci 2
tel. 0461983880
www.apt.trento.it

Hotels

Montana ★★★ &
Vason, tel. 0461948200
www.hotelmontana.it
52 rooms.
Credit cards: American Express,

Bancomat, Diners Club, Mastercard, Visa
This place is the ideal base for winter sports and summer hiking enthusiasts because of its proximity to the ski facilities and marked footpaths. A device with a video-camera enables guests to find out the weather situation and the status of the snow on piste in real time; free access to the sauna, hydro-massage and mountain bikes. Also restaurant and tennis courts.

POZZA DI FASSA

☑ **Apt della Val di Fassa**
Canazei
Strèda de Dolèda 10
tel. 0462609500
www.fassa.com

Hotels

Chalet Alaska ★★★ &
Via Larsech 11, tel. 0462764091
www.hotelalaska.net
33 rooms.
Credit cards: Bancomat, Mastercard, Visa
The perfect place to relax, with a restaurant, a sauna and a shuttle service to the ski facilities. Kids are well provided for.

Touring ★★★ & ★
Via Col da Prà 34
tel. 0462763268
www.touringhotel.info
27 rooms.
Credit cards: American Express, Bancomat, Mastercard, Visa
This typical Tyrolean building with large wooden balconies has the latest physical wellness facilities (sauna, Turkish bath, thermarium, hydro-massage); home-made cakes for breakfast and a restaurant serving Ladin and Tyrolean cuisine.

Restaurants

El Filò ⑂⑂
Via Roma 42, tel. 0462763210
Closed Wednesdays and Thursday midday
Credit cards: Diners Club, Mastercard, Visa, Bancomat
This charming venue is decorated with Venetian stuccoes and a majolica stove, and serves local dishes. Home-made pasta, bread and desserts.

PREDAZZO

☑ **APT della Valle di Fiemme**
Cavalese
Via Fratelli Bronzetti 60
tel. 0462241111
www.valdifiemme.info

Hotels

Ancora ★★★★ ★
Via IX November 1
tel. 0462501651
www.ancora.it
40 rooms.
Credit cards: American Express, Bancomat, Diners Club, Mastercard, Visa
Just a few minutes from the ski-slopes, the riding school and the Parco Naturale di Paneveggio, this hotel has a restaurant, a pool, a sauna and a well-equipped fitness center with a wellness area and a beauty farm; organized excusions and free use of bikes.

Bellamonte ★★★★ & ★
Bellamonte,
Via Prai di Mont 52
tel. 0462576116
www.bellamonte.net
44 rooms.
Credit cards: American Express, Bancomat, Diners Club, Mastercard, Visa
Well located, a good base for sports enthusiasts and families; it has a restaurant and a wellness center with a gym, a sauna and a pool.

Canada ★★★ &
Bellamonte, Via della Torba 1
tel. 0462576245
www.webhotelcanada.com
37 rooms.
Credit cards: American Express, Bancomat, Diners Club, Mastercard, Visa
Ideal for a relaxing holiday or as a base for hiking in the Parco Naturale di Paneveggio; indoor pool, sauna and restaurant serving cuisine based on typical local products.

Sporthotel Sass Maor ★★★ & ★
Via Marconi 4, tel. 0462501538
www.sassmaor.com
27 rooms.
Credit cards: American Express, Diners Club, Mastercard, Visa
This hotel offers a restaurant, a Stube, a taverna with live music, BBQs in the garden, guided hikes and evening entertainment. Also a gym, a sauna and hydro-massage.

Museums, Monuments and Churches

Museo Civico di Geologia
Piazza Ss. Filippo e Giacomo 1
tel. 0462500366
www.valdifiemme.it/museo.predazzo
Temporarily closed for restructuring work. Only the library is open.

RITTEN/RENON

> **ℹ Associazione turistica Renon**
> *Collalbo, Via Paese 16*
> *tel. 0471356100*
> *www.renon.com*

Hotels

Bemelmans Post * &**
Collalbo/Klobenstein
Via Paese 8
tel. 0471356127
www.bemelmans.com
56 rooms.
Credit cards: Mastercard, Visa
Hotel housed in a 16th-century palazzo, with an old wooden Stube, antique furniture and good facilities for physical fitness (pool, sauna, tennis courts); also restaurant.

Post-Viktoria * &**
Soprabolzano/Oberbozen
tel. 0471345365
www.sudtirol.com/hotel-post
49 rooms.
Credit cards: Mastercard, Visa
Catinaccio, the peaks of Latemar and the Sciliar massif form the background for this hotel, with a restaurant, pool and sauna.

Rural lodgings

Flachenhof
Collalbo/Klobenstein
Via Tann 31
tel. 0471352782
www.flachenhof.it
Open all year
This maso amid meadows and pine-woods, with great views of Latemar, Catinaccio and Sciliar, offers plenty of scope for horse-riding or mountain-bike enthusiasts.

Penzlhof
Longostagno/Lengstein
tel. 0471349011
www.penzlhof.it
Open all year
Credit cards: American Express, Bancomat, Diners Club, Mastercard, Visa
This historic maso with its marvelous views of Latemar, Catinaccio and Sciliar was situated on the old "Imperial Road" long before the road was built beside the river; it has a pool, and offers BBQs and guided hikes.

Restaurants

Trattoria Patscheiderhof ⫪
Signato/Signat
tel. 0471365267
Closed Tuesday
Credit cards: American Express, Diners Club, Mastercard, Visa, Bancomat

Typical Alto Adige venue in a 19th-century Stube, surrounded by vineyards and the peaks of the Dolomites; home-cured speck and meats, typical local cuisine. Don't miss their apple-strudel di mele and cheeses straight from the farm.

Museums, Monuments and Churches

Museo dell'Apicoltura
Costalovara/Wolfsgruben
Via Costalovara 15
tel. 0471345350
www.suedtirol-it.com/renon/ apicoltura.htm
April-October : Monday-Sunday 10.00-18.00. Tours for groups available on request

RIVA DEL GARDA

> **ℹ Ingarda Trentino**
> *Via Giardini Porta Orientale 8*
> *tel. 0464554444*
> *www.gardatrentino.it*

Hotels

Astoria Park Hotel ** &**
Viale Trento 9, tel. 0464576657
www.relaxhotels.com/astoria
100 rooms.
Credit cards: American Express, Bancomat, Diners Club, Mastercard, Visa
This place has a center for toning treatments; especially good for families and small kids; also has a restaurant, a pool, a sauna and an Internet point.

Brione * & ★**
Viale Rovereto 75/77
tel. 0464552484
www.hotelbrione.it
77 rooms.
Credit cards: American Express, Diners Club, Mastercard, Visa
100m from the beach, the tourist harbor and the olive-grove hike, this hotel has an Internet point, a restaurant serving traditional cuisine, a pool with a solarium and a garden.

Feeling Hotel Luise ** & ★**
Viale Rovereto 9
tel. 0464550858
www.feelinghotelluise.com
67 rooms.
Credit cards: American Express, Bancomat, Diners Club, Mastercard, Visa
Well located, with a garden and pool, this hotel has elegant reception rooms and good sports facilities; restaurant, mountain bikes and Internet facilities.

Gabry * &**
Via Longa 6
tel. 0464553600
www.hotelgabry.com
39 rooms.
Credit cards: Mastercard, Visa
Out of the center in a pleasant rural position near the beach, with a restaurant, pool, a shelter for the bikes of touring cyclists and Internet point.

Riviera * &**
Viale Rovereto 95
tel. 0464552279
www.hotelrivierariva.com
36 rooms.
Credit cards: American Express, Bancomat, Diners Club, Mastercard, Visa
Opposite the tourist harbor, most rooms have balconies facing the lake. Restaurant, sauna and a garden with a pool and a solarium.

Restaurants

Al Volt ⫪ &
Via Fiume 73, tel. 0464552570
www.ristorantealvolt.com
Closed Monday
Credit cards: American Express, Diners Club, Mastercard, Visa, Bancomat
Charming venue, furnished in keeping with the date of the building, serving cuisine from Lake Garda and the Trentino.

Museums, Monuments and Churches

Museo Civico di Riva del Garda ★
Piazza Cesare Battisti 3
tel. 0464573869
www.comune.rivadelgarda.tn.it/ museo/cultura.html
4 April-31 October: Tuesdays-Sundays 10.30-18.30. 13 June-31 August: open all year

ROVERETO

> **ℹ APT Rovereto e Vallagarina**
> *Corso Rosmini 6/A*
> *tel. 0464430363*
> *www.aptrovereto.it*

Hotels

Leon d'Oro ****
Via Tacchi 2
tel. 0464437333
www.hotelleondoro.it
56 rooms.
Credit cards: American Express, Diners Club, Mastercard, Visa
In a peaceful location, this venue has a warm, intimate atmosphere; connected to the adjoining Novecento restaurant, with picture windows.

Rovereto ★★★
Corso Rosmini 82/D
tel. 0464435222
www.hotelrovereto.it
49 rooms.
Credit cards: American Express, Bancomat, Diners Club, Mastercard, Visa
A fine late-19th-century building, perfectly preserved inside. Restaurant with a terrace.

Restaurants

Novecento ⅋⅋ ♿
Corso Rosmini 82/D
tel. 0464435222
www.hotelrovereto.it
Closed Sundays
Credit cards: American Express, Diners Club, Mastercard, Visa, Bancomat
An elegant ambience with a terrace for serving meals outside in summer. Regional cuisine and typical Trentino cheeses.

San Colombano ⅋⅋ ♿
Via Vicenza 30
tel. 0464436006
www.ristorantesancolombano.com
Closed Sunday evenings and Mondays
Credit cards: American Express, Diners Club, Mastercard, Visa, Bancomat
A typical osteria serving Trentino cuisine; there's a little room upstairs for romantic dinners.

Museums, Monuments and Churches

Casa Museo Fortunato Depero
Via della Terra 53
tel. 0464434393
Currently closed for restoration.

Museo Civico ★
Borgo S. Caterina 41
tel. 0464439055
www.museocivico.rovereto.tn.it
Tuesday-Sunday 9.00-12.00, 15.00-18.00. Closed Monday, 1 January, Easter, 5 August, 1 November, 25 December

Museo di Arte Moderna e Contemporanea di Trento e Rovereto - MART ★
Corso Bettini 43
tel. 0464438887
www.mart.trento.it
Tuesdays-Sundays 10.00-18.00; Fridays 10.00-21.00

Museo Storico Italiano della Guerra Onlus ★
Via Castelbarco 7
tel. 0464438100
www.museodellaguerra.it
Tuesdays-Sundays 10.00-18.00. Closed on Mondays (not holidays) January and February. Temporarily exhibitions open all the year

SAN MARTINO DI CASTROZZA

Hotels

Colfosco ★★★ ♿ ★
Via Passo Rolle 20,
tel. 043968224
www.hotelcolfosco.it
58 rooms.
Credit cards: American Express, Bancomat, Mastercard, Visa
Founded in the early 20th century, in the typical Alpine style, this hotel offers various leisure time activities and evening entertainment. It also has a wellness-relaxation center (with a sauna, Turkish bath, gym and solarium) and a restaurant.

Letizia ★★★ ♿
Via Colbricon 6, tel. 0439768615
www.hletizia.it
38 rooms.
Credit cards: Bancomat, Mastercard, Visa
Very handy for skiers and hikers. It also has an Internet point and facilities for keeping fit and beauty treatments.

Malga Ces ★★★
Malga Ces, tel. 043968223
www.malgaces.it
7 rooms.
Credit cards: American Express, Bancomat, Diners Club, Mastercard, Visa
Set in the Parco Naturale di Panaveggio, with splendid views of the Pale di San Martino, this small hotel expends most of its energy running the restaurant, but it also has charming rooms. The hotel overlooks the ski-slopes and is the starting-point for hikes in summer.

San Martino ★★★ ♿
Via Passo Rolle 277
tel. 043968011
www.hotelsanmartino.it
48 rooms.
Credit cards: Bancomat, Visa
On the edge of the forest, this Alpine-style hotel dates from the last century, and has an open fire in the lounge. Restaurant with Trentino cuisine, pool, sauna, tennis courts and wellness and beauty center.

SANKT KASSIAN / SAN CASSIANO

Hotels

Ciasa Salares ★★★★ ♿
Armentarola 31
strada Prè de Vì 31
tel. 0471849445
www.siriolagroup.it
42 rooms.
Credit cards: American Express,

Diners Club, Mastercard, Visa
A large baita in a rural setting: Alpine-style rooms, pool, sauna, tennis courts, Internet point and a beauty farm. Restaurant also serves meals outside.

Dolomiti Wellness Hotel Fanes ★★★★ ♿
Strada Pecei 19
tel. 0471849470
www.hotelfanes.it
50 rooms.
Credit cards: Bancomat, Mastercard, Visa
The ideal place for a relaxing holiday; also esthetic treatments and facilities for keeping fit (pool, sauna, Turkish bath, Kneipp bath, massage). Restaurant and mini-club.

La Stüa ★★★ ♿
Via Micurá de Rü 31
tel. 0471849456
www.hotel-lastua.it
24 rooms.
Credit cards: Bancomat, Visa
In a peaceful part of the old town center, with panoramic views; every week there's a Ladino evening in the tavern. Restaurant, Turkish bath, sauna, Kneipp baths, hydro-massage and an activity area for kids.

Stoeres ★★★ ♿
Via Plan 22, tel. 0471849486
www.hotelstores.it
26 rooms.
Credit cards: Mastercard, Visa
Handy base for skiers, but also suitable for summer holidays; also a restaurant and sauna.

Restaurants

La Siriola ⅋⅋⅋⅋
Armentarola, Via Pre de Vì 31
tel. 0471849445
www.siriolagroup.it
Open December-March and mid June-September, only evenings (except August); closed Mondays
Credit cards: American Express, Diners Club, Mastercard, Visa, Bancomat
Surrounded by pine-woods, this restaurant serves Alto Adige cuisine with an innovative slant and has one of the finest wine-cellars in Italy.

St. Hubertus ⅋⅋⅋ ♿
Via Micura de Rü
tel. 0471849500
www.rosalpina.it
Open December-March and mid June-October, only evenings; closed Tuesdays
Credit cards: American Express, Mastercard, Visa
This venue in one of the best hotels in the Val Badia is

a converted wooden Stube with curtains and fabrics made of loden. The cuisine is a masterly combination of innovation and tradition.

SANKT ULRICH IN GRÖDEN/ORTISEI

ⓘ Associazione Turistica Ortisei
Via Rezia 1
tel. 0471777600
www.valgardena.it

Hotels

Alpenhotel Rainell * ♿**
Via Vidalong 19, tel. 0471796145
www.rainell.com
27 rooms.
Credit cards: Bancomat, Mastercard, Visa
In a panoramic position, not far from the ski facilities and public sports facilities (entrance free), a mountain hotel with a restaurant, garden, Stube and fitness center; free guide for hikes from June to October.

Gardena-Groednerhof *** ♿**
Via Vidalong 3,
tel. 0471796315
www.gardena.it
51 rooms.
Credit cards: Mastercard, Visa
Restaurant, pool, sauna and, a special feature of the hotel, a well-equipped beauty and wellness center which includes hay baths. Ski-hire and skiing lessons arranged.

Genziana-Enzian ** ♿**
Via Rezia 111, tel. 0471796246
www.hotel-genziana.com
50 rooms.
Credit cards: Bancomat, Mastercard, Visa
Centrally located, with Tyrolean decor, this hotel has a restaurant serving traditional cuisine and a relaxation area with a pool, a sauna, a Turkish bath, hydro-massage and hay baths.

Luna-Mondschein ** ♿**
Via Purger 81, tel. 0471796214
www.hotel-luna.com
50 rooms.
Credit cards: American Express, Bancomat, Diners Club, Mastercard, Visa
In a quiet, sunny position, this 19th-century house, now a hotel, has a restaurant, a pool and a sauna.

Ronce * ♿**
Via Ronce 1, tel. 0471796383
www.hotelronce.com
24 rooms.
Credit cards: Bancomat,

Mastercard, Visa
A chalet set in a peaceful, panoramic position, with a sauna, solarium and hydro-massage pool; also restaurant and, in winter, bus service to the ski-slopes.

Restaurants

Concordia ⁉
Via Roma 41, el. 0471796276
www.restaurantconcordia.com
Closed Wednesday in low season
Credit cards: Mastercard, Visa, Bancomat
A venue with a Tyrolean Stube serving Alto Adige cuisine: fresh, home-made bread and cakes, while the ham and the salmon are smoked on the premises.

Resciesa ⁞
Via Resciesa 200,
www.resciesa.it
Open Christmas-March and June-October
This venue can only be reached by chair-lift, and has spectacular views, especially from the large terrace. The cuisine is based on traditional Alto Adige fare.

Stua Catores ⁉
Via Sacun 49, tel. 0471796682
Closed Tuesday
Credit cards: Bancomat
In a Tyrolean-style room lined with wood or the Stube you can taste the traditional rich flavors of local cuisine.

Museums, Monuments and Churches

Museum de Gherdëina
Cesa di Ladins, Via Rezia 83
tel. 0471797554
July-August: Mondays-Fridays 10.00-12.00, 14.00-18.00; Sundays 14.00-18.00. June, September-mid October: Tuesdays, Wednesdays, Fridays 14.00-18.00; Thursdays 10.00-12.00, 14.00-18.00. February-mid March: Tuesdays, Fridays 14.30-17.30. Closed mid October-January, April-May. Visits by prior arrangement for groups

SEIS/SIUSI

Hotels

Bad Ratzes *
Ratzes, Via Ratzes 29
tel. 0471706131
www.badratzes.it
48 rooms.
Credit cards: Mastercard, Visa
In the heart of the Parco Naturale dello Sciliar, in a charming position in a broad sunny meadow, surrounded by ancient spruces, by a crystal-clear stream, this hotel has a

restaurant, a pool, a sauna, recreation activities, and small kids are welcome.

Dolomiti-Dolomitenhof ** ♿**
Via Hauenstein 3, tel. 0471706128
www.dolomitenhof.it
12 rooms.
Credit cards: Bancomat
Villa with Tyrolean decor equipped for beauty treatments and keeping fit (pool, sauna).

SEXTEN/SESTO

ⓘ Associazione Turistica Sesto
Via Dolomiti 9
tel. 0474710310
www.sesto.it

Hotels

Berghotel & Residence Tirol ** ♿**
Moso/Moos, Via Monte Elmo 10
tel. 0474710386
www.berghotel.com
35 rooms.
Credit cards: Bancomat
On the panoramic side of the valley, in the middle of a huge meadow, with immediate access to the ski-slopes; restaurant serving typical local fare. Also pool and sauna.

Rainer ** ♿**
Moso/Moos, Via S. Giuseppe 40, tel. 0474710366
www.hotelrainer.com
40 rooms.
Credit cards: Visa
This hotel offers a cosmetics center and physical treatments; also restaurant, pool and sauna.

Sport e Kurhotel Bad Moos ** ♿**
Moso/Moos, Via Val Fiscalina 27
tel. 0474713100
www.badmoos.it
75 rooms.
Credit cards: Bancomat, Mastercard, Visa
Hotel with excellent sports facilities (pool) and physical and beauty treatments (sauna). Home-made cakes and jams and local cuisine.

Rural lodgings

Weber
Ferrara/Schmieden
Via Sonnwend 25
tel. 0474710081
Open all year
A riot of flowers graces this residence on the valley floor. A perfect base for hiking in summer and skiing in winter along the snowy pistes of the Sesto Dolomites. Discounts for winter holidays and for kids' ski school.

Restaurants

Tiroler Stub'n 1881 ⫪
Via del Parco 2, tel. 0474710384
www.monika.it
Open mid December-March
and mid May-mid October only
evenings; closed Mondays
(in low season)
Credit cards: American Express,
Mastercard, Visa, Bancomat
In these two charming Stuben in
Tyrolean style, with carved
wooden paneling, they serve the
specialties of local cuisine.

Museums, Monuments and Churches

Museo Rudolf Stolz
Via Dolomiti 16
tel. 0474710521
15 June-1 October: Wednesdays,
Fridays 16.30-18.30; Sundays
10.00-12.00. 15 July-1
September: Thursdays-Fridays
16.30-18.30; Sundays 10.00-
12.00. 25 December-Easter:
Wednesdays 16.30-18.30;
Sundays 10.00-12.00

STERN/LA VILLA

Hotels

Gran Ander ★★★ ★
Pedràces, Via Runcac 29
tel. 0471839718
www.granander.it
20 rooms.
Credit cards: Visa
Chalet hotel with panoramic
terrace used for breakfast and
BBQs, in an Alpine setting. Also
restaurant, Internet point and
fitness center with sauna,
Turkish bath, hay baths and
solarium.

Lech da Sompunt ★★★ ♿
Pedràces, Via Sompunt 36
tel. 0471847015
www.lechdasompunt.it
35 rooms.
Credit cards: Mastercard, Visa
The mountain peaks, the green
of the pine-woods and the blue
of a small natural lake provide
the setting for this hotel with a
restaurant, IT facilities, sauna,
Turkish bath, solarium terrace
and unusual options such as
ice-skating and curling.

Sporthotel Teresa ★★★★
Pedràces, Strada Damez 64
tel. 0471839623
www.sporthotel-teresa.com
43 rooms.
Credit cards: Mastercard, Visa
Hotel with Stube, sports
facilities (pool and indoor tennis
courts), Internet point, sauna
and restaurant serving Alto
Adige cuisine.

Restaurants

Ciastel Colz ⫪⫪⫪
Strada Marin 80,
tel. 0471847511
www.siriolagroup.it
Open only evenings;
closed Tuesdays
Credit cards: American Express,
Diners Club, Mastercard, Visa
Set in a 16th-century castle, this
venue has a charming
atmosphere; creative cooking
based on traditional Alto Adige
cuisine.

STERZING/VIPITENO

> ℹ️ **Associazione turistica Vipiteno**
> *Piazza Città 3*
> *tel. 0472765325*
> *www.vipiteno.com*

Hotels

Aquila Nera-Schwarzer Adler ★★★★
Piazza Città 1, tel. 0472764064
www.schwarzeradler.it
33 rooms.
Credit cards: Bancomat,
Mastercard, Visa
This historic venue dating from
the 14th century offers comfort
and relaxation thanks to a
restaurant serving typical local
dishes, a pool, a Turkish bath
and a sauna.

Gasteigerhof ★★★★ ♿
Casatéia/Gasteig
Via Passo Giovo 24
tel. 0472779090
www.hotel-gasteigerhof.com
34 rooms.
Credit cards: Bancomat,
Mastercard, Visa
An Alpine-style chalet with a
restaurant, pool, sauna and
fitness center offering beauty
treatments.

Rose ★★★
Prati di Vizze,
Via Prati 119
tel. 0472764300
www.hotelrose.it
29 rooms.
In the upper Valle Isarco, on the
edge of the forest, an old-
fashioned hotel, ideal for a
quiet holiday. The restaurant
serves dishes from the local
cuisine.

Restaurants

Pretzhof ⫪
Tulve,
tel. 0472764455
www.pretzhof.com
Closed Mondays and Tuesdays
Credit cards: Mastercard, Visa,
Bancomat
A typical maso situated in green

meadows offers the typical
cuisine of the valleys, with all
the nuances of the local
tradition. Also has a small shop
where you can buy jams, honey
and cheese made on the
premises.

Museums, Monuments and Churches

Museo Civico di Vipiteno e Museo Multscher
Commenda dell'Ordine Teutonico,
Via della Commenda 11,
tel. 0472766464
April-October: Tuesdays-
Saturdays 10.00-12.00, 14.00-
17.00. Closed Mondays, Sundays,
Sundays. Visits by prior
arrangement for groups

SULDEN/SOLDA

> ℹ️ **Area dell'Ortles**
> *Via Principale*
> *tel. 0473737060*
> *www.ortler.it*

Hotels

Eller ★★★ ♿
Via Principale 15, tel. 0473613021
www.hoteleller.com
50 rooms.
Credit cards: Bancomat,
Mastercard, Visa
This has been a hotel since
1865 and you can be sure of a
comfortable stay. It has a
restaurant, an Internet point and
a wellness area (pool, sauna).

Marlet ★★★★ ♿
Via Principale 110
tel. 0473613075
www.marlet.com
29 rooms.
Credit cards: Visa
In a quiet position with
exceptional views, this hotel
has a restaurant, a pool,
a sauna, a piano bar, a kids'
games room, an Internet
point and a fitness center.

Sporthotel Paradies ★★★ ♿
Via Principale 87,
tel. 0473613043
www.sporthotel-paradies.com
58 rooms.
Credit cards: Bancomat, Visa
A typical mountain hotel
with a restaurant, a pool,
a sauna and a relaxation
area offering beauty treatments.

TOBLACH/DOBBIACO

> ℹ️ **Associazione turistica Dobbiaco**
> *Via Dolomiti 3*
> *tel. 0474972132*
> *www.dobbiaco.info*

‡‡‡ ⚎ *‡* ★★★ ★★ ★ Hotels ⫪⫪⫪⫪⫪ ⫪⫪⫪⫪ ⫪⫪⫪ ⫪⫪ ⫪ Restaurants ♿ Disabled ★ Special TCI Rates

Hotels

Park Hotel Bellevue ★★★★
Via Dolomiti 23,
tel. 0474972101
www.parkhotel-bellevue.com
46 rooms.
Credit cards: American Express, Diners Club, Visa
Friendly hotel with a typical Tyrolean Stube, surrounded by a huge garden; restaurant, pool, Internet point and wellness center with Finnish sauna, solarium, hydro-massage pool, massage.

Santer ★★★★
Via Alemagna 4,
tel. 0474972142
www.hotel-santer.com
50 rooms.
Credit cards: Bancomat, Visa
In a fine position with a restaurant, and some rooms with balcony; also facilities for physical wellness: pool, sauna, Turkish bath, hay baths, hydro-massage, beauty treatments. Charming Stube with wooden ceiling. The hotel organizes theme holidays, hikes and musical entertainment (evenings). Free transfer to Treviso Airport.

Toblacherhof ★★★
Via Pusteria 8,
tel. 0474972217
www.toblacherhof.com
25 rooms.
Credit cards: Diners Club, Mastercard, Visa
Rooms and reception rooms with traditional decor; restaurant and relaxation area with sauna, Turkish bath and hydro-massage. Starting-point for hikes and trips.

Rural lodgings

Baumannhof
Via Pusteria 19
tel. 0474972602
Open all year
Accommodation in a traditional Alto Adige residence on the edge of a pine-wood. Cross-country skiing close by.

Restaurants

Genziana ¶¶
Via S. Silvestro 31
tel. 0474979072
www.ristorante-genziana.it
Closed Mondays in low season
Typical Tyrolean ambience serving traditional local fare; don't miss their home-made grappas!

Gratschwirt ¶¶
Via Grazze,
tel. 0474972293
www.gratschwirt.com

Closed Tuesdays
Credit cards: American Express, Diners Club, Mastercard, Visa, Bancomat
Tyrolean-style decor and traditional Alto Adige cuisine.

Winkelkeller ¶ &
Via Conti Künigl 8
tel. 0474972022
www.app-pichler.com
Closed Wednesdays
Credit cards: Diners Club, Visa, Bancomat
In the center of Dobbiaco Vecchio, this venue decorated with Tyrolean antiques has some charming Stuben, one of which dates from the 16C; Alto Adige cuisine.

TRENT/TRENTO

> **APT Trento e Monte Bondone**
> Via Manci 2
> tel. 0461983880
> www.apt.trento.it

Hotels

Accademia ★★★★ ★
Vicolo Colico 4/6,
tel. 0461233600
www.accademiahotel.it
42 rooms.
Credit cards: American Express, Bancomat, Diners Club, Mastercard, Visa
Medieval building not far from the Duomo; in summer, breakfast is served in the garden, restaurant with traditional cuisine.

Adige ★★★★ & ★
Mattarello,
Via Pomeranos 2
tel. 0461944545
www.adigehotel.it
80 rooms.
Credit cards: American Express, Diners Club, Mastercard, Visa
Not far from town, this hotel has a restaurant and an Internet point. Special arrangement with a beauty institute which gives guests free access to sauna, Turkish bath and hydro-massage.

America ★★★ & ★
Via Torre Verde 50
tel. 0461983010
www.hotelamerica.it
67 rooms.
Credit cards: American Express, Diners Club, Mastercard, Visa
At the beginning of the pedestrian precinct which protects the historic center, a few steps away from Castello del Buonconsiglio, it also has a restaurant.

Buonconsiglio ★★★★ & ★
Via Romagnosi 16/18
tel. 0461272888
www.hotelbuonconsiglio.it
46 rooms.
Credit cards: American Express, Diners Club, Visa
This hotel has a wide range of facilities, air-conditioned, sound-proofed rooms, orthopedic mattresses and an Internet point.

Everest ★★★ & ★
Corso Alpini 14,
tel. 0461825300
www.hoteleverest.it
113 rooms.
Credit cards: American Express, Bancomat, Diners Club, Mastercard, Visa
This spacious and well-equipped hotel has a restaurant serving Trentino cuisine and Internet facilities.

San Giorgio della Scala ★ &
Via Brescia 133,
tel. 0461238848
www.garnisangiorgio.it
15 rooms.
Credit cards: American Express, Bancomat, Diners Club, Mastercard, Visa
A garni in a charming old villa with a few, very well-appointed rooms.

Vela ★★★ ★
Vela, Via Ss. Cosma
e Damiano 21
tel. 0461827200
www.hotelvela.com
30 rooms.
Credit cards: American Express, Bancomat, Mastercard, Visa
A hotel in a quiet position; also restaurant.

Villa Fontana ★★★ & ★
Via F.lli Fontana 11
tel. 0461829800
www.villafontana.it
24 rooms.
Credit cards: American Express, Bancomat, Diners Club, Mastercard, Visa
Tastefully furnished rooms and a garage and car park with direct access to reception (included in the price of the rooms).

Villa Madruzzo ★★★ &
Cognola, Via Ponte Alto 26
tel. 0461986220
www.villamadruzzo.it
51 rooms.
Credit cards: American Express, Diners Club, Visa
On a hill, not far from the center, a 19th-century villa set in a large garden; elegant, beautifully-furnished reception rooms. Also restaurant.

Restaurants

Cantinota ♯♯ ♿
Via S. Marco 22/24
tel. 0461238527
www.corona.it/cantinota
Closed Thursdays
Credit cards: Diners Club, Mastercard, Visa, Bancomat
In the historic center, set in a 16th-century wine-cellar with characteristic furnishings and garden. Traditional cuisine based on what is available in the season; good choice of Trentino wines. Also piano bar and wine-bar.

Chiesa ♯♯ ★
Parco S. Marco,
tel. 0461238766
www.ristorantechiesa.it
Closed Sundays
Credit cards: American Express, Mastercard, Diners Club, Visa
Set in the 18th-century Palazzo Wolkenstein, with barrel-vault ceilings and rough plaster walls, this is a stronghold of true Trentino cuisine.

Osteria a le Due Spade ♯♯♯
Via Don Rizzi 11
angolo Via Verdi,
tel. 0461234343
www.leduespade.com
Closed Sunday midday and Mondays
Credit cards: American Express, Diners Club, Mastercard, Visa, Bancomat
Historic venue with characteristic barrel-vault ceilings, an original 16th-century floor and late-18th-century wooden paneling. Only a few tables (in summer they put a few more out in the small garden) and traditional Trentino cuisine.

Villa Madruzzo ♯♯ ★
Cognola, Via Ponte Alto 26
tel. 0461986220
www.villamadruzzo.it
Closed Sundays
Credit cards: American Express, Diners Club, Mastercard, Visa, Bancomat
Not far from the center, in an old villa with a lovely garden, the cuisine is a combination of old traditional dishes and various regional specialties.

Clesio ♯♯
Via Alfieri 1,
tel. 0461271000
Credit cards: American Express, Diners Club, Mastercard, Visa, Bancomat
Elegant venue with a cuisine with plenty of typical regional dishes; also piano bar.

Doc ♯♯ ♿
Via Milano 148, tel. 0461237489
Closed Saturday midday and Sundays
Credit cards: American Express, Diners Club, Mastercard, Visa, Bancomat
This restaurant serves different Trentino specialties every day, as well as a set menu of regional specialties.

Lo Scrigno del Duomo ♯♯♯
Piazza del Duomo 29
tel. 0461220030
www.scrignodelduomo.com
Closed Mondays
(except wine bar)
Credit cards: American Express, Diners Club, Mastercard, Visa
An elegant venue in a 17th-century setting on two floors: a wine bar on the ground floor and a restaurant in the basement serving Trentino specialties.

Osteria il Cappello ♯♯ ♿
Piazza B. Lunelli 5
tel. 0461235850
Closed Sunday evening and Mondays
Credit cards: American Express, Diners Club, Mastercard, Visa
Lovely downstairs dining-room with stone walls, excellent cuisine with wide range of malga cheeses.

At night

Bar Paradiso
Largo Nazario Sauro 33
Live music on Saturday or DJ on Friday.

Birreria Pedavena
Piazza Fiera 13,
www.birreriapedavena.com
A small brewery producing its own beer.
They also sell local produce.
Winter garden.

Giubbe Rosse
Galleria Torre Vanga 14
Live Music.

Museums, Monuments and Churches

Castello del Buonconsiglio - Monumenti e Collezioni Provinciali ★
Via Bernardo Clesio 5
tel. 0461233770
www.buonconsiglio.it
Winter: 9.30-17.00.
Summer: 10.00-18.00.

Mart Trento - Museo di Arte Moderna e Contemporanea di Trento e Rovereto ★
Palazzo delle Albere,
Via R. da Sanseverino 45,
tel. 0461234860
www.mart.trento.it
Tuesdays-Sundays 10.00-18.00

Mostra Permanente del Modellismo Ferraviario
c/o Stazione di Trento, binario 1

Museo Diocesano Tridentino ★
Piazza Duomo 18
tel. 0461234419
www.museodiocesanotridentino.it
June-September: 9.30-12.30, 14.30-18.00. October-May: 9.30-12.30, 14.00-17.30.
Closed Tuesday

Museo della SAT (Società Alpinisti Tridentini)
Via Manci 57, tel. 0461980211
www.sat.tn.it
Tuesdays-Fridays 15.00-19.00. Open weekends during the exhibitions

Museo Storico delle Truppe Alpine
Doss Trento, tel. 0461827248
www.esercito.difesa.it/root/Sezioni/Sez_chisiamo.asp
Summer: Tuesdays-Thursdays 9.00-12.00, 13.30-16.30; Fridays 9.00-12.00; Saturdays and Sundays by appointment. Winter: Tuesdays-Thursdays 9.00-12.00, 13.30-16.30; Fridays 9.00-12.00; Saturdays and Sundays on request

Museo Storico in Trento Onlus
Via Torre d'Augusto 41
tel. 0461230482
www.museostorico.tn.it
Temporarily closed for restoration

VAHRN/VARNA
Museums, Monuments and Churches

Abbazia di Novacella
Via Abbazia 1, tel. 0472836189
www.kloster-neustift.it
Only guided tours (from 10 people): 10.00, 11.00, 14.00, 15.00, 16.00. Mid July-mid September: also 12.00 and 13.00. Closed Sundays and public holidays. January, February and March: only by request. Visits by prior arrangement for groups

VETRIOLO TERME
Hotels

Compet ★★★
Compet, tel. 0461706466
www.hotelcompet.it
34 rooms.
Credit cards: American Express, Bancomat, Diners Club, Mastercard, Visa
Next to a pine-wood and close to the spa complex, with rooms decorated in Alpine style; typical cuisine using local products, and a sauna.

VIGO DI FASSA

Hotels

Ai Pini * ♿ TCI**
Strada Neva 97
tel. 0462764501
www.hotelaipini.net
29 rooms.
Credit cards: American Express,
Diners Club, Mastercard, Visa
In a sunny position, rooms have
typical Alpine decor. Trentino
cuisine and entertainment.
Health center offers a range of
services.

Olympic * ♿**
*San Giovanni, Strada Dolomites
4, tel. 0462764225*
www.hotelolympic.info
26 rooms.
Traditional venue with Ladin
and classic Italian cuisine,
a typical Stube, a sauna and
mountain bikes for hire.

Piccolo Hotel * ♿**
Strada Neva 70
tel. 0462764217
www.piccolohotel.net
30 rooms.
Credit cards: American Express,
Visa
A natural base for skiing
holidays or hiking in summer,
this hotel has rooms with
panoramic balconies. Stube with
a wood stove, restaurant and
tavern with a bar, Internet point
and mountain bikes for use of
guests; also Turkish bath, sauna
and hydro-massage pool.

WELSCHNOFEN/
NOVA LEVANTE

> ☑ **Associazione turistica
> Nova Levante-Carezza
> al Lago**
> *Via Carezza 21*
> *tel. 0471613126*
> *www.carezza.com*

Hotels

Posta-Cavallino Bianco ****
Via Carezza 30
tel. 0471613113
www.postcavallino.com
45 rooms.
Credit cards: American Express,
Bancomat, Diners Club,
Mastercard, Visa
This old post inn dating from
1875 is now a hotel with
wooden decor and antiques
from the local area; pool,
beauty farm, areas for physical
activities, sauna, Turkish bath,
baby-sitting service and guided
walks. The restaurant serves
vegetables from the garden and
meat from the local area.

Rosengarten * ♿**
Via Catinaccio
tel. 0471613262
www.hotelrosengarten.it
22 rooms.
Credit cards: Diners Club,
Mastercard, Visa
The hotel's unique position
below Catinaccio alone is reason
enough to come and stay here.
Traditional ambience, restaurant,
relaxation area with a sauna,
Turkish bath and hydro-
massage.

Wellnesshotel Engel ** ♿**
Via S. Valentino 3
tel. 0471613131
www.hotel-engel.com
70 rooms.
Credit cards: Bancomat,
Mastercard, Visa
This hotel in Tyrolean-style
has a restaurant, pool, sauna,
tennis courts, Internet point,
beauty center and wellness
center with various treatments
and massage. Also a mini-club
for the kids.

Rural lodgings

Vöstlhof
Via Ciscolo 2
tel. 0471613174
www.voestlhof.com
Open all year
Accommodation in a maso where
you can buy Tyrolean speck;
surrounded by meadows and
pine-woods framed by the
dolomitic rocks of Catinaccio
and Latemar.

Museums, Monuments
and Churches

Museo Locale di Nova Levante
Via Roma,
tel. 0471613126
Closed

WOLKENSTEIN
IN GRÖDEN/SELVA
DI VAL GARDENA

> ☑ **Associazione Turistica
> Selva Val Gardena**
> *Via Meisules 213*
> *tel. 0471777900*

Hotels

Alpenroyal Sporthotel *** ♿**
Via Meisules 43
tel. 0471795555
www.alpenroyal.com
36 rooms.
Credit cards: Bancomat,
Mastercard, Visa
In a rural setting, this hotel has
an Alpenstube, a garden with
garden furniture, a beauty
center and relaxation programs,

a restaurant with an excellent
wine-cellar and special menus
for kids; charming pond, pool,
sauna, tennis courts and
Internet point.

**Granvara Sport & Wellness
Hotel **** ♿**
Via La Selva 66,
tel. 0471795250
www.granvara.com
30 rooms.
Credit cards: Mastercard, Visa
Set in a large garden in a
position with exceptional views,
it has Tyrolean-style furnishings
and plenty of facilities for
keeping fit (saunas, relaxation
areas, massage) and for leisure
time (pool). Also a restaurant.

Pozzamanigoni * ♿**
La Selva 51,
tel. 0471794138
www.pozzamanigoni.com
12 rooms.
Credit cards: Mastercard, Visa
Typical Alpine-style hotel in a
panoramic position on the edge
of town; ideal for families and
hiking, fishing and riding
enthusiasts; restaurant and
wellness area with sauna and
hydro-massage.

Rural lodgings

Soleiga
Strada Daunei 77
tel. 0471795576
www.soleiga.com
Open all year
Hospitality at a maso in a
peaceful position in the
meadows surrounding the town.

Tublà
Strada Daunei 100
tel. 0471795360
Open all year
The meadows are dotted with
conifers which lead gradually up
towards the walls of dolomitic
rock; accommodation in a baita
(typical mountain house).

Restaurants

Chalet Gérard ⚑ ♿
*sulla strada per il passo
Gardena, Via Plan de Gralba 37*
tel. 0471795274
www.chalet-gerard.com
*Open December-Easter and June-
October*
Credit cards: Mastercard, Visa,
Bancomat
Charming chalet facing
Sassolungo and Sella, with
some rooms. Cuisine based on
traditional products; Tyrolean
specialties and cheeses from the
nearby valleys are served on
wooden boards.

METRIC CONVERTIONS

DISTANCE

Kilometres/Miles

km to mi	mi to km
1 = 0.62	1 = 1.6
2 = 1.2	2 = 3.2
3 = 1.9	3 = 4.8
4 = 2.5	4 = 6.4
5 = 3.1	5 = 8.1
6 = 3.7	6 = 9.7
7 = 4.3	7 = 11.3
8 = 5.0	8 = 12.9

Meters/Feet

m to ft	ft to m
1 = 3.3	1 = 0.30
2 = 6.6	2 = 0.61
3 = 9.8	3 = 0.91
4 = 13.1	4 = 1.2
5 = 16.4	5 = 1.5
6 = 19.7	6 = 1.8
7 = 23.0	7 = 2.1
8 = 26.2	8 = 2.4

WEIGHT

Kilograms/Pounds

kg to lb	lb to kg
1 = 2.2	1 = 0.45
2 = 4.4	2 = 0.91
3 = 6.6	3 = 1.4
4 = 8.8	4 = 1.8
5 = 11.0	5 = 2.3
6 = 13.2	6 = 2.7
7 = 15.4	7 = 3.2
8 = 17.6	8 = 3.6

Grams/Ounces

g to oz	oz to g
1 = 0.04	1 = 28
2 = 0.07	2 = 57
3 = 0.11	3 = 85
4 = 0.14	4 = 114
5 = 0.18	5 = 142
6 = 0.21	6 = 170
7 = 0.25	7 = 199
8 = 0.28	8 = 227

LIQUID VOLUME

Liters/U.S. Gallons

L to gal	gal to L
1 = 0.26	1 = 3.8
2 = 0.53	2 = 7.6
3 = 0.79	3 = 11.4
4 = 1.1	4 = 15.1

Liters/U.S. Gallons

L to gal	gal to L
5 = 1.3	5 = 18.9
6 = 1.6	6 = 22.7
7 = 1.8	7 = 26.5
8 = 2.1	8 = 30.3

TEMPERATURE

Fahrenheit/Celsius

F	C
0	-17.8
5	-15.0
10	-12.2
15	-9.4
20	-6.7
25	-3.9
30	-1.1
32	0
35	1.7
40	4.4
45	7.2
50	10.0
55	12.8
60	15.5
65	18.3
70	21.1
75	23.9
80	26.7
85	29.4
90	32.2
95	35.0
100	37.8

INDEX OF NAMES

GENERAL INDEX

PICTURE CREDITS

GLOSSARY

Ambo
a raised pulpit in early churches from which the Gospels were read

Apse
a semi-circular or polygonal projection of a building, esp at east end of a church

Atrium
lobby, entrance hall

Chemin-de-ronde
internal raised pathway in medieval fortifications

Codex (codices)
early, hand-written books

Embrasure
with a splayed (angled) opening

Erker
projecting window, bay window

Ghibelline
denoting support of the Holy Roman Emperor

Guelph
denoting support of the Pope

Iconostasis
screen or partition, often with tiers of icons, separating the sanctuary from the nave, esp. in early or Eastern Orthodox churches

Loggia
a colonnaded or arcaded space within the body of a building but open on one side

Loop-holes
slits for firing arrows in a medieval castle

Lunette
an area in the plane of a wall framed by an arch or vault containing a painting or sculpture

Majolica
a type of Italian earthenware covered with an opaque tin glaze

Mandorla
almond-shaped frame enclosing the figure of Christ used in early Christian art

Maso: farmhouse

Malga
mountain farm

Matroneum
overhead gallery in an early church reserved for the worship of women

Narthex
the portico in front of the nave of an early Christian or Byzantine church

Oltradige style
typical architectural style used north of the River Adige

Piano nobile
upper floor occupied by the nobility

Pilaster
shallow rectangular feature protruding from a wall with a capital and a base

pluteus (pl. plutei)
reading desk in an early library; decorated square stone slabs in Romanesque churches e.g. used vertically as base for rood screen

Predella
small painting or series of paintings below an altar-piece

Presbytery
the part of a church reserved for the officiating clergy

Pronaos
a vestibule before the main part of the church
Romanesque churches e.g. used vertically as base for rood screen
rood screen: stone or wooden balaustrade separating the main part of the church from the presbytery

Stele
upright stone slab or pillar with an inscription

Stoup
stone or marble container for holy water

Stube
tavern, private drinking club the presbytery

Transept
the major transverse part of a cruciform church

Triptych
a painting or panel with a main central part and two lateral parts

Tympanum
the space between an arch and the horizontal head of the door or window below

Notes

Trento

Foto: A. Guzzon, Medi@omnia, archivio Museo Castello del Buonconsigl.

The City of Trento

Trento is a city of art and history, and is the point at which Italian and Central European cultures meet. This Roman city was also the city of the Tridentine Council (1545-1563). Its monuments make up a heritage of art and history that has been built up over the centuries by the combination of the two cultures - Italian and Nordic, which can still be distinguished in the variety of architectural styles. The Castello del Buonconsiglio (the home for centuries of the Prince Bishops of Trento), the Cathedral with its beautiful Piazza, the houses with their frescoes, the Churches of the Council, museums, and exhibitions, are all worth a visit. The city is also home to numerous events: The "Trento mountain, exploration, and adventure film festival" that takes place in May, the Economy Festival, Traditions dating back to the renaissance with historical processions and "Feste Vigiliane" challenges in June, as well as the typical Autumn and Christmas markets. The city's numerous museums offer art exhibitions and very popular temporary exhibitions. For those looking for a holiday that combines cultural tourism with nature, Monte Bondone, the mountain of Trento, offers magical countryside in terms of light and colour, a "balcony overlooking the Dolomites" just a few kilometres from the city. An infinite range of sporting activities are available here: paragliding, horse riding, trekking, and mountain biking. In winter the perfectly snow-clad trails for Alpine and cross-country skiing are waiting for you, with up-to-date facilities and ski-lift systems.

Apples, soft fruits, walnuts, chestnuts, honey cheese, mushrooms, wine, grappa, and spumante make Trento well known among connoisseurs.

COMUNE DI TRENTO
www.comune.trento.it
Numero Verde 800.017615

Tourist information
Tel. +39 0461.983880
informazioni@apt.trento.it
www.apt.trento.it